Cases on Instructional Design and Performance Outcomes in Medical Education

Jill Stefaniak
University of Georgia, USA

A volume in the Advances in Medical Education, Research, and Ethics (AMERE) Book Series

IGI Global
PUBLISHER of TIMELY KNOWLEDGE

Published in the United States of America by
IGI Global
Medical Information Science Reference (an imprint of IGI Global)
701 E. Chocolate Avenue
Hershey PA, USA 17033
Tel: 717-533-8845
Fax: 717-533-8661
E-mail: cust@igi-global.com
Web site: http://www.igi-global.com

Library of Congress Cataloging-in-Publication Data

Names: Stefaniak, Jill E., 1984- editor.
Title: Cases on instructional design and performance outcomes in medical education / Jill Stefaniak, editor.
Description: Hershey, PA : Medical Information Science Reference, 2020. | Includes bibliographical references and index. | Summary: "This book examines the design and delivery of education programs for healthcare professionals and provides them with the foundational knowledge needed to design effective instruction for a variety of audiences and learning contexts"-- Provided by publisher.
Identifiers: LCCN 2020000781 (print) | LCCN 2020000782 (ebook) | ISBN 9781799850922 (hardcover) | ISBN 9781799850939 (ebook)
Subjects: LCSH: Medical education--Study and teaching--Case studies.
Classification: LCC R834 .C37 2020 (print) | LCC R834 (ebook) | DDC 610.71/1--dc23
LC record available at https://lccn.loc.gov/2020000781
LC ebook record available at https://lccn.loc.gov/2020000782

This book is published in the IGI Global book series Advances in Medical Education, Research, and Ethics (AMERE) (ISSN: 2475-6601; eISSN: 2475-661X)

British Cataloguing in Publication Data
A Cataloguing in Publication record for this book is available from the British Library.

Advances in Medical Education, Research, and Ethics (AMERE) Book Series

ISSN:2475-6601
EISSN:2475-661X

MISSION

Humans are living longer now than ever as a result of advances in the medical field. Having the tools available to train knowledgeable and ethical future generations of doctors and medical researchers is essential to continuing to advance our understanding of the human body and develop new ways of treating and curing sickness and disease.

The **Advances in Medical Education, Research, and Ethics (AMERE)** book series highlights publications pertaining to advancements in pedagogical practice for developing future healthcare professionals, research methods, and advancements in the medical field, as well as moral behavior and practice of healthcare professionals, students, and researchers. Featuring research-based book publications that are highly relevant to the healthcare community, this series is ideally designed for library inclusion at medical universities and research institutions as well as personal use by medical professionals, researchers, and upper-level students entering the field.

COVERAGE

- Clinical Research
- Conflicts of Interest
- Ethics in Medicine
- Healthcare Pedagogy
- Medical Curricula
- Medical Simulation
- Patient Data
- Professional Development
- Research Methods
- Scientific Misconduct

The Advances in Medical Education, Research, and Ethics (AMERE) Book Series (ISSN 2475-6601) is published by IGI Global, 701 E. Chocolate Avenue, Hershey, PA 17033-1240, USA, www.igi-global.com. This series is composed of titles available for purchase individually; each title is edited to be contextually exclusive from any other title within the series. For pricing and ordering information please visit http://www.igi-global.com/book-series/advances-medical-education-research-ethics/132365. Postmaster: Send all address changes to above address.

Titles in this Series

For a list of additional titles in this series, please visit:
https://www.igi-global.com/book-series/advances-medical-education-research-ethics/132365

Exploring Best Child Development Practices in Contemporary Society
Nava R. Silton (Marymount Manhattan College, USA)
Medical Information Science Reference • © 2020 • 305pp • H/C (ISBN: 9781799829409) • US $245.00

Building a Patient-Centered Interprofessional Education Program
Steven D. Waldman (University of Missouri-Kansas City School of Medicine, USA) and Stephanie Bowlin (Western University of Health Sciences, USA)
Medical Information Science Reference • © 2020 • 371pp • H/C (ISBN: 9781799830665) • US $225.00

Handbook of Research on the Efficacy of Training Programs and Systems in Medical Education
Ruth Gotian (Weill Cornell Medicine, USA) Yoon Kang (Weill Cornell Medicine, USA) and Joseph Safdieh (Weill Cornell Medicine, USA)
Medical Information Science Reference • © 2020 • 566pp • H/C (ISBN: 9781799814689) • US $365.00

Gender Equity in the Medical Profession
Maria Irene Bellini (Belfast Health and Social Care Trust, UK) and Vassilios E. Papalois (Imperial College London, UK)
Medical Information Science Reference • © 2020 • 339pp • H/C (ISBN: 9781522595991) • US $265.00

Preparing Physicians to Lead in the 21st Century
Valerie Anne Storey (University of Central Florida, USA) and Thomas Edward Beeman (University of Pennsylvania Health System, USA)
Medical Information Science Reference • © 2019 • 245pp • H/C (ISBN: 9781522575764) • US $245.00

IGI Global
PUBLISHER of TIMELY KNOWLEDGE

701 East Chocolate Avenue, Hershey, PA 17033, USA
Tel: 717-533-8845 x100 • Fax: 717-533-8661
E-Mail: cust@igi-global.com • www.igi-global.com

Table of Contents

Detailed Table of Contents

Clinicians and researchers are expected to educate the next generation of clinicians with little or no formal education on effective, modern instructional design. Clinicians and researchers are left to teach in the same way they were taught many years or decades ago. Medical education must adapt to meet the demands of the Generation Y student population that would benefit from the innovative use of instructional technology. This generation thrives in small groups, using social media, and has never known a world without Google. The purpose of this chapter is to demonstrate innovative curricular design strategies using technology to leverage the skills and preferences that Generation Y brings to a medical classroom.

This case study describes both the process and outcome for instructional design strategies used in the design and development of a fully online Health-System Pharmacy Administration (HSPA) M.S. degree program. The development of this online degree program was a partnership between two Midwest higher education institutions: a public research university (PRU) and an interprofessional health sciences university (HSU). The PRU had instructional designers experienced with creating fully-online graduate degree programs, while the HSU had knowledgeable faculty, staff, and administrators associated with the HSPA program. Instructional designers from the public research university designed the courses collaboratively with HSPA instructors, most of whom were health care professionals with minimal background in online teaching strategies. The instructional designers created an enhanced design process that infused the collaboration with faculty development in online teaching, as well as some amount of technology training for the Learning Management System used in the HSPA program.

This case describes the instructional design process of a workbook accompanying a four-day infection prevention and control global training. Working closely with global health professionals, the instructional designer assessed the needs, the attitudes of learners, and conducted a task analysis of the training content. Subsequently, she designed instructional strategies with special attention to cognitive load, sequencing, and generative learning. Then she created formative and summative assessment strategies and developed a prototype for testing. This case explores how the instructional designer collaborated closely with the global health team to review the content material of the training and design the workbook accordingly.

Contemporary healthcare institutions strive to provide humanistic and patient-centered healthcare. To reach this goal, healthcare systems must first look to the patient as a person, before treating a specific malady or pathology. This chapter will illustrate a humanistic approach to the provision of healthcare using the case of the My Life, My Story program in the United States Veterans Health Administration. My Life, My Story is a patient-centered, life story work intervention where learners complete a life story interview with a veteran using standardized prompts from

Research studies surrounding feedback primarily centered on frameworks designed as models for delivering feedback as well as the timing for delivering feedback. In addition, past research has also focused on individual elements that affect performance with little regard to environmental elements. This case study provides an overview of how a nurse educator utilized a performance analysis approach to providing feedback to nursing students during clinical rotations. A list of performance standards was provided to students at various checkpoints during their clinical rotation. Strategies are shared for improving the type of feedback used in healthcare settings.

This case explores the development, implementation, and ongoing evaluation of performance-based assessments (PBAs) utilized within a competency-based curriculum at Auburn University Harrison School of Pharmacy (AU HSOP). Comprised of over 270 practice-based competencies, the newly adopted curriculum was designed to equip graduates with the knowledge, skills, and abilities essential for a practicing pharmacist. Early in the curriculum development process, hands-on authentic assessment practices were identified as a key assessment strategy resulting in the integration of PBAs throughout the curriculum. This case will describe the PBA development process adopted by AU HSOP, including specific implementation considerations, and explore the role of PBAs in assessing student progression.

Healthcare leadership and department management personnel are tasked with the responsibility of ensuring safe, high-quality patient care delivered by competent and proficient staff. This responsibility often comes in the form of identification of discrepant and erroneous practices that result in subsequent employee disciplinary action process improvement discussions and implementation. This case study presents an example of a sentinel event and how Gilbert's Behavior Engineering Model (BEM) was utilized in the context of a Just Culture to ensure both processes and personnel were adequately supported to meet expected task outcomes.

Preface

Technological innovations are changing the way education is delivered. With instructional media evolving at an exponential pace, instructional designers and educators have a variety of options when deciding what tools are best for delivering their instruction. Many healthcare programs and professional fields are increasing their instructional programming efforts to enhance faculty development and meet rising accreditation standards. Medical educators are responsible for creating instruction for a variety of learning audiences, managing the logistics involved with interprofessional team training and ensuring performance improvement across the healthcare system. Technological innovations now require educators to deliver instruction across a variety of platforms beyond the traditional classroom and include distance, mobile, and simulated learning environments. Regardless of the platform, it is imperative that educators adhere to sound instructional design principles in order to yield optional learning outcomes.

Topics addressed within the case studies include the following:

- Needs assessment
- Instructional theory
- Instructional strategies and sequencing
- Virtual reality
- Medical simulation
- Leadership development
- Faculty development
- Preceptor training
- Interprofessional education and planning
- Communication and feedback
- Virtual patients

BOOK OBJECTIVE

The overall mission of this book is to provide medical educators who are involved with designing and delivering instructional to health care professionals with a series of case studies that demonstrate how instructional design practices have been applied in a medical context. This book includes 13 case studies from instructional design experts and medical educators and professionals who are responsible for delivering instruction to a variety of learners in the health care field. Each chapter highlights learning theory, instructional strategies, and suggestions for ensuring successful implementation.

To date, there is increasing attention placed on curricular programs in health care at the undergraduate, graduate, and continuing medical education levels. While medical institutions are beginning to hire instructional designers and medical educators to ensure adherence to instructional design principles, many medical educators have been appointed to lead instructional interventions based on their subject-matter expertise. Few have received formal instructional relative to designing instruction. In order to maintain accreditation, many medical institutions are required to provide documentation on a regular basis of the various types of curricular projects they are embarking on as well as any scholarly activity/research that is emerging out of their organizations. This book would provide individuals with the necessary foundational knowledge to design and implement sound instructional programs in the medical field and well as provide insights into the unique challenges instructional designers and educators are faced with when designing learning experiences for healthcare professions.

AUDIENCE

The target audience for this book consists of educators, physicians, nurses, and allied health professionals who are responsible for designing instructional activities. Many of these educators have not had any formal training in pedagogy or instructional design. This book is intended to serve as a toolkit to aid them with curriculum development and to align activities with their desired learning objectives. This book will also provide insights into how instructional designers approach instructional environments within a medical education context.

ORGANIZATION

This book contains 13 chapters that span across a variety of health care disciplines including medical education, nursing, and allied health. Each chapter presents strategies for how instructional design and performance improvement can be applied to achieve learning and performance outcomes.

Chapter 1 discusses generational differences among healthcare professionals. The authors discuss ways that medical education must adapt to meet the demands of the next generation of healthcare professionals. They demonstrate curricular design strategies that utilize technology to leverage the skills and preferences that Generation Y brings to healthcare.

Chapter 2 describes both the process and outcome for instructional design strategies used in the design and development of a fully online Health-System Pharmacy Administration degree program. The development of this online degree program was a partnership between two Midwest higher education institutions. The instructional designers created an enhanced design process that infused the collaboration with faculty development in online teaching.

Chapter 3 provides a rich account of how an instructional designer worked with global health professionals to develop training materials to promote infection prevention. Strategies for how to conduct needs assessment and formative evaluation are discussed within the case.

Chapter 4 illustrate a humanistic approach to the provision of healthcare using the case of the My Life, My Story program in the United States Veterans Health Administration. My Life, My Story is a patient-centered, life story work intervention where learners complete a life story interview with a veteran using standardized prompts from the My Life, My Story protocol. This chapter will describe the My Life My Story program at the VA Boston Healthcare System, the steps and rationale in program development and discussion of impact on the learners, the patients, and humanizing the healthcare system.

Chapter 5 describes an instructional design model that may provide a unique insight in how to use immersive VR environments to teach any learner that seeks to acquire surgical/medical professional training more efficiently and practically in a modern world of technology. This chapter describes the conceptual framework and Revinax® 180-degree stereoscopic video-based approach in addressing the academic achievement gap through conventional surgical and nurses shadowing and how immersive VR environments, may best address leveraging the learner's capability of increasing their skill acquisition, learning, and knowledge retention in a more efficient time-period, circumventing the inherent issues with conventional shadowing.

Chapter 6 discusses a variety of practices the healthcare education community can adopt from the psychotherapy literature regarding therapeutic alliance training when supervising trainees, and provides a series of recommendations, grounded in the extant literature, to bring these practices to life. In addition to describing how healthcare educators can translate Bordin's therapeutic alliance model to the medical and allied health communities, this chapter discusses aspects of therapeutic alliance facilitation and maintenance supervisors can address explicitly in supervision, including attunement to the developmental stage of trainees, using the supervisory alliance with trainees, addressing issues of diversity and multiculturalism, and increasing trainee self-awareness in the service of alliance maintenance. Specific strategies including role-play, alliance measurement, and use of video/audio recording are discussed.

Chapter 7 outlines the process of using quality improvement tools during the instructional systems design process. The clerkship curriculum of the third year of medical school was undergoing a complete reform in terms of time and content. An instructional designer was utilized to complete a needs analysis and participate in the instructional systems design process. A need for a common understanding of the language of medical education and instructional design drove the team to utilize the Institute for Healthcare Improvement (IHI), Quality Improvement tools.

Chapter 8 explores how feedback mechanisms can be improved and streamlined to support nursing students during clinical rotations. A case is presented that describes how nurse preceptors modified how they were delivering feedback to assist nursing students with identifying actional items that could help improve their performance while completing their rotations.

Chapter 9 explores the development, implementation, and ongoing evaluation of performance-based assessments (PBAs) utilized within a competency-based curriculum in a pharmacy program. Early in the curriculum development process, hands-on authentic assessment practices were identified as a key assessment strategy resulting in the integration of PBAs throughout the curriculum. This case will describe the PBA development process adopted by AU HSOP, including specific implementation considerations, and explore the role of PBAs in assessing student progression.

Chapter 10 presents a case that demonstrates how environmental analysis can be used to promote a just culture across departments in healthcare. The case presents an example of a sentinel event and how a performance improvement model was adapted to ensure both processes and personnel were adequately supported to meet task outcomes.

Chapter 11provides an overview of how protocols were developed, implemented, and evaluated in a respiratory therapy department. The case study provides specific guidelines for the analysis, creation, implementation, and evaluation of a bronchodilator protocol initiative in a respiratory therapy department. The authors also discuss the challenges that occurred during the project and implications for further improvement.

Chapter 12 shifts the focus to leadership development and describes how a needs assessment was conducted to aid in the creation of a leadership development program for a small rural hospital. Strategies for how community needs were identified and verified are discussed in detail.

Chapter 13 reviews the five elements required of a proven, comprehensive evaluation system to provide this desired organizational excellence evidence that medical educators can adopt to address the needs of stakeholders at different levels of an organization. It provides an overview of an evaluation framework, a process model, and guiding principles that are crucial elements of this methodology. The implementation of evaluative strategies is described within a case that addresses infection prevention in an intensive care unit.

CLOSING REMARKS

The premise of this book is to provide individuals who work in the area of medical education with case studies that demonstrate how instructional design practices have been applied in a variety of health care environments. The book will cover topics such as conducting a needs assessment, analyzing performance, instructional theory, developing instructional materials, and tips for managing instructional projects. To date, there are few case books that has addressed the foundational knowledge associated with instructional design for the field of medical education. It in the intent that this book would fill the void that currently exists in the medical education literature.

Chapter 1
Understanding Modern Learners, Technology, and Medical Education

Robin Bartoletti
https://orcid.org/0000-0001-9443-3947
Indiana Tech, USA

Kim Meyer
https://orcid.org/0000-0001-6216-1342
The University of North Texas Health Science Center at Fort Worth, USA

EXECUTIVE SUMMARY

Clinicians and researchers are expected to educate the next generation of clinicians with little or no formal education on effective, modern instructional design. Clinicians and researchers are left to teach in the same way they were taught many years or decades ago. Medical education must adapt to meet the demands of the Generation Y student population that would benefit from the innovative use of instructional technology. This generation thrives in small groups, using social media, and has never known a world without Google. The purpose of this chapter is to demonstrate innovative curricular design strategies using technology to leverage the skills and preferences that Generation Y brings to a medical classroom.

DOI: 10.4018/978-1-7998-5092-2.ch001

INTRODUCTION

Teaching is the most noble art, and it must improve and evolve with the times. Medical education literally has future lives in its hands which makes it worth the effort of continuous improvement. Which innovations will be successful? On which measures or assessments should change be based? An innovative curricular design that focuses on and leverages the characteristics of its learners has a great likelihood for success. The design should be solidly founded on educational theory while utilizing modern technology to meet goals and accomplish the intended learner competencies. Medical students in the year 2020 are in the older group of Millennials (Generation Y), and in just a few years, the first years of Generation Z will be entering medical programs. The generational differences between learner and teacher are distinct and must be understood in order to be a value rather than an obstruction in the learning process. Generation Y learners expect to use technology, and they should be taught to use it to improve their learning in a professional and respectful way as they interact with older generations both as instructors and future patients. Equally, instructors can utilize technology to improve their teaching and simplify their efforts. This chapter will review the characteristics of the recent generations, explore relevant learning theory, and highlight innovative curricular design strategies using technology to leverage the skills and preferences that Millennials and Generation Z bring to a medical classroom.

THE MODERN LEARNER DEFINED

Clinicians and researchers are expected to educate the next generation of clinicians with little or no formal education on effective, modern instructional design. Clinicians and researchers are left to teach in the same way they were taught many years or decades ago (Sunal et al., 2001). Medical education must adapt to meet the demands of the Generation Y student population that would benefit from an innovative curriculum using the best instructional technologies. This generation thrives in small groups, communicates using social media, and has never known a world without Google (Evans, Ozdalga, & Ahuja, 2016).

As more generations enter the workforce, a rapid change in culture and technology makes experiences of generations more divergent. Medicine demands effective interactions between members of different generations as an emphasis on teamwork, team-based care, and interprofessionalism increases. There is also a rising need for more doctors in the workforce, making retention and job satisfaction especially relevant considering that burn-out rates are climbing. Are there generational factors that are common among medical students that would allow teachers to understand and know them better? The literature brings various arguments to that effect and proves consensus in several areas in education, particularly about the fact that the values and characteristics of all students are not the same. To improve the effectiveness of teachers and professionals involved in the various stages of medical training, knowing the learners is the essential first step.

Generations are defined as the average period, generally considered to be about twenty to thirty years, in which children grow up, become adults, and have children of their own. A generation is a group of people whose characteristics are shaped and defined by the societal events that occurred during their formative years. Discussion of generational differences may be somewhat stereotypical. Individuals have characteristics of their generational group to varying degrees, but generational differences are not used for evaluation purposes. Most studies of generational characteristics are based on survey research, interviews, and sociological observations of behaviors of the general public. Generational differences measured in surveys could be based on generational experiences, age/stage of life, or accumulated life experience. Not every member of a generation will share everything in common with other members of that generation. Since generations span several years, their members still have varied experiences, and those on the "cusp" of previous or next generations may not fit stereotypes as well. For this chapter, we will examine Millennials, or Generation Y, who make up the most significant percentage of students in medical and health-related education. We will use the generational discussion of Millennials as a loose category to help improve teaching methods. The following tables give an overview of the current living generations and what makes them unique.

Table 1. Generations described by year

Generation Label	Born in Years
Generation Z	2001-present
Millennials/Generation Y	1980-2000
Generation X	1965-1980
Baby Boomers	1946-1964
Silent Generation	1928-1945
Greatest Generation	Before 1928

Pew Research Center, 2010

Table 2. What makes a generation unique? This information is based on respondents to a survey who said their generation was unique/distinct. Items represent individual, open-ended responses. This table shows the top five responses for each age group. Sample sizes for sub-groups are: Millennials, n=527; GenX n=173; Boomer n=283; Silent n=205

	Millennial	Gen X	Boomer	Silent
1.	Technology use (24%)	Technology use (12%)	Work ethic (17%)	WW II, Depression (14%)
2.	Music and pop culture (11%)	Work ethic (11%)	Respectful (14%)	Smarter (13%)
3.	Liberal/tolerant (7%)	Conservative/ Traditional (7%)	Values/Morals (8%)	Honest (12%)
4.	Smarter (6%)	Smarter (6%)	"Baby Boomers" (6%)	Work ethic (10%)
5.	Clothes (5%)	Respectful (5%)	Smarter (5%)	Values/morals (10%)

Wrobleski, 2017

Millennials

The following is a Millennial (Gen Y) generational overview for those born 1982-2002. Millennials have been researched and are described in many ways in the literature. General themes/characteristics have emerged about Millennial preferences, attitudes, and behaviors in socioeconomic and educational contexts and the subsequent attempts to briefly summarize current demographics and commonly accepted generalizations. Societal events like economic globalization, 9/11, multiculturalism, and the technology boom shaped Millennials. Their parents tended to be childhood-protective "helicopter" parents, and they have close family relationships. They are optimistic, need praise, collaborative, and keep a global outlook (Mohr et al. Academic Emergency Medicine 2011; 18:190-99). They are mobile, consumerist, and brand conscious. As for values, they are hopeful, idealistic, and value tolerance. They value cooperation, connection/communication, novelty, and conformity/perfection. The organizational style of Millennials may include: Highly affiliated with peer groups and desired affiliation with mentors/teams; Casual interpersonal style; May treat faculty as friends; Technology savvy and accepting; Expect respect based on affiliation/utility; Want to get the job done, have fun, and save the world, all with friends; Gender blind.

The educational background of Millennials has often included grade inflation and lots of positive feedback with an emphasis on individual interpretation. They will have experienced independent study, freewriting, allowed absences for trips, a relaxed or no dress codes, access to snacks throughout the day, and multiple meal options. They were protected from feelings of failure. They were told "no" often. They tend to be more educationally narcissistic and perfectionistic than previous generations (Haynes, 2008). Millennials do not learn like previous generations. As learning patterns continue to evolve, the entire medical education sector should adapt its approach. Reaching Millennials in education requires a fundamental shift in how and where learning is done. Students are experiencing a fatigue of traditional learning, and that means more significant thought, imagination, and engagement are needed to truly connect with this group.

How can these potential Millennial generational aspects be manifested in the medical academic environment? A better understanding of the Millennials will serve as a useful guide for teaching to optimize educational principles and reduce misunderstandings between students and faculty. Studies of Millennials in higher education are often qualitative and investigate attitudes and behaviors. In 2006, Borges et al. quantitatively examined personality differences between Generation Xers and Millennials at one medical school, analyzing responses from 809 students who completed a 16 Personality Factor Questionnaire.

There were significant differences in 10 of the 16 factors. Millennial students scored significantly higher in the following aspects:

- Rule-consciousness or being dutiful,
- Emotional stability or being adaptive and mature,
- Perfectionism or being organized and self-disciplined,
- Openness to change or experimenting,
- Warmth (outgoing),
- Reasoning (more abstract than concrete),
- Social boldness (adventuresome),
- Sensitivity (sentimental),
- Apprehension (self-doubting and worried).

In 2010, Borges et al. extended this work to determine if generational differences in Millennials occur in motive, a domain of human assessment apart from ability and personality, using the Thematic Apperception Test. At one medical school, a total of 426 students participated. Millennial students scored higher on the needs for "Achievement and Affiliation", which lead the authors to suggest that their findings substantiate theories that "Millennials have greater needs to belong to social groups and to share with others, stronger team instincts and tighter peer bonds, and greater need to achieve and succeed." Regarding learning preferences, Millennials gravitate to simulation, interactive group activities, workshops, and game-style presentations of knowledge.

The Millennial generation is described by another study (Janeve, 2017) study as displaying more needs for perfectionism, transparency, rules and emotional stability, and less self-reliance while setting high expectations. The study attributes traits to the global environment in which Millennials were raised and their greater exposure to it through the internet. This exposure has influenced a generation that values technology, teamwork, personalization, and mentoring in professional and educational settings. The study suggests that "Millennials are extremely socially minded and inspired to serve patients."

From a practical medical education standpoint, the research suggests that educators should make use of the following teaching methods (Eckleberry-Hunt et al., 2011):

- Group activities and team-based learning
- "Learn by doing" and actively apply knowledge and skills
- Relationship-building opportunities in the classroom or online that contribute to collaboration and teamwork
- Specified educational goals and objectives
- Avoid traditional didactic lecture formats
- Add pictures, graphics, videos and questions to didactic information
- Hands-on learning with simulations
- Contextual teaching and just-in-time learning
- The learning environment that allows students to feel safe and valued
- Frequent positive and constructive feedback
- Involve learners in developing and using new technology
- Organization is vital, with structure and proper scheduling.
- 24/7 availability of learning materials

Rapid forms of global communication mean that Millennials are interconnected and in frequent contact with each other through their social network (Hopkins et al., 2018). Their communication method and style may differ significantly from current faculty members. Aaron and Levenberg (2014) noted the following strategies that may improve communication with Millennials.

- Very explicit goals and objectives for each educational experience
- Discussion of appropriate classroom boundaries
- Utilization of peer groups
- Use 360-degree evaluations
- Feedback on how to improve
- Give written feedback and regular feedback that is concrete and immediate feedback
- Praise them since they thrive on encouragement
- Provide consistent messaging

Based on a small but growing body of research on the instructional preferences of Millennial learners, the following information is useful when designing medical education (Roberts, 2005). For Millennials, the presentation of an assessment should be objective and include constructive feedback and areas for improvement. To correct a problem, learners of this generation need to understand the reason for the required change. They must learn about the management of their learning. They must learn to recognize their mistakes and learn from them. Recognition is a crucial motivator for them. They appreciate the direct personal contact with their teachers. They must be allowed to join a cause, to get involved in a meaningful project, and to develop authentic relationships in a social group. Training to promote skills relative to leadership development is necessary. The following table highlights some teaching strategies that can be used with Millennials based on the research of Roberts (2005).

Table 3. Millennial personality and teaching strategies

Characteristics of Millennial Personality	Teaching Strategies
Lack of confidence	Clarify expectations and avoid ambiguity
Overprotected, dependent	Validate, approve, encourage, support, give frequent and immediate feedback
Were consulted on decisions during childhood	Be available, answer questions, encourage them to participate in decision-making, respect their initiative and skill
Fear stressful socio-political events, need for affiliation	Encourage them to join in a cause or to engage in a meaningful project
Still emerging adults	Provide advice to help them move towards self-sufficiency
Born with a computer mouse in hand and their world is inhabited by internet	Using new technologies while inviting rigor in the selection of information. Model contemplation, critical thinking, curiosity, dialogue with peers, the possibility of lifelong learning
Obsolete lecture methods annoy them	Innovation in didactic presentations

THEORY-BASED PEDAGOGICAL DESIGN FOR THE 21ST CENTURY LEARNER

Behaviorist Learning Theory

Studying the underlying learning theories helps faculty to create a basis for their instructional strategies. Most newer theories share pieces of these fundamental theories upon which they provide new and evolving ideas of how to best teach and learn. In the early 1900s, researchers Ivan Pavlov (Russia) and Edward Thorndike

(America), challenged the introspective ideas of learning that were prevalent at the time. They brought an objective, observable study of learning to the forefront that focused on the effect of learning is an observable behavior change. In behaviorism, as it was termed, the focus is on an environmental stimulus (S), causing a response (R) observed in the learner. In a pure behaviorist view, this excludes the internal mental processes like thoughts or motivations because those are not observable. The more "neobehaviorists," such as Clark Hull, considered that the learner has internal factors that impact the strength of the response behavior (Hull, 1952). Learning, according to behaviorists, is a mostly passive experience. The environmental stimuli are experienced by the learner, who then changes behavior as a result of that experience. Later, some behaviorists further considered the learner's thoughts and emotions. They went on to propose that the underlying assumptions of behaviorism have a more significant impact on how the behaviors are demonstrated than on the learning itself.

The principles of behaviorism are relevant in a medical classroom and practical skills lab. For classroom instruction, objectives should be written with active verbs, like discuss or appraise or compare/contrast, so the learner will know what must be done with the information that they learn. Although these are often referred to as behavioral objectives, assessing a truly behavioral objective for classroom learning would be difficult. Those are better suited for a skills lab. Behavioral objectives, such as "perform a physical exam," are ideally suited for a skills lab. The application of behavioral learning theory, especially considering the newer views on behaviorism, is best done in the skill lab. Here, learner lab experiences create or solidify learning, which can then be measured by a performance or behavior. Often, something internal to the learner, such as emotions or thoughts for example, may impact the performance of the learned behavior. When planning the curriculum, consideration of what behavior is desired in the learner who completes the curriculum can provide sound guidance during development. This is also relevant to apprenticeship or observational instruction time such as rotations or residencies. Here, what the learner observes is meant to impact how they will perform in a similar situation. Clarity and guidance for exactly what learning should occur is vital to their education.

Ivan Pavlov's Classical Conditioning Model is a well-known example of behaviorism. His study of the neutral stimulus "bell" paired with another stimulus "food" producing the response of the dog salivating because it expects food when the bell rings may seem an unlikely topic of study for healthcare educators. However, this classical conditioning extends well beyond the dinner bell to other, more relevant, involuntary responses. Aversions, anxiety, and fears seen in learners can be created accidentally. Consider that many learners suffer from an unusually heightened fear of failure due to a previous painful consequence or punishment for failure. This was likely an unintentionally created classical conditioning created by well-meaning parents or particularly cruel classmates, but it is quite real for the learner experiencing it. This classical conditioning model provides an opportunity for educators to create a neutral or positive pairing of stimulus to response for learners rather than creating an unconditioned response like this fear of failure. An example of this would be to provide a practice assessment where learners can practice until they are successful. They build up an association between the assessment and success. Conversely, repeated failure may be the stimulus for learners to fear assessment or even to fear trying new skills. Unfortunately, fear of failure in one subject may generalize to fear of failure in all subjects (Bouton, 1994).

Another behaviorist, Edward Thorndike (1898), emphasized the impact of experience on the stimulus-response connection. He termed this connectionism. Positive experiences strengthen a connection where negative experiences weaken a connection, much like reward and punishment (Thorndike, 1913). He later revised his theory because further research showed that punishment was not nearly as effective at weakening a connection as rewards were for strengthening it (Thorndike, 1932). B.F. Skinner also studied the effect of consequences on behavioral responses (1938). His theory, known as the principle of operant conditioning, stated that responses that are reinforced (positively) are strengthened and more likely to recur. In academia, this can be a double-edged sword because good behavior can be strengthened as quickly as bad behavior if it is rewarded. An encouraging word to a shy student who finally participates can strengthen that behavior. Equally, surrendering to a learner who earned a 79 but is begging for a B, can also strengthen those undesirable behaviors. Consider that the Millennial learner walking into a classroom who is greeted with a positive welcome from an instructor may be encouraged throughout the lesson by the positive learning environment.

The impact of behaviorism can be seen in education today because most agree that when a learner has the opportunity to do something (rather than passively listen), to show behavior, they are more likely to learn. Behaviorists emphasized that repeated stimulus-response behaviors strengthen the behavior to the point of habit. They concluded that practice strengthens learning, a statement to which most athletic coaches and professors alike can agree. Rewards are more effective than punishment. Furthermore, finally, a positive learning environment is essential for learning.

Social Cognitive Theory

The foundation of social cognitive theory states that learning occurs through observation and modeling (Bandura, 1977). This theory applies well to educational programs with apprenticeships like clinical rotations and residencies in medical education. Luckily for the patients, learning can occur by observing the behaviors of others together with the positive and negative consequences of those behaviors. The learner can adjust their behavior based on the consequences observed. Those who are observed are known as models (Ormrod, 2008). From the social cognitive viewpoint, the learner observes the model in order to learn, but that learning may not be demonstrated immediately. It may not be demonstrated at all. That depends on what the learner thought, what they mentally processed, about what was observed. It is precisely this mental processing that made social cognitive theory more cognitive than behaviorist. The mental processing of new material is influenced by the observed consequences that were part of the learning process. For example, a learner observes a model perform a procedure using a new technique. During this observation, the patient suffers a severe complication. The learner will be unlikely to attempt this new technique when the next opportunity presents. The learner processed the material with consideration of the consequences (Bandura, 1986). It would be natural for a learner to synthesize their learning, the positive and negative consequences, and form some expectations of future outcomes to create more desirable outcomes for themselves (Rosenthal & Zimmerman, 1978). This observational learning and modeling can be leveraged in medical education. The simulation lab offers a safe environment to imitate the behaviors learned through observation in a somewhat controlled situation. Simulation labs also foster several critical factors in learning, focused attention, and repetitive practice.

Cognitive Learning Theory

Cognitive learning theory was developed in the 1960s led by David Ausubel and Jerome Bruner. It focuses on how learners mentally respond to and think about what they experience (Ormrod, 2008). Learning can occur without a visible change because learning, to cognitivists, is a mental process not to be confused with performance. Behaviorists and even developmentalists, like Piaget and Vygotsky, influenced the development of cognitivism. These influences provided a more holistic view of learning. Piaget described knowledge as distinct units he called scheme. Scheme are smaller chunks of related facts that can be integrated to form a cognitive structure. These basic building blocks of knowledge can either fit well with existing knowledge, assimilate, or cause a shift in existing knowledge, accommodation, in order to accomplish learning. This concept helps to explain why instructors prefer to know what each group of learners should already know about their subject in order to assist with assimilation and predict those areas that may be more difficult. Learners will always attempt to make sense of new information, and it is up to the instructors to guide this "sense-making" as it progresses. The need to make sense of new information is particularly strong for Millennials. Organization of information with frequent assessment checkpoints assist this process.

Vygotsky (1962) described the zone of proximal development (ZPD) as the area where optimal learning occurs. Consider learning as a Venn diagram with the center circle being what the learner is able to do independently. The zone of proximal development is just outside of what the learner can do independently and just inside of the outermost circle which is what the learner cannot possibly do, even with assistance. This zone of proximal development is the area where an instructor can guide learning. The guidance described as scaffolding is used for complex tasks or information. Scaffolding is creating an informational structure much like scaffolding around a building is put together piece by piece. This creates an achievable step-wise set of goals for the learner, who then maintains motivation and interest as feedback is received along the way. Cognitivists emphasize that learning is more accessible when learners are actively involved with meaningful information and concrete structure (Ormrod, 2008).

Of related interest is Richard Mayer's exploration of Cognitive Learning Theory applied to multimedia learing and medical education. Mayer (2010) explores multimedia learning, or the learning from words and pictures and how it is particularly related to medical education. It is based on the idea that people have separate channels for processing words and pictures, that the capacity to process information in working memory is limited. Mayer suggests people learn better from a multimedia based lesson when they already know the names and characteristics of key concepts. For example, before receiving an explanation of how human lungs work, they should know the names and characteristics of each major part of the organ. Mayer also says students will learn better when large lessons are broken down into chunks. Rather than having several hours of multimedia content on human lungs, divide the content into discrete, logical pieces. Finally, Mayer theorizes that a multimedia lesson should be spoken rather than printed,. So, rather than having a text heavy lesson on human lungs, have an audio narrated version.

Many More Theories

The foundational learning theories guide the designing of lessons in medical education. This brief overview demonstrates the wealth of resources available to guide design, such as active participation in learning, care in the organization, zone of proximal development, and identification of scheme into appropriately sized chunks of information. A few newer theories that have grown from these foundational theories are relevant to this discussion of technology in medical education. For example, Nelson Soto (2005) wrote about developing a "pedagogy of caring." His work primarily addressed migrant children in American schools. However, considering the "imposter syndrome" suffered by many medical students who feel ill-at-ease in the medical school environment, this topic can easily apply. He argues that teachers and curricula can be adapted to better include the diverse student body by showing learners that each is a valuable member of the class. Additionally, the engaged learning theory built upon the constructivist principles by encouraging more active and engaged participation by learners during instruction (Mulford 1999). Medical simulation activities for learning cognitive processes and skills is an obvious application to medical education. Finally, Richard Mayer's book (2005) *The Cambridge Handbook of Multimedia Learning*, based his multimedia learning theory on cognitivism. It emphasized that multimedia learning goes beyond the primary assumptions that people learn by audio and visual methods (dual-processing theory) and that they have a limited capacity for processing new information. Multimedia learning, Mayer states, should have a goal to leverage dual-processing and manage the processing capacity by improving organization, reducing extraneous information that does not directly relate to objective achievement, and emphasizing the generative processing that allows the learner to make sense of the new material as they integrate it into their existing knowledge. In conclusion, the engagement with these foundational principles as well as the combining of principles will facilitate the adaptation of instructors to new generations and new curricula.

Using Technology to Reduce or Remove Existing Barriers to Effective Education

Millennial students will have access to more medical knowledge, technology, and treatment technologies than prior generations, and technology and innovative curricular approaches can help prepare them for a changing health care environment. Technology has great potential to enhance education when appropriately applied. The following table is an overview of grounding technology choices in learning theory for medical education.

Technologies that are based on learning theories and Millennial preferences have specific use cases. For example, learning management systems (LMS) such as Canvas, Blackboard, and Desire2Learn can be used to hold rich subject content and provide sequencing of materials. Survey tools found in an LMS or external tools like Survey Monkey or Qualtrics provide consistent and frequent feedback (Half, 2015) to students if used consistently by instructors. Visual presentations can be created with multimedia creation tools, open educational resources (OER), or virtual student posters that improve upon the traditional slide-deck lecture format. Alternate technologies, of which there are many to choose from, are used for varied learning preferences as Millennials are great at looking for ways to improve, improvise, and change (Half, 2015). For the purpose of making students feel safe and part of a community, Virtual Tutee System (VTS) and empathy building tools offer user-friendly resources. Group and team activities can be created with online

Table 4. Grounding technology choices in learning theory for higher medical education for Millennials

Millennial characteristics	Related learning or instructional design theory	Technology choices
Specify educational goals and objectives, add transparency to teaching.	Behaviorism (Thorndyke, 1913)	Learning management system, feedback surveys
Add pictures, graphics, videos.	Critical thinking (Cohen, 2010; Mason, 2010, Mayer, 2010)	Visual presentation tools, multimedia creation tools, Open Educational Resources (OER), virtual student posters.
Contextual teaching, just-in-time learning, 24/7.	Behaviorism (Thorndyke, 1913)	Alternate technologies for varied learning preferences.
Feel safe and valued in the learning environment; need emotional stability and personalization; sensitive.	Pedagogy of caring (Soto, 2005); Behaviorism (Thorndyke, 1913)	Virtual tutee system (VTS), empathy building tools.
Utilize group/team activities and collaboration; Provide relationship-building opportunities and contribute to collaboration.	Social Cognitive Theory (Bandura, 1977)	Online problem-based learning, virtual learning communities, social media, automated mentoring.
Learn by doing; Hands-on teaching and simulations.	Engaged Learning Theory (Mulford, 1999); Constructivism	Simulation, virtual patients.
Frequent positive and constructive immediate feedback.	Expectancy-value Theory (Peterson, 2014); Self-efficacy Theory (Bandura,1977)	Text messaging, electronic rubrics with feedback, 360 feedback tools, error correction automated tools, the ARCH model online forum.
Involve learners in developing and using new technology.	Cognitivism (Ormond, 2008); Engaged Learning Theory (Mulford, 1999)	Technology-focused research and innovation related to medical education; motivational animated pedagogical agent (MAPA), using students as teachers with technology.
Avoid traditional lecture formats. Didactic presentations may be "ancient" without embedded interactive questions or video clips.	Theory of Multimedia Learning (Mayer, 2009)	Instructional video with embedded questions, podcasts, gamified learning.

problem-based learning, virtual learning communities, and social media. Simulated virtual patients are an online resource for hands-on learning.

Frequent, positive feedback can be accomplished via text messaging, electronic rubrics with feedback, and 360 feedback tools. Specific feedback tools like Remind 101, Survey Monkey, MyEvaluations.com can further the capability of medical faculty to provide feedback. Involving learners in researching technology can be accomplished using motivational animated pedagogical agent (MAPA) as well as using students as teachers of technology in the classroom. Troester (2018) in "How Will We Train Generation Z?" directs faculty and staff trainers use the following strategies for virtual reality and gamification.

- Virtual reality (VR). Because Millennial students are familiar with learning through VR, faculty should consider how they will use this technology going forward. MIT and Stanford adopted VR into their executive education programs, enabling students from all over the world to partake in a simulated on-campus environment so that they can network and conduct group work (Johnson et al., 2016). City University of London ran a project which offered nurses a simulated clinical training experience in patient care scenarios (Ramirez, 2015).
- Gamification. Training delivery should be in a format with which Millennials are both familiar with and excited. Regarding Troester's (2018) advice, gamification can be useful when learning goals call for it.

INNOVATIVE CURRICULUM DESIGN STRATEGIES AND PEDAGOGICAL INNOVATION IN THE CLASSROOM FOR SUCCESSFUL STUDENT ENGAGEMENT

An instructor's strategy toolbox develops throughout their career. Many of the tools within are learned through trial and error, observation of others, or sheer determination. Social cognitivist theory might add social reinforcers to this toolbox, like smiling at the learners and paying attention to them as humans first and students second. Behaviorist theory adds the tool of positive feedback and activity reinforcers. These would be such things as praising good work or good effort and then allowing the learner to choose the next activity. These basic principles guide many teachers. Technology can build on these principles with additional options and resources. For example, computer-based assessment with immediate reinforcement and guidance for correct and incorrect responses. Self-paced computerized assessments that allow for mastery before moving on build not only competence but confidence as well. The following table provides some additional strategies that pair well with aspects of the Millennial generation. Further explanation follows the table.

LMS Page Templates

One frustrating factor for medical students today is the sheer volume of information and resources they must utilize and study. A critical design feature for their classes

Table 5. Technology choices and pedagogical innovations

Millennial aspect	Possible technology choices	Possible pedagogical innovation
Specify educational goals and objectives, add transparency to teaching.	Learning management system (LMS)	Keep LMS pages formatted and straightforward in a template fashion to make finding materials in every class similar.Make connections obvious.
Add pictures, graphics, videos, audio.	Visual presentation tools such as Adobe Spark, iPad tools, RISE, Explain Everything	Embed audio explanations of images.Create vodcasts for asynchronous learning.Create interactive "clickable" diagrams with Articulate RISE.
Contextual teaching: just-in-time learning.	Educreations app	Create short video answers to questions or short video tutorials to embed as a link to an online Educreations course page.
Feel safe and valued in the learning environment; need emotional stability and personalization.	Learning communities, Virtual Tutee System	Learning communities internal to the LMS or using social media build a feeling of belonging and collaboration between students.Virtual tutee systems are peer-based tutoring environments in which students teach each other virtually about the content in a course.
Utilize group/ team activities and collaboration; Provide relationship-building opportunities and contribute to collaboration.	Learning communities,Group Mindmapping,Utilize peer review	Learning communities internal to the LMS or using social media build a feeling of belonging and collaboration between students.Online mind mapping programs like Mindomo allow collaborative groups to work on one mindmap together. Anonymous peer review feedback can save endless hours of grading by correcting many problems before the final paper is submitted.
Learn by doing; Hands-on teaching and simulations.	Simulation, Virtual Patients	Simulation of all kinds: patient actors, hi-fidelity simulators, augmented, and virtual reality to supplement the mainstay of clinical experience and rotations.
Frequent positive and constructive immediate feedback.	Text messaging, electronic rubrics with feedback, 360 feedback tools, feedback in formative assessments	360-degree feedback from instructors, peers, and simulated patients is meaningful. Rubrics offer constructive suggestions for improvement rather than grade only. For every formative assessment, utilize feedback to inform both the correct and the incorrect answers.
Involve learners in developing and using new technology.	Technology-focused research and innovation related to medical education; motivational animated pedagogical agent (MAPA)	Use student for technology focused research and innovation that can be applied to courses – including course design.Motivational animated pedagogical agents use animation and video to motivate students to explore and be involved in technology.
Avoid traditional lecture formats.	Instructional video; Embedded questions; Interactive review games or case-based questions.	A flipped classroom with pre-work involving interactive modules and instructional videos followed by a classroom session. Classroom sessions with the first quiz in the form of a Quizlet game followed by case-based questions that put the pre-work into context.

is organization and systemization. This means not only organizing each LMS course within the curriculum but also standardizing that organization into a curriculum-wide template for course organization. This way, the learners can spend less time trying to find their assignments and more time working on their assignments. Standardization of other features within courses, like lessons will all be posted at least 24 hours before class sessions, is also beneficial. Another example would be to have classroom session recordings all located in the same place for easier access and review. This standardization will save precious minutes of study time.

Creating an Articulate Rise Interactive Online Module

Articulate Rise offers a helpful online platform for designing an interactive lesson for independent study. In a flipped classroom model curriculum or course, a Rise module allows the instructor to compile a concise lesson from multiple sources with audio, video, clickable images, text, and assessments in an easy to use format. The embedded audio assists with the correct pronunciation of the new terms. Video tutorials break up the reading or explain more difficult concepts. With a subscription to Osmosis.org, the cartoon-style, easy to follow Osmosis videos can be embedded into Rise. Clickable images offer a study option similar to the old children's game "Memory." The learner clicks on a symbol to identify the structure, function, or relationship of that area of the image. These work well in anatomy curricula and for physical exam skills curricula. The intermittent assessments in the form of flashcards or quiz questions, ensure mastery before learning continues. A final summary quiz may provide a numeric grade or a completion grade to transfer to the Learning Management System.

Creating a Vodcast

Individual vodcasts (a video/audio presentation) can provide asynchronous tutorials or presentations ahead of, or in addition to, classroom activities. The iPad application Explain Everything is a user-friendly and cost-effective method of recording a vodcast. Considering the average person's processing capacity for new information is 7 (+/-2) minutes/concepts, vodcasts should be restricted to a single, short topic. Complicated concepts and frequently missed questions make excellent vodcast material. The view statistics (from media platforms like Panopto, Echo 360, or Mediasite) for a vodcast can provide feedback to the instructor on the utility of the material. Vodcasts easily embed in an LMS page or module to break up written text or to explain a related image.

Figure 1. Explain Everything Screenshot – Working a Problem Together

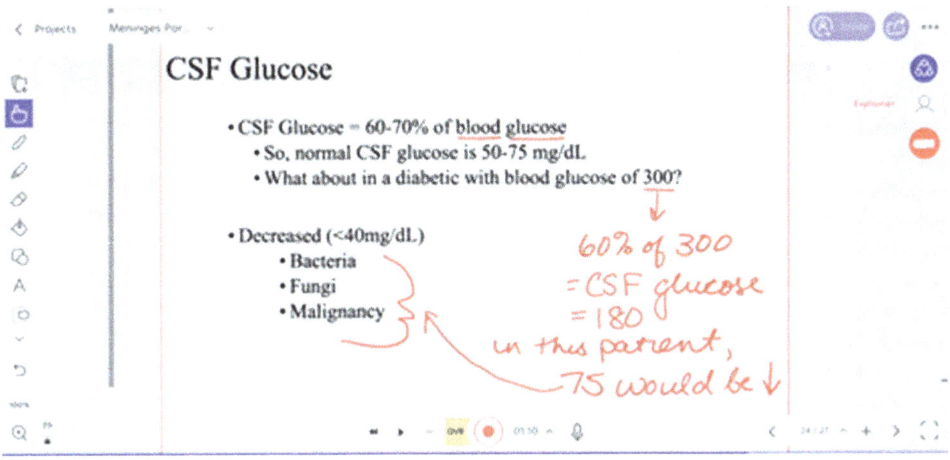

Creating an Educreations Q&A Response

Some student questions are harder to answer than others, especially asynchronously. Writing a long paragraph explanation may get to the answer, but Educreations offers a different solution. This iPad application allows the instructor to quickly capture an image, draw, and verbally explain the answer to the student's question. This quick video is then available by web link provided to the student or class. This is a timesaving and effective way to answer questions. In Figure 2 below, an instructor can assist the learner with a video drawing yellow dotted lines showing structural outlines on CT scans.

Online Collaborative Mindmapping

Mindmapping can be a useful organization and categorization tool for learning. It helps the learner to achieve meaningful learning. In meaningful learning, the network of old information is recalled, paired with the relevant new details, and stored back into long-term memory in a way that will improve recall of both old and new. A mindmap allows the learner to diagram or map their existing knowledge in preparation for a new lesson. An instructor may choose to guide the organization of the map to assist with learning the new material. The addition of new information from a class session creates a new network of information that is correctly categorized and hierarchical for improved recall (Ausubel, 1963). A mindmap allows learners to practice both internal organizations (organizing the new information within itself) and external organization (organizing the information into previously learned

Figure 2. Educreations Screenshot: Explaining a Difficult Image From Homework

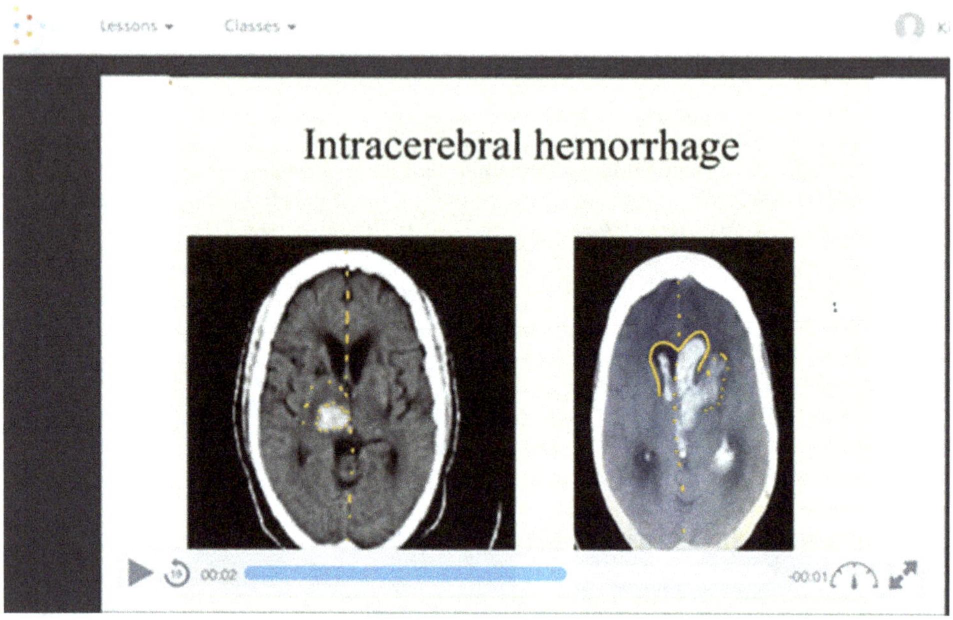

information) to improve their meaningful learning (E. Gagne, 1985). The collaborative aspect of online mind mapping is particularly attractive to younger generations who appreciate social learning. On the Mindomo platform, learners can be assigned or choose groups to work with on assignments that are linked to the LMS. Instructors can view the final product and see exactly what each group member contributed to the final product, which is a feature that high-achieving students appreciate.

Anonymous Peer Review

Peer review is a valuable tool in any program. Using peer review in the LMS has the added benefit of anonymity of the reviewer. The reviewer's comments can be thorough and critical without the threat of losing friends. The instructor who sees the identity of the reviewer can monitor for constructive and professional comments. The use of anonymous peer review could save hours of faculty grading time when used as a pre-review assignment before submission for a grade. It also offers learners the opportunity to learn from their peers' success and failure in the assignment. Learning to give constructive feedback is also an excellent skill to learn early in a medical career. This assignment is particularly useful for patient encounter write-ups like the SOAP (subjective, objective, assessment and plan) note.

Feedback Tools

At every assessment opportunity, consider constructive, immediate feedback as an invaluable instructional tool because regular feedback fosters active learning (R. Gagne, 1985). Formative assessments like a short, multiple-choice quiz, offer an opportunity for learning as well as assessment. Embedded feedback for both correct and incorrect answer choices teaches and corrects errors before they become embedded. Feedback can come from peers, instructors, and observers. An example of observer feedback would be a simulated (standardized) patient. This patient actor can provide faculty-guided feedback by completing a questionnaire regarding learner performance on a clinical encounter practical skill exam. Learners often value this feedback because they see these simulated patients as "expert" patients.

Assessments of Pre-Work

A flipped classroom offers unique challenges; one of these challenges is the confirmation that students completed the pre-work. A quiz would satisfy an assessment of pre-work, but a Quizlet Live game would do the same in a livelier and motivating way. Quizlet Live is a team quiz activity based on a bank of online flashcards (which could be provided before or after the game if desired). Teams answer questions correctly to gain points or lose all their points with a wrong answer. Team performance may act as an additional motivator to those who struggle to complete pre-work, and the game is fun. Each game lasts about 5 minutes. Post-Game analysis of frequently missed questions provides the instructor with a good starting point to the days' lesson.

Each of these tools can be considered to improve engagement, learning, feedback, or assessment. By examining the strengths and weaknesses of a given lesson as well as the intended audience, the instructor can make an educated choice on which tool to use.

CONCLUSION

There may be differences in medical students learning attitudes, behaviors, and values across generations. Too frequently these learning and developmental differences may be overlooked by medical educators who have not been trained regarding these differences. Learning differences in Millennials are due to maturation, life stage, learning stage, or other developmental factors. Providing educational opportunities tailored to Millennials helps them become competent learners and excel in their future as medical providers. Millennials need to receive specific and constant feedback so they can internalize and improve to do their jobs well in the future. All people want to feel valued and significant. Millennials especially want to be valued and involved in the decision making that affects their learning. While learners of different ages may think of respect in somewhat different terms, Millennials especially seek respect. A shift in the learning characteristics and needs of medical student needs should lead to a shift to teaching strategies, and a system of more continuous learning, training, and retraining. As technology expands and tools like augmented reality and artificial intelligence guide automation in the workplace, learning and development will be characterized by the need for critical thinking, communication, and problem solving. Fundamental human needs and similarities exist among all generations and demographics as well as differences specific to Millennials. The way forward is to explore and validate similarities among learners as well as differences. This chapter has suggested some methods for meeting Millennial students where they are in their learning. As further suggested by Roberts (2017), continue to educate yourself about the concept of generational differences and recognize the environmental and cultural forces that affect the Millennial learner.

REFERENCES

Aaron, M., & Levenberg, P. (2014). The Millennials in Medicine: Tips for Teaching the Next Generation of Physicians. *Journal of Academic Ophthalmology*, *07*(01).

Ausubel, D. P. (1963). *The psychology of meaningful verbal learning*. Grune & Stratton.

Bandura, A. (1977). *Social learning theory*. Prentice-Hall.

Bandura, A. (1986). *Social foundations of thought and action: A social cognitive theory*. Prentice-Hall.

Borges, N. J., Manuel, R. S., Elam, C. L., & Jones, B. J. (2006). Comparing Millennial and generation X medical students at one medical school. *Academic Medicine*, *81*(6), 571–576. doi:10.1097/01.ACM.0000225222.38078.47 PMID:16728812

Bouton, M. E. (1994). Context, ambiguity, and classical conditioning. *Current Directions in Psychological Science*, *3*(2), 49–53. doi:10.1111/1467-8721.ep10769943

Cohen, E. D. (2010). *Critical thinking*. Rowman & Littlefield.

Eckleberry-Hunt, J., & Tucciarone, J. (2011). The Challenges and Opportunities of Teaching "Generation Y.". *Journal of Graduate Medical Education*, *3*(4), 458–461. doi:10.4300/JGME-03-04-15 PMID:23205190

Evans, K. H., Ozdalga, E., & Ahuja, N. (2016). The Medical Education of Generation Y. *Academic Psychiatry*, *40*(382), 382–385. doi:10.100740596-015-0399-5 PMID:26283527

Gagne, E. D. (1985). *The cognitive psychology of school learning*. Little, Brown.

Gagne, R. M. (1985). *The conditions of learning and theory of instruction* (4th ed.). Holt, Rinehart & Winston.

Half, R. (2015). *Get ready for generation Z*. Retrieved from https://www.roberthalf.com/blog/the-future-of-work/get-ready-for-generation-z

Haynes, C. (2010). Generation Gaps in Medical Education: Implications for Teaching and Learning. In *AAMC Annual Meeting*. Michigan State University.

Hopkins, L., Hampton, B. S., Abbott, J. F., Buery-Joyner, S. D., Craig, L. T. B., Dalrymple, J. L., Forstein, D. A., Graziano, S. C., McKenzie, M. L., Pradham, A., Wolf, A., & Page-Ramsey, S. M. (2018). To the point: Medical education, technology, and the Millennial learner. *American Journal of Obstetrics and Gynecology*, *218*(2), 188–192. doi:10.1016/j.ajog.2017.06.001 PMID:28599897

Hull, C. L. (1952). *A behavior system: An introduction to behavior theory concerning the individual organism*. Yale University Press.

Janeve, R., Desy, J. R., Wolansky, J., & Reed, D. (2017). Milestones and Millennials: A Perfect Pairing—Competency-Based Medical Education and the Learning Preferences of Generation Y. *Mayo Clinic Proceedings*. PMID:28160874

Johnson, L., Adams Becker, S., Cummins, M., Estrada, V., Freeman, A., & Hall, C. (2016). *NMC Horizon Report: 2016 Higher Education Edition*. The New Media Consortium.

Mason, M. (2010). *Critical thinking and learning*. Wiley.

Mayer, R. E. (2009). *Multimedia Learning*. Cambridge University Press. doi:10.1017/CBO9780511811678

Mayer, R. E. (2010). Applying the science of learning to medical education. *Medical Education*, *44*(6), 543–549. doi:10.1111/j.1365-2923.2010.03624.x PMID:20604850

Miller, A., & Mills, B. (2019). 'If They Don't Care, I Don't Care': Millennial and Generation Z Students and the Impact of Faculty Caring. *The Journal of Scholarship of Teaching and Learning*, *19*(4). Advance online publication. doi:10.14434/josotl.v19i4.24167

Mulford, K. F. (1999). *A multimedia paradigm of engaged learning: An intergenerational approach.* Retrieved from https://www.semanticscholar.org/paper/A-multimedia-paradigm-of-engaged-learning%3A-An-Mulford/79ebe86bd68c5951d243c8c490cf7599d1970957

Ormrod, J. E. (2008). *Human Learning* (5th ed.). Pearson Prentice Hall.

Peterson, J., & Shibley-Hyde, J. (2014). Gender-Related Academic and Occupational Interests and Goals. *Advances in Child Development and Behavior*, *47*, 43–76. doi:10.1016/bs.acdb.2014.04.004 PMID:25344993

Ramirez, A. (2015). Augmented Reality in Higher Education: Five Tips to Get Started. *Times Higher Education.* Retrieved from https://www.timeshighereducation.com/news/augmented-reality-in-higher-education-five-tips-to-get-started/2018933.article

Roberts, D., Newman, L. R., & Schwartzstein, R. M. (2012). Twelve tips for facilitating Millennials' learning. *Medical Teacher*, *34*(4), 274–278. doi:10.3109/0142159X.2011.613498 PMID:22288944

Roberts, G. (2005). Technology and Learning Expectations of the Net Generation. In G. Oblinger Diana & J. L. Oblinger (Eds.), *Educating the Net Generation* (pp. 32–38). Educause.

Skinner, B. F. (1938). *The behavior of organisms: An experimental analysis.* Prentice-Hall.

Soto, N. E. (2005). *Caring and Relationships: Developing a Pedagogy of Caring.* Retrieved from https://digitalcommons.law.villanova.edu/vlr/vol50/iss4/11

Sunal, D. W., Hodges, J., Sunal, C. S., Whitaker, K. W., Freeman, L. M., Edwards, L., Johnston, R. A., & O'Dell, M. (2001). Teaching science in higher education: Faculty professional development and barriers to change. *School Science and Mathematics*, *101*(5), 246–257. doi:10.1111/j.1949-8594.2001.tb18027.x

Thorndike, E. L. (1913). *Educational psychology: The psychology of learning* (Vol. 2). Teachers College Press. doi:10.1037/13051-000

Thorndike, E. L. (1932). *The fundamentals of learning*. Teachers College Press. doi:10.1037/10976-000

Troester, K. (2018). How will we train generation Z? *Training Industry*. https://trainingindustry.com/blog/strategy-alignment-and-planning/how-will-we-train-generation-z/

Twenge, J. (2014). Generational changes and their impact in the classroom: Teaching Generation Me. *Medical Education*, *43*(5), 398–405. doi:10.1111/j.1365-2923.2009.03310.x PMID:19422486

Wroblewski, M. B., & Imran, I. A. (2017). *Teaching Millennials in the Clinical Environment. In Commitment to Excellence in Medical Education: Faculty Development Series*. University of Toledo.

KEY TERMS AND DEFINITIONS

Gamification: The application of typical elements of game playing (e.g., point scoring, competition with others, rules of play) to other areas of activity, in this case, learning.

Generational Differences: Based on generational experiences, age/stage of life, or accumulated life experience.

Interprofessionalism: A healthcare process by which professionals from different disciplines collaborate to provide an integrated and cohesive approach to patient care.

Learning Theories: Describe how students absorb, process, retain, and recall knowledge during learning.

Millennial (or Generation Y): Those born 1982-2002.

Mindmapping: A visual thinking tool that helps structure and organize information in a way that assists with: analysis, comprehension, synthesis, recall and generation of new ideas.

Pedagogy: The method and practice of teaching, especially as an academic subject or theoretical concept.

SOAP Note: A clinical patient encounter note divided in four primary sections: subjective, objective, assessment, and plan.

Virtual Reality: A technology-based simulated experience that can be similar to or completely different from the real world.

Virtual Tutee System (VTS): Computer characters that humans (the actual learners) teach in a virtual environment.

Chapter 2
Collaborative Instructional Design Strategies in an Online Health Systems Pharmacy Degree Program

Bethany Simunich
Kent State University, USA

Katie Asaro
Kent State University, USA

Nicole Yoder
Kent State University, USA

EXECUTIVE SUMMARY

This case study describes both the process and outcome for instructional design strategies used in the design and development of a fully online Health-System Pharmacy Administration (HSPA) M.S. degree program. The development of this online degree program was a partnership between two Midwest higher education institutions: a public research university (PRU) and an interprofessional health sciences university (HSU). The PRU had instructional designers experienced with creating fully-online graduate degree programs, while the HSU had knowledgeable faculty, staff, and administrators associated with the HSPA program. Instructional designers from the public research university designed the courses collaboratively with HSPA instructors, most of whom were health care professionals with minimal background in online teaching strategies. The instructional designers created an enhanced design process that infused the collaboration with faculty development in online teaching, as well as some amount of technology training for the Learning Management System used in the HSPA program.

DOI: 10.4018/978-1-7998-5092-2.ch002

ORGANIZATION BACKGROUND

The large public research university (PRU) has been offering online programs for over 15 years, and currently offers more than 40 online degree and certificate programs, the majority of which are online graduate-degree programs. The PRU has a dedicated office of distance education, as well as a large team of instructional designers and educated technologists, who are distributed among various colleges and university campuses. Also, the PRU utilizes a common learning management system (LMS), and has staff dedicated to the LMS maintenance, as well as other online technologies.

Additionally, with years of experience offering quality online distance education, the PRU already had a well-established instructional design workflow, comprised of separate design and development stages, which followed the Backward Design model (Wiggins & McTighe, 2008). Backward design is an instructional design model that focuses on the idea of alignment, which refers to a high degree of connection or agreement between objectives, assessments, and content (Cohen, 1987). To illustrate, instructional designers work with faculty developers who are subject matter experts (SMEs) in their field to first develop measurable learning objectives. Next, the IDs and SMEs collaboratively create both formative and summative assessments for the online course, in order to provide evidence of learning. Finally, the course is populated with relevant content in the form of textbook readings, scholarly journal articles, narrated presentations, websites, and videos that are directly aligned with course assessments.

The PRU also had experience with creating a "Master Course" – defined as a course that is designed to be replicated into multiple sections, taught by more than one instructor, and may or may not be taught by the SME/academic developer of the course. The Master Course model can use institutional resources wisely, by spending time designing one high-quality online course that ensures learning consistency between sections, rather than creating several versions of the same online course. The process also eases revision work, as changes need only occur in one place and can then be copied into the many sections being taught. In this model, the SME is added into the developing course as a student, so that they are embedded in the student experience and can see the course develop during the design process. The Master Course model was a perfect fit for the HSPA program, because it allows a program to be scaled as student enrollment grows.

Regarding the health sciences university, in its over 40-year history it has worked with community educational, research, and clinical partners to train health care professionals and researchers in a team-based, interprofessional environment. The HSU offers a dozen graduate degree options, including partnership, joint, and dual degrees. However, the HSU did not have any fully online degree programs, instructional designers, or staff who had in-depth experience with developing and delivering an online program. Additionally, the majority of the HSPA instructors/ course developers were pharmacists and other healthcare professionals, who had expertise in their field, but often did not have expertise in teaching and learning, including online pedagogy. Finally, the HSU did not have an institutional learning management system (LMS), which was needed to house the new online degree program.

SETTING THE STAGE

Administrative teams from both universities worked collaboratively to develop a relationship that was mutually beneficial. The PRU and HSU created a shared services agreement, which delineated parts of the design and development process, as well as technology sharing and compensation. The institutional collaboration began when the HSU had a desire to move their face-to-face (F2F) HSPA graduate program online, but lacked the instructional design and technology resources to do so. The public research university, however, had a team of instructional designers and an established workflow in place to develop fully online courses and programs in an efficient manner.

Additionally, the PRU also had access to project management software, file sharing services, and a learning management system -- costly investments that may have been difficult for the HSU to procure and staff in a timely manner, as the HPA would be their first fully-online degree program. In sum, the HSU benefited from the instructional design and project management expertise of the PRU, as well as their technology infrastructure and resources. Key players involved in the decision making process and shared services agreement included: the public research university's Associate Vice President of the Office of Continuing and Distance Education, the Strategic Projects Director, the Director of Online Pedagogy and Research, the Coordinator of Online Learning, a small team of instructional designers and educational technologists as well as the health-system pharmacy administration Program Director, Program Coordinator and various faculty members and subject matter experts affiliated with the interprofessional health sciences university.

The public research university, which was financially compensated for its work and resources, also benefited greatly in terms of professional development for their instructional designers. The development of the health-system pharmacy administration courses challenged their preconceptions about course design and shaped how they work with subject matter experts who lack online teaching experience. These challenges led to new skills that impacted future course development even after the health-system pharmacy administration program was fully deployed.

Additionally, the goals of the HSPA program director were to focus the course design on application, ensuring that HSPA students had opportunities to merge their own professional experience with the program topics and objectives. Thus, the instructional designers emphasized active learning, interaction, application-focused assessments in the design of each of the courses. Further, to ensure a common look and navigational experience for HSPA students, the instructional designers used an LMS template that included a custom course banner and a common navigational and organizational structure. This ensured that HSPA students would interact with a well-organized course, and could focus solely on course material without being distracted by navigation, organization, or other web-based issues.

Finally, the collaboration between the two universities involved both project and logistical management to ensure consistency and timeliness in the design process. The instructional designers worked internally with a project manager and externally with the HSPA program coordinator to create a design and development timeline that ensured that the HSPA courses were designed a semester in advance of their offering, and allowed appropriate time for the integrity and goals of the design process. Additional aspects, such as meeting accessibility guidelines and managing technology aspects, were also built-in to the design process and managed by the instructional designers, thereby allowing the HSPA instructors/developers to concentrate exclusively on the materials and assessments for the courses.

CASE DESCRIPTION

As the public research university began thinking through the process of building courses for an outside institution, it became clear that aside from the overarching goal of transitioning a face-to-face program to online, several other considerations needed to be addressed. First, the finished courses needed to be reflective of the interprofessional health science university's mission and goals. This was critical because even though the HSU students would be utilizing the public research university's learning management system and many of its resources, they still needed to feel connected to the HSU community and, specifically, to the health-system pharmacy administration program. For this reason, the public research university's marketing team developed a series of templates using the HSU branding. Everything from the banner that displayed the name of the course, to the syllabus and course schedule, to the narrated presentations and assignment documents, utilized the HSU's logo and color scheme. Aside from the "branding" aspect, this was also done as a best practice to ensure that the students enrolled in the health-system pharmacy administration program had a consistent experience as they navigated through the various courses each semester.

The second consideration that needed addressed was what do if a problem arose while the courses were being taught, and how to manage future revisions of the courses. As part of its workflow, the PRU utilized a ticketing system through which HSPA faculty can reach out for direct support as they're teaching the course, or request minor changes after the course has been taught once. Through this process, the public research university is able to ensure that an instructional designer maintains a connection to the course after it is designed, meeting the joint goal of continuous quality improvement and maintaining a high-quality experience for the student. Since the initial contract between institutions stipulated that the PRU was responsible only for designing the courses for the health-system pharmacy administration program, part of the course development process became teaching a "point person" at the HSU how to utilize the learning management system in order to function as the course support person, as this was originally missing from the inter-institutional partnership's workflow. Eventually, this became a bit cumbersome so the decision was made to give the HSU access to the ticketing system so that the PRU could adopt the role of course delivery and revision support as well.

Technology Concerns

A number of technology concerns had to be addressed prior to the instructional designers and subject matter experts beginning their work on the course design and development process. The initial technology concern to consider was how the students enrolled in the health-system pharmacy administration program would access the course, as they were using the PRU's learning management system, but were not registered PRU students. After discussion between both institutions, the decision was made that all students enrolled in the online HSPA program would receive student accounts through the public research institution. Essentially, this meant that the two universities would be sharing one learning management system to host their online course offerings. While the scope of the issues that came with sharing the learning management system go beyond the purpose of this case study, account activation and support, monetary compensation, and student data and privacy were all factors that had to be heavily considered prior to moving forward with this decision.

Ultimately though, providing student accounts with full access to the public research university's LMS proved to be a valuable step. By granting each student enrolled in the online health-system pharmacy administration program full student account access, students were able to utilize not only the learning management system, but many additional student resources as well. Access to library resources was one of such benefit that was often used in the development of the health-system pharmacy administration's online courses. For example, both the instructional designers and the subject matter experts were able to use the public research institution's library holdings and subscriptions to add valuable content to the course materials.

Additionally, students enrolled in the program could easily log in with their newly created student accounts to utilize library resources as needed to complete assignments and projects required for their coursework. Further, student accounts with the public research institution allowed the HSPA students access to a leading video platform. With this resource, the subject matter experts and instructors had the ability to enrich their content with engaging video and audio recordings. Additionally, students in the program would be able to use the video platform to record presentations and videos to complete their classwork. Ultimately, although sharing a learning management system and providing each student with an account at the public research institution took time, much negotiation, and resources, it proved to be an invaluable step in the partnership.

Another technology concern at the outset was connecting the PRU instructional designers with the HSU faculty/subject matter experts. The HSU SMEs were largely working healthcare professionals, who most often could not physically meet during the work day. Additionally, several of the subject matter experts involved in the design and development of the online courses were not local to the PRU where the instructional designers were located. To solve this issue, most of the design meetings were held through a web conferencing tool, which allowed the instructional designers and subject matter experts to meet on a weekly basis to discuss course materials, share content, and review the progress of the course in the learning management system. While this was necessary for developers who were not local to the research institution, the use of web conferencing was also an ideal way to meet with subject matter experts who were closer in proximity but did not have time to make the drive to campus for weekly meetings. Meeting remotely offered busy subject matter experts the flexibility of meeting during breaks in their day or anytime that was convenient for their schedule without having to allow time for transportation.

Design Components

One of the shared goals of the two institutions was to create high-quality online courses. For the HSU, they benefited from the fact that the PSU used the internationally-recognized design standards of the Quality Matters™ (QM) Higher Education Rubric (2018). Additionally, the IDs had completed professional development in applying the QM Rubric, and the public research university's design process and LMS design template were infused with QM Standards. This was important to the health sciences university, as they not only had accreditation requirements for quality, but they also intended on externally certifying the quality of the courses via QM Official Course Reviews.

At the course level, one of the initial challenges that had to be addressed by the subject matter expert and the instructional designer was transforming a course that was designed to be taught face-to-face in a classroom setting into a high-quality fully online course. The root of this challenge was that a significant portion of the initial, face-to-face course design focused on in-class discussions led by the instructor or subject matter expert. While each course varied in the number and point values allotted for these discussions, the end result was essentially a participation grade that comprised a large portion of the student's overall score in the course. This in-class participation grade was used as a primary method of assessing the student's understanding of the content presented and their ability to discuss the concepts and their application to health-system pharmacy. While informal discussions in a live classroom setting allow the instructor to provide immediate feedback, gauge student interest and understanding of the topic, and direct the conversation in an extemporaneous but meaningful fashion, these types of informal discussions do not lend themselves well to an asynchronous online environment. This initial challenge meant that the subject matter expert and the instructional designer could not simply re-use or make minor modifications to the assignments as they had originally been designed. In order to effectively align the course learning and program outcomes, the methods of assessment in each course needed to be heavily revised or, in many cases, developed anew.

Another design challenge that presented itself early on was that the HSU wanted to ensure that the assignments designed for the HSPA courses were application-based and meaningful to the students. Developing application-based assignments in a field in which the instructional designers had no prior experience was both challenging and motivating. Prior to beginning each project, the instructional designers were given access to the syllabus that was used for the original course in its face-to-face format, and connected with the subject matter expert who would be developing the online version of the course. For many of the projects, the subject matter expert tasked with developing the online course had previously taught the face-to-face version, but in other cases, the individuals developing the course had never taught the course in any format. With the program focused on opportunities for students to apply course concepts to their current or potential career in the medical field, however, this required the instructional designers to assume a more active role in creating assignments. While the IDs were used to collaborating with experienced academic faculty, working with the HSPA SMEs and instructors allowed the IDs to gain experience working with non-academic professionals who had a very high-degree of subject and professional knowledge. Therefore, design meetings became focused discussions with the SMEs about their experience with pharmacies in hospital settings, and how that experience could be brought back to the course. By learning what health systems pharmacists did in their daily work, the IDs were able to help locate or suggest appropriate content, and most importantly, to draft assignment ideas and prompts that reflected authentic assessments, which is "a form of assessment in which students are asked to perform real-world tasks that demonstrate meaningful application of essential knowledge and skills" (Mueller, n.d.).

An additional consideration the instructional designers and the subject matter experts needed to keep in mind was the scalability of the content and tools utilized. The HSPA program would begin with just a few students, but was projected to expand to 15 - 25 students per class within a few years. So, the challenge was that the course had to be designed to work seamlessly whether three students were enrolled or a full class of twenty-five students. This meant that although only a small number of students enrolled in the first offering of the course, the program would likely grow until it reached the enrollment cap in any given course. Building this scalability into the design of the course was difficult as the instructional designers had to consider class size when drafting assignments, particularly those that relied on learner-to-learner interaction. Class size considerations impacted not only the work that students would do, but the expected workload of the instructor as well, in terms of interacting with students and providing grades and feedback.

Further, while it could not be built into the overall design of the course itself, the instructor's teaching presence, in terms of interacting with students as the course is being delivered, would also have to be adapted based on student enrollment as well. Teaching presence is defined as "the design, facilitation, and direction of cognitive and social processes for the purpose of realizing personally meaningful and educational worthwhile learning outcomes" (Anderson, Rourke, Garrison, & Archer, 2001). It is one of the elements of the Community of Inquiry framework, along with Social Presence and Cognitive Presence (Garrison, Anderson, & Archer, 2000). Teaching presence begins with the design of course, as the content is selected, assessments are created, etc., then continues once the course begins, and must be purposefully elevated by the instructor. Due to the small class size in the HSPA courses, for example, the instructor may have to actively post and respond to the discussion boards more frequently to stimulate conversation – a strategy that may not be needed if the course enrollment increases. This pedagogical concept was new to many of the subject matter experts that developed the HSPA courses. While these individuals were experts in their field, most had no formal pedagogical training related to either face-to-face or online instruction. In addition, the newness of the online health-system pharmacy administration program meant that there was no designated training process for the subject matter experts before they taught the course. This became an additional consideration for the instructional designers to consider as they worked through the design and development process. In short, while working with the HSPA SMEs/new online faculty, the IDs had to infuse the design and development process with online teaching information and strategies as well.

For example, when creating an assignment, the IDs would go through the related prompt in detail with the HSPA faculty, discuss how the assignment supported the learning objectives, and also give suggestions for providing helpful feedback to students on the assignment. In short, the design process expanded to also become online teaching faculty development.

Additionally, while most of the developers did not have any training in online pedagogy, even fewer had experience teaching within a learning management system. This presented another professional development opportunity for the IDs, as they had to determine how to also provide some LMS training to the HSPA faculty. Therefore, pedagogical best practices as well as providing general instruction for using the grade center, the announcement tool, basic editing of content items, and the overall workings of the learning management system, became discussions that were woven into the design and development phases of the course build process.

As mentioned previously, the creation of a "Master Course" was an important step in the design process for this institutional collaboration. The utilization of the Master Course design helped establish a fluent workflow when it came time to prepare and copy the course for teaching each term that it was offered. The Master Course concept had been used successfully by the PRU for many years and had been incorporated as a best practice in their workflow, as it simplifies the process of revising courses that have multiple sections. Instructional designers can make the necessary changes in one master course and when the course is next offered, the master course can then be copied into each section that has students enrolled rather than making the changes and updates into each individual section.

The concept of using Master Courses was an important aspect of the health-system pharmacy administration program because, in addition to assisting with a smooth workflow for the revision and copy processes, it allowed the instructional designers to develop individual courses that still had the feeling of being part of a larger, more cohesive program. To promote the feeling of being part of the program, the Master Courses were all built using the same course template. In addition to creating a cohesive feel throughout the different courses in the program, the template ensured that each course utilized a similar navigational and organizational structure which allowed students to focus solely on course material without being distracted by navigation, organization, or other web-based issues. The template used for the HSPA online program was very similar to the one that the instructional designers often use in the development of fully online programs at the public research institution. This was helpful to the IDs because they were familiar with the template layout and the building process.

The public research institution made minor tweaks to its original template to ensure that the courses being designed for the health-system pharmacy administration were representative of the interprofessional health science university's branding and programmatic goals. Once such change in the course template was the course banner that appears on the landing page when students navigate to the course. This banner was designed by the public research institution's marketing team specifically for use with courses in the HSPA program, and reflected the HSU brand, including logo and color scheme. The banner was then customized for each course to include the course name and course number.

In addition to the course banner design, the marketing team for the public research institution also developed templates to use for course assignments and presentations. For example, a complete, branded assignment prompt was placed directly with each assignment item within a given course. The marketing team designed the templates for the course assignments in Microsoft® Word using a header and footer that was representative of the interprofessional health sciences university branding. Additionally, the template was designed with proper style headings that met accessibility requirements. The assignment templates included a location for the assignment's title, background information related to the assignment and why it was applicable to associated learning materials, the detailed, step-by-step instructions, grading criteria, and submission information. Once an assignment was finalized, the Microsoft Word document was exported as a PDF and attached to the assignment item in the learning management system. Each assignment in the course was provided to students in this same template. This allowed students to easily locate the details and requirements of each assignment in the course, and promoted a consistent navigational experience among all courses in the HSPA online program.

Additionally, incorporating the subject matter expert's knowledge into the course material was an essential factor in the design of each online course. Through the use of webcam video, audio recordings, and narrated PowerPoint® presentations, the expertise of the subject matter expert was infused within the learning material of each course. To help ensure a cohesive feel and a similar experience throughout the different courses in the program, the marketing team at the public research institution also developed templates for PowerPoint® presentations. Using slide masters in PowerPoint®, the marketing team again applied the colors and the logo of the interprofessional health sciences university to develop a template that could be used by all subject matter experts involved in the design and development process. The advantage to this was that all developers were using the same structure and formatting for their presentations. While this helped ensure that the look and feel of narrated presentations across the program were consistent, several courses had multiple subject matter experts involved in the creation of course content, and the PowerPoint® template also provided a consistent format for each of those individuals to contribute cohesive content to a single course.

The utilization of the templates and the course banner helped students feel that they were still part of the HSU community, even though they would be navigating to their courses through the PRU's learning management system, utilizing student accounts provided by the PRU, and accessing resources with the PRU logo and branding. The HSU branding on the templates thus allowed not only for smooth navigation and processes throughout the program, but also for students to interact in an online environment in which they still felt part of their specific program and the community of the interprofessional health sciences university.

Management and Organizational Concerns

In addition to issues regarding application-based assignments and scalability, time availability was also a concern, as the HSU subject matter experts were incredibly busy. Most worked as full-time hospital pharmacy administrators, and many of them often worked non-traditional hours. Because of this, several course developers elected to utilize "guest lecturers" for portions of their course, both because they had limited time to develop course lectures and also because it can be incredibly valuable for students to hear other perspectives. Although often beneficial for developers and students, coordinating guest lectures can pose a management and organizational issue for instructional designers.

For example, the guest lecturers were typically colleagues of the subject matter expert and, as such, were also incredibly busy working professionals. Secondly, as more subject matter experts became involved in the development process, it became a bit onerous for the ID to ensure that all best practices were being met and that content was still being received in a timely manner. Lastly, since the HSPA course developer/SME was being compensated for their work, when that work was distributed and shared with others, a new compensation model had to be developed so that all SMEs received appropriate compensation for their work.

Stakeholders from both institutions were dedicated to ensuring that the online health-system pharmacy administration program was a success. This meant establishing routes of communication, implementing measures of quality assurance throughout the design and development processes, and finding a way to assess both instructor and student satisfaction of each newly developed online course. First, the instructional designers at the public research institution checked in weekly using their online learning team's project management platform. This allowed the instructional designers to communicate seamlessly with the Strategic Projects Director and the Coordinator of Online Learning from their institution, as well as the Program Coordinator for the interprofessional health sciences university. This communication ensured that all stakeholders were aware of each project's timeline and any issues that arose throughout the process. This consistent, weekly communication also ensured that all deadlines were being successfully met in order to complete the development of each course per the agreed upon dates stipulated in the shared services agreement.

Additionally, the instructional designers met on a bi-weekly basis with the Coordinator of Online Learning. These meetings were held in person and each ID used this time to provide an update on the progress of each project. During these meetings, the Master Course was shown in the learning management system and discussed, so that the Coordinator of Online Learning was able to fully assess the current status of the project and could communicate any concerns or considerations moving forward. These meetings during the design and development process allowed for quality assurance to be monitored and elevated during development, and not just assessed at the end of work.

In addition to meeting regularly with the Coordinator of Online Learning, the instructional designers were able to speak candidly with the Director of Online Pedagogy and Research as needed, to check-in on the progress of each project, discuss concerns, and brainstorm ideas for content and assessments that meaningfully challenged students' thinking and interactions throughout the course. As previously mentioned, the HSPA Director had set a vision for the program to have applied, authentic assessments. The majority of past and future HSPA students would be employed pharmacists who were enrolled in the program to advance their training and career, but whose limited time for education demanded that coursework focus on real-world application of course material. The IDs, then, were charged with centering meetings with the HSPA faculty/SMEs on their professional experience and knowledge, so that the IDs could better suggest assignment ideas that reflected what students would be doing in the field. Discussions with the Director of Online Pedagogy and Research allowed the IDs to workshop assignment and content ideas prior to drafting up assignment prompts, storyboarding presentations, etc. to share with the SMEs for feedback and approval.

While incorporating these steps to quality assurance throughout the design and development process, it was also necessary to measure student and instructor satisfaction once the courses had been delivered. The use of anonymous student surveys in every module in all the courses provided an opportunity for students to voice their opinions about the rigor in that learning unit, the opportunities for interaction with their classmates, and anything that they found helpful or unhelpful in regards to the learning materials and assignments. Instructors could then aggregate the data retrieved from the student surveys to make future changes and adjustments to course materials to help ensure student satisfaction. Further, the instructors of each course were encouraged to make a list of items that they would like to change or address as they were actively instructing throughout the term. When the term finished, each instructor could then send the list of revisions that they would like to make to the HSPA Program Coordinator.

Once the first set of online courses was fully developed and running live with enrolled students, establishing an efficient workflow for necessary course revisions became a critical step. It was determined that the HSPA Program Coordinator would handle the collection and organization of the changes requested by each instructor. The Program Coordinator would then utilize the project management system to submit a course support ticket. The course support ticket could then be routed from the PRU's Strategic Projects Director to an instructional designer or educational technology designer who had time available in their schedule to make the necessary updates. While these managerial concerns may seem small in comparison to the scope of the overall course design process, it is worth emphasizing that while the instructional designers appear to reap the benefits in terms of knowledge gained and hands-on experience, many individuals were involved in the development of this online program and all had important roles to fulfill.

SOLUTIONS AND RECOMMENDATIONS

Although the list of challenges outlined in the previous section were notable, the instructional designers at the public research university quickly realized that a well-functioning inter-institutional partnership begins by establishing a firm foundation. In this case, realizing that there would be challenges and "growing pains" at the outset allowed both institutions time to consider how to address these issues once they arose. In terms of transforming a face-to-face course that was essentially based on classroom discussion into an online course that was both engaging and well thought-out, the instructional designers decided to assume most of the perceived workload during the design process in order to allow the subject matter expert to focus on developing high quality instructional materials. This was done in a number of ways. First, the instructional designers held a "kickoff meeting" in which the public research university's course development process was thoroughly delineated. Expectations for the subject matter expert were also made clear during this meeting, and completed courses were shown so that SME developers, most of whom had never seen or taken an online course, could understand and see from the outset what the goal was in terms of a finished, quality course.

Subsequent design meetings involved drafting an assessment plan, which often revolved around the implementation of a semester long project that was appropriately scaffolded throughout the term. These assignments were sussed out using a combination of the face-to-face version of the course's syllabus, a designated textbook, and frank discussions with the subject matter expert that centered on what they did in their day-to-day job, and how that directly related to the course being developed. Brainstorming and collaborating with other instructional designers at the public research university also proved invaluable during this time.

Once the assessment plan was in place, the instructional designers shifted their focus to development. Since the courses typically ran within days after development was finished, a short design process was essential in allowing enough time for fine-tuning course materials. The short turnaround time also meant that the instructional designers worked "behind the scenes" to alleviate as much of the subject matter expert's workload as possible, in consideration of the busy professional lives of hospital pharmacists and administrators. Thus, tasks such as alignment and rigor calculation were only mentioned if the instructional designer encountered a problem and needed to discuss with the subject matter expert how to proceed.

Overall, communication between the instructional designer and the subject matter expert played a critical role during the course development process. While the subject matter expert and instructional designer were contracted to meet weekly, due to time constraints and schedule conflicts, standing meetings became difficult. Thus, an element of flexibility was crucial in figuring out whatever worked best in terms of maintaining momentum with the course development. For example, if in-person meetings proved impractical, then virtual meetings which relied on screen sharing became the primary mode of communication. If nothing else, email coupled with editing capabilities in shared document platforms that allowed the instructional designer and subject matter expert to "track changes" allowed for frequent and substantive interactions that effectively replaced weekly meetings when necessary.

Communication on an administrative level was also crucial to the success of the inter-institutional partnership. As part of the instructional designers' "normal" workflow, weekly updates regarding the status of all course development projects is entered into a project management system. This allows the instructional designer to fully document the course development process as well as "reach out" to their superiors if a problem arises. In the case of the health-system pharmacy administration program's development, this element of transparency was essential. While a typical course development for the public research university allowed the instructional designer to communicate directly with the Coordinator of Online Learning and the Strategic Projects Director, it was decided early on that there needed to be a way for the instructional designer to communicate with administrators at the interprofessional health sciences institution as well. For this reason, the Strategic Projects Director created "client resource" accounts in the public research institution's project management system. This allowed the ID to create weekly written updates that automatically notified via email both the director and program coordinator of the HSPA program as to what was being accomplished that week in each HSPA course's design and development. In hindsight, this was probably one of the best decisions the public research university made in regards to the inter-institutional partnership. Since the PRU was not compensating the subject matter experts, the SMEs felt less attachment to the timeline, and there was little incentive for the busy developers to create content in a timely manner. However, once the subject matter experts realized that the instructional designers were communicating on a weekly basis with administrators at both institutions, the SMEs began to see the timeline as a jointly-agreed upon goal, with very little room for deviation.

In addition to open and effective communication, flexibility also proved to be essential to the success of the health-system pharmacy program's development. While working with one subject matter expert was often challenging enough, in the case of courses in which multiple guest lecturers were employed, coordinating course content inevitably proved to be an extraordinary exercise in time management. The instructional designers not only had to map out a timeline for each developer in order to hold them accountable for content creation, they also had to be available if and when each subject matter expert's schedule allowed and/or if questions arose. In some cases, this meant working outside of normal business hours or collaborating using more creative means, such as shared documents, rather than consistent meetings. Being willing to abandon some of the PRU's typical course development practices also allowed the instructional designers to compartmentalize exactly what each guest lecturer would need to know as development progressed. This allowed for better use of meeting time as the public research university already had numerous best practice handouts about creating online learning materials that could be widely distributed if necessary.

Other recommendations that the public research university can offer include the importance of discussing pedagogical concepts such as teaching presence throughout the design process, as well as completing a final walkthrough of the course with the SME before it is actually taught. Regarding introducing pedagogical concepts to new instructors, the IDs recognized this as a professional development opportunity, and worked directly with the Director of Online Pedagogy and Research (DPR) to learn faculty development techniques and strategies, and also to discuss online pedagogy and strategize for meetings with SMEs. Not only was the DPR readily available for assistance throughout the HSPA program's development, but it was also helpful that she had extensive online teaching experience. Conversely, the IDs tasked with building the courses for the program did not have online teaching experience, so felt unable to offer that perspective to the SMEs. Given the focus on online teaching that necessarily became part of the design process, however, this meant that the DPR functioned in a faculty development role for both the IDs and SMEs, as her knowledge and expertise was used as professional development in online teaching for the IDs who, in turn, were then able to discuss relevant teaching topics with SMEs during design meetings.

The final course walkthrough was essential because it provided the opportunity for the instructional designer, the Director of Online Pedagogy and Research, and the subject matter expert to review the completed course together and address any last-minute questions or concerns. The typical walkthrough was scheduled for an hour and a half and, when possible, occurred in person. During the walkthrough the instructional designer would project the course onto a large screen and walk/talk through each module. Throughout the process, any links and lectures were tested to ensure that everything was working from a technical standpoint. The syllabus and course schedule were also reviewed during this time. To further promote quality assurance, three separate checklists were completed and saved with the course files once the final walkthrough was complete. The checklists acted as both a final method of ensuring that all necessary components of the course design had been addressed, as well as an additional measure for ensuring the overall satisfaction of the subject matter expert. To this end, the subject matter expert was responsible for one overarching checklist, while the instructional designers were responsible for completing one checklist related to the technology aspects of the course, and another related to the overall design and alignment standards. To document ideas they had for future iterations of the course, or to address minor issues that were not able to be resolved in the initial development cycle, a "revision roadmap" was created. While this was a simple Microsoft® Word document that the IDs and the SMEs both contributed to in order to fully document the standing of the course at its completion, it was yet another component that reflected the truly joint nature of this partnership, while also serving as a starting point for continuous quality improvement of the courses in years to come.

CONCLUSION

Overall, the partnership between the public research institution and the interprofessional health sciences university was both highly successful and very mutually beneficial. The interprofessional health sciences university utilized the public research institution's technology, software licenses, and expertise in creating quality online courses to build a brand-new program that will, ideally, increase in enrollment. The HSPA SMEs and faculty also benefitted by experiencing an online course design and development process, which was also infused with faculty development in online teaching, as well as LMS basic instruction. The public research institution benefited by learning the multiple and often complex considerations that come with such a partnership, enabling them to improve future collaborative work. For the PRU, lessons learned included the sharing and management of technology resources, and communication and project processes between institutions. Additionally, the instructional designers experienced this as a professional development opportunity, especially because of their directing an enhanced design process, as well as increasing their knowledge of online pedagogy and their skills in faculty development. The IDs had the opportunity to utilize their complete and expansive skillset to manage a design process with multiple developers, nearly all of whom were not traditional academic faculty nor had online teaching experience.

On so many levels, this inter-institutional partnership was truly a team effort which allowed both institutions to collaboratively create a high-quality online degree program that reflected their shared efforts and goals.

REFERENCES

Anderson, T., Rourke, L., Garrison, D. R., & Archer, W. (2001). Assessing Teaching presence in a Computer Conference Environment. *Journal of Asynchronous Learning Networks*, *5*(2), 1–17.

Cohen, S. A. (1987). Instructional alignment: Searching for the magic bullet. *Educational Researcher*, *16*(8), 16–20. doi:10.3102/0013189X016008016

Garrison, D. R., Anderson, T., & Archer, W. (2000). Critical inquiry in a text-based environment: Computer conferencing in higher education. *The Internet and Higher Education*, *2*(2-3), 87–105. doi:10.1016/S1096-7516(00)00016-6

Mueller, J. (2016). *Authentic Assessment Toolbox*. http://jfmueller.faculty.noctrl.edu/toolbox/whatisit.htm

QM Higher Education Rubric. Sixth Edition. (2018). MarylandOnline, Inc. Used under license. All rights reserved. Retrieved from https://www.qualitymatters.org/myqm

Wiggins, G. P., & McTighe, J. (2008). *Understanding by design*. Association for Supervision and Curriculum Development.

KEY TERMS AND DEFINITIONS

Alignment: An instructional design concept that encompasses the connection between course elements. Alignment within the design of a course means that the course content directly supports students doing well on course assessments, which provide evidence to the instructor that the student has achieved the course learning objectives. Online courses additionally consider alignment in terms of planned interaction and chosen technology.

Authentic Assessment: Authentic assessments focus on allowing students to apply what they've learned, so they are situated at the Application Level or above in terms of the Cognitive Domain of Bloom's Taxonomy. These types of assessments not only focus on learning-by-doing, but also on creating assignments that reflect real-world application of course concepts so students directly understand the relevance and practicality of what they're learning.

Backward Design: An instructional design model that focuses on alignment, and begins with course learning objectives, or where you want students to be (in terms of their learning performance) by the end of the course. It is a results-focused instructional design approach, contrasted with the content-focused approach of beginning with the course textbook and allowing that to set the foundation for your course design.

Community of Inquiry: A framework developed to understand how the type of communication and interaction online impacts the educational experience. The Community of Inquiry framework includes the three elements of Cognitive Presence (students' cognitive engagement with course elements), Social Presence (students sense of belonging to the learning community), and Teaching Presence, which is defined below. Creating and elevating presence online is crucial to helping online students feel connected and engaged with the course, their instructor, and one another.

Health Systems Pharmacy/Health Systems Pharmacy Administration: The type of pharmacy found in traditional hospitals, as well as ambulatory care clinics, university and academic health centers, long-term care settings, etc. Regardless of the setting, the health system pharmacist serves in the role of medication expert on a team of health care providers. Within some settings, health system pharmacists might also assume an administrative role that encompasses additional managerial, organization, financial, etc. duties.

Quality Matters: An educational non-profit organization that began in 2003 with a U.S. federal education grant. Quality Matters (QM) has a design rubric that includes research-based standards for the design of online and hybrid courses, and an accompanying formal certification process whereby online and hybrid courses can be evaluated against QM Rubric design standards by trained Peer Reviewers.

Teaching Presence: One element, along with Social Presence and Cognitive Presence, of the Community of Inquiry framework. Teaching presence begins with the design of the course, as the instructor is making pedagogical choices for course content, assessments, etc., and extends through the delivery/active teaching of the course. Online, it is vital for instructors to elevate and maintain their teaching presence, as that serves as the catalyst for cognitive and social presence, and also sets the stage for learning motivation and building an online learning community.

Chapter 3
Infection Prevention and Control Training-Design of a Workbook Prototype

Suha R. Tamim
University of South Carolina, USA

Maysam R. Homsi
https://orcid.org/0000-0002-0665-246X
St. Jude Children's Research Hospital, USA

Brooke Happ
St. Jude Children's Research Hospital, USA

Miguela A. Caniza
St. Jude Children's Research Hospital, USA & The University of Tennessee Health Science Center, USA

EXECUTIVE SUMMARY

This case describes the instructional design process of a workbook accompanying a four-day infection prevention and control global training. Working closely with global health professionals, the instructional designer assessed the needs, the attitudes of learners, and conducted a task analysis of the training content. Subsequently, she designed instructional strategies with special attention to cognitive load, sequencing, and generative learning. Then she created formative and summative assessment strategies and developed a prototype for testing. This case explores how the instructional designer collaborated closely with the global health team to review the content material of the training and design the workbook accordingly.

DOI: 10.4018/978-1-7998-5092-2.ch003

ORGANIZATION BACKGROUND

Founded in 1962 by the actor Danny Thomas, St. Jude Children's Research Hospital (St. Jude) is one of the leading pediatric healthcare institutions in basic and translation research in childhood cancer treatments. Its mission is to "advance cures, and means of prevention, for pediatric catastrophic diseases through research and treatment" (St. Jude, About Us section, 2020, para. 1). The World Health Organization (WHO, 2020) reports that 300,000 children and adolescents are diagnosed with cancer annually. Most of these childhood cancers can be cured if diagnosed early and accurately, and if they are treated effectively. In fact, over the past 50 years, St. Jude helped raise the pediatric cancer survival rate from 20% to 80%, offering treatment free of cost for children from all over the world, in line with the vision of Danny Thomas that "no child should die in the dawn of life" (St. Jude, 2020, Our History section, para. 15). Unfortunately, a big gap exists in the rate of cure between high-income and low-income countries (WHO, 2020), and St. Jude aspires to reduce it. In low-and middle-income countries, (LMIC) survival is dismal due to multiple factors, many of which are linked to poor infection prevention and control practices (Caniza et al., 2015). St. Jude's global reach recently was formalized with the creation of St. Jude Global, an initiative that creates the infrastructure to support and pursue St. Jude's global vision and expand its mission worldwide. To achieve this mission, St. Jude focuses its work on three main areas: care and treatment that targets patient treatment and family support, research that aims at developing clinical and research innovations, and education and training.

Training provided at St. Jude encompasses graduate-level training for doctorate (PhD) and masters (MS or MSc) students, postgraduate training for research and clinical fellows, and advanced graduate training for healthcare providers, scientists, and other professionals. Based on specific requirements, this opportunity is accessible to the global audience to improve care for children all over the world. The goal of St. Jude Global, which is managed by the Department of Global Pediatric Medicine, is to build a network of healthcare institutions in LMICs to "improve survival rates for children with cancer and other life-threatening diseases" (St. Jude, Global Reach section, 2020, para. 2). Using education, one of three pillars (education, capacity building, and research) to improve the survival of pediatric cancer globally, St. Jude Global works to better the clinical workforce. The St. Jude Global Academy trains healthcare professionals through a combination of distance and on-site courses (St. Jude, St. Jude Global section, 2020). The St. Jude Global Academy currently offers training opportunities in Infectious Diseases, Infection Prevention and Control, Neuro-Oncology, Critical Care, and Palliative Care. The focus of this case study is on Infection Prevention and Control training.

IMPORTANCE OF INFECTION PREVENTION AND CONTROL IN A PEDIATRIC ONCOLOGY SETTING

Children with cancer are at increased risk of healthcare-associated infections because chemotherapy weakens the immune system (Dunbar et al., 2014, Simon et al., 2008). Therefore, infection prevention and control is essential for successful care outcomes, and it is attained through standard and systematic dissemination and implementation of evidence-based practices in healthcare institutions (Ariza-Heredia & Chemaly, 2018). For this reason, the goal of the Global Infectious Diseases (Global ID) Program is to improve global expertise in infection prevention and control. Global ID relies on its multiple training courses and mentorships to train clinical workforces. Central to building safer oncology care worldwide is training infection preventionists in infection prevention and control at each of the institutions caring for those children.

The Infection Control Course for Infection Preventionists is an intensive, certificate-based training program initially developed in 2005 (Caniza, 2007) and taught in Spanish 14 times to more than 360 preventionists across Latin America. In 2019, Global ID adapted this course for the English-speaking audience, while also re-launching the Spanish-based course, updating content, improving educational strategies, and harmonizing the courses across regional training hubs. This Course consists of two components: distance-learning and residential training. Based on this model, other training seminars at St. Jude were developed and successfully implemented. Students matriculate into the distance-learning component and work through four essential modules over two months by using an online educational platform. Top-performing students from the distance-learning component are then accepted into the residential training program. The residential program consists of intensive face-to-face thematic training, delivered in collaboration with healthcare institutions at global sites. These themes are called practicums. The residential program focuses on several practicums that allow participants to apply the theoretical basis of knowledge obtained during the distance-learning portion to practical situations in the clinical setting. Students are assigned to training hubs based on their language needs and geographic proximity. Currently, the residential program is offered in India, Lebanon, Egypt, and Mexico. This training enables participants to consolidate and apply what they have learned during their online sessions. The residential training spans four days and covers five infection prevention and control topics: Microbiology, Policies and Procedures, Surveillance of Healthcare-Associated Infections (Surveillance), Monitoring and Auditing of Essential Practices (Monitoring Practices), and Outbreak Investigation. Each day is divided into blocks, and each block consists of one or more of the following instructional strategies: lectures, in-class discussions, group activities, field exercises in healthcare facilities, and homework.

To enhance the residential training program and provide students with a resource to be used as a reference during and after their training, the St. Jude Global ID team partnered with an instructional designer (designer) to review and upgrade an existing companion workbook. This workbook provides a tool for practice, notes, and review during and after the training. The scope of the work included developing worksheet activities, designing reference material, and adapting lecture material into workbook content. With the re-launch of the course and the inclusion of additional residential training sites, instructional design–driven strategies were essential to continuously improve the material.

SETTING THE STAGE

The designer has several years of instructional design experience and a background in public health. She previously worked as an educational consultant for the International Outreach Program at St. Jude. Therefore, she was familiar with the nature of the organization's work. The Global ID team consists of the Director of the Global ID Program, the project coordinator, and the coordinator whose roles were to develop and support the implementation of program initiatives and who also served as the subject-matter experts for the workbook. The design of the workbook was planned to be the product of a close collaboration between the designer and the Global ID team.

To initiate the project, the Global ID team set up a preliminary meeting with the designer to discuss their vision. They presented an overview of the residential training for which the workbook was to be designed:

- The residential training spans four days.
- It covers five infection prevention and control topics: Microbiology, Policies and Procedures, Surveillance of Healthcare-Associated Infections (Surveillance), Monitoring and Auditing of Essential Practices (Monitoring Practices), and Outbreak Investigation.
- Each day is divided into blocks.
- Each block consists of one or more of the following instructional strategies: lectures, in-class discussions, group activities, field exercises in healthcare facilities, and homework.

Lecture slides from two topics were shared to begin the design work. Additionally, copies of previous versions of the workbook were provided. This first meeting created an opportunity to clarify the needs of the Global ID team and address the intended goals for the workbook. Additionally, the meeting allowed the designer to ask questions about learners' characteristics to guide the design process and fulfill their needs. Lastly, the meeting helped the designer gain a better understanding of the content and structure of the residential training program. Therefore, the stage was set for the initiation of the instructional design process.

CASE DESCRIPTION

Instructional design is a process that facilitates learning (Reigeluth, 1999). Morrison et al. (2013) defined instructional design as a "systematic process for creating instruction based on scientific research that produces effective, efficient, and reliable instruction" (p. 8). This process involves five generic phases: analysis, design, development, implementation, and evaluation (Gustafson & Branch, 2002). The designer began the analysis phase by examining the need for the workbook based on her first meeting with the Global ID team.

Needs Analysis

To gain a comprehensive understanding of the needs, she used all the data the team could provide. She broke down the needs analysis into three parts: team's needs, learner analysis, and evaluation of previous participants' attitude toward earlier drafts of the workbook.

Team's needs. The team envisioned the workbook providing learners with documentation to reinforce the in-class training, practice exercises to facilitate the learning of difficult concepts, and as a reference upon return to their home institutions to enhance the transfer of knowledge and skills. Probing more into why the workbook was desired, the designer learned the following:

- Assessment of previous training showed that participants struggled to master complex concepts and processes. Therefore, learners needed an instructional tool that would enhance the retention of the material and the application of infection control and prevention processes.
- The workbook had to include creative additions to engage learners and facilitate the learning process. The desire of the team was to enhance active learning and strengthen interactivity during the residential training. They wanted to reinforce existing instructional strategies that varied across in-class exercises, group activities, field exercises, and homework.
- Learners needed a resource in their hands to use as a reference and job aid to transfer learned skills to coworkers at their home institutions, particularly participants who worked in institutions with limited access to resources and tools.

Learner analysis. Upon review of the data from previous courses, the Global ID team described learners as novice to mid-career medical or other allied healthcare professionals who had some prior knowledge on the topics presented during the residential training. In addition, the attitude of participants toward the training was fairly positive to highly positive, due to their commitment to their professions and their enrollment in a course offered by a prestigious institution. Thus, learners were somewhat familiar with the content of the training and were motivated to participate in it.

Attitudes towards the workbook. During the preliminary meeting, the designer asked to survey past participants who received the workbook about their attitudes towards it. The Global ID team approved and, accordingly, she drafted an attitude survey that was later edited by the team. The survey examined whether previous participants found the workbook's features (e.g., the inclusion of slides, worksheets, resources, etc.) useful. Additionally, the survey asked how they have used the workbook in their home institutions, such as revisiting learned concepts, sharing with colleagues, or as a resource in their practice. It also sought recommendations for improvements. The survey revealed that almost all participants (92%) have used the workbook since the conclusion of the residential training program; they use it mostly to revisit the course materials, incorporate them as additional resources in their practice, and share them with colleagues. As for the design, they preferred to have a note-taking section with the slides and to have additional resources.

The needs analysis confirmed that the workbook was an instructional need. The Global ID team wanted to enhance the learning process through the provision of support material and the integration of active learner participation. Similarly, learners expressed an appreciation for the workbook and a use for it in their work settings. Once the needs of the team and the learners were clarified, the next step for the designer was to conduct the task analysis.

Task Analysis

A primary principle in instructional design is the determination of the types of learning to be achieved (Reigeluth, 1999), also known as task analysis. Task analysis determines what needs to be taught to achieve the goals of the training (Jonassen, 1999). Jonassen et al. (1999) recommend five steps for the task analysis process: 1) identifying tasks based on the needs assessment, 2) selecting those that will be included in the training through ranking in terms of priority; 3) describing tasks and breaking them down into component parts; 4) sequencing tasks for better learning outcome; and 5) classifying learning outcomes into types of learning and determining learning objectives.

With these task analysis principles in mind, the designer analyzed the contents of the residential training on which the workbook was based. As mentioned earlier, the residential training covered five infection prevention and control topics. However, the work initially focused on Policies and Procedures and Surveillance to create a prototype of the redesigned workbook.

It is important to note that the task analysis of this project did not need to begin with the identification of the tasks, as explained by Jonassen et al. (1999). The Global ID team had already covered that in their design of the residential training, in terms of selected content materials, so what needed to be taught had already been established. The designer picked up the task-analysis process from ranking tasks, breaking them down into component parts, and classifying them, in terms of learning outcomes. She completed these steps in collaboration with the Global ID team, guided by the PowerPoint presentation slides. For this purpose, she created a template (Figure 1) to facilitate the task-analysis process.

Figure 1. Section of a task analysis template

Objective-Slide Alignment and Ranking

Objective	Content	Ranking	Assessment
Surveillance Essentials for Healthcare-Associated Infections (slides 1- 19) **Rank from 1-6**			
Describe the objectives of HAI surveillance programs	Surveillance of HAIs is the foundation for organizing, implementing, and maintaining an effective Infection Prevention and Control program in a healthcare facility Why do we conduct surveillance? • To establish baseline rates • To identify high-risk populations, procedures, and exposures • To compare HAI rates within/between healthcare facilities • To engage clinical team to adopt best practices	1	

First, the designer used the template to suggest learning objectives for each slide and confirm the desired learning outcomes with the team. She based her work on two popular classifications of learning outcomes, Bloom et al. (1956) and Gagné's (1984). Bloom et al. defined three learning domains (i.e., cognitive, affective, and psychomotor skills), and Gagné described five types of learning outcomes that integrate Bloom's three learning domains (Driscoll, 2005). These learning outcomes are as follows: 1) verbal information relates to recall of information from memory with no analysis; 2) intellectual skills involve discriminating, learning concepts, applying rules, and problem-solving; 3) motor skills indicate an outcome of physical activity; 4) attitudes reflect tendencies to make choices and have emotional connection; and 5) cognitive strategies pertain to managing the learning process such as rehearsing, elaborating, and organizing. Therefore, the designer and the Global ID team determined the learning outcomes for the slides and specified their types and domains through the selection of appropriate learning objectives. This was an important phase of the task analysis in order to design assessment strategies that aligned with the objectives (Tyler, 1949/2017).

Second, the designer asked the team to rank the learning outcomes in terms of importance to determine which ones needed to be reinforced in the workbook. The designer recommended three considerations for ranking objectives: 1) ranking must aim at identifying content that is essential for the learners to master during the residential training, without which they cannot transfer skills to be applied in their home institutions; 2) ranking must be based on prior knowledge/skills: objectives that target knowledge/skills that learners already have or somewhat have will not be ranked as high as those that target new knowledge/skills; and 3) ranking should screen objectives to differentiate between what is important to know and what is nice to know (Jonassen, 1999).

The task-analysis template was extremely important in rethinking the design of the content. It served as a collaborative visual tool to negotiate and determine priorities and types of learning. Figure 2 shows a section of a completed form using Track Changes in Microsoft® Word.

With the analysis phase completed, the designer next considered design strategies for the instruction, assessment, and workbook prototype. Instruction and assessment strategies were developed concurrently for most learning outcomes to ensure alignment. However, for the sake of clarity, the instructional strategy will be described first.

Design of the Instructional Strategy

After negotiating and organizing the learning outcomes with the Global ID team, the designer reflected on the instructional strategy. Dick et al. (2015) defined instructional strategy as a description of "the general components of a set of instructional materials and the procedures used with those materials to enable student mastery of learning outcomes" (p. 174). Therefore, she needed to design strategies that fit the training context, in terms of time and place, the workbook, and the attainment of learning outcomes.

Reflecting on the content and the slides, the designer wanted to address essential principles of instructional design, namely information processing and cognitive load, sequencing, and instructional strategies that reduce cognitive load. She focused on

Figure 2. Completed task-analysis form

Surveillance Practicum-Objectives Alignment

Objective	Content	Ranking	Assessment
Surveillance Essentials for Healthcare-Associated Infections (slides 1- 19) **Rank from 1-6**			
Define epidemiology and the epidemiological approach (Review)	The study of the **distribution** and **determinants** of health-related states or events in specified populations, and the application of this study to the control of health problems."	6	
List the systematic measurements of the epidemiologic approach	The epidemiologic approach includes the systematic measurement and description of disease or health-related states or events. Epidemiologic systematic measurement includes: • Counting cases/health events • Describing cases/health events in terms of *person, place,* and *time* • Calculating rates • Comparing rates over time and for different groups	5	

these principles because of the complexity of the content and the limited time of the residential training. Consequently, the designer drew the attention of the team to these principles to justify the rationale behind recommendations she planned to make. Per their request, she presented an overview on these principles to bridge the gap between their mental models and to arrive at a shared vision of the design decisions. As is often the case, mismatched mental models impede change due to miscommunication, misunderstanding, and confusion (Cabrera & Cabrera, 2015; Evans, 2001; Senge, 2012). Whereas agreement in mental models supports team effectiveness, team growth, and members' satisfaction (Rentsch & Klimoski, 2001). Below is an overview of the instructional design principles the designer focused on and the related design decisions.

Information processing and cognitive load. Atkinson and Shiffrin (1968) described human memory as a system with three features: sensory memory, short-term memory, and long-term memory. They explained that learning and retention of information is sparked by environmental stimuli that act on the senses (sensory memory). This sensory information is then transmitted to the working memory, where information decays quickly if not processed further (short-term memory). Information that stays in the working memory transfers to the long-term memory, where it is stored and retained for retrieval. This is an important principle in instructional design because it draws attention to the functioning of the brain, in terms of retention of the materials to which learners are exposed. Essentially, not all that is presented is learned, especially when the knowledge and skills are novel or complex. For learning to occur, instruction needs to be designed in such a way to increase stores in long-term memory because working memory is limited in capacity and duration (Sweller et al., 2011). Pass and Sweller (2010) studied the relation between working memory and meaningful learning. Their cognitive load theory stresses the importance of selecting a design that avoids overloading the limited working memory unnecessarily. They identified three categories of cognitive load: intrinsic cognitive load that relates to the complexity of the materials, extraneous cognitive load that relates to poorly designed instruction that burdens the working memory for no learning purpose, and germane cognitive load that relates to mental resources needed for processing new knowledge (Sweller, Merrienboer, & Pass, 2019). Similarly, Merriënboer, Kirschner, & Kester (2003) concluded that although cognitive load is not the only element to be considered in the design of instruction, it is one that should be given main attention, even if it is challenging to address (Sentz, et al., 2019).

Sequencing. Instructional designers have at their hands several strategies to reduce cognitive load (Merriënboer & Sweller, 2010). One of these strategies is sequencing of learning tasks. Sequence determines the order in which content is to be taught based on relations between topics and the size of instruction (Reigeluth, 1999). Reigeluth (1999) identified two types of sequencing that span a continuum: topical on one end and spiral on the other. Topical sequencing presents the content topic by topic. Here, learners are taught each topic in depth before moving to the next. On the other hand, spiral sequencing presents the instruction gradually. Here, learners are taught the basics of several topics before revisiting them to learn more about them. According to Reigeltuh (1999), the design of instruction is a mixture of both and leans towards one endpoint or the other based on the learning needs. Similarly, Posner and Strike (1976) proposed five sequencing formats based on the order of relations between topics. Most related to the Global ID training are the following three formats: learner-centered sequencing that focuses on prerequisite skills, familiarity and difficulty of information, interest, and developmental level of learners; concept-related sequencing that follows a logical sequencing of content based on the relations between concepts; and inquiry-related sequencing that reflects the process and methodology of "generating, discovering, or verifying knowledge" (Posner & Strike, p. 676).

Design Decisions. The exchange on these instructional design principles resulted in the following design decisions. For the workbook, the team needed to select the sequence of the modules at the macro level and the sequence of concepts within each module at the micro level. At the macro level, the team decided to address the modules in a spiral sequence (Reigeluth, 1999) to provide a longer exposure to materials, extend opportunities to reflect on them with trainers, and allow for more in-depth applications at the completion of the training. For example, on the first day, students will review basic concepts on Policies and Procedures and Surveillance. On the second day, they will participate in knowledge checks and deeper discussion and practice data collection and analysis. On the final day, they will summarize their learning by presenting their findings on that particular topic.

At the micro level and contemplating the choices with the designer, the team chose a mix of a learner-centered, concept-related, and inquiry-related sequencing. Mixing sequencing strategies as such is not uncommon (Posner & Strike, 1976). Therefore, the content was sequenced from simple to complex, less difficult to more difficult, and less familiar to more familiar (learner-centered) but also highlighted relations between concepts (concept-related). For example, one of the topics addressed healthcare-associated infections surveillance systems. Here, concept-related sequencing was followed by the elements of the surveillance system, the methods of the system, the different strategies, and the different types.

Elements-Methods-Strategies-Types

Another example is the method used to conduct surveillance of healthcare-associated infections. Here, the sequencing followed an inquiry-related format, beginning with identifying the steps, then identifying data sources, followed by identifying types of data, and ending with surveillance calculations.

Steps-Sources of data-Types of data-Calculations

Infused throughout the sequencing of the content of all the modules was a learner-centered format that moved from concepts that learners were familiar with from the distance-learning portion of the course or from their practice to concepts that were new and complex. For example, learners are more familiar with the tasks of a specific surveillance method than with an understanding of the various methods and goals of surveillance programs. Similarly, identifying steps of surveillance methods is less complex than doing surveillance calculations.

Once sequencing of the content was completed, the designer looked at additional strategies to decrease cognitive load. Through her review of the training, she saw that some of these strategies were in place, while others needed to be adjusted or added, namely chunking, modality principle, completion strategy, and low to high fidelity strategy.

Chunking content into smaller parts enhances the acquisition of skills (Mayer & Moreno, 2003; Sweller et al., 2011), especially when it is supplemented with practice opportunities (Merrill, 2013). Chunking gives learners time to organize and process what is presented to them, moving from one small segment to the next, which relieves the working memory and, in turn, decreases cognitive load. So again, working with the team, the designer recommended breaking down the presentation of concepts into smaller chunks where needed, based on the prior knowledge and expertise level of the learners (Sweller et al., 2011). For instance, examples of common surveillance measures that learners were familiar with did not need be chunked in comparison to site-specific surveillance criteria that were more complex and less familiar to them.

Modality principle is another strategy that reduces cognitive load (Sweller et al., 2011). It is based on replacing text with visual information. One section of the training covered the identification and classification site-specific infections (bloodstream and urinary tract infections). The team explained that, during previous training, learners found these concepts difficult to grasp. Reviewing the related slides, the designer found them to be mostly text-based. Therefore, she suggested redesigning the slides in a way that refined the conceptual sequence and decreased cognitive load by organizing the information visually (Figure 3).

Figure 3. Example of slide redesign

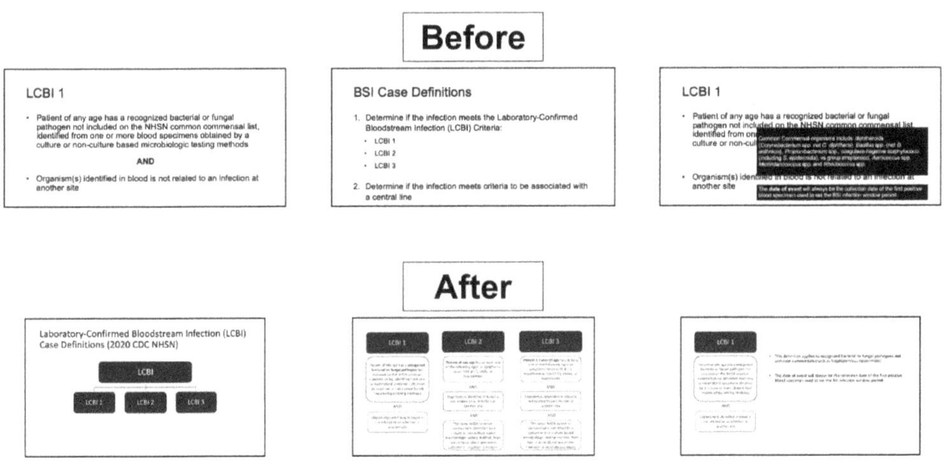

Another strategy that reduces cognitive load is completion strategy, where learners complete tasks of increasing levels of complexity (Sweller et al., 2011). For example, the Policies and Procedures module required learners to develop an infection control and prevention policy for healthcare institutions as the end product to demonstrate their learning. To decrease cognitive load, the designer recommended a sequence in which learners first review an existing policy, describe its components, then identify weaknesses and suggest improvements, and finally develop a policy from scratch.

Lastly, fidelity strategy involves learners performing a task in a simulated environment before performing it in a real-life setting. A subtopic in the training addressed the monitoring of hand hygiene practices because hand hygiene is essential in preventing infections in healthcare institutions (CDC, 2020). Therefore, learners needed to be trained to fill an assessment survey on hand hygiene practices. Initially, learners were asked to complete the survey in their home institutions before the residential training, with no previous exposure to it (high fidelity). Then, in the residential training, learners would complete the survey with representatives hosting the training (low fidelity). After a brainstorming session, the team and the designer decided that the outcome would be better if the sequence was reversed: from low fidelity, where learners first complete the survey during the residential training, with the team's support in a simulated environment, to high fidelity, where learners complete the survey in their home institutions after the training. This reversal not only helps alleviate the cognitive load but also supports the transfer of skills to practice settings.

The decisions made so far aimed to enhance the retention of the material, especially concepts that were complex and difficult to master, by selecting a sequence and reducing cognitive load based on theory. The next design decisions focused on the other goal of the workbook—to promote active learning and interactivity. Therefore, the designer suggested the inclusion of generative strategies. Generative strategies actively engage learners in ways that connect prior knowledge, skills, and experiences to newly learned materials (Morrison et al., 2013) These strategies support learners' sense making and meaning generation, (Fiorella & Mayer, 2015; Lee, et al., 2008), helping with "understanding, comprehension, and long term recall" (Wittrock, 2010, p. 43). Generative strategies guide learners in selecting relevant material, organizing it, and integrating it within prior knowledge to enable solving new problems (Fiorella & Mayer, 2015). Generative strategies not only support learning but also motivate and support thinking skills (Lee et al. 2008). They provide pausing instances during learning that chunk content, reduce cognitive load, and enhance performance. Fiorella and Mayer (2016) proposed the following ways to promote generative learning:

- Summarizing, mapping, drawing, and imaging: learners "translate to-be-learned material into a different form of representation" (p. 732).
- Selecting and organizing relevant information to integrate with existing knowledge.
- Self-testing, self-explaining, teaching, and enacting: learners elaborate on the material at a higher level with more meaningful representations.

In the task analysis, the designer identified learning outcomes and revised them with the team. Some outcomes targeted verbal information, such as listing criteria needed to conduct surveillance; some targeted intellectual skills, such as distinguishing surveillance and clinical definitions of infection; and others targeted cognitive strategies, such as interpreting basic surveillance measures. These types of learning outcomes constitute the basis for developing generative strategies (Gagné, 1984). The designer presented the team with options, and the team selected the strategies most beneficial to enhancing performance by targeting learning outcomes that needed reinforcement, based on the level of complexity and degree of learners' prior knowledge and familiarity (Dunlosky et al., 2013; Roelle & Nückles, 2019). These strategies varied between matching exercises that integrate relevant information with existing knowledge, filling out organizational charts that convert what was learned verbally into a visual form, and scenarios that require learners to explain and elaborate on the learning material at a higher level of thinking (Fiorella & Mayer, 2016). Additionally, homework assignments of the same nature were designed to enable learners to reflect and prepare for the next day's tasks.

With the instructional strategy in place, the designer again verified that cognitive load was addressed. She referred to Clark's (2008) categorization of factors that affect cognitive load in the context of training: complexity of the content, experience of learners, presentation rate and control, and instructional modes and methods. Using these factors, the designer created Table 1 to determine where in the training cognitive load is of concern and whether these concerns were addressed or if further recommendations were needed.

Table 1 shows that the review and redesign of class presentations created a good foundation for achieving stated learning outcomes by enhancing processing and retention of content. Its complexity and presentation were addressed through review of the sequence and integration of several strategies that decrease cognitive load. Instructional strategies were reviewed or added to actively engage leaners through in-class exercises, group activities, and authentic field exercises. These learner-centered strategies allow learners to solve problems using higher-order thinking skills that translate into an increased germane cognitive load and better retention of content (Jonassen, 2009; Kay, MacDonald, & DiGiuseppe, 2018; Weston & Cranton, 1986). Lecture as an instructional strategy was still necessary because the content material had to be delivered in a very short amount of time with the residential training extending over a period of four days: two days for in-class sessions, one day for field data collection, and one day for deliverables and presentations. Although lectures are not effective in promoting thought and changing attitudes (Bligh, 2000), they are effective in transmitting information, especially when well-organized and supported by active learning opportunities (Richardson, 2008).

Table 1. The designer's analysis of factors affecting cognitive load in the training

Factor affecting cognitive load	Infection prevention and control course	Impact on cognitive load as perceived by the designer	Remedies
Complexity of the content	Overall, content was complex. Not all material was new. Some of it was previously learned during the distance-learning section of the course. New material was complex and proved to be difficult to master in previous training.	Learners revisited previously learned materials. This does not add to cognitive load but supports retention of new materials by retrieving knowledge and skills from long-term memory to help process new material in working memory. It will help learners make connections and facilitate learning. New material has high intrinsic cognitive load.	The sequence and design of the new material was reviewed to address intrinsic cognitive load (complexity and difficulty).
Experience of learners	Some prior knowledge on infection prevention and control topics.	Low- to medium-intrinsic cognitive load since learners are not novices. Their experience equips them with learning that can be retrieved and connected to the new content, alleviating the cognitive load on the working memory.	Instructional strategies were developed based on the level of expertise of the learners. Strategies brushed over familiar concepts and focused on new materials.
Presentation rate and control	Long lectures with several slides with no learner control on the allotted time for presentations	High extraneous cognitive load.	Chunking of complex, less familiar concepts. Integration of practice exercises as pausing instances and room for learner control.
Instructional modes and methods	Lecture slides were mostly text-based and followed by applications in class and in the field.	The text-based nature of a good portion of the slides adds to cognitive load . Chunking alleviates cognitive load. Some slides contain visual representations, which reduce cognitive load. Parts of the program are based on in-class and field exercises that support thinking (increase desired germane load)	Varied modalities alleviate cognitive load. Revision of active learning instances enhance retention through higher-order thinking skills (germane load). Generative strategies enhance long-term memory and reduce intrinsic cognitive load.

Design of the Assessment Strategy

"Assessment is the process of determining what leaners know or are able to do" (Merrill, 2013, p. 370). If designed to enhance learners' motivations and help them set goals with effective feedback, assessment can accelerate learning (Frey et al., 2018). Assessment can be formative or summative. Formative assessment, embedded within instruction, serves as feedback on the learning process to improve learning and adjust instruction if needed, and summative assessment shows whether learning outcomes were achieved and is given at the completion of instruction (Taras, 2005; Rolfe & McPherson, 1995).

Formative assessment is an assessment *for* learning, and summative assessment is an assessment *of* learning (Taras, 2005). With that in mind, the designer and the Global ID team discussed the value of both types of assessment and marked where they could be integrated into the training and, consequently, into the workbook. The team had originally incorporated assessment strategies in their presentations. Formative assessments included verbal knowledge checks, homework, and in-class and field activities. Summative assessments included a culminating project prepared and presented by learners at the end of the training. The team and the designer explored additional opportunities for formative assessment. In fact, the generative strategies discussed earlier constituted the additional formative assessment strategies (Willis & Cowie, 2014).

The next step was to review the selected assessment strategies to determine the types and format of the assessment tools needed to measure gains in learning. It was agreed that learners would be asked to share their responses orally in the class for feedback on simple activities. More complex activities, such as developing an infection prevention and control policy, one of the culminating projects, needed rubrics for a more structured assessment. Rubrics are assessment tools designed to evaluate student performance on tasks that require a high level of thinking. They are composed of evaluative criteria that represent key attributes of learning (Popham, 1997). Therefore, existing rubrics were reviewed and adjusted accordingly and, where needed, new rubrics were developed.

Upon completion of the analysis and design phases of the instructional design process, the designer began the design and development of the workbook prototype.

Design and Development of the Workbook Prototype

So far, the instructional design process focused on the content of the training. The next step was to focus on the design of the workbook that will accompany the training. As discussed earlier, the workbook will be used in the classroom for in-class activities and provision of slide handouts and outside the classroom for homework and as a resource to support transfer. The needs analysis revealed the team's uncertainty towards including the slides in the workbook for fear of redundancy. Ultimately, the decision was made to include the slides and add space for note taking based on the following rationale provided by the designer.

Information communicated verbally, such as in lectures, is not well retained and results in diminished learning. This is what Leahy and Sweller (2016) call "transient information effect." To remedy this effect and improve instruction, they suggested presenting complex verbal information in a written format and supplementing auditory presentations with visuals. Additionally, other researchers have shown that providing learners with lecture slides enhances learning by reducing cognitive load, because it frees students to use their thinking skills to generate their own notes, instead of focusing on copying notes from the slides (Baker et al., 2018; Marsh & Sink, 2010; Worthington & Levasseur, 2015). The combination of written and visual representation provided by the slides supports the instruction transmitted during the lectures by reducing cognitive load, supporting sense generation, and enhancing retention. Therefore, the team agreed to include the slides in the workbook.

On the other hand, note taking helps learners generate thinking and construct learning (Stefanou, Hoffman, & Vielee, 2008). It acts as an "external storage…a repository of information for later review and additional cognitive processing… and further generative activities" (Armbruster, 2000, p. 222). As they take notes during lectures and review them later, learners engage in a generative process that decreases cognitive load, especially when notes are accompanied with other materials such as PowerPoint slides that act as scaffolding to the learning process and decrease the transient information effect (Leahy & Sweller; 2016; Merriënboer et al., 2003). Consequently, the team also agreed to provide a space to take notes in the workbook, next to the slides. It is important to remember that both of these decisions were supported by the results of the attitude survey, in which learners expressed an appreciation for the inclusion of slides and a space for note taking in the workbook.

Once the inclusion of slides and note-taking spaces was agreed upon and all instructional and assessment strategies were selected, the designer began working on a physical prototype, a "mock-up of the instructional events" (Merrill, 2103, p. 209) by using Adobe InDesign software. The following is a summary of design choices and the decisions that were made.

- The designer offered several options for the number of slides per page. The team chose the 3 slides per page layout
- The team expressed the desire to denote each module with a different color. These would be used in major headings.

- The team expressed the desire to include icons. These would be placed in the headers.
- The team decided to add a pocket to the workbook to add changeable materials, such as schedules, for each subsequent training.

Evaluation and Follow-Up

The design of the workbook gave rise to three future initiatives: First, the Global ID team will be hosting a Development Workshop for Educators at Global Training hubs, a 3-day workshop dedicated to training the residential teaching teams. These teams are expected to implement and lead the residential training in Mexico, India, Egypt, and Lebanon. Along with harmonizing teaching across regions and languages, this workshop aims to provide sustainability to the program and strengthen its implementation on a larger scale. As such, it will provide an opportunity for testing the workbook prototype to reveal impressions and identify strengths and weaknesses (Dick et al., 2015). The trainers' feedback will be used to refine the workbook before it goes to print in its final form.

Second, the collaboration with the designer on the review of the training and the design of the workbook raised the team's interest in instructional design principles. Therefore, the team asked the designer to create a summary of these principles in the form of a job aid to use as a reference in the design of future instructional materials.

Third, the designer suggested evaluation beyond the week of training to document evidence of program effectiveness, attitudes of learners, and long-term benefits (Morrison et al., 2013). She shared with the Global ID team the Kirkpatrick model (Kirkpatrick Partners, 2020) for evaluation of training. The model focuses on four levels of training:

- *Reaction* measures learners' attitudes towards the training. This step was already set in place by the Global ID team, in terms of training participant satisfaction surveys and through testing the prototype with trainers.
- *Learning* measures achievement of learning outcomes. Similarly, this step was covered through the revision and strengthening of formative and summative assessments that will take place during the training.
- *Behavior* measures the application of skills learned in the training in home institutions, also known as the transfer of skills. The team began the process of putting strategies in place to measure transfer. For example, they asked learners to complete the hand hygiene practices assessment survey on-site in their home institutions after being trained, to receive feedback from St. Jude experts.

- *Results* measures the actual change resulting from the training, such as reduced infection rate in pediatric cancer healthcare institutions. Though long-term and challenging, this fourth level is important to determine return on investment (Clark, 2008). The team and the designer plan to review existing follow-up surveys to incorporate as many of the Kirkpatrick levels as can be reasonably measured.

CHALLENGES AND OPPORTUNITIES

The instructional design process revealed some challenges but also opportunities for success. The first challenge for the designer was the complexity of the training material: five interrelated modules covering complex health topics, some of which were purely clinical. Thankfully, the team was always available to collaborate closely, especially on the task analysis, which took a good amount of time. Together, they navigated the process and reached an outcome that strengthened the training and the design of the workbook. On the other hand, this process helped the team to see how someone with limited familiarity with the content would process the material, what things needed clarity for less experienced or nonmedical participants, and what assumptions were made in the delivery of the instruction.

The second challenge was the first impression the designer formed about the content of the training. As mentioned earlier, cognitive load was of concern, as was the limited amount of time dedicated to the training. Once more, through close collaboration on the task analysis, the team and the designer revised the sequence of the content, chunked it, and added sound, efficient instructional strategies to reduce cognitive load within the time limits of the training. The openness of the team and their desire to explore instructional design principles eased this process immensely. Even more, they requested a job aid on these principles.

The third challenge was the interconnectedness between the workbook and the training. The original scope of work was the development of the workbook. As the instructional design process progressed, the need to review the content of the training became apparent because the workbook became an integral part of the training instead of simply being a supporting document. Again, the team's openness to change was a supportive factor in this process.

Sugar and Luterbach (2016) explained that flexibility and good rapport are key factors for the success of instructional design projects. Similarly, van Leusen et al. (2016) observed that active listening, paraphrasing, and explaining concepts and procedures are among the interpersonal skills that support trust and allow progress. The designer listened carefully to the Global ID team to understand their needs, and they listened carefully to her instructional design rationale. Additionally, every exchange was documented and shared by the Global ID team, making sure that everyone was on the same page. They all approached the project with a willingness to change and improve, which enabled a successful design process, in spite of the minor challenges.

CONCLUDING THOUGHTS

Most models describe the instructional design process as a systematic step-by-step approach. However, it is a fluid process, often completed in different sequences of steps based on context (Ertmer & York, 2009), as is the case for this project. The Global ID team and the designer established a clear need for the workbook but picked up task analysis from ranking of learning tasks since these were already set for the training. Additionally, they identified learning outcomes, ranked them, and selected instructional and assessment strategies in an iterative manner to allow for reflection and proper alignment. Last, but not least, they revised the content of the training (instructional strategy) and the workbook design (instructional product) simultaneously due to the interconnections between them. Nevertheless, by following an instructional design process, making decisions informed by theory, and collaborating closely (Sugar & Luterbach, 2016), the designer and the Global ID team enabled this project to be a positive and successful experience.

REFERENCES

Ariza-Heredia, E. J., & Chemaly, R. F. (2018). Update on infection control practices in cancer hospitals. *CA: a Cancer Journal for Clinicians*, *68*(5), 340–355. doi:10.3322/caac.21462 PMID:29985544

Armbruster, B. B. (2000). Taking notes from lectures. In Handbook of college reading and study strategy research (pp. 175–200). Lawrence Erlbaum Associates.

Association for Educational Communications and Technology. (2013). Definition. In A. Januszewski & M. Molenda (Eds.), *Educational Technology: A Definition with Commentary* (pp. 1–14). Routledge. doi:10.4324/9780203054000

Atkinson, R. C., & Shiffrin, R. M. (1968). Human memory: A proposed system and its control processes. In K. W. Spence & J. T. Spence (Eds.), *The psychology of learning and motivation: II*. Academic Press. doi:10.1016/S0079-7421(08)60422-3

Baker, J. P., Goodboy, A. K., Bowman, N. D., & Wright, A. A. (2018). Does teaching with PowerPoint increase students' learning? A meta-analysis. *Computers & Education*, *126*(August), 376–387. doi:10.1016/j.compedu.2018.08.003

Bligh, D. A. (2000). *What's the use of lectures?* (1st ed.). Intellect Books.

Bloom, B. S., Engelhart, M. D., Furst, E. J., Hill, W. H., & Krathwohl, D. R. (1956). *Taxonomy of educational objectives: The classification of educational goals*. Longmans.

Cabrera, D., & Cabrera, L. (2015). *Systems thinking made simple: New hope for solving wicked problems*. Odyssean Press.

Caniza, M. A., Maron, G., McCullers, J., Clara, W. A., Cedillos, R., Dueñas, L., Arnold, S., Williams, B. F., & Tuomanen, E. I. (2007). Planning and implementation of an infection control training program for healthcare providers in Latin America. *Infection Control and Hospital Epidemiology*, *28*(12), 1328–1333. doi:10.1086/521655 PMID:17994511

Caniza, M. A., Odio, C., Mukkada, S., Gonzalez, M., Ceppi, F., Chaisavaneeyakorn, S., Nopporn Apiwattanakul, N., Howard, S. C., Conter, V., & Bonilla, M. (2015). Infectious complications in children with acute lymphoblastic leukemia treated in low-middle-income countries. *Expert Review of Hematology*, *8*(5), 627–645. doi:10.1586/17474086.2015.1071186 PMID:26211675

Center for Disease Control. (2020). *Infection prevention and control*. https://www.who.int/infection-prevention/publications/hh_evidence/en/

Clark, R. C. (2008). *Building expertise: Cognitive methods for training and performance improvement* (3rd ed.). Pfieffer.

Dick, W., Carey, L., & Carey, J. O. (2015). *The systematic design of instruction*. Pearson.

Driscoll, M. P. (2005). *Psychology of learning for instruction* (3rd ed.). Pearson Education, Inc.

Dunbar, A., Tai, E., Nielsen, D. B., Shropshire, S., & Richardson, L. C. (2014). Preventing infections during cancer treatment. *Clinical Journal of Oncology Nursing*, *18*(4), 426–431. doi:10.1188/14.CJON.426-431 PMID:25095295

Dunlosky, J., Rawson, K. A., Marsh, E. J., Nathan, M. J., & Willingham, D. T. (2013). Improving students' learning with effective learning techniques: Promising directions. *Psychology Science in the Public Health Interest*, *14*(1), 4–58. doi:10.1177/1529100612453266 PMID:26173288

Ertmer, P. A., York, C. S., & Gedik, N. (2009). Learning from the Pros: How experienced designers translate instructional design models into practice. *Educational Technology*, *49*(1), 19–27.

Evans, R. (2001). *The human side of school change: reform, resistance, and the real-life problems of school change*. Jossey-Bass.

Fiorella, L., & Mayer, R. E. (2015). Introduction to learning as a generative activity. In *Learning as a generative activity: Eight learning strategies that promote understanding* (pp. 1–19). Cambridge University Press. doi:10.1017/CBO9781107707085.003

Fiorella, L., & Mayer, R. E. (2016). Eight ways to promote generative learning. *Educational Psychology Review*, *28*(4), 717–741. doi:10.100710648-015-9348-9

Frey, N., Fisher, D., & Hattie, J. (2018). Developing "assessment capable" learners. *Educational Leadership*, *75*(5), 46–51.

Gagné, R. M. (1984). Learning outcomes and their effects: Useful categories of human performance. *The American Psychologist*, *39*(4), 377–385. doi:10.1037/0003-066X.39.4.377

Gustafson, K. L., & Branch, R. M. (2002). *Survey of instructional development models* (4th ed.). ERIC Clearinghouse on Information & Technology.

Jonassen, D. H. (2009). Reconciling a human cognitive architecture. In S. Tobias & T. M. Duffy (Eds.), *Constructivist instruction: Success or failure* (pp. 13–33). Roultedge.

Jonassen, D. H., Tessmer, M., & Hannum, W. H. (1999). *Task analysis methods for instructional design*. Lawrence Erlbaum Associates.

Kay, R., MacDonald, T., & DiGiuseppe, M. (2019). A comparison of lecture-based, active, and flipped classroom teaching approaches in higher education. *Journal of Computing in Higher Education*, *31*(3), 449–471. doi:10.100712528-018-9197-x

Kay, R., MacDonald, T., & DiGiuseppe, M. (2019). A comparison of lecture-based, active, and flipped classroom teaching approaches in higher education. *Journal of Computing in Higher Education*, *31*(3), 449–471. doi:10.100712528-018-9197-x

Kirkpatrick Partners. (2020). *The Kirkpatrick Model*. https://www.kirkpatrickpartners.com/Our-Philosophy/The-Kirkpatrick-Model

Kirschner, P. A., Sweller, J., Kirschner, F., & Zambrano, J. R. (2018). From cognitive load theory to collaborative cognitive load theory. *International Journal of Computer-Supported Collaborative Learning*, *13*(2), 213–233. doi:10.100711412-018-9277-y PMID:30996713

Leahy, W., & Sweller, J. (2016). Cognitive load theory and the effects of transient information on the modality effect. *Instructional Science*, *44*(1), 107–123. doi:10.100711251-015-9362-9

Lee, H., Lim, K. Y., & Grabowski, B. L. (2008). Generative learning: Principles and implications for making meaning. In *Handbook of research on educational communications and technology* (3rd ed., pp. 111–124). Routledge. https://aect.org/third_edition.php

Marsh, E. J., & Sink, H. (2010). Access to handouts of presentation slides during lecture: Consequences for learning. *Applied Cognitive Psychology*, *24*(5), 691–706. doi:10.1002/acp.1579

Mayer, R. E., & Moreno, R. (2003). Nine ways to reduce cognitive load in multimedia learning. *Educational Psychologist*, *38*(1), 43–52. doi:10.1207/S15326985EP3801_6

Merriënboer, J. J. G., Kirschner, P. A., & Kester, L. (2003). Taking the load off a learner's mind: Instructional design for complex learning. *Educational Psychologist*, *38*(1), 5–13. doi:10.1207/S15326985EP3801_2

Merriënboer, J. J. G., & Sweller, J. (2010). Cognitive load theory in health professional education: Design principles and strategies. *Medical Education*, *44*(1), 85–93. doi:10.1111/j.1365-2923.2009.03498.x PMID:20078759

Merrill, M. D. (2013). *First principles of instruction: Identifying and designing effective, efficient, and engaging instruction*. Pfeiffer.

Morrison, G. R., Ross, S. M., Kalman, H. K., & Kemp, J. E. (2013). *Designing effective instruction*. Wiley.

Paas, F., van Gog, T., & Sweller, J. (2010). Cognitive load theory: New conceptualizations, specifications, and integrated research perspectives. *Educational Psychology Review*, *22*(2), 115–121. doi:10.100710648-010-9133-8

Patton, M. Q. (2018). Facilitating evaluation principles in practice. *Sage (Atlanta, Ga.)*.

Popham, W. J. (1997). What's wrong - and what's right - with rubrics. *Educational Leadership*, *55*(2), 72–75.

Posner, G. J., & Strike, K. A. (1976). A categorization scheme for principles of sequencing content. *Review of Educational Research, 46*(4), 665–690. doi:10.3102/00346543046004665

Reigeluth, C. M., & Moore, J. (1999). Cognitive education and the cognitive domain. In C. M. Reigeluth (Ed.), Instructional design theories and models (vol. 2, pp. 51-68). Lawrence Erlbaum Associates.

Rentsch, J. R., & Klimoski, R. J. (2001). Why do 'great minds' think alike?: Antecedents of team member schema agreement. *Journal of Organizational Behavior, 22*(2), 107–120. doi:10.1002/job.81

Richardson, D. (2008). Don't dump the didactic lecture; fix it. *American Journal of Physiology -. Advances in Physiology Education, 32*(1), 23–24. doi:10.1152/advan.00048.2007 PMID:18334564

Roelle, J., & Nückles, M. (2019). Generative learning versus retrieval practice in learning from text: The cohesion and elaboration of the text matters. *Journal of Educational Psychology, 111*(8), 1341–1361. doi:10.1037/edu0000345

Rolfe, I., & McPherson, J. (1995). Formative assessment: How am I doing? *Lancet, 345*(8953), 837–839. doi:10.1016/S0140-6736(95)92968-1 PMID:7898233

Senge, P. M. (2012). *Schools that learn: A fifth discipline fieldbook for educators, parents, and everyone who cares about education.* Crown Business.

Sentz, J., Stefaniak, J., Baaki, J., & Eckhoff, A. (2019). How do instructional designers manage learners' cognitive load? An examination of awareness and application of strategies. In *Educational Technology Research and Development* (Vol. 67). Springer US. doi:10.100711423-018-09640-5

Simon, A., Ammann, R. A., Bode, U., Fleischhack, G., Wenchel, H. M., Schwamborn, D., Gravou, C., Schlegel, P.-G., Rutkowski, S., Dannenberg, C., Körholz, D., Laws, H. J., & Kramer, M. H. (2008). Healthcare-associated infections in pediatric cancer patients: Results of a prospective surveillance study from university hospitals in Germany and Switzerland. *BMC Infectious Diseases, 8*(1), 1–10. doi:10.1186/1471-2334-8-70 PMID:18500998

St. Jude Children Research Hospital. (2020a). *About us.* https://www.stjude.org/about-st-jude.html?sc_icid=us-mm-missionstatement#mission

St. Jude Children Research Hospital. (2020b). *Our history.* https://www.stjude.org/about-st-jude/history.html

St. Jude Children Research Hospital. (2020c). *St. Jude global.* https://www.stjude.org/global.html

Stefanou, C., Hoffman, L., & Vielee, N. (2008). Note-taking in the college classroom as evidence of generative learning. *Learning Environments Research, 11*(1), 1–17. doi:10.100710984-007-9033-0

Sugar, W. A., & Luterbach, K. J. (2016). Using critical incidents of instructional design and multimedia production activities to investigate instructional designers' current practices and roles. *Educational Technology Research and Development, 64*(2), 285–312. doi:10.100711423-015-9414-5

Sweller, J., Ayres, P., & Kalyuga, S. (2011). *Cognitive load theory*. Springer., doi:10.1007/978-1-4419-8126-4

Sweller, J., van Merriënboer, J. J. G., & Paas, F. (2019). Cognitive architecture and instructional design: 20 years later. *Educational Psychology Review, 31*(2), 261–292. doi:10.100710648-019-09465-5

Taras, M. (2005). Assessment : Summative and formative : Some theoretical reflections. *British Journal of Educational Studies, 53*(4), 466–478. doi:10.1111/j.1467-8527.2005.00307.x

Tyler, R. (2017). Basic principles of curriculum and instruction. In D. J. Flinders & S. J. Thornton (Eds.), *Curriculum studies reader* (4th ed., pp. 73–82). Routledge.

van Leusen, P., Ottenbreit-Lefwich, A. T., & Brush, T. (2016). Interpersonal consulting skills for instructional technology consultants: A multiple case study. *TechTrends, 60*(3), 253–259. doi:10.100711528-016-0046-3

Weston, C., & Cranton, P. A. (1986). Selecting instructional strategies. *The Journal of Higher Education, 57*(3), 259. doi:10.2307/1981553

Willis, J., & Cowie, B. (2014). Assessment as a generative dance: Connecting teaching learning and curriculum. In C. Wyatt-Smith, V. Klenowski, & P. Colbert (Eds.), *Designing assessment for quality learning* (pp. 23–38). Springer. doi:10.1007/978-94-007-5902-2_2

Wittrock, M. C. (2010). Learning as a generative process. *Educational Psychologist, 45*(1), 40–45. doi:10.1080/00461520903433554

World Health Organization. (2020). *Cancer in children.* https://www.who.int/news-room/fact-sheets/detail/cancer-in-children

Worthington, D. L., & Levasseur, D. G. (2015). To provide or not to provide course PowerPoint slides? The impact of instructor-provided slides upon student attendance and performance. *Computers & Education*, *85*, 14–22. doi:10.1016/j.compedu.2015.02.002

ADDITIONAL READING

Barnett, J. E. (2003). Do instructor-provided online notes facilitate student learning? *Journal of Interactive Online Learning*, *2*(2), 1–7. http://www.ncolr.org/issues/jiol/v2/n2/do-instructor-provided-online-notes-facilitate-student-learning.html

Black, P., & Wiliam, D. (2009). Developing the theory of formative assessment. *Educational Assessment, Evaluation and Accountability*, *21*(1), 5–31. doi:10.100711092-008-9068-5

Botma, Y., Van Rensburg, G. H., Coetzee, I. M., & Heyns, T. (2015). A conceptual framework for educational design at modular level to promote transfer of learning. *Innovations in Education and Teaching International*, *52*(5), 499–509. doi:10.1080/14703297.2013.866051

Brigley, S., Hosein, I., & Myemba, I. R. (2009). Bridging the divide: Sustainability and relevance of a distance learning module for clinical officers in Tanzania. *International Journal of Phytoremediation*, *24*(2), 155–163. doi:10.1080/02680510902879486

Brown, A. H., & Green, T. D. (2018). Beyond teaching instructional design models: Exploring the design process to advance professional development and expertise. *Journal of Computing in Higher Education*, *30*(1), 176–186. doi:10.100712528-017-9164-y

Chime, J. K., Munyati, P., Musumali, M., Mweetwa, B., Kagulura, S., & Kachimba, J. S. (2016). Using e-learning for skills transfer, motivation and retention of health workers in Zambia. *Medical Journal of Zambia, 43*(2), 103-105–105.

Huxham, M. (2010). The medium makes the message: Effects of cues on students' lecture notes. *Active Learning in Higher Education*, *11*(3), 179–188. doi:10.1177/1469787410379681

Pollock, E., Chandler, P., & Sweller, J. (2002). Assimilating complex information. *Learning and Instruction*, *12*(1), 61–86. doi:10.1016/S0959-4752(01)00016-0

Smith, K. M. (2009). What do we make of design? Design as a concept in educational technology. *Educational Technology*, *49*(4), 3–17. http://eric.ed.gov/ERICWebPortal/recordDetail?accno=EJ865542

St Clair, N. E., Pitt, M. B., Bakeera-Kitaka, S., McCall, N., Lukolyo, H., Arnold, L. D., Audcent, T., Batra, M., Chan, K., Jacquet, G. A., Schutze, G. E., & Butteris, S. (2017). Global health: Preparation for working in resource-limited settings. *Pediatrics*, *140*(5), e20163783. Advance online publication. doi:10.1542/peds.2016-3783 PMID:29074610

York, C. S., & Ertmer, P. A. (2011). Towards an understanding of instructional design heuristics: An exploratory Delphi study. *Educational Technology Research and Development*, *59*(6), 841–863. doi:10.100711423-011-9209-2

KEY TERMS AND DEFINITIONS

Cognitive Load: Effort exerted by the working memory during the learning process.

Evaluation: The process by which the value of instruction, training, product, etc. is measured.

Formative Assessment: A type of assessment implemented during the learning process to give feedback on the learning process.

Generative Strategies: Strategies used during the learning process to support retention and integration of content.

Needs Analysis: A initial step of the instructional design process to establish the need for instruction.

Summative Assessment: A type of assessment implemented after the completion of the learning process to measure learning gains.

Task Analysis: Analysis and organization of learning outcomes.

Transfer of Learning: Application of learned knowledge and skills in practice settings.

APPENDIX

Questions for Discussion

- Would you have approached the design of the workbook differently?
- Would you characterize the redesign and review of the content of the training as project creep, or do you agree that this was an essential step in the design of the workbook?
- What is your perspective on the inclusion of generative strategies? Do you agree with the designer on their value in the learning process?
- What strategies might you use to obtain buy-in of teams who may not be familiar with instructional design theory? How might you convince clients of your suggested strategies?

Chapter 4
My Life, My Story:
A Narrative Life History Activity to Humanize the Veteran Patient Experience

Susan Nathan
https://orcid.org/0000-0002-0591-1378
VA Boston Healthcare System, USA & Harvard Medical School, USA

Andrea Wershof Schwartz
https://orcid.org/0000-0002-2076-6068
VA Boston Healthcare System, USA & Harvard Medical School, USA

David R. Topor
VA Boston Healthcare System, USA & Harvard Medical School, USA

EXECUTIVE SUMMARY

Contemporary healthcare institutions strive to provide humanistic and patient-centered healthcare. To reach this goal, healthcare systems must first look to the patient as a person, before treating a specific malady or pathology. This chapter will illustrate a humanistic approach to the provision of healthcare using the case of the My Life, My Story program in the United States Veterans Health Administration. My Life, My Story is a patient-centered, life story work intervention where learners complete a life story interview with a veteran using standardized prompts from the My Life, My Story protocol. This chapter will describe the My Life My Story program at the VA Boston Healthcare System, the steps and rationale in program development and discussion of impact on the learners, the patients, and humanizing the healthcare system.

DOI: 10.4018/978-1-7998-5092-2.ch004

INTRODUCTION

We can sometimes forget that our patients are more than their medical or psychiatric conditions. They are whole people with a lifetime of history that is influencing how they are coping with their condition and interacting with their providers. I think that the project allows us as providers to remember this and might also be a reminder to the patient that they are more than their medical condition. -Learner comment

Contemporary healthcare institutions strive to provide humanistic and patient-centered medical care. To reach this goal, healthcare systems must first look to the patient as a person, before treating a specific malady or pathology. To train future health professions practitioners in a way that emphasizes humanistic care, it is necessary to operationalize what it means to "know the patient as a person." This chapter will illustrate a humanistic approach to the provision of healthcare using the case of the My Life, My Story (MLMS) program in the United States Veterans Health Administration (VHA).

Life story work is a term given to biographical approaches in health care that give people the opportunity to talk about their life experiences (McKeown, Clarke & Repper, 2005). MLMS is a life story work intervention where learners complete a life story interview with a veteran patient using standardized prompts from the MLMS protocol. The interview is written up as a concise, roughly 1,000-word-first person narrative, which is then read back to the veteran. The veteran may provide feedback and adjustments before it is entered into the electronic health record with the veteran's approval, available for subsequent health care team members to view. The veteran is offered copies of the story for themselves, which they may share with family or friends. After completion of the story, interviewers can debrief their experience either in a facilitated small group setting with other learners or directly with their educational preceptor.

This program provides a direct service to the veteran, in the form of the learner bearing witness to the veteran's life story. The veteran is allowed a degree of agency in the telling and documentation of his or her own story. This is in contrast to usual healthcare, which is typically delivered in a hierarchical manner and with emphasis placed on the perspective of the healthcare system. The veteran can review and edit the story that is entered into the healthcare record, unlike the typical healthcare notes that only reflect the clinician's voice. The use of the first-person voice empowers the veteran and allows them to tell their own story as the expert in their own lived experience, rather than being relegated to the passive, third person. Rather than being a transcript of the interview, the learner writes a story, allowing the narrative to capture the associated lyricism and emotional impact on the veteran, the learner conducting the interview, and the healthcare team who have access to the final story. This chapter will describe the MLMS program at the VA Boston Healthcare System (VABHS), and the potential impact on learners, veterans, and humanizing the healthcare system.

BACKGROUND

Humanities in Health Professions Education: Filling a Critical Need

In the sufferer let me only see the human being…

These words, from a physician's oath attributed to the medieval physician and rabbi Moses Maimonides, evoke the longstanding challenge of maintaining empathy in the face of human illness for those who care for patients (Rosner, 1967). Health professions education has long turned to the humanities to maintain empathy and to humanize the clinical training experience, using a variety of different approaches, including literature, visual arts, and music (Schwartz, et al., 2009). Recent years have seen an increase in humanities-oriented activities aimed at helping health professions trainees maintain compassion during training, avoid burnout, and see patients as whole people (Peterkin & Skorzewska, 2018). In addition to promoting empathy for patients, humanities in health professions education may help trainees remain resilient and avoid burnout (Jones, 2014). For example, an undergraduate medical education course for first and second year Harvard Medical School students entitled "The Developing Physician: Lifelong Integration of Personal and Professional Growth, with Sensitive, Compassionate Care," provides an opportunity for students to share stories and reflections on the intense process of becoming a physician (Berensin, et al., 2016). Similarly, internal medicine residents from Brigham and Women's Hospital in Boston, Massachusetts participate in a program called *The Humanistic Curriculum*, which provides an opportunity for them to engage in art and reflection amidst the busy and at times emotionally difficult work of training to be a physician (Gooding, Quinn, Martin, Charrow & Katz, 2016). On a national level, the American Academy of Medical Colleges (AAMC), in collaboration and with grant funding from the National Endowment for the Humanities, is exploring the current landscape of arts and humanities in medicine to think about how best to integrate and advance the role of humanities and the arts in medical education and physician development. (Mann, 2017; The Role of Arts and Humanities in Physician Development, n.d).

Among the many modalities of arts and humanities in medicine, storytelling serves an important purpose in humanizing health professions education. Telling and listening to stories forms the core of the field of Narrative Medicine, providing training to clinicians in the art of eliciting and understanding patients' stories (Charon, 2001). Ideally, in a clinical encounter, the learner or clinician should elicit a story from the patient. However, many learners or clinicians operate in healthcare settings in which the electronic health record shapes the way in which the story is solicited, often reducing the patient's experience to a series of checkboxes (Koven, 2019). Stories may serve as 'inoculations' against the erosion of empathy, helping learners remember to fulfill those ancient words of seeing the person amidst the disease (Treadway, 2005). Examples abound of health professions trainees (Shapiro, Bezzubova & Koons, 2011) or health professionals (Silverman, 2017) sharing patients' stories with one another to help support each other to remain empathic and cope with the challenges of providing healthcare.

Despite the documented benefits of participating in humanities in general, and story-telling in particular (Bleakley, 2015), barriers remain to fully integrating these practices into health professions education. While educators and learners agree on the value of these practices, time limits and logistical considerations often stand in the way of their inclusion in curricula (Pories, et al., 2018). In many health professions programs, participation in humanities initiatives is optional. Therefore, only learners who are already interested may participate, but these may not be the learners who can benefit the most from this programming (Lam, et al., 2015). Evidence of impact is lacking in many of these programs, which diminishes their rigor in the health professions education setting and weakens the argument for their inclusion in curricula (Taylor, Lehman & Chisholm, 2017).

The My Life, My Story program addresses several of these deficits. By requiring devoted time for learners to interview a veteran, document the story, read it back to the veteran, and include it in the healthcare record, a broader swath of learners can participate and benefit from this unique patient encounter. By sharing the stories in the healthcare record, subsequent members of the health care team can learn about the veteran as a person and potentially enhance their connection to caring for that individual. Finally, both providers and veterans find the MLMS storytelling experience to be positive and meaningful, promoting trust and connection that has the potential to have a profound impact on the healthcare system (Ringler, Ahearn, Wise, Lee & Krahn, 2015).

My Life, My Story

My Life, My Story was developed at the William S. Middleton VA in 2013 through a grant from the VA Office of Patient Centered Care and has since spread to 49 other VA Healthcare Systems (Ringler, et al. 2015; VAntage Point blog, 2019).

At VABHS, MLMS has been framed as a structured educational intervention to enhance veteran-centered care competencies, with a focus on knowing the whole person, eliciting values and goals, and strengthening the therapeutic relationship. MLMS allows healthcare providers to learn who the veteran is beyond their medical problem list, and beyond the one moment in time of that encounter. It is the hope that this approach will ultimately foster increased veteran-centered healthcare.

Education is one of the four statutory missions of the United States Department of Veterans Affairs (VA). VA has a long-established historical commitment to education and has a broad impact on health professions training in the US, with the largest education and training effort for health professionals in the US. In 2018, 120,890 learners from a diverse group of health and social professions received some or all their clinical training in VA and more than forty health professions are represented by affiliations with over 1,800 colleges and universities. Over 65% of US-trained physicians, and almost 70% of VA physicians have had VA training prior to employment (Mission of the Office of Academic Affiliations, 2019). Given this position in the educational landscape, VA is well positioned to implement innovative programs that have a broad impact. The primary clinical aim of VA: "To care for him who shall have borne the battle, and for his widow, and his orphan" (Lincoln, 1865) by serving and honoring the men and women who are America's veterans and the educational mission align in the MLMS program to put the identity of the veteran at the forefront of his or her care.

Steps to Complete a My Life, My Story Interview

The MLMS process consists of finite, structured segments in a specified order, but with flexibility such that the process can be tailored to the various time and logistical constraints of the setting. MLMS has been completed in a variety of clinical settings, including but not limited to: outpatient clinic, at home, urgent care, emergency department, acute care hospital-medical/surgical wards, intensive care unit-post-acute care (i.e. subacute rehabilitation, skilled nursing facility), inpatient hospice and palliative care unit, and via telephone. All veterans are eligible to participate and should be invited to partake. It is not possible to predict who may or may not be willing to share their story. The ideal participant is anyone who says 'yes'. A foundation for MLMS is to create the space and tools in training and in the healthcare system for the veteran to tell the story and for the learner to bear witness and share that story so the veteran and their story may continue to be heard and honored by the healthcare team.

Interviews can be conducted by learners at any stage of training. Participants have included pre-clinical students, and graduate or post-graduate fellows. Stories might also be written by clinical or administrative staff and some VA sites have engaged with community-based volunteers who are trained as writers/interviewers. Learners may conduct interviews as a pair-with one as the main interviewer and both taking notes and co-writing the story. Interviewers are given a sample script on how to introduce the program to a veteran participant. This script includes an overview of the MLMS program and its purpose. Interviewers may describe the program, its growth over time, and potential benefits of participating. It is essential that the veteran understands they can talk about any topic that is important to them, which may not be related to their military service or to their healthcare. It is specified that the veteran does not have to share anything they do not want to and that the interview is not specifically focused on their military service, although basic questions about military history are asked with their permission. Some veterans will only participate if they do not have to talk about their military experience, while other veterans will focus their whole story on their time in the military.

Veterans are told that once the interview is transcribed into a story, it will be read back to them. This allows them the opportunity to make edits, additions, or subtractions. Once the veteran is in the mode of storytelling, he or she might share more than initially planned. Having the opportunity to review the story gives the veteran the chance to think about what was shared and take out components that may be too personal. While every veteran is offered the opportunity to review their story, veterans may opt not to. It is not unusual that the veteran agrees to share his or her story but does not wish to hear it back prior to it being entered into the healthcare record.

Interviews are preferentially read back rather than left with the veteran to review on their own for a variety of reasons. The impact of the experience extends beyond the interview and writing portion and into the reading back of the story for both the veteran and the learners. In hearing their own story back, the veteran has the opportunity to reflect on some of their experiences from a different vantage point, which may allow them to identify narrative, thematic arcs. At this point in the process the veteran might remark to the writer/ interviewer: "*You did a good job.*" To which the writer/interviewer might respond: "*I just listened to you and wrote down what you said.*" The reality is somewhere in between, with the veteran sharing their story which is then synthesized into the narrative that is crafted by the writer. Within the sharing of the story and the craft of synthesizing the interview by the writer there is now something unique that has been created.

There are also practical considerations in reading back the story to the veteran. The framework was designed to be mindful of variable literacy levels. For interviews done in an inpatient setting, there is a constant flow of papers, handouts, and other detritus that is accumulated and cleared away as well as other practical considerations like potential room changes. Leaving a printed story at the bedside increases the risk that the story would be thrown away without review. Additionally, in the inpatient setting there are clinical elements, including the veteran's fluctuating clinical status, that may impact the veteran's ability to read the story on their own. For the veteran who wants to review his or her story, it is not considered 'complete' until the veteran can review and make edits. The veteran may also choose to take the story and do the review on his or her own and return the edited story to the writer.

Once the veteran approves the final draft of the story and with the veteran's permission it is entered into their healthcare record and can be accessed by the healthcare team. The story is entered into the healthcare record in an easy to find location, and with a simple note-title (MY STORY), to reduce foreseeable barriers to healthcare team members being able to find it.

There are many branch points in program participation that allow the veteran to have control and agency over the degree of their participation as well as the content of the story. Participation in this program is optional. Roughly half of veterans who are offered the chance to participate will decline. Common reasons veterans offer for opting not to participate include: *I'm private; I want to leave the past in the past; I already did this; I want to focus on my medical conditions.* It is not the aim of the interviewer to convince anyone to participate, only to offer.

Of the veterans who choose to participate, they may further choose whether the story is entered in the chart. Most participants are agreeable to having the story placed into their healthcare record. Many participants will elect to share their story but will not wish to review it or have copies of the finished product. Furthermore, veterans who participate can have their story shared beyond the confines of their healthcare record. Common scenarios where stories might be shared beyond the record might be for training or education purposes-either within VA or in the community.

When the writer/interviewer is part of the clinical care team, and the story is to remain in the healthcare record only, then no special consent is required for participation, as this is a part of routine care. If the veteran is agreeable to have the story shared beyond the confines of the record then the veteran needs to sign a consent form. Or, if the person conducting the interview is not part of the clinical care team, and the veteran agrees to have the story entered into the record, the veteran signs a consent that allows the writer/interviewer to access their record, solely for the purpose of entering the story. Stories that are shared with the consent of the veteran are deidentified of protected health information and details are further obfuscated prior to being shared to protect the privacy of the veteran. Veterans will often express the desire to share their story and their experiences if it might help other veterans or if others can learn from what they have been through.

The Interview

Interviewers begin the conversation with broad introductory statements, such as: "It is important for us to understand the stories of your life. This will help us understand who you are as a person and what is important to you." Interviewers should allow veterans to share their stories and provide little re-direction to veterans as they are speaking. The interviewer might ask clarifying questions, or if the veteran shares something that the interviewer is not familiar with (i.e., military vernacular) the interviewer may ask the veteran to provide additional details. This exchange flips the typical power dynamic in the healthcare encounter, where the healthcare provider is the expert in the condition and the patient is there to seek counsel. Now it is the veteran who is the expert who can lead the encounter and share his or her specific knowledge and experience. A common starting point for the interview could be a simple question: "*Where did you grow up and what was it like?*" And that might be the only question that is asked until the end of the interview. Interviewers are advised to avoid an opening question that is too broad, i.e. "*So tell me your life story*." Often in a healthcare setting the patient is primed to tell their medical story, or their '*History of Present Illness*' and may veer into that illness story. By asking a more specific question to start off, that is intentionally non-medical, it sets the focus on veteran as person, and helps guide him or her back to the personal story rather than strictly the medical story. While there are no specific medical questions included in the interview guide, the illness story and the life story are often interwoven in the telling.

The interviewer may use open-ended prompt questions from the suggested interview question guide if additional prompts are needed to facilitate the interview. These questions can cover several topics including:

- Veteran's childhood experiences ("What were you like as a kid?", "What was it like growing up in your hometown?")
- Military service ("How did you pick the branch of the service you were in?", "What did you do after discharge?")
- Significant relationships ("Who have been important people in your life?")
- Life lessons learned ("What do you value most in life?", "What advice or wisdom would you like to pass on to others?", "What do you want your healthcare team to know that they don't already know?")
- Future plans ("What are your hopes for your future?", "How would you describe your family legacy?")

Interviewers focus less on specific dates and names, and more on the gestalt of the veteran's story. At times, the veteran may become emotional when describing life experiences. Interviewers can provide empathy and supportive statements and allow the veterans to take breaks as needed. The writer might ask the veteran if they want the difficult parts included in the story and often the response is affirmative, because it is part of the story and part of what brought the veteran to this present moment in time.

Following the interview, interviewers thank the veteran for their service and for taking the time to share his or her story and participate in MLMS.

The Write-Up

The interviewer takes written notes while the veteran is speaking. No technology is needed for the interview. The interviewer is advised to enter the conversation with a notepad and two pens. The story is written from these notes. This no technology structure serves multiple purposes. By keeping the intervention technologically streamlined, the physical and technological barrier that is often presented by the computer or the workstation in the healthcare encounter has been removed (Pearce, Arnold, Phillips, Trumble, & Dwan, 2011). As the interviewer is listening and writing intently, it reinforces that this is the time for the veteran to speak rather than time for a conversation. Because of this streamlined, no technology approach, there is no associated cost for program supplies (i.e., encrypted audio recorders), thus removing financial barriers for institutional implementation.

Interviews average 40 minutes long and the target length of the story is roughly 1000 words. This suggested story length was designed with the context in mind-specifically that this is to be accessed by a healthcare team member in the process of their clinical work. The interviewer may provide the veteran with a longer version of the story, while entering a more concisely edited version for the healthcare record. As the interviewer is listening and taking notes, he or she will develop a shorthand of sorts which will amount to editing down the interview as they go, ultimately streamlining the writing process.

At VABHS, most of these interviews have taken place in an inpatient setting. The inpatient setting provides some process advantages, in that the veteran is on site and coordinating the read-back portion of the interview is more predictable. For interviews done in an outpatient setting, additional coordination is required as to when, where and how the veteran will have the opportunity to review the first draft of the story. This might be done over the phone at a pre-determined time or might be done in person if the veteran and writer are able to coordinate a time where both parties are on site at the healthcare center. Or the writer might coordinate with the veteran around a time the veteran will already be at the healthcare center for another scheduled appointments. The veteran may be given a draft of the story to review on his or her own, which still leaves the step to coordinate the veteran returning the draft to the writer for updates. The goal is not to create additional burden to the veteran in the completion of the interview.

As part of a faculty implementation guide, several feasible implementation strategies have been outlined depending on the clinical setting and the rotation duration of the learner participant (My Life, My Story VA Boston Education, 2019).

Inpatient Setting 1: All in One Session

This works best if there is an afternoon that can be blocked off specifically for this experience. After lunch or later in afternoon often works well; early evening also can work well depending on schedules. This keeps in mind the workflow in the inpatient hospital setting, when the team conducts rounds and other direct care events are in process. This might take two hours total with some variation.

Inpatient Setting 2: In Segments Over the Course of a Few Days

Do the interview on day one. Write the interview that day or next day. Read back within next few days. This can fit more seamlessly into clinical care if a full afternoon is not able to devote to the experience. Ideal if the veteran will be inpatient for a predictable length of time.

Outpatient Setting 1: All in One Day

This might work if the veteran has a predictable day with multiple appointments or is able to spend extra time at the VA that day. The learner might do the interview in the earlier portion of the day and coordinate a time later in the day to meet and review the story.

Outpatient Setting 2: At Various Time Points

This works well if there is a longitudinal experience for the learner and a longitudinal relationship with the veteran. The interview can be done at visit one. The read back can be done at a following visit or another time when the veteran and learner are both at VA.

Outpatient Setting 3: One Question at a Time.

This works well if there is a longitudinal experience for the learner and a longitudinal relationship with the veteran and devoting a whole block of time is not feasible. The ultimate synthesis and writing of the story may take more skill but this might fit more seamlessly into a clinical encounter.

Debriefing

The interviews are a powerful experience for the learner. Following the interview, learners can meet with their faculty preceptors or mentors to discuss the impact of the interview on the trainee and on the veteran. These meetings can be conducted individually or in small groups and can focus on reflection around the learning experience. The questions below may be used as prompts to facilitate discussion or for a reflective writing exercise-either done ahead of time of the debrief and brought to discuss or done at the beginning of the session.

- What surprised you about this experience?
- What were you expecting going into the interview? How did this change by the end?
- What parts of it were comfortable? Uncomfortable?
- How was this different from other patient interactions?
- What has impacted you about this experience?
- Why was this meaningful/important?
- How will/might this impact your future practice?
- How does participating in this experience relate to competencies in your profession?

Conducting the debrief as a group can help put into words what can otherwise live on as a feeling within the participant that is not formally given a name. By having the debrief opportunity, the students can move forward from the experience with concrete examples of how to provide veteran-centered care.

What Makes a Good Story?

There are a number of features of a "good story." A good story has a linear structure with a beginning, middle, and end, and a clear narrative arc. It might be filled with tales of triumph over adversity and lessons learned. For the purposes of MLMS, a good story is one that accurately reflects the veteran's experience and the tone of the veteran. A team member reading the story might respond: 'It's like he's standing here talking to me.' There is wide variability in what a final version of a MLMS interview may look like. All these iterations are considered 'good' stories if they reflect the voice of the veteran. For two such examples of stories, please refer to sample stories included in Appendix 1.

While the activity of writing a MLMS interview might initially seem separate from other types of writing that is done as part of the healthcare encounter, there are overlapping themes and transferable skills involved. To practice in a healthcare setting in the present-day environment is to spend a significant time in writing and documentation activities. More and more time is spent in documentation and reading the chart (Mamykina, Vawdrey, Hripcsak, 2016). The task set forth with MLMS is to listen to someone's life story - which may be a large and winding entity with twists and turns, perhaps told in a non-linear fashion - and synthesize it into a concise narrative that reflects the content that the veteran has shared. This might seem different, when contrasted to a clinical interview, where a specific clinical question must be addressed. However, in the telling and ultimately writing of the clinical encounter, the answer that is provided by the patient might mimic some of features of the life story interview, in that the response to what might seemingly be a simple and straight forward question, i.e., *What brought you in today,* might similarly have an indirect course in getting to that answer, that must then be synthesized and documented in a way that accurately reflects the information provided and in a way that might be used to guide additional care by team members going forward.

Impact

From April 2016 to December 2019 over 800 stories total have been written at VABHS. Over 500 learners from various health professions training programs including, physician assistant, medicine, social work, pharmacy, psychology, speech and language pathology, occupational therapy and nursing, have participated.

Program evaluation was conducted using voluntary and anonymous electronic surveys sent to the learner after completion of the MLMS experience (Nathan, et al., 2019). The survey consisted of two parts. In the first part learners were asked to rate themselves in five patient-centered-care domains and asked how participation in MLMS affected those competencies (not at all, somewhat, a great deal). The survey design was based off the CARE (Consultation and Relational Empathy measure) questionnaire - a validated tool designed to be administered to patients in an outpatient setting, where the patient is asked to rate their provider on a variety of domains with a focus on empathy (Mercer, Maxwell, Heaney & Watt, 2004). VABHS MLMS program coordinators reviewed the 12 item CARE questionnaire and identified questions most aligned with PCC using the Mead & Bower framework (Mead & Bower, 2000). The following domains were selected:

- Make the patient feel at ease (introducing yourself, explaining your position, being friendly and warm towards patients, treating patients with respect; not cold or abrupt).
- Let the patient tell their story (giving time to fully describe their condition in their own words; not interrupting, rushing or diverting).

- Really listen (pay close attention to what the patient is saying, not looking at notes or computer as patient is talking)
- Be interested in the patient as a whole person (asking/ knowing relevant details about the patient's life and situation; not treating the patient as "just a number")
- Show care and compassion (seeing genuinely concerned, connecting with the patient on a human level; not being indifferent or detached).

The survey also contained several open-ended questions:

- What did you find most valuable about participating in the "My Life My Story" project?
- Why (if at all) do you think this is an important thing to do? If we wanted to convince others to do more of this in the VA, why is it important? How does it affect you? the family? the patient?
- Is there anything you would change or anything you would suggest we do differently in the future?

Thematic analysis was conducted on open-ended survey responses. These responses were collected during a two-year period from 3/31/2017-4/2/2019. During this time frame learners completed 482 stories and evaluation was done on 141 available survey responses. The most stories in this time frame were completed by physician assistant students, followed by learners in medicine (students, residents and fellows), pharmacy (students and residents), social work interns, mental health (psychology and psychiatry students, interns, residents and fellows), nursing students and a few individuals from other professions (speech language pathology, health administration). Themes were grouped into three main categories: perceived effects on patient-centered care competencies, perceived effects on health outcomes, and perceived positive impact for the family, patient and professional. Regarding perceived effects on patient centered care competencies, the most frequently observed comment related to better understanding the whole person. For example:

Getting to know a patient beyond the medical side of things that is often lost while caring for patients in the hospital; I think it is important because it allows you to more wholly know the patient; treat them more as an individual than just another patient. I think it is important for these reasons; I got the opportunity to witness how important her family is to her and the joys and hardships she has dealt with and deals with. -Learner comment

The subsequent most common comment related to perceived effects on improved empathy, followed by comments on how the activity built the relationship with the veteran. For example:

This is important to do to let the patient know we are here to help them and genuinely want to work with them for their best interest. This affects me, because I now am able to develop a relationship with the patient. -Learner comment

Additional comments were made relating to improvement in the ability to really listen or 'hear' the veteran in a different way and building knowledge of values and goals. Under the umbrella theme of *Perceived Effects on Health Outcomes* the most prevalent theme was that the MLMS experience provides a contrast to usual healthcare.

The most common elements of constructive feedback included length restrictions, questions around use of the first-person voice in the story and in that same vein, concerns about accurately reflecting the veteran voice without the use of audio recording.

FUTURE DIRECTIONS

The aim during the pilot and implementation phase of MLMS within VABHS was to institute the program in a manner that was feasible and that would be framed in such a way as to be relevant for learners across professions and levels of training as a veteran-centered care educational activity. Attention was paid to create a process that could be directly integrated into both clinical care and the clinical educational experience in a way that complemented already established learning objectives and curricular requirements.

As program growth continues there are additional avenues of program development and scholarship that may be pursued. Further program development and targeted outreach and intervention may be instituted with the specific aim to reach veteran populations where amplifying individual stories may have an added element of advocacy. The MLMS program has the potential to amplify the voice of groups of people who are marginalized within VA or society as a whole, including veterans with medical, mental health or social conditions that might be stigmatizing.

Presently program evaluation has been focused on MLMS as an educational intervention and the impact on the learners. Further evaluation is needed to assess the impact on the veterans who participate in this program and elucidate how participation might affect the veteran experience, health outcomes, engagement with the healthcare system. Additional assessment is needed to understand the impact on the healthcare team members who read the stories in the matter of course of providing direct care to the veteran, including the impact on staff engagement and burnout.

CONCLUSION

My Life, My Story is an example of a life story work intervention that has been successfully implemented and evaluated as an educational intervention that is effective at enhancing veteran-centered care competencies in learners across professions and across levels or training and has a direct impact on the veteran and the learner. It is the hope that this educational tool can be adopted by other educational healthcare settings as a means of teaching humanistic and patient-centered healthcare and improving the quality of care provided to patients.

ACKNOWLEDGMENT

The authors would like to thank the all the veterans who have shared their stories and the two veterans who shared their story for this chapter. The authors would also like to thank the leadership at VA Boston Healthcare System for ongoing support of this program, all the learners who have participated in writing these stories, program and evaluation mentor Dr. Jennifer Moye PhD, ABPP, health science specialist Ms. Kelly Doherty and national program lead Mr. Thor Ringler MFA, MS.

This program and evaluation within VABHS received no specific grant from any funding agency in the public, commercial, or not-for-profit sectors. This material is the result of work supported with resources and the use of facilities at the VA Boston and New England GRECC. The contents do not represent the views of VA or the United States Government.

REFERENCES

Beresin, E. V., Milligan, T. A., Balon, R., Coverdal, J. H., Louie, A. K., & Roberts, L. W. (2016). Physician Wellbeing: A Critical Deficiency in Resilience Education and Training. [PubMed]. *Academic Psychiatry*, *40*, 9. doi:10.100740596-015-0475-x

Bleakley, A. (2015). *Medical Humanities and Medical Education: How the medical humanities can shape better doctors*. Routledge. doi:10.4324/9781315771724

Charon, R. (2001). Narrative medicine: A model for empathy, reflection, profession, and trust. *Journal of the American Medical Association*, *286*(15), 1897–1902. doi:10.1001/jama.286.15.1897 PMID:11597295

Gooding, H. C., Quinn, M., Martin, B., Charrow, A., & Katz, J. T. (2016). Fostering Humanism in Medicine through Art and Reflection. *Journal of Museum Education*, *41*(2), 123–130. doi:10.1080/10598650.2016.1169732

Jones, D. S. (2014). A Complete Medical Education Includes the Arts and Humanities. *AMA Journal of Ethics*, *16*(8), 636–641. doi:10.1001/virtualmentor.2014.16.8.msoc1-1408 PMID:25140687

Koven, S. (2016). *As hospitals go digital, human stories get left behind.* https://www.statnews.com/2016/04/06/electronic-medical-records-patients/

Lam, M., Lechner, B., Chow, R., Chiu, L., Chiu, N., Lam, H., Popovic, M., Milakovic, M., DeAngelis, C., Chow, E., & Henry, B. (2015). A review of medical humanities curriculum in medical schools. *Journal of Pain Management*, *8*, 289–298.

Lincoln, A. (2016, June). *Lincoln's second inaugural address.* Champaign, IL: Boulder, CO: Project Gutenberg;

Mamykina, L., Vawdrey, D.K., & Hripcsak, G. (n.d.). How Do Residents Spend Their Shift Time? A Time and Motion Study With a Particular Focus on the Use of Computers. Academic Medicine, 91(6), 827–832. PubMed doi:10.1097/ACM.0000000000001148

Mann, S. (2017). *Focusing on Arts, Humanities to Develop Well-Rounded Physicians.* Retrieved from https://www.aamc.org/news-insights/focusing-arts-humanities-develop-well-rounded-physicians

McKeown, J., Clarke, A., & Repper, J. (2006, July). Life story work in health and social care: Systematic literature review. *Journal of Advanced Nursing*, *55*(2), 237–247. doi:10.1111/j.1365-2648.2006.03897.x PMID:16866815

Mead, N., & Bower, P. (2000). Patient-centredness: A conceptual framework and review of the empirical literature. *Social Science & Medicine*, *51*(7), 1087–1110. doi:10.1016/S0277-9536(00)00098-8 PMID:11005395

Mercer, S. W., Maxwell, M., Heaney, D., & Watt, G. C. (2004). The consultation and relational empathy (CARE) measure: Development and preliminary validation and reliability of an empathy-based consultation process measure. *Family Practice*, *21*(6), 699–705. doi:10.1093/fampra/cmh621 PMID:15528286

Mission of the Office of Academic Affiliations. (2019). Retrieved from https://www.va.gov/oaa/oaa_mission.asp

My Story, My Life. (2019). *VA Boston Education*. Retrieved from https://www.vabostoneducation.org/my-life-my-story

Nathan, S., Fiore, L. L., Saunders, S., Vilbrun-Bruno, S. O., Hinrichs, K. L., Ruopp, M. D., Schwartz, A. W., & Moye, J. (2019, September 9). My life, my story: Teaching patient centered care competencies for older adults through life story work. *Gerontology & Geriatrics Education*, 1–14. Advance online publication. doi:10.1080/02701960.2019.1665038 PMID:31498034

Pearce, C., Arnold, M., Phillips, C., Trumble, S., & Dwan, K. (2011). The patient and the computer in the primary care consultation. *Journal of the American Medical Informatics Association*, *18*(2), 138–142. doi:10.1136/jamia.2010.006486 PMID:21262923

Peterkin, A. D., & Skorzewska, A. (Eds.). (2018). *Health Humanities in Postgraduate Medical Education: A Handbook to the Heart of Medicine*. Oxford University Press. doi:10.1093/med/9780190849900.001.0001

Pories, S. E., Piawah, S., Abel, G. A., Mullangi, S., Doyle, J., & Katz, J. T. (2018, December). What is the Role of the Arts in Medical Education and Patient Care? A Survey based Qualitative Study. *The Journal of Medical Humanities*, *39*(4), 431–445. doi:10.100710912-018-9530-4 PMID:30076508

Ringler, T., Ahearn, E. P., Wise, M., Lee, E. R., & Krahn, D. (2015, June). Using Life Stories to Connect Veterans and Providers. *Federal Practitioner*, *32*(6), 8–14. PMID:30766066

Rosner, F. (1967). The Physician's Prayer Attributed to Maimonides. *Bulletin of the History of Medicine*, *41*(5), 440–454. PMID:4865040

Schwartz, A. W., Abramson, J. S., Wojnowich, I., Accordino, R., Ronan, E. J., & Rifkin, M. R. (2009). Evaluating the impact of the humanities in medical education. *The Mount Sinai Journal of Medicine, New York*, *76*(4), 372–380. doi:10.1002/msj.20126

Shapiro, J., Bezzubova, E., & Koons, R. (2011, July). Medical Students Learn to Tell Stories about Their Patients and Themselves. *American Medical Association Journal of Ethics.*, *13*(7), 466–470. PMID:23134794

Silverman, E. (2017, Aug. 21). Sharing and Healing Through Storytelling in Medicine. *JAMA Intern Med*. doi: . doi:10.1001/jamainternmed.2017.2996

Taylor, A., Lehmann, S., & Chisolm, M. (2017). Integrating humanities curricula in medical education: A literature review. *MedEdPublish*, *6*(2), 28. doi:10.15694/mep.2017.000090.2

The Role of Arts and Humanities in Physician Development: From Fun to Fundamental. (n.d.). Retrieved from: https://www.aamc.org/what-we-do/mission-areas/medical-education/humanities

Treadway, K. (2005). Notes to the Class— First Day. *The New England Journal of Medicine*, *352*(19), 1943–1944. doi:10.1056/NEJMp048298 PMID:15888691

VA geriatric scholar uses the power of story to improve patient care. (2019). *VAntage Point blog*. Retrieved from: https://www.blogs.va.gov/VAntage/69524/va-geriatric-scholar-uses-power-story-improve-patient-care/

ADDITIONAL READING

Epperly, T. (2012). Person-centered medical education: North American approaches. *International Journal of Patient-Centered Medicine*, *2*(1), 38–42.

Frank, A. (1995). *The Wounded Storyteller: Body, Illness, and Ethics*. University of Chicago Press. doi:10.7208/chicago/9780226260037.001.0001

Kleinmann, A. (1989). *The Illness Narratives: Suffering, Healing & The Human Condition*. Basic Books.

Kumagai, A. K. (2008). A conceptual framework for the use of illness narratives in medical education. *Academic Medicine*, *83*(7), 653–658. doi:10.1097/ACM.0b013e3181782e17 PMID:18580082

McKeown, J., Clarke, A., Ingleton, C., Ryan, T., & Repper, J. (2010). The use of life story work with people with dementia to enhance person-centred care. *International Journal of Older People Nursing*, *5*(2), 148–158. doi:10.1111/j.1748-3743.2010.00219.x PMID:20925716

Pennebaker, J. W., & Seagal, J. D. (1999). Forming a story: The health benefits of narrative. *Journal of Clinical Psychology*, *55*(10), 1243–1254. doi:10.1002/(SICI)1097-4679(199910)55:10<1243::AID-JCLP6>3.0.CO;2-N PMID:11045774

Rathert, C., Wyrwich, M. D., & Boren, S. A. (2013). Patient-centered care and outcomes: A systematic review of the literature. *Medical Care Research and Review: MCRR*, *70*(4), 351–379. doi:10.1177/1077558712465774 PMID:23169897

KEY TERMS AND DEFINITIONS

Interprofessional Education: Collaborative educational activities that involves either learners or educators from at least two health professions backgrounds with aim to foster collaborative practice and learning.

Medical Humanities: An interdisciplinary field within medicine that incorporates the arts and humanities into medical education and medical practice.

Narrative Medicine: A medical approach that seeks to enhance clinical practice and patient care with the use of patient narrative and reflection to enhance narrative competence.

Patient-Centered Care: A philosophical approach to medical care that involves partnership with the patient and family to engage in shared decision making that is informed by the patient's values and goals.

Veterans Health Administration: The largest integrated health care system in the United States with the express aim to provide health care to people who have service in the active military, naval or air service.

APPENDIX

Below are two examples of My Life, My Story interviews. These stories are shared with consent of the veterans. Details have been changed to protect the identity of the veterans.

My Life, My Story

I was born in Delaware - in an era where segregation was the norm - I spent the first 11 years of life raised by my grandfather, who had been born a slave. However, with hard work and diligence, my grandfather became a successful landscaping gardener, after the emancipation proclamation.

Even though I applied to and received rejections from nursing schools all over Delaware (due to the color of my skin), I never gave in to the discrimination. In the early 50's, I graduated from nursing school at Freedmen's Hospital S.O.N at Howard University. And a few years later I joined the United States Airforce Nurse's Corp.

When I first entered the Air Force Nurse's Corps for basic training, I was sent down to Montgomery, Alabama, during the time of the bus boycotts after Rosa Parks' arrest. While there, I got to witness Martin Luther King delivering speeches every Thursday at the local church. This sparked my extensive and lifelong advocacy for affirmative action and equal rights.

In the mid-60s, I went on to become the first African American nurse in the clinics of Mass General Hospital, Boston. But I did not stop there - in pursuit of further academic excellence, I went on to Boston University where I pursued a bachelor's degree in Education and a master's degree in Counseling Psychology.

I have paved the way chairing several committees. I was the Board Chair of the Boston YWCA, vice president of the Board of Trustees of Bunker Hill Community College, chair of the Advisory Committee of the Statewide Head Injury Program, president of the Board of Boston Senior Home Care Services and current president of the Mass Senior Action Council. I am most proud of my work with this council, resulting in approximately 40,000 more seniors being able to access the Medicare Savings Program. My favorite part of advocacy is working together with legislators to improve access and resources for others.

I value reflection and have reflected on the headway I have made throughout my life. I hope others can see the progress of people of color and recognize the odds of leading a successful life of advocacy, during segregation. My advice to healthcare providers is to be more open-minded in order to gain an appreciation about people from different backgrounds, cultures, and religions.

Most importantly, I believe one should cherish one's family. My son lives in another state but has taken after me with the same passion for helping others and advocating on behalf of veterans and civilians who have experienced traumatic brain injuries.

My Life, My Story

I grew up nearby, but I've lived all over. My life has taken me from the East Coast, to the South, out West, Vietnam, Oklahoma and back.

When I was growing up, I had a hard time in school and while I had a home it was abusive at times. I bounced between my grandmother and aunt's houses as a result. I'll admit- I was sort of a punk in the early years. I skipped school and didn't make it past the 9th grade, but a lot of this was to escape what was going on at home. At one point it was so bad that I skipped school for several months without my mom knowing. When it finally came out, I was forced to go to a correctional facility as a teenager. That was the first real scare I had and it definitely changed me, but it also built character. Some of the inmates suggested I try the military to straighten out. My father had been a WWII veteran and I figured I might as well try it out.

Unfortunately, I got turned down by recruiter after recruiter because of my lack of education. My last option was the Marine Corps. I took their test and flunked it too, but just by a few points. The recruiter asked me how bad I wanted to go and I told him I felt like it would make me a better man. He stepped back into his office for a few minutes and when he returned, he told me they had made a mistake in grading my test and that I had passed. He also reassured me that since I was the only boy in my family to carry on the family name, I wouldn't be sent to Vietnam for combat. I did Bootcamp at Parris Island and then basic training at Camp Lejeune in North Carolina. While I was on leave from training I received notice I was heading to San Francisco for overseas training. When I arrived there they told me I was headed to Vietnam, despite what I'd been told. I was 18 at the time. And so, I went, and I served for a year.

The Marine Corps made me more mature. When it came time to renew my commitment, they told me I couldn't continue because I didn't finish school. I tried for my GED at that time but missed it by 2 points so I was forced to come back to the states.

Sometimes I wonder if this was an omen, if my military time was not meant to be. At first it was hard. When I returned home, I bounced between over a 100 jobs-- from curtain factory to fishing vessel to tractor trailer driver, you name it. I got into fights and I struggled with post-traumatic stress. I was a loner. I walked away when others brought up the war. Finally, I ended up in a program for my PTSD with a psychiatrist. It was the best thing that happened to me when I got home. He helped bring me back. He taught me to search my soul, to figure out what I want and to stick to it. "You need to stomp your feet on the ground and say, 'I'm Home."

This advice he gave me always stuck and helped me to keep out the bad thoughts and find the good. I learned how to talk about my experiences-that's what will heal you, it's about getting it all out of you. If you dwell on the negative, you never escape the negative.

I met a friend in the program who convinced me to move to Oklahoma to work on a hog farm. He was a great friend, so I decided to take the risk and make an investment to get him started. At this point in my life I was in a better place to learn and focus. I got my GED and went to college to study computer science. While I was living in OK, I had another experience that left me asking "What If? What if things had been different?" I was supposed to be at an appointment in the building that was blown up in the OKC bombings in 1995 but since I changed my schedule the week before, I was home instead that day. While I watched the news coverage I thought to myself, "You need to do something!" I met with the Mayor and my college dean and organized a fundraiser in support of efforts to fix all the damage and aid those affected by the bombings.

After growing up in a difficult family situation I was lucky to find love at various times in my life. I was married 4 times, and my last wife just passed away three years ago. She was an amazing woman and not a day goes by that I don't think about her and miss her. She gave me the opportunity to live with and love a family like I never did growing up. I have many children and now 5 grandchildren from 1 year old to 13-year-old. When she had the chance to take anyone, she wanted to her first school dance, my oldest granddaughter invited me. I was so excited I decided to buy a nice new suit with a marine corps collar. I spent $300 on it only to have her veto it when I arrived to take her to the dance, but it was still such an honor to be her guest. She will be a force to reckon with!

What if things were different? There's so much of life out there that none of us have ever touched. I like to think about all the possibilities and try to use those thoughts to make good choices. But what-if questions can play tricks on you. You can get wrapped up in decisions and miss out on life in front of you.

If I could do everything over again, sure I would do things differently. But would I change it all now? No. No, because I'm only me because of the experiences, good and bad, that I have lived through in my life. I've lived well and loved, and I found a balance of give and take to make the most of my time.

Chapter 5
Virtual Reality Stereoscopic 180-Degree Video-Based Immersive Environments:
Applications for Training Surgeons and Other Medical Professionals

Maxime Ros
https://orcid.org/0000-0002-2149-165X
Revinax®, France & Educational Sciences Department, University of Montpellier, France

Lorraine Weaver
Thompson Rivers University, Canada

Lorenz S. Neuwirth
https://orcid.org/0000-0002-8194-522X
SUNY Old Westbury, USA & SUNY Neuroscience Research Institute, USA

EXECUTIVE SUMMARY

The theoretical and practical applications of immersive VR, although relatively new, have accomplished much in the area of pedagogical learner applications. This chapter describes the conceptual framework and Revinax® 180-degree stereoscopic video-based approach in addressing the academic achievement gap through conventional surgical students and nurses shadowing and how immersive VR environments may best address leveraging the learner's capability of increasing their skill acquisition, learning, and knowledge retention in a more efficient time-period, circumventing the inherent issues with conventional shadowing. Further, these VR experiences through

DOI: 10.4018/978-1-7998-5092-2.ch005

first-person Point of View (POV), although simulated and artificial, evoke mirror neurons, and can recruit neurocircuitry that are imperative for skill acquisition and later skill application. As such, the Revinax® instructional design model may provide a unique insight in how to use immersive VR environments to teach any learner that seeks to acquire surgical/medical professional training more efficiently and practically in a modern world of technology.

INTRODUCTION

New technological programs, tools, and devices often create excitement and curiosity as people seek to learn about new technologies and their potential future applications. This is especially true for individuals that given their specific job/training roles, could find ways in which technology can help them complete their work more effectively and efficiently. Thus, it is not surprising that many educators and future generation learners are currently increasingly exposed to pedagogical approaches targeted at technology-dependent learning instruction over conventional approaches. Such modern pedagogical technology-dependent approaches have already begun, yet as many emerge, a clearer understanding of their utility, generalization, and translational application(s) from the learning environment into real-world contexts, become the greatest sought after outcome measure. Further, some of these technology-dependent applications may be less educationally immersive (*e.g.,* avatar simulations, 2-D video simulations, passive video recording instruction, etc.), while others can be more educationally immersive (*e.g.,* virtual reality [VR], stereoscopic first-person point-of-view [POV] instruction, etc.). Therefore, during such a technologically expansive, exciting, and necessary time-period, educators are seeking novel and effective approaches for elucidating which technological programs, tools, and devices would be best suited for their pedagogy is warranted. In order to shed light on this very issue, the present study offers an unbiased assessment of how VR can be used in novel evidence-based ways for assessing educational training of surgeons and other medical professionals.

As such, VR has evolved significantly from its inception in the 1950s (*For Review See* Mandal, 2013) and is presently emerging as a versatile pedagogical tool that can be used to train surgeons more effectively and efficiently across a number of medical interventions (Alaker, Wynn & Arulampalam, 2016; Vaughn, Dubey, Wainwright & Middleton, 2016; Aim, Lonjon, Hannouche & Nizard, 2015; Ragan et al., 2015; Anderson, Winding & Vesterby, 2011; Gurusamy, Aggarwal, Palanivelu & Davidson, 2008; Aggarwal et al., 2007; Haque and Srinivasan, 2006). Despite the fact that VR encompasses a wide range of user experiences that are appropriate for different training objectives and applications, it has also been shown to have an increasing demand and interest in the educational training of more medical applications (Kamińska et al., 2019; Górski, Bun, Wichniarek, Zawadzki & Hamrol, 2017;). Consistent with these current trends, Revinax® has uniquely integrated VR technology with the use of a stereoscopic 180-degree video-based intervention to provide surgeons and other medical professionals with a first-person POV of the surgical procedures that they will be trained on, in addition to accessing other relevant patient data as part of the curriculum for a surgical training program. The goal of this surgical training program was to: 1) provide video-based evidence of the value of stereoscopic 180-degree VR; 2) establish the importance of its technological and curricular design; 3) discuss what the field can learn from modeling, validating, reliably testing, and/or building upon such pedagogical technologies; and 4) how such technology can be effectively used for educating medical students and professional on surgical interventions through more immersive experiences.

WHAT IS VIRTUAL REALITY (VR)?

There are many definitions of VR, partly because of the wide range in which it is executed in order to achieve the context-specific goals of the design team. Some current examples of VR definitions are: creating digital worlds/environments suitable for real-time human learning (Górski, Bun, Wichniarek, Zawadzki & Hamrol, 2017), an environment for users to interact with artificial stimuli in a somewhat naturalistic way (Concannon, Esmail & Roduta-Roberts, 2019), "an artificial three-dimensional environment…presented to a person in an interactive way" (Kamińska et al., 2019, p. 2), and as an environment which promotes immersion, interactivity and imagination (Concannon et al., 2019; Kamińska et al., 2019). These VR definitions provide the theoretical framework from which pedagogical instructional designers can begin to envision the kinds of artificial, somewhat naturalistic, and immersive environments that they would like to create as part of their curriculum. Further, the exact time-points or active learning opportunities that they envision, can then be pre-determined within these VR environments to control and investigate through evidence-based means, how the student users' interactivity within and responsivity to the VR environment can be investigated. This latter point is pivotal since the instructional design of VR environments have varying levels of user immersion, and without such proper instructional design intention and controls in place, identifying an evidence-based pedagogical approach through VR would be obscure. Arguably, the levels of user immersion within the VR environment, directly relates to whether or not a user can experience aspects of the VR environment that will facilitate them in obtaining a simulated sensory experience of the real-world (Concannon et al., 2019). Moreover, the levels of immersion experienced by the user directly affects how *"actively present"* the user feels within the VR experience (Górski et al., 2017). Kamińska et al. (2019) notes that the *"level"* of immersion that the user experiences should be adjusted based upon the curricular training goals with the lowest-level of immersion being used for knowledge acquisition (*i.e.,* the short-term learning objective), a moderate-level for skills acquisition (*i.e.,* sustained learning acquisition and skills maintenance), and a high-level of immersion for problem solving (*i.e.,* applied learning, contextual (re)organization, and generalization of skills learned from one environment to another). According to Fowler et al. (2015) the most important factors that are used as criteria to obtain a successful 3D VR learning environment/experience for the user are: 1) presence (*i.e.,* the user feels as if he or she were within the environment), 2) co-presence (*i.e.,* the user feels as if other people were within the environment), and 3) interactivity (i.e., the user feels as if they can manipulate, explore, or become apart of the environment). Thus, immersive VR (*i.e.,* accompanied by a headset otherwise referred to a head mount display [HMD]) can achieve and/or fulfill all of these factors, thereby meeting the criteria for an effective and user optimized 3D VR learning environment/experience.

Indeed, beyond immersion-dependent learning processes, an equally important instructional design feature of VR environments are the varying levels of interactivity that provide opportunities for how the user and their (in)actions can relate to how the users can manipulate the VR environment (Concannon et al., 2019). Some examples of interactivity are input devices that can include motion-sensing gloves, controllers or photo sensors that allow the user to see and use their hands within the VR environment (Concannon et al., 2019; Górski et al., 2017). Some VR environments also provide haptic (*i.e.,* tactile vibration-dependent sensory reception or proprioception) feedback or resistance to simulate an immersive sensory experience (Concannon et al., 2019; Górski et al., 2017). The amount of control that a user has within the VR environment can directly influence how *"real"* the experience is perceived and whether or not the user feels *"present"* within the VR environment (Concannon et al., 2019). Notably, how closely "the user's actions, senses and thought processes…resemble those that would be experienced while in the same situation…in the real world" (Concannon et al., 2019, p. 4) is known as fidelity (*i.e.,* influence of believing the *"realness"* of such VR environments). It is imperative that the physical, functional, and psychological fidelity of the VR environments in which the users experience be examined separately to address where the instructional design and curricular content provide the most interactivity for the user to achieve an optimal and believable learning outcome (Concannon et al., 2019). This would promote the user's perception of a high fidelity VR environment that would simulate real-world training and generalization. However, using such VR instructional design should be cautioned as it can be extremely expensive to recreate 100% matched simulations to real-world events, may not be practical in some circumstances, and are not always required in order to reach the educational learning and training goals sought after.

DECIDING WHEN VR INSTRUCTIONAL DESIGN WOULD BE BENEFICIAL

Despite how luring VR environments might appear if they were to be used in an educational instructional design, educators should caution themselves as VR environments may be advantageous for some learning/training objectives, but may equally have pedagogical limitations. Thus, it is essential to understand both the benefits and challenges associated with using VR environments pedagogically, in order to understand the ceiling and floor effects of VR environments within the pedagogical context of instructional design **(Fig. 1)**.

Despite the number of levels created within an immersive VR environment, the instructional designer must be cognizant of the practical limits in overwhelming the user with too many immersive aspects (*i.e.*, ceiling effect), and ensuring to provide just enough immersive aspects (*i.e.*, floor effect) to optimize the user's attention and learning. Moreover, it is important to highlight that the immersive VR environment helps to reduce cognitive load and if too many pedagogical approaches are given at once, it may be counterproductive.

Figure 1. Instructional design concept map for understanding the ceiling and floor effects of an immersive VR environment

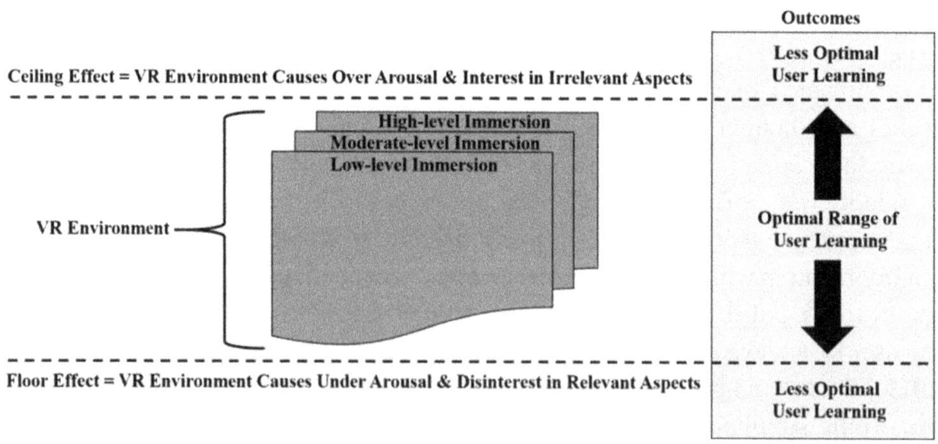

By following this instructional design concept map, the outcome would be an immersive VR environment optimized for the user's education. This outcome could then maximize the user's learning benefits by reducing unnecessary distractions (Harrington et al., 2018), and overcome the user's learning obstacles by making the content just surpass the most minimal arousal levels. Further, this concept map would help overcome the inherent issues with VR environments where an instructional designer's vision must meet a user's adaptation to and ongoing engagement within the VR environment to develop an ideal pedagogical application for training/educational programs. Notably, these user benefits and challenges may differentially influence the instructional design and training objectives of VR environments. Górski et al. (2017) suggested that there were three distinct, yet different, levels within the educational medical VR environment applications: 1) general (*i.e.,* conceptual skills), 2) procedural (*i.e.,* behavioral/ adaptive skills), and applied knowledge (*i.e.,* practical/ generalization skills). **Figure 2** illustrates the conceptualized differences between the user's knowledge levels directly related to the instructional design variations are required to reduce any potential academic achievement gaps when constructing an effective VR environment for pedagogical applications (Górski et al., 2017).

BENEFITS OF IMMERSIVE VR ENVIRONMENTS: ACCESSIBILITY, AUTONOMY & COST

Accessibility Within Immersive VR Environments

"Accessibility refers to the user's ability to find what is needed, when it is needed. Improved access to educational materials is crucial, as learning is often an unplanned experience." (Ruiz, Mintzer & Leipzig, 2006, p. 208). Consistent with this quote, VR environments can allow users anywhere in the world to access the same training so long as they have access to the required technological devices to permit them to become immersed within the experience (Kamińska et al., 2019). Accessibility of an effective education is perhaps best captured by the following quote: "Learning is a deeply personal experience: we learn because we want to learn." (Ruiz, Mintzer & Leipzig, 2006, p. 208). However, knowing the needs of the prepared and/or underprepared user is a critical factor in which their autonomy within an immersive VR environment may help to facilitate their learning and produce better educational outcomes, irrespective of the academic achievement gap.

Figure 2. Illustrates the conceptualized instructional design for the developing VR environments for ensuring optimal educational outcomes for the user based on the models proposed by Górski et al. (2017)

(A) *displays the venn diagram of the Górski et al. (2017) model when the VR user's experience is balanced in learning content across conceptual, behavioral/adaptive, and practical/generalization skills* **(B)**. *Further, instructional designers should be aware to permit flexibility for the user to adapt within such VR educational environments whereby at time they may need more conceptual than practical skills* **(C)**, *more practical than conceptual skills* **(D)**, *more behavioral than conceptual skills* **(E)**, *and more behavioral than practical skills* **(F)**. *Permitting such flexibility may create more immersive VR environments with greater educational gains for the user.*

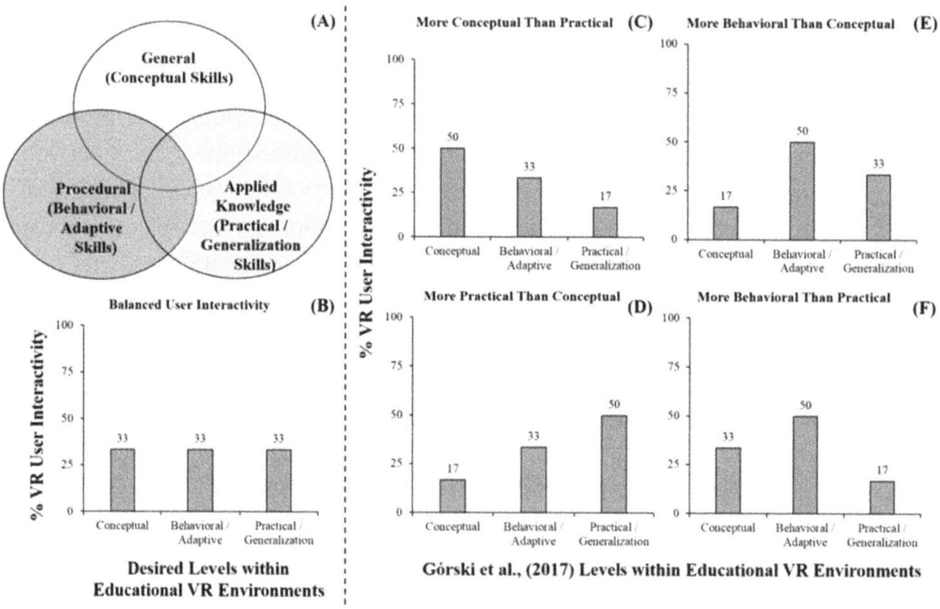

Autonomy Within Immersive VR Environments

Beyond accessibility, VR environments differ in the degree of autonomy that individual users might experience when accessing the identical VR environments repeatedly over time. Some VR environments can be accessed and experienced by the user, while others require an instructor to set them up or run the experience for a single or group of prospective users (*i.e.*, shared VR experience), and lastly, some are designed to require other users to interact with the main user (*i.e.*, cooperative VR experience) within the VR environment to complete a single experience (Kamińska et al., 2019). Therefore, the degree of the user autonomy is directly influenced by the desired educational goals of the training and the instructional design of the VR environment, in turn, defining the user's VR overall experience. However, identifying how much user autonomy is needed for the instructional design is a critical factor in determining the cost of developing immersive VR environments for pedagogical purposes.

Cost of Developing Immersive VR Environments

Monetary savings can be achieved over time when comparing the use of VR with 3D, 2D, and real models, as well as, tissues or patients (Górski et al., 2017). However, in the initial development stages of any technological tool, device, or software costs can be exorbitant. Because of these financial challenges in developing VR environments, a balance must be achieved between leveraging the expenses that go into developing the VR instructional curriculum and design, while maximizing the pedagogical/educational outcomes and detailing such cost comparisons for future research and development of VR experiences (**Fig. 3**). Such information can help future educational instructional designers of high-quality high-return investments compared to low-quality low-return investments when developing new VR environments for applied pedagogical instruction. Further, knowing such information may be essential in motivating and capturing the interest of users to seek engagement in VR environments within an educational context.

Figure 3. Probability squares of assessing cost and returns for developing effective applied learning technologies in VR Environments for conceptual (**A**)*, behavioral* (**B**)*, and practical* (**C**) *instructional design*

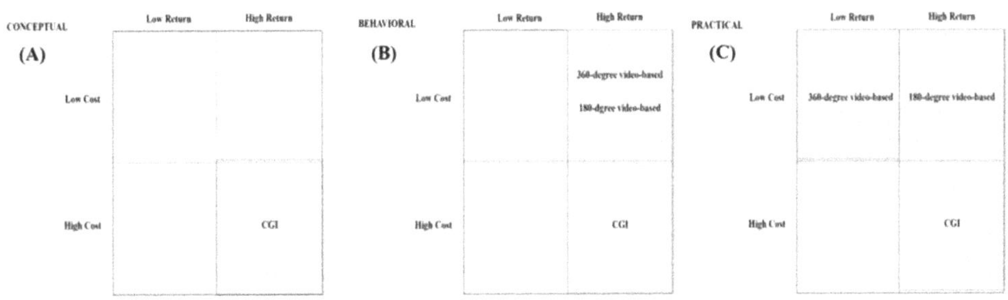

The ideal situation is to maximize high returns from the lowest cost across each of these three factors, but often times that may be less than ideal.Novel VR enviornments might require high cost to initially develop high returns and over time can be economically reassessed.

It is also imperative to understand how such a pedagogical immersive VR environment can transcend a wide-range of conceptual parameters to increase the user/learner's ability to fully comprehend what is being presented to them (**Fig. 4**).

Figure 4. Illustrates a conceptual framework for designing the most optimal immersive VR environment across a number of factors (i.e., conceptual – CGI, practical – CGI, practical 180-degree vide-based, and behavioral 360-degree video based) as they would relate to low and high returns (i.e., the financial investments that go into creating the technological and the pedagogical gains achieved by the user/learner).
© 2020, Ros & Neuwirth. Used with permission

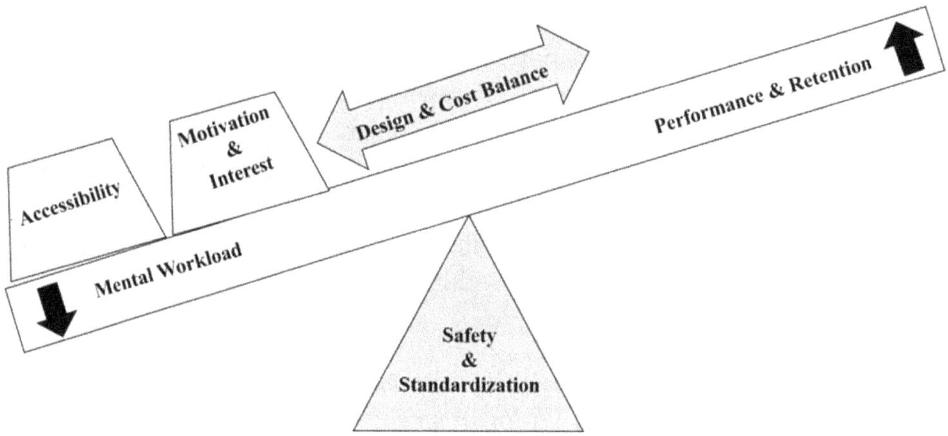

Obtaining and Sustaining User Motivation and Interest Within Immersive VR Environments

The use of exploring VR environments in grade school curriculums (*i.e.,* "VR field trips" in middle school students' social studies) has been shown to increase educational motivation and interest (Kamińska et al., 2019). Further, studies focusing on the use of VR technology in different learning contexts supports the findings that learners are more engaged and self-report that they understand the content being taught better. These benefits may come from the lower "task-unrelated images or thoughts" (Harrington et al., 2018, p. 993) (*i.e.,* improved attention) that are brought out through the immersive characteristic of these VR experiences. These findings are further supported by data showing that blinding students to the actual VR environments that they will be immersed into actually increases their focus upon entering the VR-environment. Harrington (2018) showed a significantly higher student level of engagement (*i.e.,* 360 video-based instructional content) and the student's preferred it when compared to a 2D video of the same content. This might be a key factor that warrants further investigation in developing VR immersive environments that encapsulate meaningful engagement for the learner through depth perceptual processing and/or visual feedback, which is critical for transferable pedagogical outcomes in VR environments. Ultimately, this type of learning could positively influence student's preference for a VR curricular format over others that in turn, promotes an increase in student motivation and educational interest.

Ekstrand (2018) stated that VR prevented *"neurophobia"* (*i.e.,* a fear of learning neuroanatomy), which provided insight in expanding the pedagogical approach from just viewing content to include exposure and re-exposure of the same content to increase user acceptability of the information being presented/taught. Using Computer-Generated Imagery (CGI) to reconstruct the neuroanatomy among 175 students, of which, 94% were willing to have VR integrated in their educational curricula because it helped them to improve their understanding of the course content. Thus, students directly report that having a better understanding of educational content can be achieved through VR, and then having the luxury of going over it multiple times, can facilitate a self-regulated means of adapting to and desensitizing students to their own inherent fear(s) of learning neuroanatomy. This latter point is compelling as it provides invaluable insight into the utility of VR when the user can determine how frequent they would like to experience the course content. This could further provide the instructional designers to anticipate the learners with the ability to augment and adapt within the VR environments to increase their motivational and educational interests in response to uninteresting, aversive, or noxious educational content. Such insightfulness can help the instructional designers to create supportive VR environments that may best address their academic achievement gaps with course content that intimidates them such as neuroanatomy and other forms of biological dissection of tissues (*i.e.,* both human and non-human).

Further, *"neurophobia"* has been an emerging issue that can also deter students from entering the biological and medical science fields and may reduce future medical professionals in the science, technology, engineering, and mathematics (STEM) fields if left unaddressed (*For Review See* Neuwirth, Dacius, & Mukherji, 2018); yet, VR might be able to leverage this very issue in a responsible and ethical manner through creative instructional design of VR environments that combine exposure/re-exposure immersion levels that desensitize the user to content that they might find aversive. By providing the user with the control to regulate how much they would like to tolerate in becoming immersed in such VR content, this may actually decrease their mental workload and increase learning. Further, if the user can control the VR environment this may increase engagement from students who would otherwise view the material as aversive and mostly result in course attrition, to follow through with the curriculum and perhaps continue to learn more content beyond the VR module.

Reduced Mental Workload Through Immersive VR Environments

Notably, VR can increase the user's motivation and interest, which makes it an attractive technology for integrating educational content with an immersive experience that is uniquely memorable. However, as with any attentional task, one's attention span and cognitive load can either be limited or limit how much information one attends to at a given moment in time (Feldon, 2007; Barrouillet, Bernardin, Portrat, Vergauwe & Camos, 2007; Oviatt, 2006). Unlike standard visual and attentional processing where humans are easily distracted by events, actions, objects, and movements within their visual field, VR headsets block out these competing peripheral and background distractors and increase the user to focus their attention on the foreground of the VR environment. The attention to the VR environment is also enhanced due to its novelty (Roussou, 2000). Thus, it can be argued that through these inherent features of VR, it may reduce the user's attentional load and free up more cognitive capacity stores for increasing skill acquisition and learning retention (Andersen, Mikkelsen, Konge, Cayé-Thomasen & Sørensen, 2016) to be freely available to become increasingly or fully immersed within the VR experience; thereby, facilitating the user's learning, memory, and post-educational outcomes.

Moreover, since VR also facilitates the first-person POV, this particular feature has also been suggested to further reduce the user's cognitive load to increase their learning capacity just by using the first-person POV. The first-person POV has been shown to improve the learning of new gestures. Mirror neurons are usually activated when the learner sees someone else performing a procedure. If this procedure is viewed from a first-person perspective, cognitive load is less important, and trainees are more able to replicate the procedure. (Fiorella, Van Gog, Hoogerheide & Mayer, 2017).

This latter point is critical as mirror neurons are the neurobiological/ neuropsychological basis for empathy (Iacoboni, 2009), vicarious reinforcement, (Bandura, Ross & Ross, 1963), and more relevant to this VR context and enriched sense of learning that is validated by the user's brain responsivity to VR and their brain's ability to perceive the POV as being the user's own first-person experience. Thus, the first-person POV constitutes a powerful way in which 3D 180-degree stereoscopic VR experiences directly influencing the user's brain in ways that can optimize learning through VR environments that provide sound evidence that it can offer unique pedagogical benefits to the learner/user by improving their skill acquisition and memory retention.

Improved Learning Skill/Performance Acquisition and Memory Retention Through Immersive VR Environments

Several studies have begun to address the issues of learning performance and retention when using VR environments. In order to address this issue, the pedagogical designer's instructional plan must be comprised of a step-by-step approach that directly scaffolds the short-term learning objectives with the desired long-term learning outcomes of the curriculum. However, despite even the most well-defined and structured curriculum in VR, some difficulties might arise from the wide variety of and different intentions for how the VR environment was implemented within a given curriculum. Together, this begets the questions, which VR studies are consistent, reliable, and comparable in best addressing the issue of standardizing key factors for using VR in best pedagogical practices for educating the next generation learners. It may very well depend on the type of VR that is studied (*e.g.*, CGI, 360-degree video, 180-degree video, etc.), since the pedagogical objectives (*i.e.*, theoretical, procedural, practical knowledge, etc.) and what they are compared against (*e.g.*, books, videos, lecture, physical simulator, etc.) may be more important in capturing the user/learner's attention and sustaining their cognitive loads, while diminishing distractors to improve learning outcomes. Further, it has been shown that non-immersive VR can lead to improved educational performance (*i.e.*, less errors and reduced time to complete the task) in reproducing complex tasks, when compared to technical manuals and multi-media films. For simple tasks, there were no differences observed between non-immersive VR and multi-media films regarding the number of errors, but non-immersive VR did speed-up the time to complete tasks (Chao et al., 2017).

Another study by Smith (2018) aimed to compare computerized-images displayed between immersive VR, flat-screen VR, and written notes after having watched a video. They assessed the performance on a mannequin and measured their time to completion. The results showed that they failed to observe any short-term or mid-term (*i.e.*, 6 months follow up) differences between the groups, when compared to immersive VR. Surprisingly at mid-term, the non-immersive solutions produced significantly faster time to task completion when compared to baseline, but again without any significant difference between groups. Sheik-Ali (2019) mentioned that the speed to meet criteria is an important variable, but more importantly, in a surgical training context, the speed of surgical skill acquisition is arguably more important in order to become proficient enough to complete a later surgical task. They concluded that many studies have consistently shown a positive linear relationship between the use of VR/AR in surgical training and surgical skill acquisition, despite the tools used being rather different. To be clear, there is only one immersive VR tool, which uses hand-tracking instead of remotes. Regarding the influence of immersive

VR with CGI to complete a task, Smith et al. (2018) found no difference between the group using immersive VR and the group receiving conventional training. The authors further showed the same post-interventional outcomes with gradual improvements and lower retention scores at 6-months follow up. Thus, they stated that VR was at least as good as conventional training but did not surpass it. In a recent study, Andersen et al. (2018) showed that using VR with CGI for practical knowledge before a training course increased the benefits of the course and allowed the students to achieve better learning outcomes. They also showed that the more people were trained repeatedly in VR, the better their results were when compared to a single training of VR. This suggested that VR has additional educational gains influencing skills acquisition and memory retention through repeated exposures.

Regarding the theoretical knowledge and skill acquisition in healthcare, user-cases are similar to industrials cases: the possibility to enter a 3D reconstruction of a *"machine"* provides a better conceptual understanding. The possibility offered by VR to uniquely explore the educational content through an *"anatomy journey"* (*i.e.,* through VR moving through a biological organ to view new perspectives and connections within and across systems). Using a 3D CGI reconstruction of an organ, which is literally put in front of the learner to let the user artificially enter through and rotate this organ with intent that the user will become more familiar with the course content regarding knowledge of the organ. This way the user can explore the organ under every angle and have a better understanding of the different tissue layers and the relations between organs. Further, this experience offers the learner the ability to adopt a new perspective, that could not otherwise be achieved, without the VR environment. This finding is not only fascinating, but offers an endless range of new pedagogical possibilities. Therefore, VR is not only an entertaining way to learn new skills through technology, but it actually improves the learners *"visual field"* (*i.e.,* a VR-induced Proprioception) thereby expanding their understanding and approach to finding additional solutions to conventional learning problems. The exposure to these unique perceptual angles and vantage points is perhaps the largest advantage of using immersive VR environments over other forms of technology and conventional educational learning. Since these VR environments are based upon CGI that is directed by the theoretical knowledge underlying the course content, which are then aimed at increasing skill acquisition and retention of the content to be learned by the user. Concerning neuroanatomy, Ekstrand et al. (2018) found no difference in effectiveness between VR and textbooks as learning tools. However, they showed that VR prevented *"neurophobia"* among 175 students, and the authors stated that the results were encouraging. This may be perhaps due to the user being able to alter the imagery in the VR environment when compared to the fixed imagery presented by the textbook.

In cardiac anatomy, Maresky et al. (2018) found improvements in the user's results after learning through immersive VR environments. Thus, VR helps students to gain a better understanding of the organ itself, its structure-function relationships, its spatial connections, and its interfaces within systems biology, that can create a greater comprehensive understanding of the material within minutes in an immersive VR environment that would otherwise require reading hundreds of pages and weeks to months to achieve such understanding through conventional means. Another important feature is that VR environments in the biomedical fields help to overcome a real educational resource issue. Most dissections and surgical techniques are done in a time restricted and sample/organ tissue availability-dependent course (*i.e.,* the dissection or surgical laboratory). These laboratory courses require many students to shadow the instruction with little to no hands-on experience and often times result in less than optimal time viewing the actual procedure or details of the procedure that reduce the skills acquisition and applied learning of these concepts. Through VR environments, these learning gaps can be reconciled, improved, and even enhanced to prevent such learning gaps from occurring. These finding beg the question, how can immersive VR environment improve the user's learning retention? It is hypothesized that because immersive VR environments probably facilitate the user to understand better theoretical questions by being able to manipulate the structures/organs and understand how it works in a constructivist approach, or to acquire practical knowledge by being able to literally *"live in an educational experience"* and its different steps. Becoming fully aware, the user/learner has all what they need to gain a better understanding of the course content, which may then foster better skills acquisition and memory retention for generalization of applied learning. Altogether, the immersive VR environment may optimize the benefits of a lesson beyond convention pedagogical approaches, but would require standardization in order to accomplish this task.

Standardization of Immersive VR Environments

Similar to e-learning Ruiz et al. (2006) showed that the use of immersive VR environments standardizes the educational content and provides the same information and learning experience to all students, when compared to conventional learning. Further, the experience that is created in the immersive VR environment by the instructional designer and experienced by the user are equivalent to the teacher designing the curriculum and the student learning from the conventional educational experience. However, when an immersive VR environment is used for pedagogical purposes, this standardization may begin to exceed the expectations and expand the potential limits for the user/leaner; albeit, still within a standardized curriculum/environment.

Safety of Immersive VR Environments

The immersive VR environment often allows the user to acquire the necessary training to do things that would otherwise be too dangerous (*i.e.*, an animal dissection, dissecting a brain, or human organ, calculating a drug dosage to give a patient, etc.) for most people to experience as a first time exposure within a real life situation (Concannon et al., 2019). Thus, such use of immersive VR environments can improve both the safety of the user/trainee/student as well as the individuals they might have to help post-training in real situations that are dangerous. Using a similar logic with respect to surgical education, the use of immersive VR environments can allow the user to acquire technical skills in a simulated environment without the possibility of harming patients (Concannon et al., 2019). This enhances the ethical component of the pedagogical approaches through immersive VR environments and further can increase the user/trainee's skills, confidence and decrease surgical risks that might otherwise occur in patients. Alternatively, immersive VR environments can be used for a situation that one specialist must know, and further through repetitious learning/exposure/re-exposure, it can help the younger students/professionals to be ready faster, which was one of the first immersive VR tutorials created by Revinax® (Ros et al., 2017). Moreover, immersive VR environments can help the user to face/experience situations that are rare, while increasing the user's readiness for real-life situations based upon their VR training. For example, Vankipuram (2014) developed an immersive VR simulator for resuscitation illustrating the utility of VR in this very generalizable translation of knowledge across VR to real-world contexts/ environments. **Figure 5** below summarizes the overall instructional design goals for creative optimal immersive VR environments, in which the Revinax © model endorses and applies to their pedagogical framework for creating educational VR experiences with content that is learned faster, remembered more, and promotes skill acquisition and generalization from VR to real-world applications.

The goal is to balance the user's accessibility, cost, motivation and interest, amongst safety and standardization. The adaptive ability of the immersive VR environment should address decreasing the user's mental workload and increasing their performance and retention as a validity and reliability measure for successful pedagogical applications.

CONSIDERING SELF-REPORTED ADVERSE EFFECTS OF VR

Nausea and dizziness (*i.e.*, called VR sickness, motion sickness, simulator sickness and/or cyber sickness) can also occur for a temporary time-period when participants are immersed in the VR environment (Concannon et al., 2019; Kamińska et al.,

Figure 5. illustrates the conceptual model for developing an optimal immersive VR environment
© 2020, Ros & Neuwirth. Used with permission.

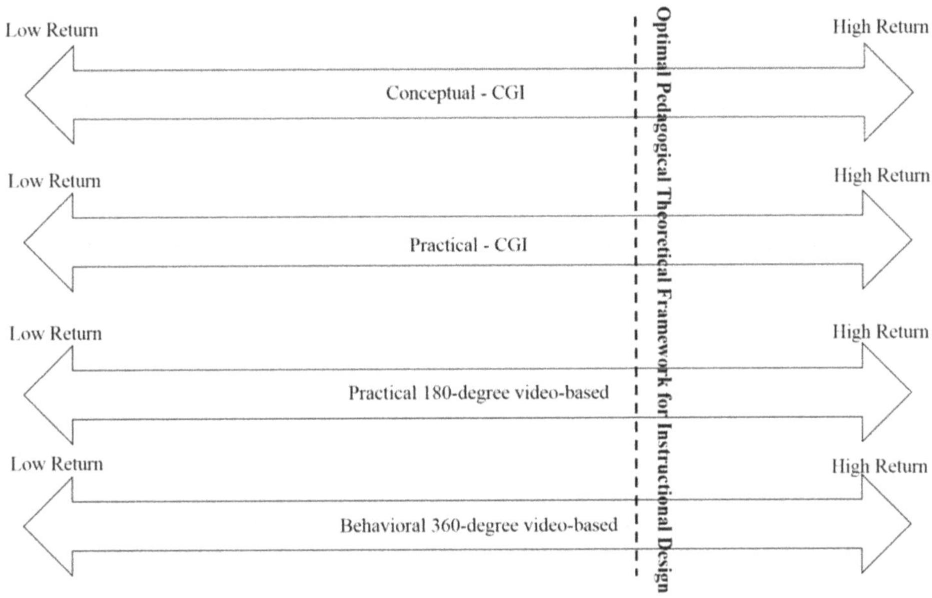

2019). This occurs when participant's movement within the VR environment does not match their movement in the physical world (*i.e.,* a perceptual kinesthetic mismatch). Besides people who suffer from internal ear dysfunction, several factors can potentially contribute to experiencing sensations in VR that may result in this feeling. Consequently, the hardware used (*i.e.,* VR headset), the resolution quality of the VR displayed, and the refresh rate of the video frames captures, are among the main contributing factors for VR sickness. Alternatively, the quality of the content: frames per second, resolution, and movements can also contribute to VR sickness. Notably, VR sickness happens infrequently, but can occur in people who do not suffer from motion sickness, but is brought on by the novelty of the first time they are exposed to VR combined with feelings of nervousness due to the uncertainty of this new experience.

REVINAX® STEREOSCOPIC 180-DEGREE ENVIRONMENT

A Peculiar Instructional Design

The immersive VR environment that is typically created is often based upon either CGI or 360-degree video-based experiences. Additionally, CGI helps to recreate an environment and make an artificial environment seem more realistic to the user, whereas in contrast, 360-degree video-based experiences simply display real footage. Thus, CGI is interesting as it offers a unique platform in which to represent things that cannot be recorded and played back. Since CGI attracts much interest due to its full user interaction within the immersive VR environment, as a by-product, its pedagogical value becomes increasingly important. However, the main problem in developing immersive VR environments with such pedagogical value is that the cost to create this content is rather expensive (*i.e.,* additional design features and the more realistic the desired experience the more it will be expensive). Moreover, the time to create and deploy this high-value pedagogical immersive VR environment will still require hardware for it to be used in a dedicated/restricted area (*i.e.,* which are not totally standalone). The 360-degree video-based experiences can supplement the immersive VR environment by helping people to project/insert themselves within the VR content, context, and/or situation that is pedagogically designed by the instructor.

The user interaction comes from the unique experience (*i.e.,* perceived simulation of a first-person POV) and what is then captured by embedded questions or decision trees testing the users/learners comprehension of the task within the immersive VR environment as it appears on the movie through these 360-degree video-based displays. These videos are faster to produce than CGI, the content is intrinsically realistic (*i.e.,* as they are pre-recorded from real-life events) and it is therefore easier to deploy even outside of the traditional VR HMD. However, the problem arises in 360-degree video-based displays when the user is trying to learn how to complete a procedure (*i.e.,* practical knowledge), since they are not fully capable of positioning themselves within the first-person POV to activate their mirror neuron systems to fully immersive themselves within the VR pedagogical content as intended. Revinax® produced in 2014 a stereoscopic 180-degree 3D video-based recording of an actual surgical procedure in real-time and since 2015 has been dedicated to advancing and further developing this technology as a pedagogical tool based on user feedback. Revinax® accomplishes this by creating a tutorial that involves three steps: 1) the surgical procedure is recorded in 3D video-based format from the surgeon's point of view (*i.e.,* using the equipment worn by the surgeon performing the procedure in real-time); 2) the 3D movie is then organized into chapters corresponding to the different steps of the surgery (i.e., with calibration and synchronization of the two videos); and 3) clinical imaging and data are then incorporated into the tutorial to make it a pedagogical immersive VR environment.

Among the content created, the surgical video covering the medical procedures for carrying out an external ventricular drainage, was instrumental in allowing trainees/students to view the procedure from a first-person POV perspective with the following educational intervention-based goals: 1) enhancing their memorization, 2) increasing their understanding of and confidence in implementing the procedure, 3) minimizing error when conducting the procedure, and 4) ultimately the training/educational intervention would decrease both surgery risks and time in surgery. Trainees/students could also access other patient data that underwent the same procedure to help them draw comparative assessments, weigh out any other alternative risks and/or concerns that they might have in replicating the procedure, and increasing their reliability of the procedure to better understand the case study with deeper analytical, critical, and clinical thinking. Further, theses resources were supplemented in the immersive VR environment with the patient's Computerized Tomography (CT) scan and an educational 3D model of the organ in which the surgery would occur. Taken together, this immersive VR environment in theory provides in a *"hands-free"* manner, virtual surgical, clinical, and educational resources that could be potentially be used in real-time within an operating room prior and during surgical interventions. However, it is also important to note that while in the operating room, the trainee/student/surgeon user could pause or replay the immersive VR 180-degree stereoscopic video-based intervention and view patient data, without actually making decisions to guide the surgery or actively influence their environment. The unique experience that Revinax® designed was, in this particular context to allow an immersive view of the surgery while allowing access to other patient information. The first-person POV allows the user to see themselves as if they were the actual surgeon performing the operation(s). In other experiences, Revinax® recorded simultaneously the first-person POV of different members of the surgical team. The ability to switch to other views allows the learner to envision what other members of the surgical team are doing at specific points within the surgery.

As described in Ros et al. (2017), when surveyed, a large majority of participants viewing the immersive VR environment tutorial saw the benefit of using it as a part of the teaching program and felt that it had a beneficial effect on their learning outcomes. One of the interesting results obtained from this study was that there were no age differences observed (*i.e.,* cohort was composed of a wide range of healthcare professionals from young students to old practitioners). Indeed, as this is a video-based environment, people may be familiar with the context. This helps to bridge and reduce/attempt to eliminate the technical gap, which can be perceived across real/VR environment and the academic achievement gap observed by students based on their learning styles (Neuwirth, Ebrahimi, Mukherji & Park, 2018; 2019) and how redefining student diversity may further influence these outcomes across generations (Mukherji, Neuwirth & Limonic, 2017). Other studies have been launched, including more than 450 participants attempting to address these very issues at the core of modern learning and immersive VR environment integration as a powerful pedagogical tool. The first set of results have helped increase how to understand the place and/or setting in which using immersive VR environment would be most optimal for the learner within this environment. One way this was achieved was to assess the retrieval, reconsolidation, and retention of knowledge by comparing a group that read a technical note versus another group that had been exposed to the same technical note plus access to the immersive VR environment. Students who were trained with the immersive VR environment showed significantly better immediate memorization than students trained without the immersive VR environment. The same trend was observed (*i.e.,* without reaching significance) in the groups six months post-training. Another study aimed to assess hands-on training within immersive VR environment compared to another group who had a traditional lecture. The results showed that the immersive VR environment helped to speed up the time to complete the procedure. Interestingly, both groups had the same results while checking the items corresponding to the different steps of the procedure. This controlled for the key differences the users experience through the immersive VR environment. The outcomes showed that the lecture group performed better in answering theory-based questions prior to completing the procedure. One of the values of developing immersive VR environment tutorials are: the tutorial is affordable, easy to comprehend, and facilitates efficient learning; these benefits can help address the problems reported by the World Health Organization (WHO) (2015) concerning surgical training globally. Indeed, not everyone can afford to have access to a laboratory or an operating room with the highest caliber of technology, but a simulation training center may help to leverage the financial and practical problems surgeons face globally by expanding telemedicine through such applied VR pedagogical applications.

Challenges of Immersive VR Environments and How the Revinax® Model Addresses Them

Some VR hardware requires the trainer or educator to have specialized knowledge (Concannon et al., 2019), which can be a barrier to deploying the *"full"* VR experience. Some VR environments lack visual realism due to the limits of producing accurate graphics, while inaccurate or unrealistic details can further deviate away from the intended immersive VR experience; thereby, detracting the user from the believability of the immersive VR experience (Kamińska et al., 2019). As such, creating a more realistic environment can increase the cost of producing the VR experience or lead to other restrictions such as limiting the interactivity of the VR experience (Kamińska et al., 2019). One of the reasons that Revinax® chose to use the 180-degree video-based immersive VR environment first-person POV experience was that trainers did not require much specialized knowledge to use the technology. Further, it also allows the user to create content that is intrinsically realistic and more familiar to the user. Thus, the users can adapt to the content easily, which may help to integrate it in a wide-range of educational training programs. Further, video-based immersive VR environments helps to decrease the price to create content, and is able to represent a wide range of situations as pedagogical context for instructional use. Although, there are various ways to create video, the first-person POV has been proven to be an important pedagogical tool with more efficiency over other video content. Finally, Revinax® has committed to make content available through easy deployment and provide users the choice of a cross-platform approach in order to deliver the content in a VR standalone headset along with smartphones.

INCORPORATING VR INTO A TRAINING PROGRAM

Changing an already existing training program or creating a new training program should always begin with a user needs assessment. During this assessment phase, multiple options for training delivery should be assessed and the decision to use immersive VR environments as part of the training program along with the justification should be documented. Although Concannon, Esmail & Roduta Roberts (2019) found a positive outcome for immersive VR environments in 35 out of 38 experiments they reviewed (*i.e.*, 92% efficacy rate), caution should be exercised as immersive VR environments is not the solution for every training problem nor should it be used just because it is an attractive technology. Regarding the theoretical knowledge, immersive VR environments can be used as mentioned for a conceptual/structural understanding. Likewise, the procedural and practical knowledge for immersive VR environments should be considered when the training problem that needs to be addressed is related to experiential training. Experiential Training corresponds to the fact the learner needs to live the situation, to understand, gain experiences and thus will be able to become proficient. How to define when experiential training is indicated? When it is only the fact to have lived the experiences, which allows the trainee to have a full understanding. When you wonder how to show people and you are thinking the best way would be to take everyone in that context to make them live the experience, experiential training is indicated. Although technology and learning pedagogies have developed considerably over the last 15 years, the approach that Ruiz, Mintzer & Leipzig (2006) provided helps the field to better understand the pedagogical value of incorporating different learning methods into immersive VR environments. "Traditional instructor-centered teaching is yielding to a learner- centered model that puts learners in control of their own learning" (Ruiz et al., 2006, p. 207). Specifically, experiential learning and social constructivist learning theory accompanies the incorporation of immersive VR environments into any training program (Concannon et al., 2019). Adults learn better, when they are able to determine what they need to learn, explore the topics themselves, and then apply their knowledge actively. The autonomous and experiential nature of virtual reality makes it a good-fit with adult learning theory. Consistent with this approach, this is why Revinax® wanted to create a learner-centered experience in which the user feels being directly immersed within the middle of any immersive VR learning environment to have access to everything he or she needs surrounding them to enhance their learning.

Once it is determined that virtual reality should be used, it is important to define which kind of *"VR"* would be the best pedagogical and instructional method to answer the users' training objectives: Through CGI – when the context cannot be represented for practical or for conceptual knowledge / 360-degree based-video display to understand a given context, can be considered procedural. In contrast, the 180-degree first-person POV for teaching practical or procedural content with the goal to be deployed at large scale. Of course, the cost of the content creation, its volume, the hardware used to deploy it, and the number of people who have to undergo the experience can increase the variability of the outcomes and the potential applied cross-applications of any given pedagogical VR intervention.. However, Górski et al. (2017) identified a sound methodology for building Knowledge-Oriented Medical Virtual Reality (KOMVR), which is a six-step process: 1) identification, 2) justification, 3) knowledge acquisition, 4) knowledge formalization, 5) application and 6) implementation. From such a pedagogical needs assessment, the educator can define the user group and what they want the learner to accomplish during the training. As such, the theoretical framework for the KOMVR maps directly onto the training objectives to facilitate a deeper level of knowledge and from there to produce a range of acquired skills that may be useful for theoretical, practical, procedural, yet generalizable behaviors with the intent for applied purposes, within the immersive VR environment and potentially the real-world.

The second stage of KOMVR is justification, which includes planning who should be a part of the development team, estimating the work hours, calculating hardware and software costs, obtaining funding or developing a business plan and assessing the project risks (Górski et al., 2017). During the development process, the immersive VR environmental experiences should be tested by a diverse group of potential users/stakeholders to obtain feedback relating to functionality, effectiveness and the capability that addresses whether or not the experience adds to the training program (Kamińska et al., 2019). This can be done with a combination of survey questions targeting usability such as the System Usability Scale (Kamińska et al., 2019) and open questions to determine simple improvements that could enhance learning and the user experience. It is important to obtain feedback from a range of users as well as teachers and surgical experts in the field as the system and the experience will be viewed very differently by these groups.

CONCLUSION

The motivation and impetus to develop the immersive VR environment tutorial was brought on by the experiences users reported from the training program. Due to the practical limitations of shadowing surgeons within crowded operating rooms, the inherent set backs were the difficulty of medical professionals being allowed an appropriate/optimal view it of the surgical and nursing procedures that would increase their pedagogical applications of what they learned via direct observation of every procedure. The surgeon "mentoring" via shadowing within the operating room happens with the trainees /medical professional assisting the mentor. Since the trainee/medical professional is usually shadowing beside, behind, or even facing the surgeon the learning/pedagogical vantage point/perspective may be a self-limiting variable within the pedagogical approaches in acquiring skill acquisition of the surgical technique under study. Even when the user can see accurately what on the surgeon is doing via shadowing in real-time, they may not have the correct vantage point in order to acquire, consolidate, reconsolidate, and generalize the correct translational application of the surgical technique under study through natural observation means. Thus, the human brain has arguably some learning limitations through which it can optimally acquire information in which it may not fully/correctly memorize information in which it is presented. Further, the human brain can inadvertently make mistakes during the learning acquisition period, when the individual is tasked with attempting to (re)produce the surgical procedure from conceptual to practical generalizations. This is one explanation as to why it increases learning competency to acquire the skill acquisition procedures to reproduce these practical skills. Moreover, the observer through this shadowing/naturalistic observation methods may have learned something through the process, but due to the constraints of the human attention span and environmental distractors, how much is accurately learned in order to generalize and apply to practical application may be more limited than once thought. Thus, it poses the question, how can one address this inherent learning gap when trying to acquire new information during real-time surgical shadowing/observation (*i.e.*, which is what is conventionally considered the status quo)?

Additionally, through this comprehensive, yet conceptualize understanding of the limitations of shadowing and naturalistic observations, the present study proposes that it was not possible to provide/optimize these experiences to surgeons locally or abroad in other countries. A Lancet report (2015) for WHO stated that surgery should be considered as one of the top priority medical interventions for advancing global health. The catalyst for this is that five billion people globally do not have access to surgery. Further, to maintain this insufficient medical coverage, the surgical workforce (*i.e.,* not only surgeons, but inclusive of all medical health professionals participating in surgeries) needs to double by 2030 to address this very issue. Teaching people essential surgeries (across ~44 medical procedures) could save up to five millions lives per year. The theory behind this proposes the question, how then can we achieve that goal? The answer may lie at the interface of training people in remote areas with telemedicine through immersive VR environments from more advanced medical areas globally? From these immersive VR experiences, a global telemedicine workforce may be assembled to address these very issues. Further, to provide surgeons/surgical students and medical professionals with a portable/accessible tool, which can help them to have a better conceptual and translational understanding of a surgical procedure through immersive VR, may help to circumvent the pedagogical inherent issues in natural shadowing/observations through a more immersive VR environment as with the Revinax® model that addresses these issues to optimize the pedagogical outcomes of the surgeon/medical professional to increase future generations of biomedical educators in the field.

REFERENCES

Aggarwal, R., Ward, J., Balasundaram, I., Sains, P., Athanasiou, T., & Darzi, A. (2007). Proving the effectiveness of virtual reality simulation for training in laparoscopic surgery. *Annals of Surgery*, *246*(5), 771–779. doi:10.1097/SLA.0b013e3180f61b09 PMID:17968168

Aïm, F., Lonjon, G., Hannouche, D., & Nizard, R. (2016). Effectiveness of virtual reality training in orthopaedic surgery. *Arthroscopy*, *32*(1), 224–232. doi:10.1016/j.arthro.2015.07.023 PMID:26412672

Alaker, M., Wynn, G. R., & Arulampalam, T. (2016). Virtual reality training in laparoscopic surgery: A systematic review & meta-analysis. *International Journal of Surgery*, *29*, 85–94. doi:10.1016/j.ijsu.2016.03.034 PMID:26992652

Andersen, C., Winding, T. N., & Vesterby, M. S. (2010). Development of simulated arthroscopic skills. *Journal Acta Orthopaedica*, *82*(1), 90–95. doi:10.3109/17453674.2011.552776 PMID:21281257

Andersen, S. A. W., Foghsgaard, S., Cayé-Thomasen, P., & Sørensen, M. S. (2018). The effect of a distributed virtual reality simulation training program on dissection mastoidectomy performance. *Otology & Neurotology*, *39*(10), 1277–1284. doi:10.1097/MAO.0000000000002031 PMID:30303946

Anderson, S. A. W., Mikkelsen, P. T., Konge, L., Cayé-Thomasen, P., & Sørensen, M. S. (2016). Cognitive load in mastoidectomy skills training: Virtual reality simulation and traditional dissection compared. *Journal of Surgical Education*, *73*(1), 45–50. doi:10.1016/j.jsurg.2015.09.010 PMID:26481267

Bandura, A., Ross, D., & Ross, S. A. (1963). Vicarious reinforcement and immitative learning. *Journal of Abnormal and Social Psychology*, *67*(6), 601–607. doi:10.1037/h0045550 PMID:14084769

Barrouillet, P., Bernardin, S., Portrat, S., Vergauwe, E., & Camos, V. (2007). Time and cognitive load in working memory. *Journal of Experimental Psychology. Learning, Memory, and Cognition*, *33*(3), 570–585. doi:10.1037/0278-7393.33.3.570 PMID:17470006

Cates, C. U., Lönn, L., & Gallagher, A. G. (2016). Prospective, randomised and blinded comparison of proficiency-based progression full-physics virtual reality simulator training versus invasive vascular experience for learning carotid artery angiography by very experienced operators. *BMJ Simulation and Technology Enhanced Learning*, *2*(1), 1–5. doi:10.1136/bmjstel-2015-000090

Chao, C. J., Wu, S. Y., Yau, Y. J., Feng, W. Y., & Tseng, F. Y. (2017). Effects of three-dimensional virtual reality and traditional training methods on mental workload and training performance. *Human Factors and Ergonomics in Manufacturing*, *27*(4), 187–196. doi:10.1002/hfm.20702

Concannon, B. J., Esmail, S., & Roduta Roberts, M. (2019). Head-Mounted Display Virtual Reality in Post-secondary Education and Skill Training. *Frontiers in Education*, *4*(August), 1–23. doi:10.3389/feduc.2019.00080

Ekstrand, C., Jamal, A., Nguyen, R., Kudryk, A., Mann, J., & Mendez, I. (2018). Immersive and interactive virtual reality to improve learning and retention of neuroanatomy in medical students: A randomized controlled study. *CMAJ Open*, *6*(1), E103–E109. doi:10.9778/cmajo.20170110 PMID:29510979

Feldon, D. F. (2007). Cognitive load and classroom teaching: The double-edged sword of automaticity. *Educational Psychologist*, *42*(3), 123–137. doi:10.1080/00461520701416173

Fiorella, L., Van Gog, T., Hoogerheide, V., & Mayer, R. E. (2017). It's all a matter of perspective: Viewing first-person video modeling examples promotes learning of an assembly task. *Journal of Educational Psychology*, *109*(5), 653–665. doi:10.1037/edu0000161

Fowler, C. (2015). Virtual reality and learning: Where is the pedagogy? *British Journal of Educational Technology*, *46*(2), 412–422. doi:10.1111/bjet.12135

Górski, F., Bun, P., Wichniarek, R., Zawadzki, P., & Hamrol, A. (2017). Effective design of educational virtual reality applications for medicine using knowledge-engineering techniques. *Eurasia Journal of Mathematics. Science and Technology Education*, *13*(2), 395–416. doi:10.12973/eurasia.2017.00623a

Gurusamy, K., Aggarwal, R., Palanivelu, L., & Davidson, B. R. (2008). Systematic review of randomized controlled trials on the effectiveness of virtual reality training for laproscopic surgery. *British Journal of Surgery*, *95*(9), 1088–1097. doi:10.1002/bjs.6344 PMID:18690637

Haque, S., & Srinivasan, S. (2006). A meta-analysis of the training effectiveness of virtual reality surgical simulators. *IEEE Transactions on Information Technology in Biomedicine*, *10*(1), 51–58. doi:10.1109/TITB.2005.855529 PMID:16445249

Iacoboni, M. (2009). Immitation, empathy, and mirror neurons. *Annual Review of Psychology*, *60*(1), 653–670. doi:10.1146/annurev.psych.60.110707.163604 PMID:18793090

Izard, S. G., Juanes, J. A., García Peñalvo, F. J., Estella, J. M. G., Ledesma, M. J. S., & Ruisoto, P. (2018). Virtual reality as an educational and training tool for medicine. *Journal of Medical Systems*, *42*(3), 1–5. doi:10.100710916-018-0900-2 PMID:29392522

Jensen, L., & Konradsen, F. (2018). A review of the use of virtual reality head-mounted displays in education and training. *Education and Information Technologies*, *23*(4), 1515–1529. doi:10.100710639-017-9676-0

Kamińska, D., Sapiński, T., Wiak, S., Tikk, T., Haamer, R. E., Avots, E., ... Anbarjafari, G. (2019). Virtual reality and its applications in education: Survey. *Information (Switzerland)*, *10*(10), 1–20. doi:10.3390/info10100318

Mandal, S. (2013). Brief introduction of virtual reality & its challenges. *International Journal of Scientific & Engineering Research, 4*(4), 304–309.

Maresky, H. S., Oikonomou, A., & Ali, I. (2018). *Virtual reality and cardiac anatomy: Exploring immersive three-dimensional cardiac imaging, a pilot study in undergraduate medical anatomy education.* Clin Anat N Y N. doi:10.1002/ca.23292

Meara, J. G., Leather, A. J. M., Hagander, L., Alkire, B. C., Alonso, N., Ameh, E. A., Bickler, S. W., Conteh, L., Dare, A. J., Davies, J., Mérisier, E. D., El-Halabi, S., Farmer, P. E., Gawande, A., Gillies, R., Greenberg, S. L. M., Grimes, C. E., Gruen, R. L., Ismail, E. A., ... Yip, W. (2015). Global Surgery 2030: Evidence and solutions for achieving health, welfare, and economic development. *Lancet, 386*(9993), 569–624. doi:10.1016/S0140-6736(15)60160-X PMID:25924834

Mock, C. N., Donkor, P., Gawande, A., Jamison, D. T., Kruk, M. E., & Debas, H. T. (2018). Essential surgery: Key messages from Disease Control Priorities. *Lancet, 391*(10125), e11–e14. doi:10.1016/S0140-6736(15)60091-5 PMID:25662416

Mukherji, B.R., Neuwirth, L.S., & Limonic. (2017, Apr.). Making the case for real diversity: Redefining underrepresented minority students in public universities. *Sage Open,* 1-10.

Neuwirth, L. S., Dacius, T. F. Jr, & Mukherji, B. R. (2018). Teaching neuroanatomy through a historical context. *Journal of Undergraduate Neuroscience Education, 16*(2), E26–E31. PMID:30057504

Neuwirth, L. S., Ebrahimi, A., Mukherji, B. R., & Park, L. (2018). Addressing diverse college students and interdisciplinary learning experiences through online virtual laboratory instruction: A theoretical approach to error-based learning in biopsychology. In A. Ursyn (Ed.), *Visual approaches to cognitive education with technology integration* (pp. 283–303). IGI. doi:10.4018/978-1-5225-5332-8.ch012

Neuwirth, L. S., Ebrahimi, A., Mukherji, B. R., & Park, L. (2019). Addressing diverse college students and interdisciplinary learning experiences through online virtual laboratory instruction: A theoretical approach to error-based learning in biopsychology. Hershey, PA: IGI. doi:10.4018/978-1-5225-8179-6.ch025

Oviatt, S. (2006). Human-centered design meets cognitive load theory: Designing interfaces that help people think. *Proceedings of the 14th AMC International Conference on Multimedia*, 871-880.

Ragan, E.D., Bowman, D.A., Kopper, R., Stinson, C., Scerbo, S. & McMahan, R.P. (2015). Effects of field of view and visual complexity on virtual reality training effectiveness for a visual scanning task. *IEEE Transactions on Visualization and Computer Graphics, 21*(7), 794-807.

Ros, M., & Neuwirth, L. S. (2020). Increasing global awareness of timely COVID-19 healthcare guidelines through FPV training tutorials: Portable public health crises teaching method. *Nurse Education Today, 91*(104479), 1–6. doi:10.1016/j.nedt.2020.104479

Ros, M., Trives, J. V., & Lonjon, N. (2017). From stereoscopic recording to virtual reality headsets: Designing a new way to learn surgery. *Neuro-Chirurgie, 63*(1), 1–5. doi:10.1016/j.neuchi.2016.08.004 PMID:28233530

Roussou, M. (2000). Immersive interactive virtual reality and informal education. *Proceedings of i3 Workshop on Interactive Learning Environments for Children*, 1-9.

Ruiz, J. G., Mintzer, M. J., & Leipzig, R. M. (2006). The impact of e-learning in medical education. *Academic Medicine, 81*(3), 207–212. doi:10.1097/00001888-200603000-00002 PMID:16501260

Sheik-Ali, S., Edgcombe, H., & Paton, C. (2019). Next-generation Virtual and Augmented Reality in Surgical Education: A Narrative Review. *Surgical Technology International, 35*, 27–35. PMID:31498872

Smith, S. J., Farra, S. L., Ulrich, D. L., Hodgson, E., Nicely, S., & Mickle, A. (2018). Effectiveness of Two Varying Levels of Virtual Reality Simulation. *Nursing Education Perspectives, 39*(6), E10–E15. doi:10.1097/01.NEP.0000000000000369 PMID:30335708

Sturm, L. P., Windsor, J. A., Cosman, P. H., Cregan, P., Hewett, P. J., & Maddern, G. J. (2008). A systematic review of skills transfer after surgical simulation training. *Annals of Surgery, 248*(2), 166–179. doi:10.1097/SLA.0b013e318176bf24 PMID:18650625

Sutherland, J., Belec, J., Sheikh, A., Chepelev, L., Althobaity, W., Chow, B. J. W., Mitsouras, D., Christensen, A., Rybicki, F. J., & La Russa, D. J. (2019). Applying modern virtual and augmented reality technologies to medical images and models. *Journal of Digital Imaging, 32*(1), 38–53. doi:10.100710278-018-0122-7 PMID:30215180

Van Gog, T., Paas, F., Marcus, N., Ayres, P., & Sweller, J. (2009). The mirror neuron system and observational learning: Implications for the effectiveness of dynamic visualizations. *Educational Psychology Review*, *21*(1), 21–30. doi:10.100710648-008-9094-3

Vankipuram, A., Khanal, P., Ashby, A., Vankipuram, M., Gupta, A., DrummGurnee, D., Josey, K., & Smith, M. (2014). Design and development of a virtual reality simulator for advanced cardiac life support training. *IEEE Journal of Biomedical and Health Informatics*, *18*(4), 1478–1484. doi:10.1109/JBHI.2013.2285102 PMID:24122608

Vaughan, N., Dubey, V. N., Wainwright, T. W., & Middleton, R. G. (2016). A review of virtual reality based training simulators for orthopaedic surgery. *Medical Engineering & Physics*, *38*(2), 59–71. doi:10.1016/j.medengphy.2015.11.021 PMID:26751581

Chapter 6
Training Healthcare Providers to Establish Therapeutic Alliances With Patients:
Lessons From Psychotherapy Training

Nicholas R. Morrison
https://orcid.org/0000-0002-7268-1170
VA Boston Healthcare System, USA & Harvard Medical School, USA

David R. Topor
VA Boston Healthcare System, USA & Harvard Medical School, USA

EXECUTIVE SUMMARY

This chapter discusses a variety of practices the healthcare education community can adopt from the psychotherapy literature regarding therapeutic alliance training when supervising trainees, and provides a series of recommendations, grounded in the extant literature, to bring these practices to life. In addition to describing how healthcare educators can translate Bordin's therapeutic alliance model to the medical and allied health communities, this chapter discusses aspects of therapeutic alliance facilitation and maintenance supervisors can address explicitly in supervision, including attunement to the developmental stage of trainees, using the supervisory alliance with trainees, addressing issues of diversity and multiculturalism, and increasing trainee self-awareness in the service of alliance maintenance. Specific strategies including role-play, alliance measurement, and use of video/audio recording are discussed. Supervisors can apply these nomothetic concepts to their scopes of practice and address idiographic concerns with trainees that emerge in their patient populations.

DOI: 10.4018/978-1-7998-5092-2.ch006

INTRODUCTION

The patient-provider relationship is a cornerstone of medical practice. This relationship impacts all clinical interactions and is recognized by the healthcare and lay communities as an integral part of treatment. Healthcare providers across disciplines have considerable latitude to adjust their approaches to the patient-provider relationship to maximize the benefit to clinical care (Beach, Inui, & Relationship-Centered Care Research Network, 2006; Dorr Goold & Lipkin, 1999; Szasz, Knoff, & Hollender, 1958).

The strength of the patient-provider relationship is linked to increased patient satisfaction with clinical care, increased treatment adherence, and better treatment outcome (Chipidza, Wallwork, & Stern, 2015; Fuertes et al., 2007; Fuertes, Toporovsky, Reyes, & Osborne, 2017). Birkhäuer and colleagues (2017) conducted a meta-analysis examining a patient's trust with their healthcare provider and its relation to clinical outcome, and found a small to moderate correlation between patient trust and self-rated subjective health outcomes (e.g., adherence to medication, health-related quality of life). They also found a large correlation between trust and patient satisfaction. Conversely, poor clinical outcomes as noted by objective measures or standardized subjective metrics have been found when patients feel unheard, disrespected, or otherwise out of partnership with their physicians (Chipidza, Wallwork, & Stern, 2015; Gordon & Beresin, 2016; Ong, de Haes, Hoos, & Lammes, 1995).

Attention to the relationship is advocated by multiple healthcare professional organizations. The American Medical Association's (AMA) Code of Medical Ethics highlights the importance of patient-provider relationships, stating "the practice of medicine, and its embodiment in the clinical encounter between a patient and a physician, is fundamentally a moral activity that arises from the imperative to care for patients and to alleviate suffering" (AMA, 2016). The American College of Physicians Ethics Manual also stresses the importance of the patient-provider relationship:

At the beginning of and throughout the patient–physician relationship, the physician must work toward an understanding of the patient's health problems, concerns, values, goals, and expectations. After patient and physician agree on the problem and the goals of care, the physician presents one or more courses of action, with a specific recommendation for the patient. (Sulmasy & Bledsoe, 2019, p. S3)

Given the stated importance of this relationship, it is critical for healthcare providers across disciplines to learn to cultivate strong patient-provider relationships. Thus, this chapter describes several strategies that can be used to teach trainees ways to strengthen the patient-provider relationship.

Lessons From Psychotherapy Training

Strategies to enhance the patient-provider relationship can be found in the methods through which psychotherapy skills are taught to trainees in the mental health professions. These strategies have broad applicability to the training of other healthcare professionals. Notably, how clinicians build the therapeutic patient-provider relationship is one of the most studied constructs in the psychotherapy literature (Elvins & Green, 2008; Horvath, Del Re, Flückiger, & Symonds, 2011; Wampold & Imel, 2015). This relationship is a key component of psychotherapy and is consistently related to improved patient care (Flückiger, Del Re, Wampold, & Horvath, 2018).

Although there are a number of definitions of the patient-provider relationship, the authors use Bordin's (1979) definition, and will continue to use the term *therapeutic alliance* to describe the patient-provider relationship throughout this chapter. The alliance is defined as the degree to which 1) patient and provider agree on the *goals* of treatment (e.g., what does the patient want to be different as a result of treatment), 2) patient and provider agree on the *tasks* of treatment (e.g., how will the patient accomplish the identified goals), and 3) patient and provider address the treatment in the context of a collaborative and affective *bond*. Given its ubiquity across the modalities and theoretical orientations of psychotherapy, the therapeutic alliance has been conceptualized as the "quintessential integrative variable" (Wolfe & Goldfried, 1988) and the "flagship common factor" (Constantino, Castonguay, & Schut, 2002).

A number of provider factors contribute to the development of a strong therapeutic alliance. These factors include both provider attributes (e.g., warmth and patience) and provider behaviors (e.g., communication of empathy and facilitation of affect expression) (Ackerman & Hilsenroth, 2003; Del Re, Flückiger, Horvath, Symonds, & Wampold, 2012). Conversely, other attributes (e.g., rigidity and defensiveness) and behaviors (e.g., maintaining directiveness despite a patient's desire to control the appointment) relate negatively to alliance quality (Ackerman & Hilsenroth, 2001). In addition to developing these positive attributes, providers must be taught how to address and repair problems in the therapeutic alliance (Safran, Muran, & Eubanks-Carter, 2011).

The American Psychological Association (APA) guidelines for clinical supervision in health service psychology call for education and training in relationship formation, maintenance, and rupture and repair (2014). There are a number of ways to teach trainees to develop stronger alliances with patients (e.g., Eubanks-Carter, Muran, & Safran, 2015; Muran & Barber, 2010; Smith-Hansen, 2016), including those recommended by the Interdivisional APA Task Force on Evidence-Based Therapy Relationships (Norcross & Wampold, 2011). The Task Force established demonstrably effective elements of the therapeutic relationship, including attending to the alliance, exhibiting empathy, and collecting patient feedback, as well as probably effective elements of the therapeutic relationship, including goal consensus, collaboration, and positive regard for the patient. The Task Force's training recommendations included having training programs provide competency-based training in the demonstrably and probably effective elements of the therapy relationship, having training programs provide competency-based training in adapting psychotherapy to the individual patient in ways that demonstrably and probably enhance treatment success, and having accreditation bodies develop criteria for assessing the adequacy of training in evidence-based therapy relationships.

Supervisors in the broader healthcare professions might consider these recommendations in their training programs and consider specific strategies regarding therapeutic alliance development, such as those discussed below. However, it is important to recognize that there are a plurality of approaches supervisors might consider when training their supervisees to establish strong therapeutic alliances with their patients, and that the strategies below do not represent an exhaustive list. Indeed, one therapeutic alliance researcher once remarked, "the concept of a gold standard [of therapeutic alliance training] seems somewhat problematic, and it is more useful for people to develop different ways of working with the relationship and studying it so that different approaches may emerge" (Constantino, Morrison, MacEwan, & Boswell, 2013, p. 287).

Developmental Attunement

Supervisors need to take into account the developmental level of the trainee when providing supervision and attending to the therapeutic alliance. For example, trainees early in their training may be nervous or apprehensive working with patients. They may be pre-occupied with thinking about many facets of the clinical encounter, including knowledge needed to address the patient's concerns, ability to foster a relationship with the patient, concern over how to correctly complete documentation for the healthcare record, and their supervisor's evaluation. For beginning trainees, supervisors can gradually integrate discussion of the therapeutic alliance into supervision. This can be done through discussions, role-plays, or assigning short readings (e.g., Muran & Barber, 2010; Safran, Muran, & Eubanks-Carter, 2011). The following vignette highlights how a supervisor can discuss the alliance with a new physical therapy trainee.

Supervisor: *So, you've had a chance to read a bit of background about the patient, and have a game plan for treatment. I do want to discuss your alliance with the patient, as this is key to the treatment plan. Can you recall the three aspects of the alliance from the assigned reading?*

Trainee: *The bond, goals, and tasks of treatment?*

Supervisor: *Right; so what does that mean to you when you think about your upcoming first patient?*

Trainee: *Well, I know from the initial chart review that the patient is reporting chronic pain in his left leg and difficulty getting around, so I suppose I should be thinking about how to talk about what his goals are for treating those concerns.*

Supervisor: *Okay, that's part of it. We want to be thinking in these first appointments about how the two of you will negotiate the treatment goals, and the tasks of the work that will emerge from our agreed upon approach. So in thinking about this patient, how might you develop a good working rapport?*

Trainee: *Um...maybe thinking about how difficult it must have been for him to get here with the pain in his leg?*

Supervisor: *And what do you think is difficult about that for him?*

Trainee: *Well I think it was hard physically and mentally. The patient is in pain and getting to this appointment was difficult. I think the patient is also worried that the pain will never go away.*

Supervisor: *Definitely. We're not sure if he is anxious about his first physical therapy experience, or if he is struggling with feelings of shame about being unable to ambulate like he used to. Or something else. Creating space and allowing him to express these concerns with you will help facilitate the bond as you address the patient's goals and the technical work of the tasks. Any questions about that?*

Trainee: *No I don't think so. That makes sense.*

Supervisor: *This will in many ways serve as the cornerstone of your work and will be an area you will re-visit throughout treatment. So, let's talk a little about how you are going to bring up the discussion of goals during your first session.*

This example demonstrates how a supervisor can call explicit attention to alliance-fostering strategies with a beginning trainee. When working with a more experienced trainee, supervisors may want to focus on having the student reflect on the clinical encounter and the alliance. At all levels of psychotherapy training, directly addressing the alliance in supervision can lead to a stronger therapeutic alliance (e.g., Crits-Christoph et al., 2006; Hilsenroth, Ackerman, Clemence, Strassle, & Handler, 2002). By including this discussion as a part of all supervision sessions, supervisors can continue to gauge trainee growth in this area over time, adjust recommendations, and potentially shift supervisory style as the trainee gains more skills and experience (Barnett, Erickson Cornish, Goodyear, & Lichtenberg, 2007). Supervisors will also be better able to help trainees modify their approach as the patient's relational abilities and style change over time (Crits-Christoph, Crits-Christoph, & Gibbons, 2010).

Using the Supervisory Alliance

For more advanced trainees, supervisors can use the trainee-supervisor alliance as a means of teaching aspects of the therapeutic alliance. Bordin (1983) recognized the natural extension of the therapeutic alliance to the *supervisory alliance* (1983). He posited that both alliances have similar goals, tasks, and bonds, and noted the following:

Just as the terms of the therapeutic working alliance permit us to transcend the varieties of therapeutic traditions and their associated goals, the supervisory working alliance allows us to incorporate the varieties of goals that have been posed for supervision. (Bordin, 1983, p. 37)

Patton and Kivlighan (1997) measured trainee ratings after each of four supervision sessions on the Supervisory Working Alliance Inventory and measured patient ratings after each counseling session on the Working Alliance Inventory. They found that trainees' perceptions of the supervisory alliance were significantly related to patients' perceptions of the therapeutic alliance. DePue and colleagues (2016) found that the supervisory alliance (from the perspective of trainees) was positively associated with the trainees' perspectives of the therapeutic alliance with their patients; trainees who rated the supervisory relationship as high were more likely to rate the therapeutic alliance as high.

There are a number of variables that are related to a positive supervisory alliance, including higher trainee self-efficacy regarding ability to provide clinical care, increased trainee well-being, greater perceived effectiveness of supervision, and more discussions of culture in supervision (Watkins, 2014). Alternatively, a weak or unfavorable supervisory alliance was related to higher degrees of perceived stress, increased exhaustion and burnout, and more frequently perceived occurrences of negative supervision events. Thus, the supervisory alliance has implications for the trainee's supervision, training, and clinical practice.

Supervisors can help trainees increase their sense of self-efficacy by highlighting areas of clinical care that the trainee is performing well. Supervisors can regularly check-in with the trainee about the trainee's own health and well-being, being mindful of signs of burnout. Supervisors can also routinely check in about the effectiveness of supervision and what changes need to be made in supervision to be most helpful to the trainee. To reflect on the supervisor-trainee alliance, supervisors can identify communication patterns that occur in supervision, or note specific behaviors the trainee exhibits in supervision, and ask the trainee to reflect on how these patterns and behaviors might occur when the trainee is meeting with patients. The following vignette provides an example of how a supervisor might explicitly work to attend to the supervisory alliance with a trainee.

Supervisor: *Per our discussion last week, I thought it would be helpful to check in to see how things are going between the two of us in here. I was able to write down some thoughts and hope you were, too.*

Trainee: *Yes, I was able to jot some notes down.*

Supervisor: *Great. Maybe we can start by talking about what seems to be going well. What do you feel is working well in supervision?*

Trainee: *I really appreciate how open and transparent you are. I think we're able to talk about any clinical issues that come up, which I really appreciate. I also like how we're able to structure our meetings at the outset to talk through whatever we agree is most important.*

Supervisor: *I agree; our communication also seems to me to be open and honest. I feel like you've been willing to bring up clinical concerns as they arise. Where do you feel like I'm missing the mark in here, and how can I do better?*

Trainee: *I mean I think things are generally going really well.*

Supervisor: *I notice that you say "generally" going well. What comes to mind for you when you think of times things weren't going well?*

Trainee: *Well, I think I wanted to focus a little more on learning [X technique] like we discussed at the outset of the rotation, and feel we really haven't been able to do that with all the other responsibilities that have come up.*

Supervisor: *I'm really glad you brought that to my attention. We can set aside some more time each week to address that area. That's exactly the kind of thing I hope you continue to share with me in supervision. Is there anything else we can do differently in here?*

Trainee: *No, I really think that's the only thing.*

Supervisor: *Okay great; let's both agree to continue checking in with each other to be sure you're getting what you need out of this process.*

In this instance, the supervisor gently presses the trainee to share what is awry in supervision. Supervisors are encouraged to be mindful of the power differentials in the supervisory relationship, and to recognize that careful attention to subtle behavioral patterns or wording of trainee responses like the word "generally" above can serve as process markers for supervisors to attend explicitly to the supervisory relationship. For explicit strategies on addressing the alliance in supervision with trainees, see examples presented by Friedlander (2015).

Therapeutic and Supervisory Alliance Measures

Supervisors can use established, empirically validated measures to assess the trainee's therapeutic alliance with their patient. While most providers are interested in clinical outcomes, it can be helpful to also monitor the clinical process to ensure patient and provider are in agreement about the trajectory of their work together. The Working Alliance Inventory (WAI) is a tool to quickly, efficiently, and systematically examine the therapeutic alliance (Horvath & Greenberg, 1989). Both the patient and the provider can complete the WAI to gauge each person's experience of the alliance. Once the measure has been administered, the provider can score the measure on the subscales of goals, tasks, and bond in the relationship, which can then help the provider to have a conversation with the patient about where there may be disagreement between the provider and patient. This measure is easily accessible to providers online, and providers can also use a psychometrically validated revised short version of the Working Alliance Inventory (Hatcher & Gillaspy, 2006).

Moving beyond the field of psychotherapy, as many as 19 distinct instruments assessing the patient-provider relationship exist (Eveleigh et al., 2012). Many of these instruments are short and do not take long to administer. For example, the Patient-Doctor Relationship Questionnaire (PDRQ-9; Van der Feltz-Cornelis, Van Oppen, Van Marwijk, De Beurs, & Van Dyck, 2004), which emerged from the psychotherapy literature, consists of nine short statements about a patient's relationship with his or her primary care physician. Although these measures are readily accessible, it is unclear how frequently providers are using them. Supervisors can work to shift the culture and attitude of trainees around these process measures by directly and explicitly encouraging trainees to use them in clinical encounters. The measures and scores can then be reviewed in supervision.

Supervisors might consider modeling using measures between the patient and provider by using measures of the supervisory alliance between the trainee and supervisor. As before, a number of measures are available to supervisors, including the Supervisory Relationship Questionnaire (SRQ; Palomo, Beinart, & Cooper, 2010) and the Short Supervisory Relationship Questionnaire (S-SRQ; Cliffe, Beinart, & Cooper, 2016). The S-SRQ may be of particular interest to healthcare educators across disciplines, given its short length, ease of administration, and broad applicability to a host of training environments. Incorporation of psychometrically validated measures of the supervisory relationship over the course of supervision models how trainees might implement alliance measures with their patients, provides a forum for discussing what appears to be going well and not going well in supervision, and offers a medium for supervisors and trainees to evaluate whether they have been able to address supervisory problems in the alliance over time.

Role-Plays

Supervisors can engage in role-playing with trainees to simulate a patient encounter. These role-plays can occur either in a group supervision setting with multiple trainees, or one-on-one with a supervisor and single trainee. Role-plays allow the trainee to practice certain behaviors in the "safe" confines of the supervisory relationship, assuming that the supervisor has worked to facilitate a positive and supportive learning environment. When role-playing, trainees can practice the role of patient and/or provider. For example, in a one-on-one setting, the trainee can practice developing a treatment plan with a patient.

When teaching trainees to grapple with new material, it may be helpful for them to first play the role of the patient. This will allow them to first observe the supervisor demonstrate what it is the supervisor hopes the trainee will communicate, and learn different techniques the supervisor might use in various clinical situations. Then, the pair can swap roles and can role-play the same clinical interaction. The trainee can then receive direct feedback from the supervisor. At the end of the role-play, both the supervisor and trainee debrief about the role-play and discuss what went well and what needs to be changed in the future.

When in a group setting, it can be helpful to have a more advanced or proficient trainee role-play with the supervisor. This can help more junior or less proficient trainees observe the desired clinical interaction, especially if the supervisor does not have archived video/audio recordings of ideal patient-provider interactions. Additionally, supervisors can encourage the observing trainees to note what they feel does and does not go well in the role-play. Once the role-play is completed, the group can discuss the interaction as a whole. This approach helps facilitate more active learning among trainees. For additional considerations when using role-play with healthcare trainees, see Joyner and Young (2006).

Addressing Issues of Diversity and Multiculturalism With Patients

Building an alliance with a patient requires the provider to be attuned to issues of diversity and multiculturalism. These issues need to be discussed with the trainee. For example, the multicultural guidelines put forth by APA (2017) invite both the therapist and the patient to engage in conversations with each other regarding identity as part of the alliance-building process. Given the plethora of identities that may be salient for each patient, direct and ongoing conversations with supervisors about the potential for issues of diversity to present themselves during the treatment is needed.

Further, a conversation on how to address issues of diversity in the treatment room as part of the therapeutic alliance can be especially informative for trainees at an early developmental stage, as they have yet to navigate these issues. For example, it may be the case that patients from certain backgrounds may be more mistrusting of healthcare providers (Ward, 2002). Fuertes and colleagues (2006) found that in therapy dyads, there were strong associations between patients' ratings of therapist multicultural competence and ratings of the therapeutic alliance, therapist empathy, and satisfaction. Importantly, multicultural competence is not achieved and simply applied across cases, but rather is unique to each therapy dyad. Thus, supervisors are encouraged to help trainees consider diversity and multiculturalism with their patients to build the alliance.

There are a number of strategies supervisors can use to increase the trainee's ability to incorporate a patient's cultural background into clinical care. Supervisors can identify readings that provide practice guidelines, such as recommendations for addressing intersectionality of patient identities in clinical contexts (e.g., Eckstrand, Eliason, St. Cloud, & Potter, 2016; Wilson, White, Jefferson, & Danis, 2019). Supervisors can role-play being the patient with the trainee, where the trainee can practice bringing up cultural background. Supervisors can watch archived video recordings of clinical sessions with trainees and discuss ways to increase integration of the patient's cultural identity into care. Explicit conversations about diversity with supervisors may help mitigate trainees' anxiety about how to address these issues in clinical situations.

Supervisors might consider engaging with trainees in a manner similar to the vignette below. In this example, a supervisor helps a resident consider issues of diversity and multiculturalism when thinking about how best to help a patient adhere to post-surgery instructions. The patient identifies as a 26-year-old, Hispanic, man. He is recovering from surgery in his right wrist following a car accident that has left him unable to load and unload the cargo required for his job.

Supervisor: *Okay, so you'll be meeting with Mr. Ramos a little later today and will have a chance to discuss discharge instructions with him. What are some of the multicultural factors we might want to keep in mind that might affect his recovery?*

Trainee: (Brief pause) *I'm not quite sure what you mean.*

Supervisor: *I'm wondering if you've had a chance during any of your coursework or rotations to think about the role identity has played in the treatment of your patients.*

Trainee: *We've learned a bit about it, and I've reflected on that to some degree.*

Supervisor: *I think it can be difficult sometimes to talk about these issues, both with me and with your patients, for fear of saying or doing the wrong thing. I'm wondering if you might feel somewhat apprehensive as we're talking about this right now?*

Trainee: *Yeah, maybe just a little.*

Supervisor: *That's understandable. These things can be tricky, and at the same time they're important to consider. One way that we might think about this is through intersectionality of patient identities, or the different cultural factors that may affect the patient as a whole. So, let's break this down a bit. What might be some of the considerations to think about regarding Mr. Ramos?*

Trainee: *Well, I know in talking with him he's pretty stressed about how being out of work is going to affect him and his family financially. He has a baby at home and is concerned about how he's going to make ends meet.*

Supervisor: *Okay, and so what might that mean for his recovery?*

Trainee: (Brief pause) *I suppose he might be more inclined to rush his recovery and push himself to go back to work.*

Supervisor: *That's definitely something that could happen. Also, when we think about systemic issues, it's possible he is unfamiliar with how to navigate issues related to medical leave or benefits. It would be helpful to have a conversation with Mr. Ramos about those concerns to show you are invested in him and his situation. Even if you don't have the answer, you can still validate his concerns.*

Trainee: *I can do that.*

Supervisor: *What would you want to be thinking about in terms of the patient's ethnicity?*

Trainee: *Um…I really don't know.*

Supervisor: *Well, if we're thinking about intersectionality, we might think about Mr. Ramos' various identities. We know from the empirical literature that Hispanic patients are less likely to seek medical care than non-Hispanic peers. Also, when we take this information and couple it with his age, gender, and this being his first clinical experience like this, he may be particularly reluctant to reach out for help. This might not be at all true about Mr. Ramos, but when we think about the intersection of his identities, it will be important to think about and explicitly address with him potential barriers to his seeking out additional care if he needs it. I'd like to try to role play this conversation with him. First, you can play the role of Mr. Ramos and I'll play you to model the interaction. Then, we'll switch roles so you can get some practice. Does that sound okay?*

In this vignette, the supervisor encourages the trainee to consider a multicultural perspective. The supervisor assesses the trainee's knowledge to gauge the conversation, and also validates the difficulty for some trainees to engage in this conversation with both patients and supervisors. Then, rather than simply instruct the trainee about how to proceed, the supervisor poses open-ended questions to help the trainee to think critically about the issues at hand.

Self-Awareness and Alliance Repair

Teaching trainees to be more self-aware of their thoughts, feelings, and behavior when meeting with patients can help to improve the therapeutic alliance, and can lead to improvements in the alliance when the relationship breaks down. Supervisors can regularly ask trainees about the trainee's own thoughts and feelings about the relationship with patients. Trainees should be encouraged to pay particular attention to their thoughts and feelings when implementing a new procedure, when there has been little progress in treatment, when a patient's goals for treatment change, or when a conflict begins to arise. These are all times of change in the therapeutic alliance and may elicit both trainee and patient thoughts and feelings about the care being provided.

This is especially true for trainees working in time-limited settings, where they may feel pressure to address some of the more technical aspects of the work and may be less attentive to the markers of relationship process in treatment. This can lead to an *alliance rupture*, or a breakdown in the therapeutic alliance. When this occurs, supervisors might encourage supervisees to focus on self-awareness and consider engaging in metacommunicative strategies with patients. Meta-communication, or "communication about communication," allows patient and provider to talk openly about the alliance and any perceived miscommunication that may be occurring.

Safran and colleagues (2011) acknowledge the importance of addressing alliance ruptures as they occur and offer similar strategies to the provider to facilitate the repair. Immediate repair strategies may involve clarifying a treatment rationale, changing goals or tasks, or clarifying misunderstandings. Trainees might also consider inviting the patient to engage in collaboration (instill a sense of "we"-ness), track the patient's response to treatment, and/or explore the trainee's own contributions to the alliance rupture (Muran, Safran, & Eubanks-Carter, 2010). Supervisors might even model these processes in the context of addressing ruptures in the supervisory alliance (Eubanks-Carter, Muran, & Safran, 2015). The following vignette illustrates how this type of situation might arise for a medical student working to address a patient's obesity.

Trainee: *I don't know, I'm just having a hard time getting buy-in from this patient.*
Supervisor: *Tell me more about that.*
Trainee: *I was very careful at the outset of treatment to gauge his expectations for change, ask about his preferences for treatment, and talk about the importance*

of a healthy diet and exercise. He was on board at the time, but now I just feel like we keep butting heads over our treatment goals. I'm really trying to be understanding, but it's tough trying to be supportive and understanding when the patient doesn't seem to want to go along with what we both agreed and set out to do. I have reiterated the importance of a healthy diet and the health risks associated with the patient's continued lifestyle but it doesn't seem to change anything.

Supervisor: *It sounds like you're both maybe out of sync in terms of what you're expecting from the work.*

Trainee: *Yeah, that's how it feels. It's just hard, because I worked really hard to establish an effective working relationship at the outset of treatment, and I am finding it awkward to be continuously asking the patient about weight gain.*

Supervisor: *That can definitely be a difficult thing to do. It sounds like you did a good job laying the groundwork for treatment in the earlier sessions. I'd like for you to try a less prescriptive and directive approach for the next appointment and focus on the therapeutic relationship. Being able to show flexibility is important, and your genuine attention to the relationship may end up helping the patient to feel more apt to hear you out. Focus on addressing those aspects of the relationship that don't seem to be going well, and we'll take it from there.*

Trainee: *It seems like if I do that, the patient is only going to gain more weight, though.*

Supervisor: *Potentially, yes. However, you also run the risk of the patient withholding their genuine concerns or dropping out of treatment altogether. I think directly addressing the matter is important. For example, you might say something like, "I'm wondering if we can maybe pause for a moment and talk about what your goals are for your physical health. What are your current goals for treatment? I think that would really help me to understand where you're coming from and get us on the same page of what we're working toward together." When you notice yourself working hard to convince the patient to do something, that actually might serve as a cue to pause and make sure you are both working toward the same goal.*

In this example, the supervisor helps the trainee consider the role of the therapeutic alliance in a more integrative way. The supervisor also helps the trainee identify specific language that can be used when addressing the discrepancy between the treatment goal and the patient's behavior. By increasing self-awareness, and communicating openly about alliance ruptures, trainees can be more attuned to their actions when meeting with patients and make adjustments to their behavior as needed. For example, if a trainee is becoming frustrated, the trainee can realize this frustration and use strategies (e.g., take a few minutes break) to be able to re-focus and work with the patient in a collaborative way.

Video/Audio Recording

Using video and/or audio recordings of sessions in supervision can give the supervisor another vantage point by which to evaluate the therapeutic alliance. It is important that patients know they are being recorded and that there are privacy guidelines in place to keep these recordings confidential. Work with the institution's privacy officer to establish such guidelines. At no time should recordings be made from a personal recording device (i.e., mobile phone), as they are not secure. Recordings need to be consented to by the patient.

Reviewing video/audio is an excellent way to help trainees develop interpersonal skills with their patients, and eliminates potential biases in the trainee's recollection of the clinical encounter. The use of video provides particular nuance to the supervision process. Among some of the benefits are the reduction in trainees' need to worry about reporting selective or biased memories in supervision, and the supervisor's ability to attend to nonverbal behavior exhibited by both the trainee and the patient (Haggerty & Hilsenroth, 2011). At a more specific level, reviewing video can be an important aspect to the development of alliance-fostering and alliance repair strategies (Eubanks-Carter et al., 2015).

Despite the potential benefits of reviewing video/audio in supervision, many trainees may be hesitant or reluctant to do so (Topor, AhnAllen, Mulligan, & Dickey, 2017). Aside from direct observation, they may feel vulnerable and worried about criticism. To help alleviate these concerns, supervisors can emphasize the importance of reviewing the work for the explicit goal of a trainee's learning and validate the trainee's apprehension about reviewing their clinical work. Further, supervisors can show videos of their own clinical sessions to normalize the process. Supervisors can ask trainees to bring to supervision video segments of positive aspects of the clinical encounter and segments where trainees have questions about the alliance. While trainees' discomfort may persist despite these strategies, trainee trepidation about reviewing their performance may decrease. The vignette below expands upon the physical therapy example from earlier in the chapter.

Supervisor: *What video are we watching today?*

Trainee: *Well, I had my initial evaluation with the patient, which I think went well, and we then met a second time, which is the session I would like to discuss today. The initial evaluation seemed a bit easier, because it felt more formulaic to get through the diagnostic procedures and logistics of the clinic before our time was up. I tried my best in this session we are about to watch to attend to* *the therapeutic alliance in the way we discussed during our last supervision meeting, but it was pretty difficult.*

Supervisor: *How so?*

Trainee: *I just felt like there were a lot of balls in the air. I had to check in about how the initial evaluation went, present the therapeutic rationale for our treatment plan, follow up with the patient's concerns for that week, and address the therapeutic relationship. It was hard enough to do those tasks, and I had to keep reminding myself to be warm, empathic, and genuine, which felt pretty disingenuous!*

Supervisor: *Sure, it makes a lot of sense you would feel that way in your first session after the initial evaluation. You have a lot of stuff you want to cross off of your "To Do List," and you still want to keep the patient engaged in a way that makes them feel heard, safe, and at ease. It sounds like you had all of the right ideas in mind. Did you have a chance to talk about the goals of the therapy per our discussion last time?*

Trainee: *Yes.*

Supervisor: *Okay, great. Why don't we start by reviewing how that went? Find the place in the video where you begin to talk about the goals. Before we start watching, tell me a little bit about what you were thinking in that moment, and what you hoped to accomplish with the patient. We can then watch for a bit, and discuss how things went. Does that plan sound okay?*

Trainee: *Yes.*

Supervisor: (After watching 10 minutes of video) *So I see a number of things went well here. What do you think went well?*

Trainee: *Hmmm...the patient seems to buy into the treatment plan?*

Supervisor: *I agree. What else? What do you feel you did well that facilitated patient buy-in?*

Trainee: *Um...I took the time to review the protocol in depth.*

Supervisor: *I agree. You can really see it in what you are saying both with your words and your body language. That's excellent. How about areas you think you would like to improve for next session?*

Trainee: *There were a few times I got nervous talking about the treatment. Was it noticeable?*

Supervisor: *That is great you are able to identify aspects you would like to change for next session. For next time, see if you can slow down a bit more to really be "in the moment" with the patient. You can see starting around the 5-minute mark when you begin discussing some of the technical aspects of treatment that you become a bit anxious. When you notice that happening, see if you can take a deep breath to help you slow down. This will help you to facilitate the relationship and prioritize what's most important to that meeting.*

In this instance, the supervisor is able to comment on the trainee's interpersonal process with the patient. As a result of reviewing the video, the supervisor can provide direct feedback on how the trainee addressed the patient's goals and tasks of treatment, and was also able to advise the trainee to slow down and approach the work more deliberately. While watching the video, both supervisor and trainee realized that the trainee appeared anxious to get through everything prepared in advance. The trainee would not have received that important feedback if the supervisor had only relied on the trainee's recollection of the session and not viewed the video recording.

The supervisor is also encouraged to take the time to validate the trainee's experience, including the potential for feelings of vulnerability and incompetence. A supervisor's decision to genuinely listen and validate the trainee is likely to facilitate a more trusting, open, and transparent process both in that supervisory session and future sessions. This supervisory stance helps to cultivate a stronger supervisory bond between the supervisor and the trainee. A stronger emotional bond between supervisor and trainee from early to late in supervision has been correlated with trainees perceiving supervisor performance and trainee behavior in supervision more positively (Ladany, Ellis, & Friedlander, 1999).

CONCLUSION

The aforementioned recommendations and vignettes highlight some of the practical approaches supervisors might consider when teaching their trainees to establish therapeutic alliances with their patients. Supervisors are encouraged to explicitly and deliberately teach their trainees to effectively cultivate and maintain strong therapeutic alliances with their patients, and can do so in a variety of ways.

Supervisors are encouraged to consider the developmental status of their trainees. Although a more seasoned trainee may not need to have the role of the alliance explicitly described to them, they may need to develop a greater understanding of how the alliance relates to the therapeutic approach from which they are practicing. For example, trainees on new rotations may find themselves practicing in an entirely novel environment with an unfamiliar patient population. Trainees in novel environments will need to learn to recalibrate their clinical skills, including in some instances their relational styles and alliance-fostering strategies.

In these situations, the supervisory alliance is especially important. Supervisors might be particularly attentive in these contexts to having trainees gauge their learning needs in supervision, complete supervisory self-assessments, and establish supervisory contracts or agreements that outline, among other domains, supervisor and trainee roles, supervision structure, and evaluative procedures (Watkins & Scaturo, 2013).

Supervisors are encouraged to be mindful about helping trainees to address issues regarding multiculturalism and diversity with their patients, and to consider these issues across varied clinical situations and contexts. Relatedly, trainees can benefit from greater self-awareness of their thoughts, feelings, and behaviors with their patient populations. This self-awareness is critical to addressing alliance ruptures as they arise.

Supervisors also have practical tools at their disposal to help trainees to develop and maintain therapeutic alliances with their patients, including therapeutic alliance measures, role-play strategies, and video/audio recording options. Supervisors are encouraged to think creatively about how to most effectively employ these strategies, and to integrate them into their current training practices. The reader will note that there is considerable overlap between the recommendations in this chapter, which the authors hope will prompt supervisors to consider mixed approaches to training.

The recommendations in this chapter are not without their limitations. Although the recommendations are grounded in theoretical and empirical psychotherapy literature, it is unclear how well these practices generalize to the broader practices of physicians and allied health professionals. Further research is warranted to determine how well the therapeutic alliance construct and its cultivation and maintenance translate outside of the psychotherapy context. Additionally, these are nomothetic recommendations that must be crafted to idiographic situations of discipline-specific settings, procedures, and patient populations. However, it may be the case that more explicit attention to the alliance may help facilitate better patient outcomes, and clinical supervisors are encouraged to extrapolate on the aforementioned recommendations and consider innovations for their own disciplines regarding best practices in alliance training.

DISCLOSURES

This material is the result of work supported with resources and the use of facilities at the VA Boston Healthcare System. The contents do not represent the views of the VA or the United States Government.

REFERENCES

Ackerman, S. J., & Hilsenroth, M. J. (2001). A review of therapist characteristics and techniques negatively impacting the therapeutic alliance. *Psychotherapy (Chicago, Ill.)*, *38*(2), 171–185. doi:10.1037/0033-3204.38.2.171

Ackerman, S. J., & Hilsenroth, M. J. (2003). A review of therapist characteristics and techniques positively impacting the therapeutic alliance. *Clinical Psychology Review*, *23*(1), 1–33. doi:10.1016/S0272-7358(02)00146-0 PMID:12559992

American Medical Association. (2016). *AMA principles of medical ethics*. Retrieved October 1, 2019, from https://www.ama-assn.org/delivering-care/ama-principles-medical-ethics

American Psychological Association. (2014). *Guidelines for Clinical Supervision in Health Service Psychology*. Retrieved from http://apa.org/about/policy/guidelines-supervision.pdf

American Psychological Association. (2017). *Multicultural Guidelines: An Ecological Approach to Context, Identity, and Intersectionality*. Retrieved from http://www.apa.org/about/ policy/multicultural-guidelines.pdf

Barnett, J. E., Erickson Cornish, J. A., Goodyear, R. K., & Lichtenberg, J. W. (2007). Commentaries on the ethical and effective practice of clinical supervision. *Professional Psychology, Research and Practice*, *38*(3), 268–275. doi:10.1037/0735-7028.38.3.268

Beach, M. C., & Inui, T. (2006). Relationship-centered care: A constructive reframing. *Journal of General Internal Medicine*, *21*(S1), S3–S8. doi:10.1111/j.1525-1497.2006.00302.x PMID:16405707

Birkhäuer, J., Gaab, J., Kossowsky, J., Hasler, S., Krummenacher, P., Werner, C., & Gerger, H. (2017). Trust in the health care professional and health outcome: A meta-analysis. *PLoS One*, *12*(2), e0170988. doi:10.1371/journal.pone.0170988 PMID:28170443

Bordin, E. S. (1979). The generalizability of the psychoanalytic concept of the working alliance. *Psychotherapy (Chicago, Ill.)*, *16*(3), 252–260. doi:10.1037/h0085885

Bordin, E. S. (1983). A working alliance based model of supervision. *The Counseling Psychologist*, *11*(1), 35–42. doi:10.1177/0011000083111007

Chipidza, F. E., Wallwork, R. S., & Stern, T. A. (2015). Impact of the doctor-patient relationship. *The Primary Care Companion for CNS Disorders*, *17*. Advance online publication. doi:10.4088/PCC.15f01840 PMID:26835164

Cliffe, T., Beinart, H., & Cooper, M. (2016). Development and validation of a short version of the supervisory relationship questionnaire. *Clinical Psychology & Psychotherapy*, *23*(1), 77–86. doi:10.1002/cpp.1935 PMID:25504780

Constantino, M. J., Castonguay, L. G., & Schut, A. J. (2002). The working alliance: A flagship for the "scientist-practitioner" model in psychotherapy. In G. S. Tryon (Ed.), *Counseling based on process research: Applying what we know* (pp. 81–131). Allyn and Bacon.

Constantino, M. J., Morrison, N. R., MacEwan, G., & Boswell, J. F. (2013). Therapeutic alliance researchers' perspectives on alliance-centered training practices. *Journal of Psychotherapy Integration, 23*(3), 284–289. doi:10.1037/a0032357

Crits-Christoph, P., Crits-Christoph, K., & Gibbons, M. B. C. (2010). Training in alliance-fostering techniques. In J. C. Muran & J. P. Barber (Eds.), *The therapeutic alliance: An evidence-based guide to practice* (pp. 304–319). Guilford Press.

Crits-Christoph, P., Gibbons, M. B. C., Crits-Christoph, K., Narducci, J., Schamberger, M., & Gallop, R. (2006). Can therapists be trained to improve their alliances? A preliminary study of alliance-fostering psychotherapy. *Psychotherapy Research, 16*, 268-281. doi:500268557 doi:10.1080/10503300

Del Re, A. C., Flückiger, C., Horvath, A. O., Symonds, D., & Wampold, B. E. (2012). Therapist effects in the therapeutic alliance-outcome relationship: A restricted-maximum likelihood meta-analysis. *Clinical Psychology Review, 32*(7), 642–649. doi:10.1016/j.cpr.2012.07.002 PMID:22922705

Dorr Goold, S., & Lipkin, M. (1999). The doctor-patient relationship: Challenges, opportunities, and strategies. *Journal of General Internal Medicine, 14*(S1), S26–S33. doi:10.1046/j.1525-1497.1999.00267.x PMID:9933492

Eckstrand, K. L., Eliason, J., St. Cloud, T., & Potter, J. (2016). The priority of intersectionality in academic medicine. *Academic Medicine, 91*, 904–907. doi:10.1097/ACM.0000000000001231 PMID:27166867

Elvins, R., & Green, J. (2008). The conceptualization and measurement of therapeutic alliance: An empirical review. *Clinical Psychology Review, 28*(7), 1167–1187. doi:10.1016/j.cpr.2008.04.002 PMID:18538907

Eubanks-Carter, C., Muran, J. C., & Safran, J. D. (2015). Alliance-focused training. *Psychotherapy (Chicago, Ill.), 52*(2), 169–173. doi:10.1037/a0037596 PMID:25150677

Eveleigh, R. M., Muskens, E., van Ravesteijn, H., van Dijk, I., van Rijswijk, E., & Lucassen, P. (2012). An overview of 19 instruments assessing the doctor-patient relationship: Different model or concepts are used. *Journal of Clinical Epidemiology, 65*(1), 10–15. doi:10.1016/j.jclinepi.2011.05.011 PMID:22118265

Flückiger, C., Del Re, A. C., Wampold, B. E., & Horvath, A. O. (2018). The alliance in adult psychotherapy: A meta-analytic synthesis. *Psychotherapy (Chicago, Ill.), 55*(4), 316–340. Advance online publication. doi:10.1037/pst0000172 PMID:29792475

Friedlander, M. L. (2015). Use of relational strategies to repair alliance ruptures: How responsive supervisors train responsive psychotherapists. *Psychotherapy (Chicago, Ill.), 52*(2), 174–179. doi:10.1037/a0037044 PMID:25111380

Fuertes, J. N., Mislowack, A., Bennett, J., Paul, L., Gilbert, T. C., Fontan, G., & Boylan, L. S. (2007). The physician-patient working alliance. *Patient Education and Counseling, 66*(1), 29–36. doi:10.1016/j.pec.2006.09.013 PMID:17188453

Fuertes, J. N., Stracuzzi, T. I., Bennett, J., Scheinholtz, J., Mislowack, A., Hersh, M., & Cheng, D. (2006). Therapist multicultural competency: A study of therapy dyads. *Psychotherapy (Chicago, Ill.), 43*(4), 480–490. doi:10.1037/0033-3204.43.4.480 PMID:22122138

Fuertes, J. N., Toporovsky, A., Reyes, M., & Osborne, J. B. (2017). The physician-patient working alliance: Theory, research, and future possibilities. *Patient Education and Counseling, 100*(4), 610–615. doi:10.1016/j.pec.2016.10.018 PMID:27773600

Gordon, C., & Beresin, E. V. (2016). The doctor-patient relationship. In T. A. Stern, M. Fava, T. E. Wilens, & J. F. Rosenbaum (Eds.), *Massachusetts General Hospital Comprehensive Clinical Psychiatry* (2nd ed., pp. 1–7). Elsevier.

Haggerty, G., & Hilsenroth, M. J. (2011). The use of video in psychotherapy supervision. *British Journal of Psychotherapy, 27*(2), 193–210. doi:10.1111/j.1752-0118.2011.01232.x

Hatcher, R. L., & Gillaspy, J. A. (2006). Development and validation of a revised short version of the Working Alliance Inventory. *Psychotherapy Research, 16*(1), 12–25. doi:10.1080/10503300500352500

Hilsenroth, M. J., Ackerman, S. J., Clemence, A. J., Strassle, C. G., & Handler, L. (2002). Effects of structured clinician training on patient and therapist perspectives of alliance early in psychotherapy. *Psychotherapy (Chicago, Ill.), 39*(4), 309–323. doi:10.1037/0033-3204.39.4.309

Horvath, A. O., Del Re, A., Flückiger, C., & Symonds, D. (2011). Alliance in individual psychotherapy. *Psychotherapy (Chicago, Ill.), 48*(1), 9–16. doi:10.1037/a0022186 PMID:21401269

Horvath, A. O., & Greenberg, L. S. (1989). Development and validation of the Working Alliance Inventory. *Journal of Counseling Psychology*, *36*(2), 223–233. doi:10.1037/0022-0167.36.2.223

Joyner, B., & Young, L. (2006). Teaching medical students using role play: Twelve tips for successful role plays. *Medical Teacher*, *28*(3), 225–229. doi:10.1080/01421590600711252 PMID:16753719

Ladany, N., Ellis, M. V., & Friedlander, M. L. (1999). The supervisory working alliance, trainee self-efficacy, and satisfaction. *Journal of Counseling and Development*, *77*(4), 447–455. doi:10.1002/j.1556-6676.1999.tb02472.x

Muran, J. C., & Barber, J. P. (Eds.). (2010). *The therapeutic alliance: An evidence-based guide to practice*. Guilford Press.

Muran, J. C., Safran, J. D., & Eubanks-Carter, C. (2010). Developing therapist abilities to negotiate alliance ruptures. In J. C. Muran & J. P. Barber (Eds.), *The therapeutic alliance: An evidence-based guide to practice* (pp. 320–340). Guilford Press.

Norcross, J. C., & Wampold, B. E. (2011). Evidence-based therapy relationships: Research conclusions and clinical practices. *Psychotherapy (Chicago, Ill.)*, *48*(1), 98–102. doi:10.1037/a0022161 PMID:21401280

Ong, L. M. L., de Haes, J. C. J. M., Hoos, A. M., & Lammes, F. B. (1995). Doctor-patient communication: A review of the literature. *Social Science & Medicine*, *40*(7), 903–918. doi:10.1016/0277-9536(94)00155-M PMID:7792630

Palomo, M., Beinart, H., & Cooper, M. (2010). Development and validation of the supervisory relationship questionnaire (SRQ) in UK trainee clinical psychologists. *British Journal of Clinical Psychology*, *49*(2), 131–149. doi:10.1348/014466509X441033 PMID:19457275

Patton, M. J., & Kivlighan, D. M. Jr. (1997). Relevance of the supervisory alliance to the counseling alliance and to treatment adherence in counselor training. *Journal of Counseling Psychology*, *44*(1), 108–115. doi:10.1037/0022-0167.44.1.108

Safran, J. D., Muran, J. C., & Eubanks-Carter, C. (2011). Repairing alliance ruptures. In J. C. Norcross (Ed.), *Psychotherapy relationships that work: Evidence-based responsiveness* (2nd ed., pp. 224–238). Oxford University Press. doi:10.1093/acprof:oso/9780199737208.003.0011

Smith-Hansen, L. (2016). The therapeutic alliance: From correlational studies to training models. *Journal of Psychotherapy Integration*, *26*(3), 217–229. doi:10.1037/int0000012

Sulmasy, L. S., & Bledsoe, T. A. (2019). American College of Physicians ethics manual: Seventh edition. Annals of Internal Medicine, 170, S1-S32. doi:10.7326/M18-2160

Szasz, T. S., Knoff, W. F., & Hollender, M. H. (1958). The doctor-patient relationship and its historical context. *The American Journal of Psychiatry*, *115*(6), 522–528. doi:10.1176/ajp.115.6.522 PMID:13595126

Topor, D. R., AhnAllen, C. G., Mulligan, E. A., & Dickey, C. C. (2017). Using video recordings of psychotherapy sessions in supervision: Strategies to reduce learner anxiety. *Academic Psychiatry*, *41*(1), 40–43. doi:10.100740596-016-0605-0 PMID:27558629

Van der Feltz-Cornelis, C. M., Van Oppen, P., Van Marwijk, H. W. J., De Beurs, E., & Van Dyck, R. (2004). A patient-doctor relationship questionnaire (PDRQ-9) in primary care: Development and psychometric evaluation. *General Hospital Psychiatry*, *26*(2), 115–120. doi:10.1016/j.genhosppsych.2003.08.010 PMID:15038928

Wampold, B. E., & Imel, Z. E. (2015). *The great psychotherapy debate: The evidence for what makes psychotherapy work* (2nd ed.). Routledge. doi:10.4324/9780203582015

Ward, E. C. (2002). *Cultural competence, cultural mistrust, working alliance and racial ethnic minority clients' experience of counseling: A mixed methods study*. University of Wisconsin Press.

Watkins, C. E. Jr. (2014). The supervisory alliance: A half century of theory, practice, and research in critical perspective. *American Journal of Psychotherapy*, *68*(1), 19–55. doi:10.1176/appi.psychotherapy.2014.68.1.19 PMID:24818456

Watkins, C. E. Jr, & Scaturo, D. J. (2013). Toward an integrative, learning-based model of psychotherapy supervision: Supervisory alliance, educational interventions, and supervisee learning/relearning. *Journal of Psychotherapy Integration*, *23*(1), 75–95. doi:10.1037/a0031330

Wilson, Y., White, A., Jefferson, A., & Danis, M. (2019). Intersectionality in clinical medicine: The need for a conceptual framework. *The American Journal of Bioethics*, *19*(2), 8–19. doi:10.1080/15265161.2018.1557275 PMID:30784384

Wolfe, B. E., & Goldfried, M. R. (1988). Research on psychotherapy integration: Recommendations and conclusions from an NIMH workshop. *Journal of Consulting and Clinical Psychology*, *56*(3), 448–451. doi:10.1037/0022-006X.56.3.448 PMID:2899579

Chapter 7
Consensus Building Using Quality Improvement Tools During the Instructional Design Process

Julie A. Bridges
https://orcid.org/0000-0003-0567-1703
Eastern Virginia Medical School, USA

Mily J. Kannarkat
Eastern Virginia Medical School, USA

Brooke Hooper
Eastern Virginia Medical School, USA

Catherine J. F. Derber
Eastern Virginia Medical School, USA

Bruce Britton
Eastern Virginia Medical School, USA

Gloria Too
Eastern Virginia Medical School, USA

Andrew Moore
Eastern Virginia Medical School, USA

Jessica Burgess
Eastern Virginia Medical School, USA

Kyrie Shomaker
Children's Hospital of The King's Daughters, USA

Samantha Schrier Vergano
Children's Hospital of The King's Daughters, USA

EXECUTIVE SUMMARY

This case outlines the process of using quality improvement tools during the instructional systems design process. The clerkship curriculum of the third year of medical school was undergoing a complete reform in terms of time and content. An instructional designer was utilized to complete a needs analysis and participate in the instructional systems design process. A need for a common understanding of the language of medical education and instructional design drove the team to

DOI: 10.4018/978-1-7998-5092-2.ch007

utilize the Institute for Healthcare Improvement (IHI) Quality Improvement tools. The reform took 11 months, involved six clerkship directors, multiple administrators, and resulted in consensus among the clerkship directors regarding the knowledge, skills, and attitudes appropriate for a third-year medical student curriculum.

ORGANIZATION BACKGROUND

The medical school was facing a scarcity of resources, an upcoming accreditation process, complex business processes, and data overload. Third year clerkship directors were time impoverished; took care of patients and worked with an average of 25 students per rotation. Adding to their anxiety, several directors were new or had been in the position three or fewer years. Student satisfaction measures in the Graduation Questionnaire (GQ) collected by the Association of American Medical Colleges (AAMC), were below benchmark levels in perception of quality, and with an upcoming accreditation visit looming, the clerkship directors of the institution were charged with improving these measures by the institutional Dean/President/Provost.

The charge to the clerkship directors was to reduce learner time and improve quality in the traditional third year clerkship of medical school curriculum. The time available between the charge and the implementation was 11 months. Six clerkship directors in the areas of family medicine, internal medicine, obstetrics and gynecology, pediatrics, psychiatry and surgery gathered in team meetings to meet this challenge. The diverse group of leaders faced considerable design challenges. These challenges included viewing the curriculum as whole, identifying needs, prioritizing experiences for learners, aligning assessments with the step examinations and institutional competencies. The main task was to identify the knowledge, skills and attitudes appropriate for a third year medical student that would prepare learners to meet the requirements of residency directors hiring the learners upon completion of the four-year program of study.

The large group of clerkship leaders had competing interests, limited time, and varying past measures of quality perception from learners. Past learner performance in cognitive measures of the Step 2 Clinical Knowledge (Step 2 CK), were slightly above the national average. Past measures of clinical performance on the Step 2 Clinical Skills (Step 2 CS) examination, were slightly below the national average. The task was to reduce the time in core clerkships from eight to six weeks, include an elective clerkship for specialty and career exploration. Additionally, the task was to increase opportunities for learners to prepare for Step 2 CS and improve quality perception in all clerkships. A leadership decision to include a full instructional systems design (ISD) process resulted in an effective and peaceful decision-making experience. During the needs analysis phase, the inclusion of the Institute for Healthcare Improvement (IHI) Quality Improvement tools during ISD process enabled consensus building and increased efficiency of group decision-making (Quality Improvement Essentials Toolkit, n.d.). Initial consensus on design decisions resulted in immediate quality perception improvements as well as improvements in key areas for the ongoing clerkships.

The initial needs identified by leadership were a restructuring of the time allotted to each clerkship to allow for a specialty and career exploration clerkship, additional faculty for teaching and coordinators for administrative duties during the clerkships. Co-clerkship directors were identified or hired to serve in a teaching role and the percentage of time allotted to each director was increased. Additionally, co-clerkship coordinators were identified or hired to assist in the administrative duties for the clerkship. A new associate dean for clinical education led the reform effort. New faculty were brought on board with the explicit understanding that they were critical to the reform process and existing faculty now had the bandwidth to orient the new faculty to the educational process due to the support provided by additional coordinators. A new associate dean for program evaluation and assessment and director of assessment were hired to assist in these areas.

The restructuring of time in the clerkships changed from an 8-week structure to a six-week structure for the family medicine, pediatrics, obstetrics and gynecology, psychiatry, and surgery clerkships. The time in Internal medicine clerkship increased from an eight week to a 12-week clerkship to include geriatrics and neurology. The remaining six weeks in the 48-week curriculum contained a career exploration and specialty clerkship. The restructuring would reduce the number of students in each rotation from 25 to 20.

CASE DESCRIPTION

The institution had massive data available through end of clerkship satisfaction surveys, performance measured through subject examinations, standardized patient encounter measurements through checklists and rubrics, and clinical performance measurements through a uniform rubric completed by attending physicians, residents, and preceptors. The massive data had yet to be converted to meaningful information and was regularly delivered to the clerkship directors who found the bulk of the data to be overwhelming and disheartening. The associate dean for program evaluation and assessment began by bringing the massive data into a single report that to tell a story easily understood by the clerkship directors. The report included visualizations that allowed the clerkship directors to see their measures against the benchmarks. Previous reports included the entire GQ benchmarking report that appeared in table format. The new reports used data visualization principles that allowed the directors to identify the need for change (Tufte, 2001). Table 1 and Figure 1 is a comparison of data from the GQ table format to the visualization format.

Table 1. Sample Results of Examinations in Table Format (Not Actual Institutional Data)

	Benchmark	Total
2014	96	99
2015	96	98
2016	97	98
2017	96	97
2018	95	95
2019	95	93

Figure 1. Results displayed visually to show trends

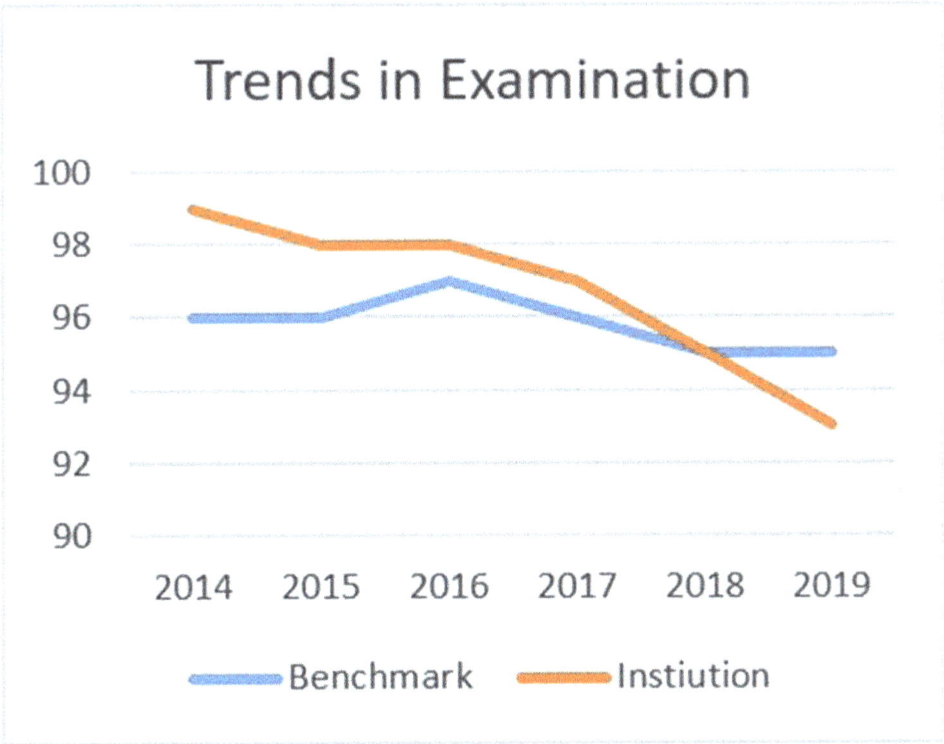

With the problem presented in visual format, it was easy to spot areas where satisfaction and/or performance were below benchmark.

Pre-meetings

When the new faculty were onboard and oriented, the dean of clinical education, the instructional designer, and the director of assessment met with each set of clerkship directors to review the story of the data for each clerkship in small group meetings. At these meetings, the tone was collegial and supportive with the clinical education dean reviewing the issues and concerns of the clerkship directors and gathering requests for additional educational resources. At the individual meetings, discussion of concerns regarding the change occurred in a safe environment. The dean listened carefully to each concern and suggested ways to implement the six-week curriculum. The team took a supportive approach and appreciated the input of an instructional designer to help with the entire process. The clerkship directors did not have to analyze and interpret all the performance data alone because they had the help of the director of assessment. During the pre-meetings, a shared mental model was agreed upon that a six-week clerkship curriculum could be successful, that support was available, and a structured, scientific and evidence based approach to instructional design would be used. At the end of the pre-meetings, all directors agreed to spend one year working on the design of the curriculum with the goal of moving to a six-week clerkship for all clerkships except internal medicine. Internal medicine would be12 weeks in length in order to house geriatrics (previously taught in family medicine) and neurology (previously taught in psychiatry). All directors agreed that it would be very useful for all directors to attend monthly meetings to review the entire third year curriculum for redundancies, gaps, and measures for the institutional competencies as well as the institutional competencies.

Low hanging fruit. During the individual meetings, several low-hanging fruit opportunities were identified for immediate improvement. These opportunities included dropping extra assignments and redesigning the LMS course for one of the lower rated clerkships, usage of standardized syllabi for all clerkships, and a standardized student activity card to summarize required activities for each clerkship.

Monthly Meetings

A schedule of monthly meetings was developed based on availability of directors and the first Thursday of the month at 7 a.m. was determined to be the best available time for all directors. Hot breakfast was served and the meetings were affectionately named “the bacon meetings”. A central repository for all agendas, reports and supporting documents was created in the learning management system. The LMS

Figure 2. Timeline for design

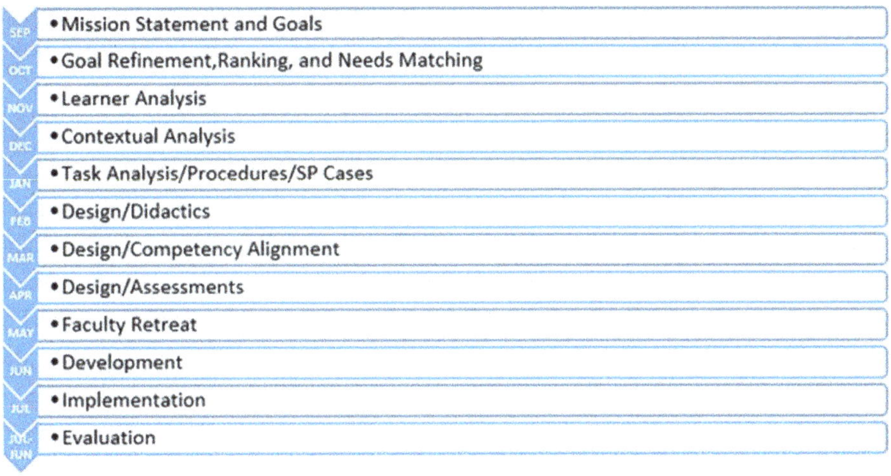

provided a reference point and document sharing mechanism during the process. At the first meeting, a timeline for design was introduced.

The instructional designer explained each step of the process, and the team unanimously agreed that the entire process should be followed including five months of analysis. The next step was deciding to adopt an instructional design model and committing the time to do the entire process of instructional systems design including asking the important question of why the instruction was needed during the analysis phase (Morrison, Morrison & Kalman, 2019).

Design Process

With the meeting schedule created, the team had to decide upon a process for design. The team used terminology that included language from the instructional design model and from quality improvement. The team included an instructional designer from the beginning of the process, and relied upon their expertise in choosing a model to follow during the design process. A modified version of the Kemp Design Model (Morrison, et al., 2019) was chosen. The model served the team's needs because the iterative nature of the model matched the iterative processes suggested by our accreditation agencies, Liaison Committee on Medical Education (LCME) and Southern Association of Colleges and Schools Commission on Colleges (SACSCOC). The model was adapted to include additional quality improvement tools for the project because the clerkship directors already used QI tools in their regular practice and felt familiar with the language. One major challenge presented during the model adoption phase, was the translation from educational terminology to medical terminology.

Choice of QI tools. The choice to use the IHI quality improvement tools ("Institute for Healthcare Improvement: Quality Improvement Essentials Toolkit," n.d.) occurred during the initial project phase because clerkship directors often used quality improvement descriptors to articulate their visions for the clerkship design process. This natural integration provided a level of familiarity to the instructional design process that seemed to reduce the complexity of the problem and provided a kind of Rosetta stone between the language of education and the language of medical practice. Directors reached an understanding of the iterative nature of the design process including the quality improvement process. This understanding resulted in the adoption of an instructional design process model to resolve the needs of the clerkship directors.

IHI tools. The clerkship directors commonly used quality improvement terminology to identify areas for improvement, and the choice to use the IHI tools was a perceived as a natural fit during the decision making process because of their familiarity. Tools were chosen for use at appropriate times during the process based on the needs of the team and the functions of the tools (Bunney & Dale, 1997; Jafari & Setak, 2010).

The instructional design process is a systematic approach to analyze, design, develop, implement and evaluate instruction. Instructional design resides within the context of curriculum organization while both are directly related to goals, objectives and measurements of performance and satisfaction (Brauer & Ferguson, 2015). A systematic approach to an integrated curriculum, aligned instructional events, and increased measures of success is outlined in the following design plan. The first step in instructional design is to complete a needs analysis.

Needs Analysis. The needs analysis contains four phases of planning, collecting data, data analysis, and final reporting. The audience for the instruction was defined as third year medical students in their clerkship experiences. The participants in the design process include clerkship directors, clerkship coordinators, administrators, and students. Stakeholders identified are LCME, EVMS leadership, students, clerkship directors and coordinators, department chairs, faculty, residents, and simulation center members. The initial question asked in the needs analysis was regarding the necessity of the instruction. Initially, this question was confusing until it was clarified by asking: What aspects of clerkship instruction are needed for third year undifferentiated physicians? In adding the idea that particular material would be appropriate for residents, but not third year medical students, the question regarding the necessity of instruction became real. The team looked to the existing data to answer these questions.

Data were collected from the results of the National Board of Medical Examiners (NBME) Step 2 Clinical Knowledge (CK) and Clinical Skills (CS) Examinations and from the Graduation Questionnaire (GQ). Data analysis from the previous year's focus groups revealed the following themes:

- Grading inconsistency
- Organization and consistency among clerkships
- Balance of patient care and study time
- Inclusion as part of the team
- Quality feedback
- Availability of preceptors

Recent trends in the Graduation Questionnaire (GQ), collected from the Association of American Medical Colleges (AAMC) showed learner dissatisfaction with both the learning environment and the learning material. Recent trends in learner performance on standardized board examinations showed above average proficiency in the domain of knowledge (Step 2 CK) but showed mixed results in clinical skills (Step 2 CS). The measure of communication on Step 2 CS was above average while the measure of integrated clinical examination was below average. Comments from the GQ were analyzed to reveal the following themes:

- Increased class size stress on the institution
- Lack of administrative resources/lack of organization within the clerkships
- Lack of consistency across clerkships

Administrators had the resources to conduct a thorough needs analysis and found the following needs:

- Experiences that will improve integrated clinical encounter performance
- Observed history taking with feedback for improvement
- Observed physical exam with feedback for improvement
- Improved mid-clerkship experiences
- Improved clerkship organization/consistency across clerkships
- Improved faculty teaching in all clerkships
- Improved resident teaching in all clerkships

At times, conducting a complete needs analysis is not possible due to time or resource constraints but a possible alternative is to conduct a goal analysis (Morrison, et al., 2019). The medical school as fortunate to have time to do both the needs analysis and the goal analysis. The administrators completed the needs analysis with the assistance of the instructional designer, and the clerkship directors completed the goal analysis. To frame the goal analysis, a mission statement, based on the institutional mission statement, was created by the team and proved a valuable exercise in developing a shared mental model of the clerkship goals.

The clerkship experience will provide quality experiences for learning and progression in the areas of dedication to patient care, collaboration, teamwork, lifelong learning, continuous improvement, and service to the community. Our clerkships have been purposefully created by aligning goals and objectives with needs focused on knowledge skills and attitudes of a well-rounded physician of any specialty. Our curriculum is designed to provide supportive opportunities helping learners find their path and maximizing their full potential. We hold the belief that communication and learning are two-way streets, with responsibilities to teach and learn shared in a collaborative manner. Given our unique focus on service to the community, learners will emerge from year three of the curriculum with a renewed passion for medical service.

The next step in the design process was the goal analysis. The Nominal Group Technique (NGT), allowed for a silent collection of information without long emotional and political discussions for the choices (Dobbie, Rhodes, Tysinger, & Freeman, 2004). Using a silent NGT group technique, goals were collected in written form from individuals, arranged in categories, and consensus reached for the initial goals:

1. Experiential learning with clinical immersion for learners
2. Maximize main faculty time with learners for the longest time possible
3. Clinical reasoning taught in a controlled environment
4. Simplified goals and objectives for clerkships aligned with needs (and core competencies) and focused on an undifferentiated third year medical student
5. Core exploration with personalized plans for subspecialty exploration

A brief discussion provided the consensus of reined goals ranked in the following order:

1. Experiential learning with clinical immersion for learners
2. Aligned goals and objectives with needs focused on knowledge skills and attitudes of a well-rounded physician of any specialty
3. Clinical reasoning taught in a controlled environment with patient oriented interactive learning focused on clinical reasoning based on institutional competencies and preparing for subject examinations.

4. Maximize main preceptor time with learners for the longest time possible, recognizing excellence with awards and focusing on residents as educators
5. Core exploration with personalized plans for subspecialty exploration

To unify the needs analysis provided by administration, and the goals provided by the directors, an exercise to match the needs to goals provided opportunity for rich discussion.

Table 2. Needs Matched to Goals

Needs	Goals
Experiences that will improve integrated clinical encounter performance experiences (Step 2 CS ICE)	3,2
Observed history taking with feedback for improvement	1,3,4
Observed physical exam with feedback for improvement	1,3,4
Improved mid-clerkship and ongoing feedback	4
Improved organization/consistency across clerkships	2
Improved faculty teaching in all clerkships	3,2
Improved resident teaching in all clerkships	3,2
Improved student evaluations and assessments of student in all clerkships	4
Career exploration opportunities	5
Improved learning environment/mistreatment measures on GQ	all

After the matching process, the directors all agreed that their own goals matched the administration's needs analysis. The matching of process provided a level of trust that the goals of the clerkship directors were considered important, aligned with the institutional needs, and all agreed to proceed to the learner analysis.

Learner analysis. Directors voiced concerns that learners were not completely prepared to meet the demands of the curriculum coming into the clerkship year. A Pareto Analysis was utilized to reveal the top areas of concern from the clerkship directors and allowed the group to accept that everyone had the same common issues. The Pareto analysis, often called the 80/20 rule, where 80% of the effect was due to 20% of the causes, was used to collect the largest to smallest contribution to the effect. The top 20%, or "vital few" causes were visualized in a chart for easier identification and facilitated a focused and productive discussion. The issues identified were larger, general attributes of the learner. Each area of concern was a large issue that required more information to understand. A cause and effect diagram was used to fully understand the area of perspective. A root cause analysis was utilized to expand on the idea of "perspective" found in the Pareto Analysis and revealed the categories of patient focus, expectations, grade focus, role of learner on the team, missing knowledge and skills.

The rich discussion that resulted from the cause and effect diagram process revealed the need for further individual discussions regarding each category in the diagram. The Clerkship Directors were in a unique position to understand and further define necessary attributes of the entering the clerkships. Through a facilitated discussion, the Clerkship Directors came to consensus on the following key 13 attributes of a "Day 1" M3 student:

1. Perspective
2. Seek feedback and utilize for improvement
3. Adaptable, Flexible, Resilient

Figure 3. Pareto chart

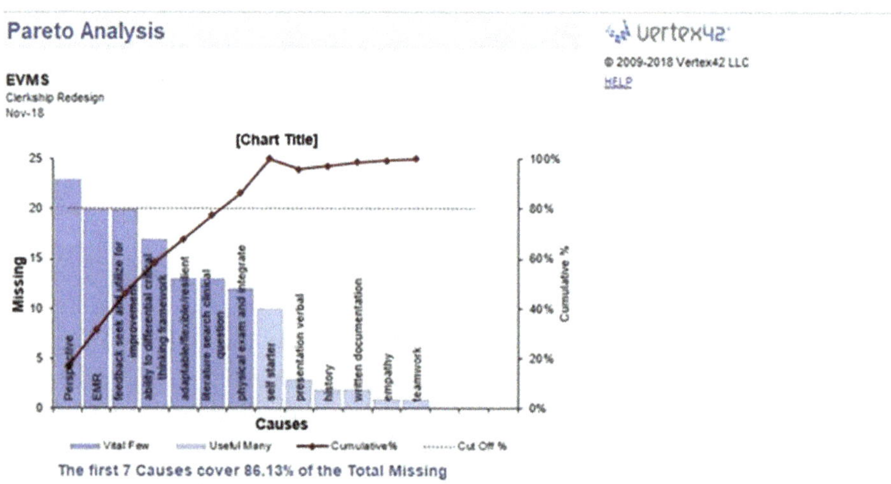

Cumulative Percentage Cutoff: 80%

#	Causes	Missing	Cumulative%
1	Perspective	23	16.8%
2	EMR	20	31.4%
3	feedback seek and utilize for improvement	20	46.0%
4	ability to differential critical thinking framework	17	58.4%
5	adaptable/flexible/resilient	13	67.9%
6	literature search clinical question	13	77.4%
7	physical exam and integrate	12	86.1%
8	self starter	10	100.0%
9	presentation verbal	3	95.6%
10	history	2	97.1%
11	written documentation	2	98.5%
12	empathy	1	99.3%
13	teamwork	1	100.0%

Insert new rows above this line

Vital Few Useful Many Cut Off %

Figure 4. Cause and effect analysis of perspective category

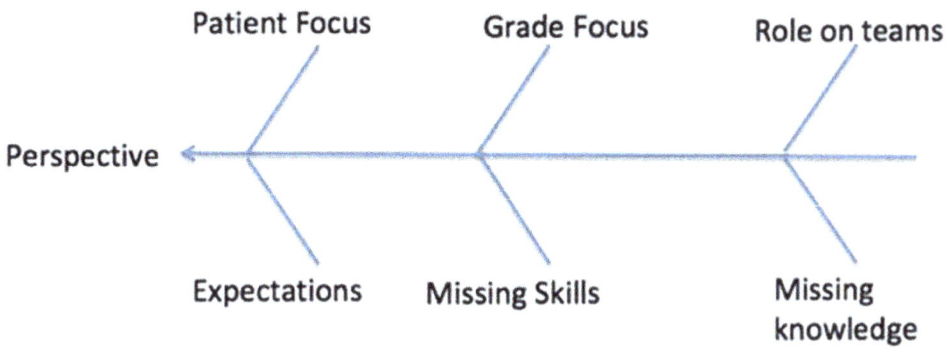

4. Self-starter
5. Empathy
6. Teamwork
7. Ability to develop differential diagnosis, have framework for critical thinking
8. Form clinical question, perform literature search
9. Perform history
10. Perform physical exam and integrate
11. Oral presentation
12. Written documentation
13. EMR

It is important to note that these 13 attributes represent the expectations of the clerkship directors as it relates to the knowledge, skills, and attitudes of a Day 1 M3 student. There is inherent overlap to these attributes. As such, it was important to further define and clarify the meaning behind each of these "attributes." the Associate Dean for Clinical Integration, met individually with each of the Clerkships (Clerkship Directors representing General Surgery, Internal Medicine, Family Medicine, Pediatrics, Ob/Gyn, Psych) to revisit these 13 attributes, ensure continued consensus, and where needed clarify the meaning behind these attributes.

Perspective. The following descriptions were agreed upon to explain the clerkship director expectations perspective. The learner:

- Can transition into clinical environment where patient care is the primary focus (e.g. student learning is part of the process, but structure of day is centered around patient's needs)
- Can identify ways to contribute to the team and still meet individual learning needs.

- Can recognize that all core clerkships have important concepts central to patient care (e.g. can "keep an open mind" regardless of specific interests)
- Finds value in patient care and learning within the clinical experience (e.g. motivated beyond grade/numbers)
- Can appreciate time commitment and sacrifice inherent in medicine (e.g. beyond "9am-5pm on Mon-Fri mentality)

Seek feedback and utilize for improvement. The following descriptions were agreed upon to explain the clerkship director expectations perspective. The learner:

- Is intrinsically motivated to improve (motivation extends beyond grade/numbers)
- Can define his/her self-identified goals and reflect on one's performance prior to asking for feedback.
- Can recognize appropriate time, place, and context to ask for feedback.
- Can ask for feedback.
- Can recognize different types of feedback when given in real time (e.g. can recognize short snippets of feedback while rounding, not always a sit down meeting)
- Is mentally prepared to hear and accept feedback as a normal process of self-improvement. This includes recognizing the breadth of potential feedback which could range from perception of student attitude, style of conversation, knowledge level, etc.

Adaptable, flexible, and resilient. The following descriptions were agreed upon to explain the clerkship director expectations perspective. The learner:

- Can manage one's time in different environments (e.g. can use time in between scheduled clinical activities effectively, can use gaps over the course of the day effectively)
- Can adjust to the needs of other team members as it relates to patient care (ex. can adapt to the needs of the receiver of information for an oral presentation).
- Can navigate and adjust to change (e.g. change in preceptor and student schedule, differences that exist between clerkships, etc.).
- Can understand that day-to-day schedules in medicine are not identical between providers.
- Can recognize one's own limitations (e.g. can recognize the difference between something being inherently difficult vs. recognizing when one needs to ask for additional help)
- Has appropriate boundaries with patients.

- Can account for and listen to the perspective of others while maintaining sense of self => "not crushed by 1 comment on 1 evaluation, can keep going" (academic buoyancy)
- Can be flexible to guidance and appreciates that "there can be more than one way to do something"
- Can balance competing responsibilities for one's time (clinical care as part of a team, reading for patients, studying for exam, personal responsibilities, etc.)

Self-starter. The following descriptions were agreed upon to explain the clerkship director expectations perspective. The learner:

- Can actively observe, listen, and gather info on how team functions (without having to be told explicitly).
- Can seek out new opportunities and offer help concordant with one's abilities and scope of practice ("knows when to do vs. when to watch")
- Can establish study schedule and balance different responsibilities.
- Can intellectually engage even when discussion of medicine is not directly directed toward the student (team's patient but student not directly pre-rounding on patient)
- Can prepare and "be ready for rounds"

Empathy. The following descriptions were agreed upon to explain the clerkship director expectations perspective. The learner:

- Is nice! (nice to the patient, the team, and him/herself)
- Can listen and genuinely seek to understand where patient is coming from (especially in circumstances when patient background could be very different from their own). Examples cited as different background could include "life experiences to include loss of loved ones," "different socioeconomic standing," "dysfunction in one's life," "history of abuse".
- Can demonstrate a genuine appreciation for patient's story through nonverbal communication. (e.g. can "actively listen in a way that transcends words")

Teamwork. The following descriptions were agreed upon to explain the clerkship director expectations perspective. The learner:

- Can recognize the important roles of others on a team.
- Can recognize "it's a win if everyone does well" (e.g. "not feeling like you have to outshine your peers to be/look good")

- Can respect and listen to all team members (e.g. "values input from all team members, not just the attending")
- Can recognize the team's responsibility to care for patients (e.g. "team's patients are my patients")
- Is courteous and polite to everyone ("nice to staff and attending physician")

Develop a differential diagnosis. The following descriptions were agreed upon to explain the clerkship director expectations perspective. The learner:

- Can independently develop a differential diagnosis (e.g. list 5-10 diagnoses) for common symptoms**
- Has a framework for clinical reasoning
- Recognizes the process from patient symptom to diagnosis
- Can translate initial differential diagnosis into pertinent/hypothesis driven H&P
- Can recognize the importance of discriminating and distinguishing features in an illness script
- Can recognize the varied application of a differential diagnosis (e.g. differential diagnosis for symptom vs. differential diagnosis for an abnormal lab value)
- Can recognize variables that might influence the development of a differential diagnosis (site of care, prevalence of a disease, life threatening/can't miss diagnoses)

Form clinical question, perform literature search. The following descriptions were agreed upon to explain the clerkship director expectations perspective. The learner:

- Has intellectual curiosity, can self-identify gaps in knowledge and perform focused reading
- Can access resources to answer background questions (e.g. what is standard of care for a condition?)
- Knows "basic biostats"
- Can recognize statistical significance

IM clerkship – specific expectation for student presentation

  - Is familiar with interconnected process of "Ask, Acquire, Appraise, and Advise"
  - Can ask a background question and utilize self-directed learning to define foreground (PICO) question

    - Can use appropriate resources as part of self-directed learning
    - Can perform a pub med search using search filters
    - Knows which study designs can answer what types of clinical questions

Note: Expectation is not to be a complete EBM expert on Day 1 M3, but rather to be familiar with process of EBM, able to access available resources, and use those resources to facilitate answering questions about patients.

Perform history and perform physical exam and integrate findings. The following descriptions were agreed upon to explain the clerkship director expectations perspective. The learner:

- Can approach a patient one on one, gather a history, and perform a physical exam
- Can appreciate the similarities and differences between types of visits
    - New visit vs. f/u visit, Inpatient vs. outpatient, Reason for visit - manage chronic Illness vs. acute illness vs. acute exacerbation of chronic illness
- Can identify relevant history and exam in patient presenting with common symptoms**
- Can gather a clinically relevant social history ("Social History is more than Tobacco/EtOH/Drugs" – e.g. can elicit and explore support system, functional status, social determinants of health)
- Can identify and describe normal physical exam findings.
- Can perform "close to Pass" on domain of History and Physical on clinical evaluation form

Oral presentation and written documentation. The following descriptions were agreed upon to explain the clerkship director expectations perspective. The learner:

- Can perform "Close to Pass" on domain of oral presentation on clinical evaluation form
- Can share patient story accurately

Electronic medical record (EMR). The following descriptions were agreed upon to explain the clerkship director expectations perspective. The learner:

- Can recognize the importance of supplemental sources of information.
- Can apply hypothesis driven approach and verbalize information needed from EMR ("know what you are looking for so you can focus/actively search for information within the EMR").

Note: Can learn nuances of different EMR as an M3, just in time EMR training is reasonable.

**A*s listed on M3 Clerkship Student Objectives Card:*

Abdominal pain, Altered mental status, Back Pain, Chest pain, Cough, Diarrhea, Dizziness, Dysuria/Male GU symptoms, Fever, Gastrointestinal bleeding, Headache, Leg swelling, Nausea/Vomiting, Shortness of breath/Dyspnea, Upper respiratory tract symptoms (runny nose, sore throat), Rash, Abnormal uterine bleeding, Pelvic pain.

With the learner analysis complete, the next step of contextual analysis, the team utilized driver diagrams to conceptualize solutions to the common goals of the clerkships based on the group consensus.

Contextual analysis. During the contextual analysis, the team considered the instructional environment issues such as requirements, hospitals, locations, preceptor availability, resident availability, clerkship director availability, etc. The team used the driver diagrams shown below to define the optimum aim of each context (i.e. 4:1 faculty student ratio) and the primary drivers that could make that happen (i.e. co-module director, dedicated faculty, residents as teachers training, etc.). These diagrams were completed using pencil and paper, scanned and emailed to the designer in between meetings. The designer converted the drawn diagrams to digital format and projected them during the next meeting following the diagram completion. The diagrams were used to frame the meeting discussions regarding the contextual analysis.

The most pressing issue was the time and quality spent with the attending/preceptor. Several important decisions were made on business processes that were taking time out of the physicians' teaching schedule that could be offset to the new curriculum coordinators such as scheduling. Other items were accountability for completing evaluations of students that could be solved with a simple report from the current system. Several important curriculum discussions emerged regarding focusing on presenting main signs and symptoms, preparation during the basic science years on clinical reasoning skills, and opportunities to provide feedback on student note taking.

Many solutions sprung from the discussion about learner clinical reasoning including refocusing the standardized patient encounters, choosing didactic topics to prepare learners for subject examinations, and the need to refocus basic science education to clinical reasoning regarding presenting signs and symptoms instead of disease based instruction.

The thought process diagram added more dimension to the clinical reasoning diagram to drill into what is learned during clinical skills in first and second years of the curriculum. The consensus was to focus the learner on the thought processes of why the differentials were correct.

Figure 5. Drivers and restrainers diagram of maximize time/quality with preceptor

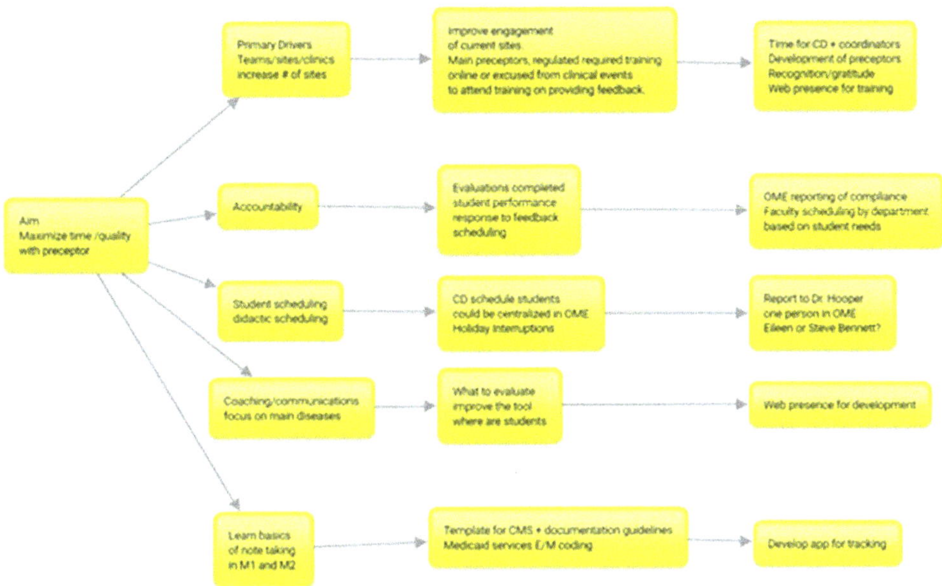

Figure 6. Drivers and restrainers diagram of clinical reasoning

All discussions referred to the diagrams as each item was addressed. When the discussion lost focus, the diagram was projected to allow refocus and resolution.

Task analysis. During the next monthly meeting, clerkship directors created a master list of procedures, distributed the procedures among the clerkships, and provided a checklist or grading rubric for each procedure. Directors considered utilizing the simulation center for practice on procedures when possible, developed

Figure 7. Drivers and restrainers diagram of thought process problem

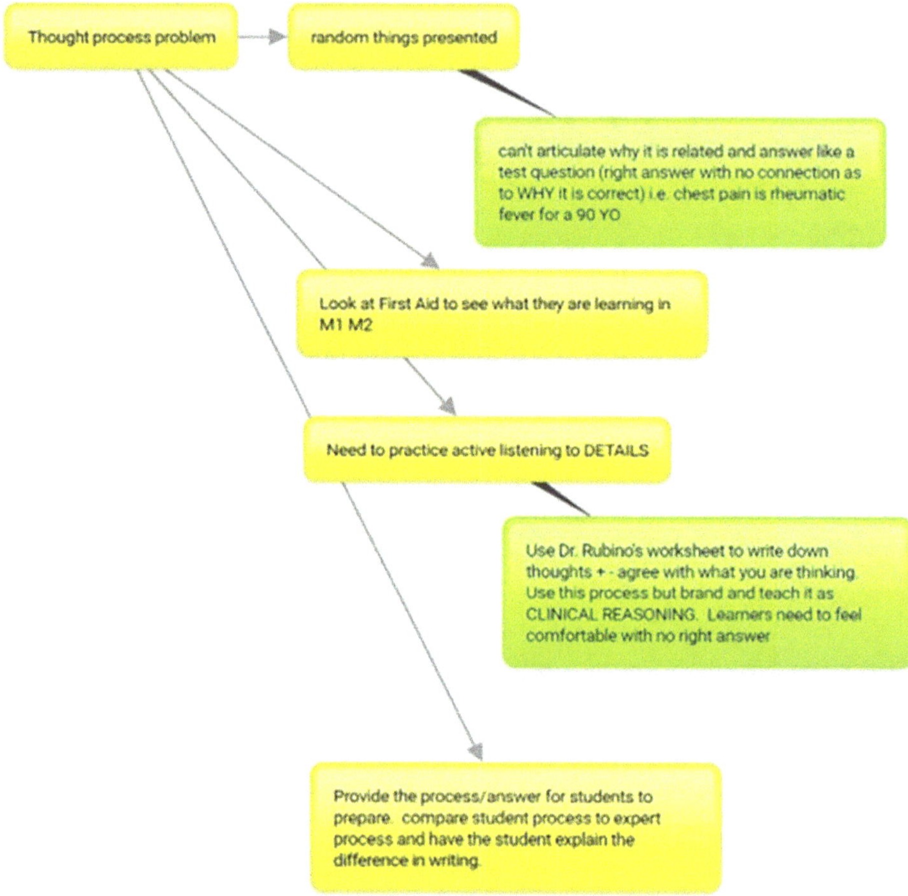

a simulation, and standardized patient schedule. A master list of procedures was created using a sample list to begin the process (Thompson, Exline, Leung, Way, Clinchot, Bahner, & Khandelwal, 2016).

Didactics. Didactics and assessment were aligned with the competencies to make sure no overlaps and gaps were present. Content Area Item Analysis Summary reports from the NBME subject examinations were used to identify any areas in need of improvement and didactics were eliminated if they did not support competencies for medical knowledge (subject examination) or clinical knowledge. A worksheet provided directors the opportunity to align the didactic sessions to the competencies. The time spent on the topic was compared to the weighting in the NBME subject exam item analysis to make sure enough time was spent on appropriate topics.

Diseases. Directors compiled the list of diseases/disorders required for each clerkship and narrowed their lists down to the top ten required in each clerkship. A list of each of the top 100 diseases taken from First Aid (Le, & Bhushan, 2018). was utilized to identify where each item was covered in the basic science modules. Analysis of the session objectives in the basic science years revealed a need for focus on clinical skills reasoning and a need for more defined depth and breadth of topics covered in the basic science years. This is now an ongoing process led by a new Dean of Clinical Integration appointed based on the identification of the needs of the clerkship directors.

Competency alignment and assessments. All clerkship assessments were aligned to institutional competencies. The unified clinical knowledge form proved invaluable because the majority of competencies were measured with the form. Other competencies were assessed with the subject examination, and simulations. Remaining competencies were assessed with a project in the family medicine clerkship or during service learning experiences in first, second or fourth years.

Once the design phase was completed, a faculty retreat provided an opportunity to decide on a unifying grading system to reduce confusion between clerkships and the perception among learners regarding inconsistency in grading. The process of team building during the meetings had created a trust among the directors and administration so agreement on the last item of unified grading (weighting of subject examinations, clinical evaluations, and "other" categories) was achievable. The hard work of the directors and coordinators as well as the administrative leaders of the team was acknowledged with a great meal and a small gift of appreciation.

Development

Once the design plan was in place, the instructional designer created the course shells according to the standardized design. Items from old courses were brought over and placed in the appropriate content areas, and new content was created by faculty, if necessary. Clerkship directors spent one month reviewing and updating the master courses that would be used for copying into each block of the clerkship. The administrative portion of the team (instructional designer, director of assessment, and the dean of clinical education) created the standardized syllabi, student activity cards, and reviewed all material to make sure the content matched the design plan. A central network drive contained all documents including the last version of each affectionately referred to as final-final-final.doc. This pressure-filled month was made easier by the design document, humor, and large quantities of coffee.

Implementation

The first block of courses was deployed in the learning management system one week prior to clerkship beginning. During the first block of clerkships, student feedback was heavily solicited by the clerkship directors and during our first monthly meeting of the second year, edits suggested by student representatives were made for the second block of courses. One of the most valuable aspects of the process was the perception of students who had just utilized the standardized course layout and documentation. One area of improvement noted by students was the organization of sub folders, especially those of the standardized patient encounters.

Immediate Results and Future Planning

Using the IHI tools, Nominal Group Technique (NGT), Pareto Analysis, Root Cause Analysis, and Driver Diagrams, helped bring swift and easy consensus to the design process because of the familiarity of the tools and processes. The written NGT provided a silent method to collect information that had emotional and institutional political charge. The silent collection method saved a great deal of time by collecting the information, categorizing the items, and voting on the top categories to reach consensus.

Quality. After the curriculum change, perceived quality from the last block of the old curriculum to the first block of the new curriculum remained relatively the same or improved in all clerkships except one clerkship due to a loss of coordinators at the beginning of the year.

Observed history. The benchmark of 95% of students observed taking a history was met or exceeded by all clerkships. Data were gathered from mandatory end of clerkship surveys completed by students.

Observed Physical Examination. The benchmark of 95% of students observed completing a physical examination was met or exceeded by all clerkships. Data were gathered from mandatory end of clerkship surveys completed by students.

The monthly meetings continued through the next year as additional items were identified for continuous improvement. Identified areas for continuing improvement were:

- Improving perception of the quality of mid-clerkship feedback from students by adjusting the timing so preceptor evaluations can be included in the feedback and reviewing a patient note created by the students.
- Communication of expectations around the standardized patient encounter.

Continuous improvement processes were implemented by incorporating the student feedback and making rapid changes when possible to clarify processes for assessment especially those for the standardized patient encounters during the first block of deployment. As a result of the student feedback, an entire area for improvement was identified to standardize all information provided to students regarding expectations around the SP process and a new team formed to address this for next year. Standardization of the design documentation process with a modified ASPE template for SP case design will be utilized to improve communication from the simulation center to the clerkship design team (including directors, coordinators, and administration). Future processes for improvement include calibration of faculty and student expectations around all assessments, and targeted faculty development in the feedback process.

REFERENCES

Bunney, H. S., & Dale, B. G. (1997). The implementation of quality management tools and techniques: A study. *The TQM Magazine*, *9*(3), 183–189. doi:10.1108/09544789710168966

Dobbie, A., Rhodes, M., Tysinger, J. W., & Freeman, J. (2004). Using a modified nominal group technique as a curriculum evaluation tool. *Family Medicine*, *36*(6), 402–406. PMID:15181551

Institute for Healthcare Improvement (IHI). (2018). *Institute for healthcare improvement: Quality improvement essentials toolkit-Flow Chart*. doi:10.4102/hts.v71i1.2874

Jafari, S. M., & Setak, M. (2010). Total Quality Management Tools and Techniques: the Quest for an Implementation Roadmap. *Proceedings of the AGBA 7th World Congress*, *1*(3), 1–12. 10.1111/conl.12206

Le, T., & Bhushan, V. (2018). *First Aid for the USMLE Step 1*. McGraw Hill Professional.

Morrison, G. R., Ross, S. J., Morrison, J. R., & Kalman, H. K. (2019). *Designing effective instruction*. Wiley.

Quality Improvement Essentials Toolkit | IHI - Institute for Healthcare Improvement. (n.d.). Retrieved January 30, 2020, from http://www.ihi.org/resources/Pages/Tools/Quality-Improvement-Essentials-Toolkit.aspx

Thompson, L., Exline, M., Leung, C. G., Way, D. P., Clinchot, D., Bahner, D. P., & Khandelwal, S. (2016). A clinical procedures curriculum for undergraduate medical students: The eight-year history of a third-year immersive experience. *Medical Education Online*, *21*(1), 29486. doi:10.3402/meo.v21.29486 PMID:27222103

Tufte, E. R. (2001). *The visual display of quantitative information* (Vol. 2). Graphics Press.

APPENDIX

Questions for Discussion

1. As an instructional designer, what do you think was gained by spending time in the analysis phase of design?
2. How did the use of the IHI Quality Improvement tools improve the process of curriculum reform?
3. What advantages can you see to adding the instructional systems design process to the curriculum reform process?
    a. Is there a difference between instructional systems design and curriculum design?
4. What do you think are the next steps in the design and/or quality improvement process?
5. What are some ways the school can measure success of this curriculum?
    a. Is there a difference between instructional systems design and program evaluation?

Objectives

Explain the utility of the analysis phase during the ISD process
Analyze the use of QI tools during the ISD process
Differentiate between ISD and curriculum design
Discuss measures of evaluation within the context of ISD
Differentiate between ISD and program evaluation

Chapter 8
Creating an Infrastructure to Deliver Meaningful Feedback to Nursing Students

Jill Erin Stefaniak
University of Georgia, USA

Melanie E. Ross
Northrop Grumman, USA

EXECUTIVE SUMMARY

Research studies surrounding feedback primarily centered on frameworks designed as models for delivering feedback as well as the timing for delivering feedback. In addition, past research has also focused on individual elements that affect performance with little regard to environmental elements. This case study provides an overview of how a nurse educator utilized a performance analysis approach to providing feedback to nursing students during clinical rotations. A list of performance standards was provided to students at various checkpoints during their clinical rotation. Strategies are shared for improving the type of feedback used in healthcare settings.

BACKGROUND

Since delivering meaningful and effective feedback is an acquired skill, it is necessary to train nursing educators to provide feedback, especially since very few empirical studies focused on the training the providers received for delivering effective feedback (Al Wahbi, 2014; Dobbelaer, Prins, & van Dongen, 2013; Mitchell et al., 2013). In nurse education, feedback is often known as debriefing or clinical evaluation.

DOI: 10.4018/978-1-7998-5092-2.ch008

Debriefing is used to provide nursing students structured, formative feedback during and/or after experiential learning opportunities that primarily occur in simulation settings (Cant & Cooper, 2011). During a learning opportunity, debriefing affords the learner the ability to adapt to a variety of situations as they occur, as well as to address errors or changes in the environment (Huggard, 2013). When debriefing sessions occur after a learning opportunity, learners are guided through a purposeful discussion relating to the experience (Huggard, 2013). This guided discussion aids in drawing out the explanations behind the individual's performance and highlights progress while also enabling the individual to develop strategies to enhance future performance (Cant & Cooper, 2011).

Clinical evaluation is also a term commonly used for providing feedback in nurse education clinical settings where students care for patients during hands-on rotations (Hendricks, Wallace, Narwold, Guy, & Wallace, 2013). For years, clinical skills of nursing students have been studied to assess the effects of different media, methodologies, and tools on measuring the clinical performance of nursing students (Hawkins, Osborne, Schofield, Pournaras, & Chester, 2012; Hendricks et al., 2013; Walsh, Jairath, Paterson, & Grandjean, 2010). Despite the varying terminology based on simulation or clinical rotations, both are designed to provide nursing students with structured feedback to assess performance regarding a variety of skills. For purposes of this research study, the terms feedback, debriefing, and clinical evaluation were used interchangeably.

Despite the varying definitions of effective feedback, for feedback to be effective, the nursing educator must communicate the desired behavior in a receptive manner for the nursing student to receive, understand, and physically accomplish the behavior (Rasheed, Khan, Rasheed, & Munir, 2015). If the accomplishment is not a result of the changed behavior, the feedback provided was ineffective. Although effective feedback is necessary to promote performance improvement, the environment, individual competencies, and training are several factors that contribute to a nursing educator's ability to provide effective feedback. Nursing educators cannot be expected to provide effective feedback to nursing students without the proper resources and skills gained through training.

Feedback in Nursing

Occurring in both clinical and simulation-based learning environments, debriefing is situation-dependent and is commonly used to correct errors, discuss different ways to handle similar events the next time, encourage self-assessment, and promote reflective thinking (Rivera-Chiauzzi, Lee, & Goffman, 2016). Debriefing sessions in clinical situations allows the nursing student to manage and/or reduce stress while improving the ability to develop strategies to improve quality and patient safety

(Rivera-Chiauzzi et al., 2016) and effectively cope with sudden, overwhelming, and unexpected situations (Huggard, 2013). Debriefing sessions in simulation-based learning environments enhance the practice of clinical skills in a safer learning environment due to the exposure to rare, but critical events without a real patient (Rivera-Chiauzzi et al., 2016).

Similar to feedback sessions found in different industries, debriefing is unique to the situation and can occur collective or individually; dictated by the nature of the debriefing session, which can focus on daily required tasks and procedures or adverse events surrounding tasks and procedures or stressful and unusual traumatic events (Huggard, 2013). For example, a nursing educator may wish to conduct an organization debriefing session as a group to discuss an error made in administering medication to a patient. During this group setting, the nursing educator will meet with the cohort of nursing students to identify the cause of the error as well as discuss future policies and procedures to safeguard future instances (Huggard, 2013). Also, they may discuss what went well, what did not go well, and what lessons were learned during the event (Huggard, 2013; Rivera-Chiauzzi et al., 2016). Contrary to the organizational debrief, the nursing educator may wish to conduct a psychological debrief one-on-one with a nursing student to allow the student to validate feelings and emotions experienced during a stressful or unusual traumatic event; contributes to reducing potential psychological harm due to talking about the experiences (Huggard, 2013). This one-on-one session allows for the nursing student to make sense of the situation and the adverse outcome while understanding and validating their feelings. A psychological debriefing session can also occur in small groups.

The debriefing sessions above require the use of two-way communication between the nursing educator and the nursing student; however, debriefing can also occur through reflective practices, such as journaling. The act of journaling allows nursing students to reflect upon their experiences to decompress and manage feelings associated with adverse outcomes, ethical dilemmas, conflicts, and other situations (Andersen, 2016; Santiago & Abdool, 2011). Reflective debriefing also allows for nursing students to reflect upon experiences in a nonthreatening environment, thus potentially reducing anxieties and improving clinical judgment when experienced in clinical practice (Davies, 1995; Lavoie, Pepin, & Boyer, 2013). In some instances, nurse educators may use self-reflection practices in conjunction with organizational and psychological debriefing sessions to further enhance the learning opportunity. As mentioned previously, debriefing sessions are situation-dependent where nursing educators will often employ a variety of techniques to debrief their students; all techniques are implemented to improve the quality of healthcare and patient safety during critical and non-critical procedures.

Nursing educators understand feedback is necessary to improve performance; however, there is no prescribed number of times to deliver feedback in a specified period to invoke a change in behavior. Despite not knowing an exact number of times to provide feedback, research has found that receiving feedback too frequently leads to a decrease in performance due to excessive focus on and more systematic processing of recent data rather than comparing information received from multiple periods (Lurie & Swaminathan, 2009). Similarly, receiving feedback too frequently may interfere with a nursing student's ability to learn tasks due to an overload of information (Hemayattalab & Rostami, 2010).

Feedback Models in Healthcare

Roberts, William, Kim, and Dunnington (2009) proposed the Briefing, Intraoperative, Teaching, Debriefing (BID) Model for teaching in the operating room. This model was developed due in part to infrequent opportunities for teaching in the operating room. The BID Model is great for strategically engaging the learner before, during, and after surgery in a fast-moving, demanding field. It begins with the surgeon briefing the learner for two to three minutes to assess the needs of the learner, for the learner to assess individual needs, and to collaborate to identify and establish objectives for the operation; the learner is responsible for selecting one to two objectives to focus on during the operation (Roberts, Williams, Kim, & Dunnington, 2009). The next step includes intraoperative teaching where the surgeon uses teaching scripts to have didactic discussions with the learner based upon the established learning objectives to guide the learner through the surgery (Roberts et al., 2009). The last step in the BID model includes debriefing where the attending physician asks the learner to reflect upon the performance concerning the established objectives; learners are required to assess what they learned while listening to the attending surgeon diagnose identified problems (Roberts et al., 2009).

Despite the frequent interactions between surgeons and learners in the operating room, the BID Model possesses several limitations. Rather than developing a plan to observe and debrief a learner, the BID Model promotes opportunistic teaching where the surgeon teaches the learner in the current moment. Since situations rarely ever mimic one another entirely, the situations in which feedback is delivered will differ, thus potentially confusing due to different feedback delivered and/or received each time. Similarly, with the BAF Model, learners are involved in the debriefing process through constant communication about the present and future behaviors whereas the BID Model employs a passive transfer of information, as the surgeon walks the learner through the surgery while emphasizing the established objectives. Although the BID Model is designed for surgeons to avoid spending time debriefing learners outside the operating room, it fails to provide adequate time to allow surgeons to provide the necessary feedback for learners to improve performance as well as for them to reflect upon and process their experiences. The BID Model fails to incorporate any environmental elements that could affect performance; it offers severely limited feedback using a narrow scope of passive information focusing only on the individual and their performance (Roberts et al., 2009).

The 3D Model of Debriefing developed by Zigmont, Kappus, and Sudikoff (2011) is a debriefing model that focuses on defusing, discovering, and deepening the experience of the performer. Defusing allows the performer to express any emotions, struggles, or events that occur during simulated events or first-hand experience. Discovering allows the performer to analyze and evaluate their performance by reflecting upon experiences as well as discovering mental models for exhibiting specific behaviors (Zigmont, Kappus, & Sudikoff, 2011). Deepening allows for the performer to develop connections learned in simulation to create cues to implement in clinical practice; it discusses how the relationship of performance during the simulation period can be related to the clinical setting (Zigmont et al., 2011). Although this comprehensive model allows performers to identify discrepancies in performance during the discovery stage, this model relies heavily upon the performer, to be honest about experiences and emotions exhibited during experiences. This model fails to incorporate an element that requires the facilitator to observe the performer in the learning and practice environments, thus relying heavily upon information from the performer. Performers may be dishonest out of fear of feeling silly or behind when compared with peers.

The 3D Model of Debriefing utilizes elements from the Learning Outcomes Model, which focuses on the importance of the learner, experience, and environment to promote effective learning (Zigmont et al., 2011). The learner element focuses on intrinsic motivation, prior knowledge and experience through mental models, competence and reasoning, and emotions while the environmental element of the model focuses on the learning and performance environments, to include skilled mentors, location of learning and equipment available, and policies in place during practice (Zigmont et al., 2011). The experience is based on Kolb's Experiential Learning Cycle, which promotes active learning where previous experiences are considered alongside new experiences to make connections (Zigmont et al., 2011); experiences may be positive or negative and can occur during simulation or with patients (Zigmont et al., 2011). This model only discusses resources and fails to articulate the data or incentives in the environment that could influence performance. This particularly focuses on the performer's orientation, analogical reasoning, and mental models rather than the knowledge, capacity, and motives that influence performance.

The Ask-Tell-Ask (ATA) Model was initially adapted and implemented at the Cleveland Clinic in 2005 to assist medical trainees with reflecting upon and assessing their own skills (French et al., 2015). The rater asks performers to conduct a self-assessment before the facilitator sharing observations, concerns, strengths, and weaknesses. It then seeks to check the performer's understanding before discussing a plan for improvement (French et al., 2015). Although this model aligns with the BAF in that it utilizes direct observation and addresses a maximum of one to two objectives per session, it fails to provide the instructor or supervisor specific elements to focus on in the feedback session. Since there are individual and environmental elements that are known to affect performance, it is imperative to surround the feedback sessions around these elements. Without focusing feedback around these elements, it is highly possible that the information delivered will not affect performance in the way the instructor or supervisor hopes. Table 1 provides a summary of the feedback models used in healthcare settings.

Previously explored feedback models tend to serve as a framework for providing feedback, as they provided insight into how feedback should be structured, but failed to deliver specifics for delivering feedback. Due to the nature of the nursing environment and the understanding that patient's lives are in the hands of nursing students, nursing educators need a prescriptive feedback model for delivering behavior-specific feedback surrounding the elements that are known to influence a change in behavior. Research on feedback found the individual elements that affect performance are secondary to the environmental elements (Gilbert, 2007).

In clinical environments, nursing educators constantly step into situations to deliver immediate feedback that is specific to the student's behavior. Although immediate feedback is necessary, research proves delayed feedback leads to better retention of information over time for later usage, which contributes to improved performance over time (Butler et al., 2007; Mullet et al., 2014; Phye et al., 1976).

SETTING THE STAGE

Rebecca Murphy is an experienced nurse educator who has been a preceptor for Covenant Hospital for over 20 years. Over the years she has served in many leadership roles as a nurse educator for the medical-surgery unit. As an educator, one of her responsibilities is to oversee nursing students from the local university who complete their clinical rotations on her unit.

A challenge Rebecca faces is providing the nursing students with adequate and timely feedback that they can use while they complete their rotations. Due to the shift work and the high volume of nurses that work on her unit, the nursing students interact with and are supervised by several nurses during their rotation. It is Rebecca's responsibility to gather feedback from all of the nurse preceptors who interact with the students and consolidate feedback that is useful to the student.

Table 1. Summary of Feedback Models in Healthcare Settings

Model	*Author*	*Advantages*	*Disadvantages*	*Context*	*Elements of the BEM Included*
The BID Model	Roberts, Williams, Kim, & Dunnington	· Utilizes a teaching script that focuses on student-selected objectives; promotes self-reflection.	· Employs passive transfer of information in a short amount of time. · Limited feedback focuses only on an individual's performance for that particular situation.	Healthcare: Operating Room	Individual · Knowledge: Training Program
The 3D Model of Debriefing	Zigmont, Kappus, & Sudikoff	· Focuses on defusing by expressing through emotion, discovering through reflection, and deepening experiences through developing connections.	· Information about performance comes from the performer, which requires honesty about emotions and experiences. · It does not allow for performance to be observed.	Healthcare: Clinical Setting	Individual · Knowledge: Knowledge, Skills, Experience · Motives: Placement
The ATA Model	Cleveland Clinic	· Promotes self-assessment of skills and reflection, and promotes observations and discussions.	· No specific guidance is provided for what to focus on during the feedback session.	Healthcare: Clinical Setting	Individual · Knowledge: Training Program
Multi-Rater Feedback Approach	Wachter & Lion	· Utilizes peer feedback and instructor and self-evaluation on an on-going basis to develop the skills and confidence needed to perform.	· Subjective · May not be truthful due to boost own performance.	Healthcare: Operating Room	Individual · Knowledge: Training Program · Capacity: Ability · Motives: Alignment

In the past, Rebecca has found that feedback is written and delivered to the nursing students after they have completed their clinical rotation and have moved onto their next clinical assignment. There is no opportunity for her to remediate the students and provide formal formative feedback during their rotation.

After meeting with several other nurse preceptors, Rebecca has decided that she wants to try a new approach for delivering feedback to the nursing students that will involve delivering formative feedback at several different checkpoints during their clinical rotation. While the students have been receiving informal feedback on an ongoing basis, Rebecca wants to ensure that this feedback is adequately documented.

CASE DESCRIPTION

Rebecca met with nursing students who had recently completed their clinical rotation with her unit. She asked them to share what types of feedback would be most helpful to them. Many of the students that she spoke with shared that a lot of the feedback was superficial and did not provide constructive feedback to help them make changes to their performance. They also expressed a need to receive feedback earlier in their rotation so that they would have time to make modifications under the guidance of their nurse preceptors.

The students also shared with Rebecca that feedback was delivered inconsistently by the preceptors. Some of the preceptors provided formal feedback while others relied solely on informal means of communication. The students said that it would be easier if a consistent mechanism was established in the unit.

Rebecca also met with nurse preceptors in her unit as well as colleagues who worked in other units of the hospital. She asked them to identify the challenges they encounter while providing feedback. Some of the concerns they raised included finding the time to deliver feedback to the nursing students. While there is always a degree of impromptu feedback that is provided as students are assisting with patient care, it is difficult to find time to sit down with the nursing student and have a one-on-one conversation to reflect on the day's events.

A few of the preceptors also expressed that they were uncomfortable delivering negative feedback as they did not want to be an obstacle for the nursing students' professional development. They shared that it would be helpful if there was a structure that they could all follow in the unit.

After reviewing several clinical feedback models, Rebecca decided to adapt the behavioral analysis feedback model to her clinical setting. The Behavioral Analysis Feedback (BAF) Model serves as a prescriptive feedback model designed to continuously provide feedback while accounting for the environmental and individual elements that influence behavior (Ross & Stefaniak, 2019). Comprised of four steps, the BAF Model utilizes a supervisor-centered approach with performer input for reinforcing and modifying behaviors. Table 2 includes the four steps needed for delivering feedback after the performance has been observed. Although the steps appear to be linear, due to the constant evaluation for each of the components and the ability to revisit any step at any point, the BAF Model and the four-step approach is considered recursive.

Table 2. Four-Step Approach

Step	Activity	Actions
1	Ask	· Select one individual or one environmental element to be discussed. · Ask nursing students to think about where they were in terms of their current performance. · Ask nursing students where they would like to go in terms of the element.
2	Discuss	· From direct observations and relating to the factors, identify specific behaviors that need to be reinforced or corrected. · Provide behavior-specific suggestions for improvement.
3	Ask	· Ask nursing students what they need to reach the desired performance. · Develop a plan of action including a proposed timeline. · Check the performer's understanding.
4	Evaluate	· Continuously evaluate the nursing students' performance based on the established plan of action. · Revisit each step as needed, and evaluate performance again.

Rebecca met with each of her nurse preceptors to look at the BAF model. They followed the four-step approach in Table 2 and agreed to use this format when communicating with their nursing students.

Nursing Student Performance

As predicted by the body of research surrounding effective feedback (Al Wahbi, 2014), the present case uncovered evidence that the nursing educator needs to provide on-time and specific feedback for nursing students to reach their full potential, as it provides nursing students the information needed to improve performance. Current research shows that simply providing nursing student's surface-level feedback, such as praise or the right answer, does not support the nursing student's ability to comprehend or understand the effects of their performance or use the information to help achieve or exceed the pre-established goals (Schartel, 2012). Similarly, research has found that delivering behavior-specific feedback has been proven to be more beneficial than delivering surface-level feedback because it provides the performer the desired result and the behaviors needed to achieve the desired result (Austermann Hula et al., 2008;

Zigmont et al., 2011). By employing a set of performance standards, the nursing educators were required to deliver behavior-specific feedback to the nursing student. Using a list of performance standards to achieve in the performance environment led to the overall improvement of performance among nursing students. Similarly, it was uncovered that nursing students demonstrated consistent techniques between the learning environment and the performance environment.

Similarly, the frequency and timing of the feedback also played a role in improving performance among nursing students. While there is no prescribed number of times to deliver feedback in a specified period to invoke a permanent change in behavior, too much or too little feedback is known to be detrimental (Hemayattalab & Rostami, 2010; Lurie & Swaminathan, 2009). The use of the BAF Model required the nursing educator to communicate behavior-specific feedback during two or three formal debriefing sessions depending on the length of the clinical rotation. By employing a set number of formal debriefing sessions, the results of the BAF Model demonstrated the number of debriefing sessions conducted were adequate for improving performance (Lurie & Swaminathan, 2009) while avoiding hindrance of the nursing student's ability to perform the required tasks due to information overload (Hemayattalab & Rostami, 2010). This coincided with the current research that shows that providing too much feedback can cause a performer to lose the ability to self-reflect on their performance and correct any errors (Rivera-Chiauzzi et al., 2016) while providing too little feedback may allow a performer to exhibit the wrong behavior far too long. Since the BAF Model employed only two or three formal debriefing sessions throughout the clinical rotation, the feedback that was delivered was considered delayed. Nursing educators assessed their student's performance and provided feedback the following week during the formal feedback session. The use of delayed feedback with the BAF Model supports the current research that delaying feedback contributes to prolonged improvement over time, as it hinges on the performer's curiosity by encouraging them to anticipate the answer, which can ultimately increase their attention when feedback is received

Nursing Educator Feedback Perception

Three elements, including the need for training, personal experiences, and the follow-on interview, contributed to influencing the nursing educator's perception of delivering feedback. Nursing educators were required to participate in a self-paced training program surrounding the utilization and implementation of the BAF Model with specific regards to communicating behavior-specific feedback. The utilization of the BAF Model uncovered an overwhelming agreement that the nursing educators developed the skills needed to deliver behavior-specific feedback as well as motivated them to provide behavior-specific feedback to their nursing students.

This coincides with the current research that suggests direct supervisors should participate in feedback training geared towards causal analyses to identify, determine, and bridge the identified gaps in performance (Van Tiem, Moseley, & Dessinger, 2012), which goes beyond the interpersonal communication, professionalism, adequacy, and resources needed to provide effective feedback to nursing students (Mitchell et al., 2013).

Similarly, the nursing educator serves as a direct supervisor to the nursing students and is responsible for guiding what is deemed acceptable for proper performance (Ashford & Cummings, 1983; London & Smither, 2002). Not only is it important for the nursing educator to know what the acceptable performance includes, but also how to communicate it in a way the nursing student can accept and understand. Results from this research study uncovered an overwhelming agreement from the nursing educators that the use of the BAF Model led to increased communication between the nursing educator and nursing student and encouraged feedback to be behavior-specific. This supports the current research that nursing educator's need to communicate desired behaviors in a receptive manner to nursing students, so they can receive, understand, and physically accomplish the behavior (Rasheed et al., 2015).

While trialing new feedback models, Rebecca realized that many of her nurse preceptors experienced challenges with delivering feedback during and regarding stress situations. The performance context for nursing educators and nursing students alike includes the potential for stressful situations with adverse outcomes and the overall feelings and emotions experienced during such an event. Although nursing educators may feel apprehensive and anxious before, during, and after feedback sessions, the nursing educator must provide the nursing student with behavior-specific feedback that leads them to achieve the desired behavior. While this may not always be easy, there are some quick principles the nursing educator could apply to assist with alleviating any feelings of apprehension and anxiety. Similarly, these principals may also assist with nursing students feeling less anxious and apprehensive towards receiving feedback.

- To ensure feedback is delivered to nursing students in a receptive manner, the nursing educator should use neutral, non-judgmental language focusing on observable behaviors.
- To ensure nursing students are paying attention to the conversation at hand, have the learner repeat the desired behavior and the actions he or she will need to conduct to reach the desired behavior.
- If the nursing student does not engage in the conversation with the nursing educator, the nursing educator should conduct a think-aloud approach where the nursing student walks the nursing educator through the required procedures to reach the desired result.

- If the nursing student continues to repeat mistakes or fails to reach the desired behavior after repeated debriefing sessions, the nursing educator should provide the nursing student one or more worked examples in the performance environment with a step-by-step demonstration of how to perform the task or how to solve the problem.
- To invoke a change in performance, the nursing educator should look at the three perspectives – information, instrumentation, and motivation – and compare the elements at the environmental level with the individual level to determine where deficiencies lie. *E.g. compare data with knowledge, resources with capacity, and/or incentives with motives to determine if it is an issue at either the environmental or individual level or both that is affecting performance.*

CONCLUSION

Feedback in nursing education is critical, as performance can be the result of life or death outcomes for patients in the nurse's care. Although feedback is often handled on-the-job, the need for formal feedback sessions is imminent for performance improvement. The use of the BAF Model in nursing education may enhance the overall feedback process. By following the model, nurse educators are required to deliver behavior-specific feedback with explicit objectives in mind based on assessed performance. This in conjunction with the timing, language, and format of the debriefing session will aid in the continuity of the sessions, thus minimizing surprises that may lead nursing students to exhibit negative feelings about receiving feedback.

The use of the BAF Model may assist with removing barriers for delivering and receiving feedback, thus enhancing the quality of learning and teaching. Nursing educators and nursing students are required to participate in an on-going dialogue surrounding performance. From identifying areas for improvement to developing a plan of action to achieve the behaviors discussed, nursing educators and nursing students are in constant communication beyond the formal debriefing sessions. This may contribute to fostering better relationships between the nursing educator and nursing student, which may lead to better decision-making abilities amidst times of chaos. It may also open the eyes of nursing educators and students about resources that might be missing in the environment, which would contribute to more efficient and effective practices during such situations. Also, with a better relationship developed, nursing educators may feel more comfortable delivering feedback since they are better prepared to deliver behavior-specific feedback. Similarly, nursing students may feel more receptive to the feedback being delivered since they know what to expect during the debriefing sessions.

With educators feeling better prepared to deliver behavior-specific feedback and nursing students more receptive towards receiving feedback, the quality of learning and teaching may be enhanced. With a positive relationship and minimal to no barriers present, nursing students may feel more inquisitive and less apprehensive seeking out their instructor's knowledge and expertise. On the other hand, nursing educators who previously worried about hurting nursing student's feelings when delivering negative feedback may no longer feel this way this since feedback is delivered the same way each time with an emphasis on specific behaviors that need to be modified.

Similar to nursing education, feedback is inherent for improving performance regardless of the industry. On a broader scale, using the BAF Model at the individual, organizational, and societal levels may improve performance. At the individual level, the performer would no longer have to decipher the surface-level feedback received from their supervisor to determine the adequacy of their performance. Feedback would be meaningful and behavior-specific. Similarly, performers would not have to wait weeks or months to receive meaningful feedback, as it would be delivered regularly. Rather than being passive receivers of information, performers would be required to participate in meaningful discussions with their supervisor. Similarly, inadequate performance exhibited by the performer may not be due to performance incompetence; the meaningful discussions might facilitate discovery that resources are missing from the performer's environment to adequately perform the task. Ultimately, this may contribute to performers exhibiting positive feelings and behaviors towards receiving feedback and supervisors exhibiting positive feelings and behaviors towards delivering feedback since potential blame for inadequacy may shift from the performer to the environment; performers may not feel as though they are being picked on or attacked for inadequacy, especially if it is discovered that something missing in the environment is contributing to the inadequacy of performance. When performers are more apt to receiving feedback and supervisors are more apt to delivering feedback, not only does the performer reap the benefits, but so does the organization.

At the organizational level, the results of this study have implications for positive social change for improving performance across nursing educators and students nationwide. An organization's goals are discussed explicitly in the company's strategic organizational plan. As previously mentioned, with an improvement in individual performance, the performer will be able to yield better products and/or services, thus upholding the organization's vision and goals. Similarly, supervisors will be able to determine whether the performance is relevant to achieving the goals as well as ensuring the necessary resources are allocated appropriately to achieve the goals.

The use of the BAF Model may be considered innovative for many organizations that lack feedback models for delivering timely, behavior-specific feedback.

While the focus of feedback surrounds performance and does not distinguish between individual and environmental elements, this study suggests that feedback delivered using the BAF Model assists with identifying the gaps in performance with relation to the individual and environmental elements. Similarly, the results of this study uncovered the need for on-going, active communication where both the nursing educator and nursing student are active participants in the conversation. This technique contributed to the nursing educator's and nursing student's ability to identify issues within the environment that affected individual performance, which then became the focus during debriefing sessions to mitigate any unwarranted performance behaviors. More specifically, the use of the BAF Model broke down the individual and environmental elements that affected performance and allowed the nursing educator to gain a better understanding about how the organizational resources align with the skill set of the performer as well as effect and contribute to the overall performance of the nursing students.

REFERENCES

Al Wahbi, A. (2014). The need for faculty training programs in effective feedback provision. *Advances in Medical Education and Practice*, *5*, 263–268. doi:10.2147/AMEP.S62889 PMID:25170287

Andersen, E. (2016). Enhancing the clinical reflective capacities of nursing students. *Nurse Education in Practice*, *19*, 31–35. doi:10.1016/j.nepr.2016.04.004 PMID:27428689

Ashford, S. J., & Cummings, L. L. (1983). Feedback as an individual resource: Personal strategies of creating information. *Organizational Behavior and Human Performance*, *32*(3), 370–398. doi:10.1016/0030-5073(83)90156-3

Austermann Hula, S. N., Robin, D. A., Maas, E., Ballard, K. J., & Schmidt, R. A. (2008). Effects of feedback frequency and timing on acquisition, retention, and transfer of speech skills in acquired apraxia of speech. Journal of Speech, Language & Hearing Research, 51(5), 1088-1113.

Butler, A. C., Karpicke, J. D., & Roediger, H. L. III. (2007). The Effect of Type and Timing of Feedback on Learning from Multiple-Choice Tests. *Journal of Experimental Psychology. Applied*, *13*(4), 273–281. doi:10.1037/1076-898X.13.4.273 PMID:18194050

Cant, R. P., & Cooper, S. J. (2011). The benefits of debriefing as formative feedback in nurse education. *The Australian Journal of Advanced Nursing*, *29*(1), 37–47.

Davies, E. (1995). Reflective practice: A focus for caring. *The Journal of Nursing Education*, *34*(4), 167–174. PMID:7782884

Dobbelaer, M. J., Prins, F. J., & van Dongen, D. (2013). The impact of feedback training for inspectors. *European Journal of Training and Development*, *37*(1), 86–104. doi:10.1108/03090591311293301

French, J. C., Colbert, C. Y., Pien, L. C., Dannefer, E. F., & Taylor, C. A. (2015). Targeted feedback in the milestones era: Utilization of the ask-tell-ask feedback model to promote reflection and self-assessment. *Journal of Surgical Education*, *72*(6), e274–e279. doi:10.1016/j.jsurg.2015.05.016 PMID:26123726

Gilbert, T. F. (2007). *Human competence: Engienering worthy performance*. Pfeiffer.

Hawkins, S. C., Osborne, A., Schofield, S. J., Pournaras, D. J., & Chester, J. F. (2012). Improving the accuracy of self-assessment of practical clinical skills using video feedback - The importance of including benchmarks. *Medical Teacher*, *34*(4), 279–284. doi:10.3109/0142159X.2012.658897 PMID:22455696

Hemayattalab, R., & Rostami, L. R. (2010). Effects of frequency of feedback on the learning of motor skill in individuals with cerebral palsy. *Research in Developmental Disabilities*, *31*(1), 212–217. doi:10.1016/j.ridd.2009.09.002 PMID:19864110

Hendricks, S. M., Wallace, L. S., Narwold, L., Guy, G., & Wallace, D. (2013). Comparing the Effectiveness, Practice Opportunities, and Satisfaction of the Preceptored Clinical and the Traditional Clinical for Nursing Students. *Nursing Education Perspectives*, *34*(5), 310–314. PMID:24245381

Huggard, J. (2013). Debriefing: A valuable component of staff support. *International Journal of Palliative Nursing*, *19*(5), 212–214. doi:10.12968/ijpn.2013.19.5.212 PMID:23971303

Lavoie, P., Pepin, J., & Boyer, L. (2013). Reflective debriefing to promote novice nurses' clinical judgment after high-fidelity clinical simulation: A pilot test. *Dynamics (Pembroke, Ont.)*, *24*(4), 36–41. PMID:24616950

London, M., & Smither, J. W. (2002). Feedback orientation, feedback culture, and the longitudinal performance management process. *Human Resource Management Review*, *12*(1), 81–100. doi:10.1016/S1053-4822(01)00043-2

Lurie, N. H., & Swaminathan, J. M. (2009). Is timely information always better? The effect of feedback frequency on decision making. *Organizational Behavior and Human Decision Processes*, *108*(2), 315–329. doi:10.1016/j.obhdp.2008.05.005

Mitchell, J. D., Holak, E. J., Tran, H. N., Muret-Wagstaff, S., Jones, S. B., & Brzezinski, M. (2013). Are we closing the gap in faculty development needs for feedback training? *Journal of Clinical Anesthesia*, *25*(7), 560–564. doi:10.1016/j.jclinane.2013.05.005 PMID:24008192

Mullet, H. G., Butler, A. C., Verdin, B., von Borries, R., & Marsh, E. J. (2014). Delaying feedback promotes transfer of knowledge despite student preferences to receive feedback immediately. *Journal of Applied Research in Memory and Cognition*, *3*(3), 222–229. doi:10.1016/j.jarmac.2014.05.001

Rasheed, A., Khan, S.-U.-R., Rasheed, M. F., & Munir, Y. (2015). The impact of feedback orientation and the effect of satisfaction with feedback on in-role job performance. *Human Resource Development Quarterly*, *26*(1), 31–51. doi:10.1002/hrdq.21202

Rivera-Chiauzzi, E., Lee, C., & Goffman, D. (2016). Debriefing after adverse outcomes. *Contemporary Ob/Gyn*, *61*(2), 24–32.

Roberts, N. K., Williams, R. G., Kim, M. J., & Dunnington, G. L. (2009). The briefing, intraoperative teaching, debriefing model for teaching in the operating room. *Journal of the American College of Surgeons*, *208*(2), 299–303. doi:10.1016/j.jamcollsurg.2008.10.024 PMID:19228544

Ross, M., & Stefaniak, J. (2019). Promoting a Holistic Approach to Delivering Performance Feedback: Introducing the Behavioral Analysis Feedback Model. *Performance Improvement*, *58*(6), 17–27. doi:10.1002/pfi.21882

Santiago, C., & Abdool, S. (2011). Conversations about challenging end-of-life cases: Ethics debriefing in the medical surgical intensive care unit. *Dynamics (Pembroke, Ont.)*, *22*(4), 26–30. PMID:22279847

Schartel, S. A. (2012). Giving feedback – An integral part of education. *Best Practice & Research. Clinical Anaesthesiology*, *26*(1), 77–87. doi:10.1016/j.bpa.2012.02.003 PMID:22559958

Van Tiem, D. M., Moseley, J. L., & Dessinger, J. C. (2012). *Fundamentals of performance improvement: Optimizing results through people, process, and organizations* (3rd ed.). Pfeiffer.

Wachter, A., & Lion, R. W. (2016). Multi-Rater Feedback: Improving Students' Readiness for the OR. *Techniques - American Vocational Association*, *91*(3), 44–49.

Walsh, T., Jairath, N., Paterson, M. A., & Grandjean, C. (2010). Quality and Safety Education for Nurses Clinical Evaluation Tool. *The Journal of Nursing Education*, *49*(9), 517–522. doi:10.3928/01484834-20100630-06 PMID:20672776

Zigmont, J. J., Kappus, L. J., & Sudikoff, S. N. (2011). The 3D Model of Debriefing: Defusing, Discovering, and Deepening. *Seminars in Perinatology*, *35*(2), 52–58. doi:10.1053/j.semperi.2011.01.003 PMID:21440811

Chapter 9
Designing, Implementing, and Evaluating Performance-Based Assessments Within a Competency-Driven Curriculum

Channing R. Ford
Harrison School of Pharmacy, Auburn University, USA

Erika L. Kleppinger
Harrison School of Pharmacy, Auburn University, USA

EXECUTIVE SUMMARY

This case explores the development, implementation, and ongoing evaluation of performance-based assessments (PBAs) utilized within a competency-based curriculum at Auburn University Harrison School of Pharmacy (AU HSOP). Comprised of over 270 practice-based competencies, the newly adopted curriculum was designed to equip graduates with the knowledge, skills, and abilities essential for a practicing pharmacist. Early in the curriculum development process, hands-on authentic assessment practices were identified as a key assessment strategy resulting in the integration of PBAs throughout the curriculum. This case will describe the PBA development process adopted by AU HSOP, including specific implementation considerations, and explore the role of PBAs in assessing student progression.

DOI: 10.4018/978-1-7998-5092-2.ch009

ORGANIZATION BACKGROUND

Established in 1885, the Auburn University Harrison School of Pharmacy (AU HSOP) offers a Doctor of Pharmacy (PharmD) degree in addition to Masters and PhDs in Pharmaceutical Sciences. Students entering into the PharmD program complete four years of study, three years of didactic coursework with the final year being comprised of experiential clinical rotations. In addition to Auburn and Mobile, Alabama, students may complete their clinical rotations in areas near Birmingham, Huntsville, Montgomery, or Tuscaloosa, as well as near Columbus, Georgia. PharmD students entering AU HSOP are predominately from in-state (~77%), white (~77%), and female (~65%). On average 50%-60% have completed a bachelor's degree prior to enrollment. Class cohorts average 150 students across two campuses, Auburn and Mobile, with 125 completing course work in Auburn, and 25 in Mobile. The Mobile site was established in 2006 and is housed on the University of South Alabama's campus. As a result of the dual campuses, the integration of video conferencing has been essential to allow for synchronous learning and for student interactions across campuses.

AU HSOP is comprised of three academic departments (Pharmacy Practice, Health Outcomes Research and Policy, and Drug Discovery and Development), and four administrative divisions (Academic Programs, Clinical Affairs and Outreach, Faculty Affairs and Strategic Initiatives, and Research). This organizational framework encourages collaborations across the departments as faculty are immersed not only in their academic department but also within the administrative divisions which include representation from all departments within the school.

With an administrative reorganization in 2019, the establishment of multiple director roles were implemented, providing oversite of the Doctor of Pharmacy (PharmD) program to the Director of Professional Programs. The Director of Professional Programs works closely with all faculty within the new practice-ready curriculum (PRC), while also directing the first-semester of the PharmD curriculum. During this transition, the Dean also named three faculty from the Pharmacy Practice Department to serve as the Skills Lab Coordinator for each program year to collaborate with faculty to develop, implement, and evaluate skills-based activities and performance-based assessments (PBAs). A Director of Assessment was also named and works with faculty across all academic years for all assessments including PBAs. The Skills Lab Coordinators and Director of Assessment work closely together to promote consistency between the classroom and skills lab activities, and the development of the PBAs.

In fall of 2017, AU HSOP implemented the new competency-driven PRC, steeped in positive pedagogical teaching and learning approaches that immerse students in authentic learning experiences including aspects of active and team-based learning.

With the release of the Accreditation Council for Pharmacy Education (ACPE) accreditation standards in 2016 (ACPE, 2015), AU HSOP established a curricular team to initiate the transition from the legacy curriculum to the practice-ready curriculum. This curricular team represented a cross-section of faculty representatives in addition to experts in curricular development and academic assessment. The team was tasked with developing and implementing the new curriculum with several members serving as the Learning Community (LC) Chairs (i.e. instructors of record responsible for collaborating with members of the teaching teams) for the first academic year. The collaborative nature of the development process influenced the overall curricular design, resulting in course units taught by teams of faculty, eliminating silos. Teaching teams are comprised of faculty experts from multiple academic departments and are responsible for the development and delivery of assigned content areas. The LC Chair collaborates with all teaching teams within their assigned academic semester, providing feedback on content and assessment development.

The PRC strives to prepare student pharmacists for entry into the pharmacy profession by instilling the knowledge, skills and abilities needed for practice while shaping the students' professional identity by providing them with experiences that will shape their overall attitudes regarding the profession, the patients they serve, and the healthcare team. To accomplish this feat, AU HSOP recognized that innovative teaching, learning, and assessment practices would be crucial to prepare graduates for entry into practice. This case will explore the development, implementation, and ongoing evaluation of performance-based assessments utilized throughout this practice-ready curriculum, and the role of PBAs to assess student progression.

SETTING THE STAGE

As a health professions training program, AU HSOP was an early adopter of objective structured clinical examinations (OSCE) (McDonough, Kleppinger, Donaldson, & Helms, 2015) as a form of PBAs. While an already established assessment practice in schools of medicine (Harden, 1988; Harden, 2015), the integration of OSCEs in a PharmD curriculum is still relatively new in the United States (Shirwaikar, 2015). However, this trend is changing as these assessments allow for the holistic evaluation of a student's knowledge, skill, and ability within a set clinical objective.

Legacy Curriculum

Within the legacy curriculum, OSCEs were a common assessment approach for the skills-based courses within the Contemporary Aspects of Pharmacy Practice sequence. OSCEs were completed at the end of each semester, were comprised of

4-6 stations, and totaled 40% of students' course grades. Stations within the OSCE assessed students on content from the current semester and examples of stations included blood pressure assessment, patient counseling, over-the-counter product recommendations, and sterile/non-sterile compounding. Typically, each station was a total of 10 minutes and students were evaluated on their clinical knowledge and skills, and overall ability to communicate with the simulated patient/caregiver/healthcare provider. Non-interactive stations excluded the communication component for grading. While grading was completed in real time utilizing video conferencing software, standardized persons (SPs) evaluated student performance using paper checklists prior to the transition to ExamSoft, a web-based assessment software program (ExamSoft Worldwide, Inc., 2019).

To evaluate student readiness for clinical rotations, in 1997, AU HSOP implemented Milestone exams which were OSCEs that included content from across all three academic years (McDonough et al., 2015). Milestone exams included 6-8 stations and each station was 10 minutes in length. These assessments were not part of student coursework but were used to assess a student's readiness for practice. Data from these early assessments were used to inform administrators regarding student progress and were not shared with students. In 2012, the intent of Milestones was reevaluated and the assessment was transitioned to a high-stakes exam. With this change, a predetermined cut point was established. Any student failing to meet the specified cut point after two evaluations would not progress to rotations. Milestones remained a high-stakes assessment until the conclusion of the legacy curriculum in 2019.

Practice-Ready Curriculum

Created using a backward design approach (Wiggins & McTighe, 2005; Daugherty, 2006; Emory 2014), the development of the PRC occurred over a two-year period. This integrated curriculum is influenced by over 270 practice-based competencies that directly stem from 11 ability-based outcomes identified as essential to practicing pharmacists (Wright, Hornsby, Marlowe, Fowlin, & Surry, 2018). As the curriculum is driven by competencies, the integration of hands-on, authentic assessments was essential to ensure that student pharmacists completing the PharmD curriculum were prepared for entry into practice.

To assess for readiness, performance-based assessments were incorporated into the overall curricular assessment plan and are offered at the end of each integrated learning experience (ILE). As each ILE is six weeks in length, students complete at least two PBA events each semester. The inclusion of these assessments allows educators to evaluate students on their knowledge, skills, and abilities, while also striving to incorporate critical thinking strategies that are essential for future healthcare providers to practice safely and effectively. Due to the complexity of these types of assessments and needed resources, PBAs are often viewed as high-stakes since a significant portion of the student's course grade is tied to their overall success within the examination.

Mirroring the expectations of the curriculum development teams, all performance-based assessments are developed by a collaborative team that includes members of the LC teaching teams, the Skills Lab Coordinator for that academic year, and the Director of Assessment. The team is responsible for preparing the assessment, providing feedback both before and following the assessment, and training the standardized persons (if needed) prior to implementation.

With the evolving nature of technology, the utilization of online resources during testing has become essential which is a change from the previous curriculum. Paper-based resources have been limited and the integration of software programs and web-based resources have become common place. To mimic real-world practice and to prepare students to utilize systems that they will encounter upon entry into practice, faculty have consistently integrated this technology throughout the practice-ready curriculum and regularly evaluate students on their ability to navigate, interpret, and utilize these resources in their simulated patient encounters in the classroom, lab activities, or performance-based assessments. Further discussion of the technology used is covered later in the case.

CASE DESCRIPTION

AU HSOP defines performance-based assessments as assessments that require students to perform or complete a clinical skill or series of skills, interact with a simulated patient/caregiver/healthcare provider, or demonstrate technical skills (i.e. sterile and non-sterile compounding). PBAs can be interactive or non-interactive in nature. With over 270 skills-based competencies driving the curriculum, PBAs were identified as a key assessment strategy early in the design process as an effective skills assessment approach. The complex nature of these types of assessments can seem overwhelming to those unfamiliar with the process; the following sections will discuss how AU HSOP develops, implements, and evaluates PBAs for the PharmD curriculum.

PBA Personnel and Logistical Needs

The robust nature of PBAs requires a unified team dedicated to the overall assessment mission. Within AU HSOP, the OSCE team is comprised of multiple members with varied expertise and years of experience. To ensure that a skilled licensed pharmacist is present for all testing events, faculty members from the Department of Pharmacy Practice are assigned as Skills Coordinators for each of the three academic years. Two of the three faculty members are located on the Auburn Campus, with the third located in Mobile. To provide additional support during the actual implementation of the testing event in Mobile, a curriculum coordinator who is also a licensed pharmacist was recruited to manage PBAs for the first and third-year students. The Director of Assessment is responsible for overseeing all PBAs and to ensure consistency in assessment development and implementation. Administrative support is provided by two staff members, one in Auburn and one in Mobile, who are responsible for document preparation, SP hiring and support, and logistics support. Lastly, the most essential members of the OSCE team are the instructional technology (IT) specialists. These team members manage all the IT needs for PBAs to include: identifying, purchasing, and managing equipment; staging audio and visual components; recording and processing student recordings; and providing onsite technology support during testing administration. The IT specialists are responsible for staging equipment (i.e. laptops, cameras, printers) for both interactive and non-interactive assessments.

In addition to the core OSCE team, further support is provided by faculty involved within the relevant course to assist with initial station review and SP debriefing during PBA implementation. This additional support is essential as it allows members of the OSCE team to be available for troubleshooting without devaluing the intent of the station review. These faculty are tasked with watching and evaluating both student and SP performance on an assigned station. This allows them to provide real-time feedback to SPs during the debriefing session for both patient portrayal and student grading, and to provide the OSCE team with potential issues or concerns they identified. The debriefing session will be discussed in further detail later in the case.

Identifying testing space is a key aspect to consider as PBAs are designed and implemented. Within AU HSOP, space was allocated on both campuses for lab activities to include the implementation of performance-based assessments. These spaces are divided into two areas that include a large teaching space with moveable tables that allow for multiple classroom configurations and an area with multiple patient exam rooms (10 in Auburn, 3 in Mobile). The large teaching space and each individual patient room is wired for audio-visual needs and various connections for power and data. However, with the transition to the PRC, the space needed has increased as a result of the variability of PBA approaches utilized to assess student learning, the overlapping assessment weeks across cohort years, and the complex class schedule which requires specified quiet time when no PBA testing can occur. To overcome these challenges, the OSCE team identified alternative space in Auburn and Mobile that was not initially designed for assessments and worked with AU HSOP IT to prepare the space for PBA utilization.

Design

As a component of the backward course design process, faculty developing a new curriculum should begin with the end in mind, which essentially demands that educators consider how they will assess student learning, and how these assessments will correlate to their teaching approach (Wiggins & McTighe, 2005). To identify focus areas for PBA cases, LC teams would consider the disease states, course-related learning objectives, and competencies to identify potential clinical scenarios that would assess related clinical skills and abilities. As the assessment plan was finalized, the LC team would evaluate the overall percentage PBAs would comprise of the student's overall course grade.

To support faculty as they developed these cases, the OSCE team provided case authors with standardized case templates for each type of PBA approach. These templates include all components necessary for case administration such as case synopsis, SP prompts and responses, case rationale, patient profiles, props, technology needs, administration logistics, learning objectives, analytical checklist (including grading criteria) tagged to competencies, and the communication rubric. These templates serve as guides for essential information needed for training the standardized persons to be able to effectively complete the student interactions. To ensure that each interactive PBA is applicable to practice, the analytical checklist template is organized using the Pharmacists' Patient Care Process (Joint Commission of Pharmacy Practitioners, 2014) steps to prompt case authors to consider the entire process as they develop their assessments, and to allow students to reflect in a more meaningful manner as they review their performance report. However, it is important to note that these templates serve only as guides and faculty can include, exclude, or add items to the document as appropriate for the assessment. Prior to initial development, case authors are also provided with a timeline, outlining deadlines for each aspect of case development (i.e. first draft, final draft, etc.).

Once the design process begins, case authors have access to select members of the OSCE team including the Skills Lab Coordinator for the academic year and the Director of Assessment to brainstorm and discuss potential scenarios, review resources, and to provide feedback as cases are developed and refined. Feedback is provided throughout the development process and focuses on the authenticity, feasibility, and overall content developed. A key component of the review process is assessing developed scenarios and whether the time allotted within the case is appropriate for assessment completion. For example, scenarios that are data collection heavy, such as noninteractive webEHR cases, may require longer than the traditional 10 minutes as seen in many OSCEs; as a result, the team will discuss how much time is needed for a student to adequately complete the outlined task. While case authors are key resources during this process, they are not responsible for assessment implementation. It is the role of the entire OSCE team to identify the resources needed for implementation such as potential pharmaceutical products, devices (simulation arms, inhalers, etc.), technology needs, faculty and non-faculty graders, standardized persons needed for role portrayal, and space. As case development progresses, the team must also take into consideration the Mobile campus and the resources available for implementation at that site.

To encourage authentic assessment, the case authors are encouraged to explore different PBA approaches. To date, AU HSOP has offered traditional patient, caregiver, or healthcare provider interactions, data collection from electronic health records, pharmaceutical product preparation, product labeling and dispensing, product checking, clinical documentation, and progressive scenarios that require multiple steps to complete. These PBAs are designed to introduce new clinical skills or build upon previously demonstrated skills to assess continued professional development prior to clinical rotations.

Noninteractive stations, to include those assessing data collection, product checking, and clinical documentation, require students to provide written documentation addressing specific questions or tasks. These stations are graded using rubrics specifically designed for the PBA and include clear cut-points within the criteria description for grading consistency. As students are not interacting with a SP during these encounters, 100% of the station grade is allocated to the pre-determined rubric. Traditionally, AU HSOP utilizes faculty or graduate teaching assistants with a pharmacy background to grade these assessments instead of standardized persons.

Interactive stations typically include two grading components, an analytical checklist designed specifically for the station and a standardized communication rubric that is used across the curriculum (Ford, Garza, Kavookjian, & Kleppinger, 2019). Eighty percent of the overall station grade is allocated to the analytical checklist with 20% to the communication rubric. Case authors are asked to provide clearly defined expectations within the analytical checklist to foster consistency when grading. Within the school, SPs serve as PBA graders for both the analytical checklist and the communication rubric. The inclusion of clearly defined criteria is essential to ensure that the SP graders are able to evaluate if a student is meeting the expectation of the designed interaction.

Each interactive station is developed with the intention of authentically assessing students in situations that would occur in real practice; however, academicians often highlight ideal practice situations instead of those more commonly seen outside academic environments. In order to promote pharmacist best practices among students, case authors are encouraged to incorporate a patient-centered approach with interviewing, counseling, and educating patients regarding their healthcare needs into learning and assessment activities. Incorporation of these best practices in both the learning and assessment activities will foster practice change within AU

HSOP graduates, resulting in positive patient outcomes and improved best practices in the community.

PBAs may include anywhere between 2 and 8 cases, depending on the academic course. The number of cases and the allotted number of days for testing will determine how the PBA is administered and how students will complete the assessment. For example, in the spring semester of student pharmacists' first year, the LC team developed non-interactive, interactive, and team-based PBA cases that had to be completed over the course of three days. To accomplish this goal, the OSCE team recognized that at least a day and a half was needed to administer the team PBA; this meant that the interactive and non-interactive cases had to be administered at the same time within the remaining day and a half. To accomplish this goal, the team had to identify additional space and resources that had not been included in the preliminary planning stage. However, due to some out of the box thinking and the willingness of the OSCE team and staff to try new things, the assessment was a success and met the goals of the learning community.

To prepare students for these assessments, case authors are encouraged to integrate similar preparatory learning activities into their classroom or lab experiences. These activities can include having students learn the appropriate way to use a device (i.e. glucometer, blood pressure cuff, etc.), counsel on a new product, or complete an exercise using the dispensing or webEHR software; these experiences are intended to provide the foundational principles needed to interact with patients in future scenarios. Case authors have the opportunity to utilize SPs in their classroom activities to simulate counseling experiences that students could encounter within these high-stakes assessments. These activities should include a mechanism for students to receive feedback regarding their performance within the activity, either from an instructor, facilitator, peer, or SP. Case authors are also encouraged to provide specific learning objectives and a skill guide when appropriate to offer guidance regarding how students will be assessed. An example of a product selection and counseling skill guide provided to student pharmacists is included in the Appendix.

Once the LC team have determined the number and type of PBAs being offered, a student schedule is developed. Depending on the types of PBAs used to evaluate student learning, students may receive multiple testing times; it is not unusual for students to complete a non-interactive station at a different time than an interactive station in order to maximize the available resources for the testing event. Using a random number generator, students are assigned a specific date and time to complete their assessments. Due to the complexity of scheduling, the team decided early on that students would be required to complete their assessment during their assigned time and that no student would be allowed to request a time switch with another student. While initially frustrating for students, they have come to appreciate the consistency and fairness this approach has provided. Once finalized, these student schedules are distributed using the school's learning management system. Students utilizing testing accommodations complete their PBAs separately to allow the OSCE team to meet students' testing needs and are contacted via email with their assigned dates and times.

While OSCEs and performance-based assessments have long been a part of health professions education (Harden 1988; Harden 2015; Shirwaiker 2015), students entering into the pharmacy curriculum are often unsure what to expect. To prepare first-year student pharmacists for their initial PBA, members of the OSCE team host an orientation session to educate students about the role of OSCEs/PBAs within the curriculum, how students will be evaluated, and what those experiences can look like. Offered as a required two-hour small group lab activity, students are introduced to the communication rubric and have the opportunity to watch recordings of a positive patient interaction and a negative patient interaction. Following the videos, students are asked to evaluate the simulated student's communications skills and to provide feedback on steps that the student could take to improve. These exercises are intended to prepare students for the types of feedback they will receive following their own PBA experiences. Table 1 is a sample schedule for the student OSCE/PBA orientation.

Implementation

SP Training

Prior to the implementation of any PBA, considerations must be taken into account for preparing SPs to serve in their roles within the assessment. As part of the onboarding process, standardized persons must complete a half-day workshop dedicated to introducing them to the OSCE process, their roles/responsibilities as a SP (to include yearly FERPA training), and participation in structured grading activities. Table 2 is an example of the SP Workshop agenda. These grading activities introduce the SPs to both the standardized communication rubric, the format of the analytical checklist used for traditional interactions, and approaches for giving written feedback. These mini-sessions are completed in small groups and led by members of the OSCE team. These workshops are held at the start of each academic semester, and all new and returning SPs are required to attend one session in order to work that academic year. These workshops provide the team with the opportunity to share curricular changes, new assessment approaches, and technology updates. These workshops also allow SPs to meet in a non-testing environment which fosters comradery and team building, and provides the OSCE team with the opportunity to recognize SPs for their years of service.

Table 1. Example student OSCE/PBA orientation schedule

Time Allocated	Discussion Topic
20 minutes	Introductory information • Define performance-based assessments & OSCEs • Describe PBA/OSCE station procedure and flow
10 minutes	Confidentiality & grading overview • Review confidentiality agreement • Describe grade breakdown
15 minutes	Analytical checklist • Review steps in Pharmacists' Patient Care Process (collect, assess, plan, implement, follow-up) • Introduce "CAMO" questions ∘ Ask about medical problems/conditions (C) ∘ Ask about drug allergies (A) ∘ Ask about prescription medications (M) ∘ Ask about OTC medications (O) • Review Product Selection & Counseling Skill Guide (see Appendix)
20 minutes	Communication rubric • Review all communication rubric domains (introduction, appropriate terminology, confidence, patient-centered approach, information delivery, conclusion, professional demeanor) • Describe global assessment
30 minutes	Communication rubric grading practice • Watch 2 different simulated SP encounter videos (1 poor performance, 1 good performance) • Students independently score encounter using communication rubric • Students share answers & discuss as a group
10 minutes	PBA review & challenge information • Describe ExamSoft reports • Required & open review policies • Grade challenge procedures

Table 2. Example of SP workshop agenda

Time Allocated	Discussion Topic
60 minutes	Introductory session for New SPs only • Overview of policies • Logistics of OSCE operations • Overview of grading procedures (analytical checklist and communication rubric)
10 minutes	Welcome of all SPs
10 minutes	Review of new checklist formats
120 minutes	Standardization Exercises • 3 stations (breakouts – 40 minute rotations) 1. Analytical exercise 2. Communication exercise 3. Feedback exercise
40 minutes	Overview of software programs
10 minutes	Announcements

To prepare for each PBA, SPs are assigned to a specific scenario, receiving their case information for review prior to attendance at a required one-hour training event. These training events occur up to a week before the assessment and focus on introducing SPs to the case scenario, familiarizing them with potential products and props, and addressing any questions they may have. Due to the dual campuses, synchronous training occurs using the school's video-conferencing system. The simultaneous training is essential as it allows for uniformity across campuses and ensures that SPs at both locations understand the intent of the scenario and best practices for navigating their roles. Scenario authors or a member of the OSCE team serve as trainers for these training events. If scenario authors are unable to attend the required training, they have the option to complete a pre-recording that is used within the in-person sessions. These recordings are then supplemented by a member of the OSCE team so questions can be addressed in real-time. Training time is also dedicated to reviewing the grading criteria to include the case-specific analytical checklists, communication rubric, or any other graded materials. SPs are also provided with opportunities to ask questions prior to the start of the assessment day and throughout testing periods should additional questions arise following training.

A benefit of the one-hour training events is the feedback provided by the SPs prior to assessment implementation. As a result, the OSCE team has been alerted to potential inconsistencies with case information and props, additional prompts and responses needed, and clarifications and adjustments required within the grading criteria. SP feedback has also allowed for the enhancement of the scenario template as the OSCE team recognized that the inclusion of pronunciation guides for drug names would allow SPs to feel more at ease when entering into the scenario with students.

Performance-Based Assessment Events: Interactive Stations

Prior to the start of an assessment day, the testing environment must be staged for the intended interaction (standing or sitting stations) with all necessary products, props, and technology (webEHR, online resources, etc.). The staging of the testing environment is dependent on the assessment needs and may include small patient rooms or a larger skills lab. For grading purposes, the SPs who are watching the encounters via live video feed are located in an isolated grading area with reduced noise and traffic, while SPs serving in the actor capacity are located in a holding area close to student testing. The OSCE team are located in the student testing area, easily accessible by both students and SPs.

Due to the complexity of implementing and managing the assessment, the OSCE team identified a SP to serve as Lead to manage the flow of the assessment day. The Lead SP is responsible for overseeing SPs, keeping time for stations and breaks, and assisting the team with overall assessment implementation. SPs report to the testing location 30 minutes prior to the start of the assessment to receive final information and to prepare for the day. SPs are then paired in teams of two and switch throughout the day between the patient and grader roles. When serving as the patient, SPs are responsible for evaluating students using the paper communication rubric; whereas, those serving in the grader role are responsible for assessing students with the scenario-specific analytical checklist directly on ExamSoft. These pairs are tasked with portraying the patient role consistently throughout the assessment by providing real-time feedback to each other.

Students are instructed to arrive 15 minutes prior to their scheduled assessment time. Prior to the PBA, students receive a written instruction sheet and confidentiality agreement for their review and signature. The instruction sheet includes logistics such as station time frames (i.e. number of minutes for prep and number of minutes for SP interaction) and final reminders relevant to the testing environment. At the initiation of the assessment, students enter the testing environment and find their assigned starting station. Once all students have found their station, a whistle is blown by the Lead SP to indicate the start of the PBA. The whistle also serves as the indicator to transition to the next station and to conclude the testing event.

For each station, students are allotted specific time frames for each component of the assessment. Traditionally, most interactive PBA stations are designed for a total of 10 minutes with students receiving two minutes to prepare and eight minutes for the encounter. The preparation time may be used to familiarize themselves with the products available in the room, to review information available in the online drug information resource, or to review the patient profile. The encounter is led by the student with SPs providing responses or engaging the students with pre-determined questions as specified by the case authors. Once the student concludes the encounter, the SP leaves the room but remains directly outside the door until just before the conclusion of the station time. Students who complete the interaction prior to the whistle are allowed to call the SP back into the exam room should any additional questions/counseling points need to be addressed.

During the initial rounds of student testing, members of the OSCE team review in real-time the PBA scenarios. Throughout these reviews, members of the OSCE team are assessing SPs for continuity, delivery of required prompts, and overall performance. They are also using this time to assess students for overall performance and to identify potential challenges in SP grading (i.e. unexpected student questions and counseling points). Following these rounds, the OSCE team meet with the SPs to debrief and discuss their findings. Time allotted for debriefing sessions varies and is dependent on the number of scenarios; however, a typical debrief session is 30-45 minutes. Following debrief, the OSCE team relies on SP pairs to identify inconsistencies, provide peer feedback, and to notify the team of any issues that arise.

As SPs serve in both the patient and grader roles, they serve as an essential member of the evaluation team. Both the patient and the grader are encouraged to provide focused written feedback in addition to evaluating student performance within the specified checklist/rubric criteria. All SP feedback is reviewed by the OSCE team prior to student review.

Performance-Based Assessment Events: Non-interactive Stations

The variability of the types of non-interactive stations offered makes it difficult to describe every potential implementation strategy. However, one of the first steps of implementing these assessment approaches is to determine whether the non-interactive stations will be embedded within the interactive stations or if they need to be assessed independently. If assessed independently, the OSCE team must then identify space, resources, and technology needs for implementation. For these stations, the OSCE team utilizes SPs as room monitors to allow the OSCE team to transition between the multiple assessments. Due to the technical requirements of many of these types of assessments, the OSCE team also found that students often requested assistance that was not permissible; utilizing SPs as monitors reduced the likelihood of students requesting help that could not be given.

As with the interactive stations, the testing environment must be staged to provide students with the resources needed to complete the task. For documentation or dispensing stations, often this requires either lab or classroom space, laptop devices, label printers, and documentation materials. For the purposes of testing, laptops must include access to needed software and cameras for recording assessment activity. For pharmaceutical compounding, lab space is required in addition to the necessary supplies needed for the preparation. Typically, these stations are not graded in real time and require faculty to evaluate student documentation following the testing event.

Students with Testing Accommodations

Over the last 10 years, the number of students utilizing testing accommodations within HSOP for performance-based assessments has increased. These accommodations can include extra testing time, the need for a separate, quiet environment, or other specific individualized needs as directed by the Office of Accessibility. Testing accommodations may be utilized for all performance-based assessments except for those that deal with life or death scenarios that require completion within an allotted timeframe (i.e. simulated codes, CPR, etc.). It is important to note that when implementing these accommodations, students must be held to the same testing practices as students without testing accommodations. Therefore, testing time for each component of the station (i.e. prep, SP interaction) will be expanded to the allotted timeframe and students will not be able to rotate to the next station until the entire station time has elapsed. For example, if a student has an accommodation for double time (i.e. 20 minutes per station), they will have four minutes of preparation time and 16 minutes with the SP. Should that student complete the interaction with several minutes to spare, the student must wait for the entire 20 minutes to pass before rotating to the next station. To reduce administrator burden, overall implementation costs, and when feasible, students with the same accommodation needs may be tested together.

Sequestering

Traditionally, faculty have not chosen to sequester students during their performance-based assessments due to the number of days required for testing. However, with the implementation of progressive PBAs, second-year student pharmacists were sequestered for their assessments at the conclusion of their spring semester. This decision was made due to the complexity of the assessment and the instructors concerns regarding confidentiality compliance. As the PBAs occurred during an assessment heavy period, case authors developed four unique scenarios that would be offered over the course of two days. Students were then randomly assigned to a specific group and completed their assessment within the four-hour window assigned to each scenario. This reduced student sequestering from a full day to a half-day. With the growing number of progressive PBAs being designed and implemented in the PRC, the likelihood of increased sequestering is high.

Performance Feedback and PBA Reviews

After the OSCE team has reviewed all station grading for a given PBA, limited results are released for student review in addition to the overall station grade. While full details of the graded communication rubric are released for each station, only limited information is released from the analytical checklist. The report indicates each item on the checklist as "completed" or "not completed" and an indication to the step of the Pharmacists' Patient Care Process (PPCP) to which it relates (Joint Commission of Pharmacy Practitioners, 2014). Students must attend a review session if they would like to review the details of the analytical checklist. All narrative comments included on both the analytical checklist and communication rubric are released for student review.

Approximately 1-2 weeks after completion of the PBA, a review session is held over a four-hour period. Students who score <70% or miss a critical skill on any station are required to attend the review session. During the required review, the case scenario and checklist is reviewed with a small group of students. A member of the OSCE team leads a discussion which engages the students and assists them in identifying the errors made during the station in hopes of preventing similar errors on future PBAs. Students who fail to meet the minimum threshold for multiple stations may participate in a more directed mentoring session with one or more members of the OSCE team. These sessions allow for an individualized discussion on areas where development is needed. All other students may attend during an open review time if desired. Throughout the review, a member of the OSCE team is present to answer any questions that arise regarding the case scenarios. At this time, students are unable to personally view their station recordings due to limitations with the recording technology.

After reviewing the detailed station evaluation criteria, all students have the option to challenge their station grade if they feel they were unfairly scored. Challenges are allowed for PBAs since SPs are completing a majority of the grading and may not be able to distinguish certain subtleties in the student's questioning and counseling points. When students challenge a station, a member of the OSCE team views the recording and re-grades the student using both the analytical checklist and the communication rubric. As a result, the student's station grade can go up, go down, or remain the same. For many scenarios, the encounter is watched several times to ensure accurate grading.

Evaluation

Assessment design is an iterative process requiring constant monitoring regarding the effectiveness of designed assessments to evaluate students on intended learning outcomes. Following each testing period, the Skills Lab Coordinator for that academic year and Director of Assessment evaluate each PBA regarding students' overall performance, individual station item analysis, and when applicable, performance history across program years prior to grades being released. During the item analysis, team members also consider feasibility and consistency issues within each station such as a significant number of students running out of time, SPs failure to deliver required prompts, and so forth. Further analyses include an evaluation of the alignment between classroom or lab activities and the corresponding assessment to determine if poor performance was due to a lack of student preparation or misalignment. At the conclusion of this review, the instructor of record is contacted regarding potential station adjustments, and is provided with station averages and rubric analyses for their individual review.

At the conclusion of the testing period, the Skills Lab Coordinator and Director of Assessment communicate with case authors regarding overall station performance, issues or concerns that arose during the implementation process, and any relevant notes provided by the SPs as they navigated the assessment process. This feedback is communicated via email, as a component of the course review process, or prior to the next PBA development period. The supplied data drives assessment change and can result in revisions to the curriculum when appropriate. Feedback is also used to evaluate the effectiveness of the teaching strategies used within the classroom to prepare students for future assessments.

As PBAs occur throughout the year, the OSCE team identifies and tracks inconsistent SP performance issues as well as areas in which confusion is present. The collected data informs the next year's workshop and influences PBA specific training throughout the year. The team also seeks out SP formal and informal feedback as assessment instruments are designed, new PBA approaches are implemented, and training formats are updated. Furthermore, SPs are periodically surveyed for information regarding how they evaluate students for global feedback, so faculty and students can gain a better understanding of what expectations they have for future practicing pharmacists.

Technology Components and Concerns

As the OSCE team navigated the first implementation year of the PRC, additional technology resources were identified as a result of changes to the curriculum, the practice-based technology utilized in classroom/lab activities, and online resources available for all student pharmacists. With this integration, the OSCE team determined that a technology upgrade was essential to allow for authentic PBAs to occur. To meet these assessment demands, the patient exam rooms were equipped with a 40-inch television, mounted laptop computer (to include an external wireless keyboard and mouse), and panoramic high-def camera. Each laptop was loaded with the relevant practice-based software and also serves as the device for video conference recordings during the assessment. For monitoring purposes, this upgrade also permits screen capturing to occur which allows the OSCE team to review student performance in navigating these programs. As a result, the technology upgrade has provided faculty with the data needed to assess students on their understanding of practice-based technology, specifically their ability to navigate the electronic health record, dispensing software, and online drug information website. Specific descriptions of the implemented software programs are provided.

Panopto™ and Zoom

All OSCEs and PBAs are recorded using Zoom (Zoom Video Connections, Inc., 2019), an AU provided web-based video and audio conference recording system. To accommodate the testing format within AU HSOP, members of the OSCE team worked with the IT Specialists to acquire additional Zoom numbers for each patient exam room on the Auburn and Mobile campus. This collaboration was vital as the IT Specialists were best prepared to navigate the usage requirements outlined by the university regarding Zoom number allocation.

The Zoom integration has allowed the OSCE team to record not only SP interactions but to also monitor student performance on non-interactive stations through its screen capture feature. These recordings capture the student's computer navigation and allow graders to assess if they utilized programs or online features that were prohibited during the assessment. This feature also allows graders to identify where students may have encountered difficulties when completing the assigned task.

However, while Zoom serves as an excellent audio and video conferencing system, it is not ideal for watching student performance after the event. Once Zoom recordings are processed, the IT specialists transition the files to Panopto™ (Panopto, 2019), an online video platform supported by the university. The usability of Panopto™ allows for easy video review, providing a single place for Zoom recordings from multiple accounts to be housed. The system also allows users to be added or removed when necessary to ensure FERPA compliance, and offers video viewing features not available in Zoom such as rewind and fast forward.

While these programs allow for faculty to review student performance, further enhancements could be made to the recording process that would allow students to holistically evaluate their overall performance. At this time, the AU HSOP PBA recording system does not provide a video processing system that lends itself to cutting or editing student videos in a timely manner. Therefore, student pharmacists are unable to review their own PBA performances for peer or self-assessment. While recording systems do exist that would allow students to review their performance, the overall costs for these types of programs are cost prohibitive at this time.

ExamSoft

Prior to the implementation of the PRC, AU HSOP adopted ExamSoft (ExamSoft Worldwide, Inc., 2019) as the school's assessment software for the PharmD curriculum. With this implementation, the Director of Assessment worked with faculty to transition from the university's learning management system to ExamSoft for course assessments, which included multiple faculty development sessions and support as the transition occurred. At that time, OSCEs and PBAs had been graded on paper requiring manual grade entry and limited usable student data outside of the formalized review process. With the integration of ExamSoft and its reporting features, the Director of Assessment worked with course instructors offering OSCEs as an assessment strategy to integrate this software into OSCE implementation. These faculty were early adopters of the rubrics feature within ExamSoft, and helped foster faculty acceptance of the feasibility of rubric utilization in other areas of the curriculum due to the robust data available. Integration occurred over a 12-month period and required extensive and ongoing training with the SPs to ensure that they were prepared to transition from grading on paper to a computer. This transition reduced faculty grading time by eliminating data entry and made tracking student outcomes and analyses for performance trends easier.

With the transition to the PRC, the preexisting use of ExamSoft for PBA assessment helped minimize potential challenges affiliated with student progression tracking. Each PBA's line item of the analytical checklist and communication rubric is tagged to corresponding disease states, curriculum competencies, and foundational knowledge when applicable. Therefore, at the conclusion of the assessment period, students receive not only their overall performance scores but a detailed report outlining their overall performance, how they scored within each individual focus area, and where their performance stands among their peers. Lastly, these reports allow students to assess how they perform within these focus areas over time.

Lexicomp®

It is essential for pharmacists to be able to navigate various drug information resources in order to make appropriate and accurate recommendations. Historically, a drug information book was provided for PBAs due to concerns with academic integrity; however, with the upgraded hardware installed in the past year, AU HSOP has replaced text-based drug information resources with Lexicomp® (Wolters Kluwer Clinical Drug Information, Inc., 2019), an online, electronic drug information resource. While multiple electronic drug information resources are available for students to utilize, Lexicomp® is the one most often used by both students and faculty for classroom activities. One advantage to transitioning to an electronic resource for PBAs is the availability of additional features, notably drug interaction checks, IV compatibility, drug identification, patient education resources, and various calculators in addition to standard drug information such as dosing, adverse drug reactions, product availability, and precautions. In addition to simulating a more authentic environment, utilization of an electronic drug information resource allows case writers to incorporate a wide variety and increased complexity of tasks into PBA activities.

WebEHR

In order to simulate an electronic health record for ambulatory care or clinic-based services, AU HSOP adopted CGMwebEHR™ (CompuGroup Medical, Inc., 2019) for student use throughout the curriculum. This software is fully web-based with separate systems created for educational purposes (with mock patient information) and real clinic patients (followed by students during experiential activities). At this time, most student interaction with the webEHR is through data collection and assessment. For PBAs, faculty can input all relevant patient information for students as they would see in a medical chart, including medication lists, patient history information, labs, vital signs, and SOAP notes. Students access this information to complete questions on a worksheet for non-interactive stations or to look up information prior to interacting with an SP. While students are capable of entering data into the webEHR, this is not used for PBAs since each student would need to enter information under a unique patient name with all patients visible to all students. Also, there are some challenges from a faculty perspective with preparing patient information for student review. First, data must be entered close to the student activity since information cannot be inputted with future dates. If patients are utilized for multiple years, some information can be hidden and updated, however medication information is perpetual and cannot be deleted.

PioneerRx

Since many pharmacists work in community pharmacy settings, introducing students to electronic dispensing software was essential. As a result, AU HSOP adopted PioneerRx (PioneerRx Pharmacy Software, 2019), a community pharmacy dispensing software system marketed for independent pharmacies. Since this software is not web-based, students can only access the program when they are on computers dedicated for lab activities and PBAs. As a result, students are given several opportunities to practice with the software prior to testing. Students learn how to create a new patient in the system, input insurance information, verify patient profile information, enter a new prescription, and print a prescription label. Currently, PioneerRx is used solely for non-interactive PBA activities, however consideration is being made to replace paper patient profile scenarios for interactive cases with patient profiles in either the webEHR or PioneerRx, depending upon the setting of the scenario.

CURRENT CHALLENGES FACING THE ORGANIZATION

Design

Overall, AU HSOP has a well-established approach for integrating PBAs into the existing PharmD curriculum. The identification of specific faculty and staff to support the PBA infrastructure greatly benefits this assessment approach. However, more integration is needed across the academic years to ensure that critical clinical skills are reassessed regularly as well as prior to the start of fourth-year clinical rotations.

Implementation

As faculty and the OSCE team continue to implement PBAs, ongoing technology upgrades will need to occur to remain up to date with practice expectations and to reduce grading burden. The integration of ExamSoft has reduced the grading burden associated with the analytical checklist; however, members of the OSCE team still manually enter data from the communication rubric. Also, ongoing communication with the Dean and other key stakeholders remains essential as the costs for integrating a PBA recording and management system would need to be budgeted multiple years in advance.

Ongoing efforts are also needed to ensure that assessment practices remain consistent across the two campuses. While all SPs complete training as a team, due to the significantly smaller class size on the Mobile campus, identifying and resolving potential case discrepancies is limited as there are fewer rounds after debriefing.

The continued growth and complexity of PBAs has allowed AU HSOP to assess students for their preparedness for future practice. Yet, continued work is needed to evolve and enhance the PBAs already in place. But to do so, additional assessment space is needed for a variety of reasons. This would allow students from multiple academic years to be assessed simultaneously, for richer and more authentic assessments to occur, for larger more robust assessments to be designed, and to provide enough assessment space that multiple types of PBAs could be implemented at the same time. Finally, the ability to include additional stations would enhance the reliability and validity of the assessments (Munoz, O'Byrne, Pugsley, & Austin, 2005).

Evaluation

With the transition to the new practice-ready curriculum, student pharmacists' progression is no longer limited to course performance but is also tied to their ability to successfully benchmark the 270+ competencies that inform the HSOP curriculum. As a result, the LC must consider how each assessment impacts a student's progression within the competencies. As these competencies primarily focus on clinical skills and abilities, utilization of PBAs to monitor student progression has allowed faculty to create assessments closely tied to one or more competencies, often building on previous assessment tasks to promote critical thinking and refinement of clinical skills. This approach has also allowed for perpetual analyses of student performance to identify students in need of remediation prior to progression throughout the curriculum.

Yet, faculty are often unsure how to develop these high-stakes assessments and when created, are hesitant to establish specific thresholds for student success or failure. To successfully meet the goals of the curriculum, faculty should consider the final assessment approach needed to benchmark each competency and how previous assessments have prepared learners for this high-stakes assessment. For example, each PBA assesses students' clinical skills and abilities, yet may focus on only one component of an overall competency. However, when developing the benchmark, faculty should develop assessments that evaluate the entire clinical process. But to do so, they must first evaluate if students have been adequately prepared and assessed to meet the outlined performance level expected within the benchmark which may include multiple competencies that were not previously assessed together. This is a critical area where faculty development is needed prior to developing and implementing high-stakes benchmarking.

While several benchmark assessments have been created and implemented, specific progression thresholds have not been finalized. These benchmarks are often incorporated into an existing testing period and may or may not be tied to a course grade. Students who fail to meet the threshold may be required to complete a formal remediation plan or may not be allowed to progress to the next stage of the curriculum. However, the nature of the remediation strategies for these benchmarks are still in development.

To evaluate the effectiveness of SP grading, the OSCE team also struggles with having time to assess grading consistency throughout the PBA testing period due to competing demands, limited staffing, and troubleshooting needs. Limited monitoring of grading consistency does occur as a result of the student challenge process as members of the OSCE team track, share, and discuss grade changes after watching and regarding the encounter. While a positive first step, this evaluation occurs after the fact and would best serve the students and SPs if implemented in real-time during the PBA.

SOLUTIONS AND RECOMMENDATIONS

Design

Further collaboration among the Skills Lab Coordinators and Director of Assessment across the academic years should result in improved incorporation of clinical skills and abilities throughout the curriculum. As AU HSOP moves towards the complete integration of its new PRC, improved collaboration between all Skills Lab Coordinators and the Director of Assessment across academic years will ensure that clinical skills are repeated and retained, while increasing the overall rigor of these assessments as more attention is given to the spiraling nature of the curricular content.

Implementation

Significant strides have been made to the overall PBA implementation process over the last couple of years to create uniformity across the campuses, to integrate technology to simulate real-world practice, and to reduce faculty grading burdens. However, the OSCE team recognizes that more work is needed and that ongoing technology integration will occur. A next step that the team hopes to achieve is the integration of iPads into the testing environment to eliminate paper grading for the communication rubric portion of the interactive stations. Due to the increased number of smart phone users across the generations (Zickuhr & Madden, 2012), preparing SPs, who are typically considered older adults, to use these devices should be less challenging as they already use similar devices in their daily lives. To assess SP readiness for this integration, some SPs have piloted iPad use during testing events. Overall, the feedback has been positive with multiple SPs asking to utilize the devices at future PBA events.

The improved collaboration between Skills Lab Coordinators and Director of Assessment could also allow for improved consistency throughout the assessment periods as this could enhance cross-coverage during testing events. While there are additional personnel present prior to the debrief period, these individuals are not available for the duration of the testing event. Increased collaboration could provide the resources needed to allow for periodic check-ins for SP grading accuracy throughout all PBAs. Consistency across campuses continues to be a challenge and further brainstorming is needed to determine realistic strategies for overcoming these complexities.

Evaluation

Preparing faculty to develop and implement high-stakes assessments will require multiple faculty development sessions to effectively establish best practices. These sessions should focus on rubric development, strategies for setting grading thresholds, and assessment results interpretation. To allow for faculty reflection and acceptance, the sessions will need to occur over a period of time and should be supported by the OSCE team.

The collaboration among Skills Lab Coordinators and the Director of Assessment will allow for improved student progression tracking to occur as increased communication between the teams will allow for closer monitoring of students in potential jeopardy. These collaborations will also support the LC Chairs as they assess student learning outcomes to determine if changes are needed within the curriculum.

Creating and refining remediation plans for individual students will continue to prove challenging as AU HSOP completes the implementation of the new PRC, especially as these plans should consider not only the competencies and content deficits requiring remediation but also the individualized nature of the plans needed to ensure student success. More formalized processes for student remediation are currently in development for high-stakes benchmarking assessments.

Final Thoughts

Structured performance-based assessments are still a relatively new assessment strategy within the health professions overall. While this case study comes from a school of pharmacy, the authors feel the lessons learned from their experience are valuable to all health professions programs undergoing a curriculum shift. Unfortunately, no two programs will experience identical successes and challenges; yet, reviewing the AU HSOP case could provide insights on potential resources and strategies for overcoming barriers unique to one's own institution.

REFERENCES

Accreditation Council for Pharmacy Education. (2015). *Accreditation Standards and Key Elements for the Professional Program in Pharmacy Leading to the Doctor of Pharmacy Degree ("Standards 2016")*. Retrieved from https://www.acpe-accredit.org/pdf/Standards2016FINAL.pdf

CompuGroup Medical, Inc. (2019). *CGM webEHR*. CompuGroup Medical.

Daugherty, K. K. (2006). Backward course design: Making the end the beginning. *American Journal of Pharmaceutical Education*, *70*(6), 135. doi:10.5688/aj7006135 PMID:17332861

Emory, J. (2014). Understanding backward design to strengthen curricular models. *Nurse Educator*, *39*(3), 122–125. doi:10.1097/NNE.0000000000000034 PMID:24743175

ExamSoft Worldwide, Inc. (2019). *ExamSoft* [assessment software]. Available from https://www.examsoft.com

Ford, C. R., Garza, K., Kavookjian, J., & Kleppinger, E. L. (2019). Assessing student pharmacist communication skills: Development and implementation of a communication rubric. *Currents in Pharmacy Teaching & Learning*, *11*(11), 1123–1131. doi:10.1016/j.cptl.2019.07.018 PMID:31783958

Harden, R. M. (1988). What is an OSCE? *Medical Teacher*, *10*(1), 19–22. doi:10.3109/01421598809019321 PMID:3221760

Harden, R. M. (2015). Misconceptions and the OSCE. *Medical Teacher, 37*(7), 608–610. doi:10.3109/0142159X.2015.1042443 PMID:26075956

Joint Commission of Pharmacy Practitioners. (2014). *Pharmacists' Patient Care Process*. Retrieved from: https://jcpp.net/wp-content/uploads/2016/03/PatientCareProcess-with-supporting-organizations.pdf

McDonough, S. L. K., Kleppinger, E. L., Donaldson, A. R., & Helms, K. L. (2015). Going "high stakes" with a pharmacy OSCE: Lessons learned. *Currents in Pharmacy Teaching & Learning, 7*(1), 4–11. doi:10.1016/j.cptl.2014.09.017

Munoz, L. Q., O'Vyrne, C., Pugsley, J., & Austin, Z. (2005). Reliability, validity, and generalizability of an objective structured clinical examination (OSCE) for assessment of entry-to-practice in pharmacy. *Pharmacy Education, 5*(1), 1–12. doi:10.1080/15602210400025347

Panopto. (2019). *Panopto™* [web-based video platform]. Available from https://www.panopto.com/

PioneerRx Pharmacy Software. (2019). *PioneerRx* [pharmacy dispensing software]. PioneerRx Pharmacy Software.

Shirwaikar, A. (2015). Objective structured clinical examination (OSCE) in pharmacy education – a trend. *Pharmacy Practice, 13*(4), 627. doi:10.18549/PharmPract.2015.04.627 PMID:26759616

Wiggins, G., & McTighe, J. (2005). *Understanding by design*. Association for Supervision and Curriculum Development.

Wolters Kluwer Clinical Drug Information, Inc. (2019). *Lexicomp®* [web-based drug information resource]. Available from https://online.lexi.com/lco/action/home

Wright, B. M., Hornsby, L., Marlowe, K. F., Fowlin, J., & Surry, D. W. (2018). Innovating pharmacy curriculum through backward design. *TechTrends, 62*(3), 224–229. doi:10.100711528-018-0283-8

Zickuhr, K., & Madden, M. (2012). Older adults and internet use. *Pew Internet & American Life Project*. Retrieved from https://pewinternet.org/Reports/2012/Older-adults-and-internet-use.aspx

Zoom Video Connections, Inc. (2019). *Zoom* [web-based video conferencing system]. Available from https://zoom.us/signin

KEY TERMS AND DEFINITIONS

Analytical Checklist: A comprehensive list of items specific to a performance-based assessment scenario that students must complete to successfully achieve the outlined clinical skill or task. This is graded as achieved or not achieved for each item.

Interactive Scenario: A performance-based assessment station that requires the student to engage with a standardized person to complete the task.

Learning Community: A team of faculty tasked with developing, implementing, and evaluating content and assessments within an academic semester.

Non-Interactive Scenario: A performance-based assessment station that does not require the student to engage with a standardized person to complete the task.

Objective Structured Clinical Examination (OSCE): A form of performance-based assessment used to measure clinical competence. Introduced initially as an assessment method in medical education, an OSCE is a series of stations designed to evaluate clinical skills correlated to various disease states, often interacting with standardized persons in a variety of healthcare settings.

Performance-Based Assessment (PBA): An assessment that evaluates learners on their ability to complete a clinical skill or series of skills, interact with a simulated patient/caregiver/healthcare provider, or demonstrate technical skills (i.e. sterile and non-sterile compounding).

Rubric: An assessment tool for grading performance-based activities that includes performance levels, specific criteria, and criteria descriptions. Written feedback can also be included to support the overall performance level selected.

Staging: The process of arranging the space for a testing experience, to include the set-up of technology components, drug products, physical props, and furniture placement.

Standardized Person (SP): An individual hired to play the role of a patient/caregiver/healthcare provider within a structured scenario. SPs may also serve in a grading capacity utilizing a provided checklist or rubric to evaluate student performance.

WebEHR: A web-based electronic health record for storage and management of patient health information, also utilized for simulated patient health information for educational purposes.

APPENDIX

Table 3. Product Selection & Counseling Skill Guide - OTC or Prescription Medications

COLLECT	• Ask about a further description of the main symptom – quality, changes, frequency • Ask about symptoms other than the chief complaint (if applicable) • Ask about a further description of other symptom(s) (if applicable) • Ask if symptoms have changed • Ask if patient has had these symptoms before • Ask how patient has treated these symptoms in the past (if patient had symptoms previously) • Ask when the current symptoms began • Ask where is the problem located (if applicable) • Ask what makes the symptom(s) worse • Ask what makes the symptom(s) better • Ask if patient has tried anything for the current symptom(s) • Ask appropriate disease-specific questions (symptom and lifestyle management) • Ask about medical problems/conditions • Ask about drug allergies OR confirms drug allergies on profile • Ask about current prescription medications OR verifies patient profile • Ask about OTC medications
ASSESS	• Assess patient understanding with 3 prime questions for a new prescription counseling or product recommended by another health care professional. ◦ What did the doctor tell you this medication is for? ◦ How did the doctor tell you to take this medication? ◦ What did the doctor tell you to expect from this medication? • Assess patient adherence to medication and/or therapy • Identify/assess patient barriers to education (e.g. socioeconomic, physical, cultural, language, health literacy) • Identify the patient's primary problem • Determine if the patient is an appropriate self-care candidate or requires referral • Assess patient understanding through teach-back (typically at the end of the encounter)
PLAN	• Counsel patient on goals of therapy • Choose a specific product and tell patient the product name • Provide a rationale or indication for the selected product • Counsel on appropriate dose and frequency
IMPLEMENT	• Counsel on appropriate duration/length of therapy • Counsel on onset of symptom relief • Counsel on missed dose management for scheduled medications (if applicable) • Counsel on adverse effects (most common and/or significant ADRs) • Counsel on proper medication storage (if applicable) • Counsel on appropriate non-drug treatment for symptoms (if applicable)
FOLLOW-UP	• Instruct patient when to seek further medical attention (specific length of time or condition) • Instruct patient when to follow up with pharmacist (if applicable) • Ask patient if they have any questions

Chapter 10
Performance Improvement in Healthcare:
Integrating Gilbert's Behavior Engineering Model Within a Just Culture

Candice Freeman
Old Dominion University, USA

Jill Erin Stefaniak
University of Georgia, USA

EXECUTIVE SUMMARY

Healthcare leadership and department management personnel are tasked with the responsibility of ensuring safe, high-quality patient care delivered by competent and proficient staff. This responsibility often comes in the form of identification of discrepant and erroneous practices that result in subsequent employee disciplinary action process improvement discussions and implementation. This case study presents an example of a sentinel event and how Gilbert's Behavior Engineering Model (BEM) was utilized in the context of a Just Culture to ensure both processes and personnel were adequately supported to meet expected task outcomes.

EMPLOYEE BACKGROUND

Alec Trager is a phlebotomist working third shift at Saint Tomas Medical Center in Sharmaine, North Carolina. His regular shift starts at 20:00 and ends at 06:00, and he is the only phlebotomist staffed during the third shift. He works Monday through Friday and every fourth weekend. Alec's responsibilities include a collection

DOI: 10.4018/978-1-7998-5092-2.ch010

of timed, scheduled, and stat patient testing for all inpatients within the hospital; this includes a collection of morning AM collections, which start at 04:00. During this time, there is only one phlebotomist collecting morning rounds, which must be completed by 07:30.

A new phlebotomist, Alec has been with Saint Tomas for ten months, and this is his first full-time job in healthcare. He graduated from a three-month phlebotomy certificate program at a local community college; he completed his clinical training at Saint Tomas and was immediately hired upon course completion. During the past 10 months, Alec's performance has slowly declined, changing from exemplary to needing improvement. The phlebotomy supervisor, Betty Murphey, has counseled Alec on several occasions regarding proper patient identification procedures and customer service skills and had extended his probationary period by 3 months, according to Betty. Alec completed his probationary period 9 months after his first day of employment.

SETTING THE STAGE

Saint Tomas Medical Center is a 72-bed critical access hospital with an emergency department that treats an average of 93 patients per day. In addition to emergent care, the facility houses a medical/surgical wing, intensive care unit, and labor and delivery with a nursery. The surgical suite includes two operating rooms and is staffed by one general surgeon and one obstetrician. On average, the facility has a census of 34 inpatients per day, with approximately 23 of those having AM labs to be collected.

The medical center is located in one of the most rural parts of North Carolina, serving an underrepresented, underserved population of patients who rely heavily on the medical expertise of the healthcare professionals. The majority of patients treated at the facility receive indigent care services and have limited knowledge of healthcare service lines and quality of care. Little to no patient engagement in healthcare-related decisions transpire between the patient and the healthcare provider, as most of the patients are ill-informed of care needs concerning their chief medical complaint and prognosis. Rarely do they ask probing questions about services rendered.

During a typical third shift rotation, Alec has a considerable amount of downtime due to the decrease in patient volume coming through the ED and the fact that timed and routine lab work is rarely ordered for collection before 4:00 am. Much of this downtime is spent assisting the testing personnel with instrument maintenance, quality control procedures, and inventory management. At approximately 2:45 am each morning, scheduled, morning patient testing labels automatically print in the phlebotomy work area; it is Alec's job to organize the labels and verify that all ordered lab work has a corresponding collection label. This is done through reconciliation to a specimen collection log, which Alec prints from the laboratory information system (LIS).

Once Alec organizes the collection labels, he stocks his collection tray with enough supplies to ensure that all samples may be collected efficiently and effectively. A surplus of collection supplies are housed in the lab supply room, and Alec is responsible for managing all phlebotomy supplies. Alec has also been tasked with ordering phlebotomy supplies as needed and per frequency of use.

After Alec completes morning lab collections, he returns to the lab, logs in the specimens into the LIS, and begins to process the samples in preparation for testing. These tasks are generally completed by no later than 6:00 am. Alec is scheduled to clock out at 6:45 am and may not incur any overtime. Alec typically works Monday through Thursday, 10 hours per shift.

CASE DESCRIPTION

On Friday morning, Alec gathered the morning round labels, which were generated at 02:45 am and began to organize them based on his planned collection route. Alec always starts his rounds in the intensive care unit, moving to the obstetric unit, and finally wraps up his collection round in the medical/surgical unit; however, this morning, a nurse in obstetrics requested that her patients be collected first, preferably by no later than 5:00 am. Alec collected the unit as requested.

In the obstetric unit, there were only three patients: a 61-year-old in room 301, a 35-year-old in 303, and a 15-year-old in room 315. Alec did have lab orders for patients in rooms 301 and 303; there was no lab work ordered for the patient in room 315. Proceeding in order, Alec entered room 301 to collect the patient's specimen.

Upon entering the patient room, Alec placed his cart against the wall, reviewed the patient collection label for name and date of birth, and then proceeded to identify the patient before sample collection. After he identified the patient, he returned to his cart, grabbed the labels and collection supplies, and returned to the bedside.

During venipuncture preparation, the patient requested that Alec not collect the specimen at that time and return later that morning to complete it. Alec attempted to convince the patient to allow collection at that time; however, the patient was insistent about waiting. Alec agreed, documented that someone would return, and exited the room. He made this documentation on the top of the patient label. At that time, Alec proceeded to room 303 and successfully collected the patient sample as ordered.

Alec returned to the lab, logged in his samples, and began processing specimens for the lab techs. At 6:30 am he handed off the labels for room 301 to the day shift phlebotomist and instructed her to collect the labs as soon as possible. The phlebotomist immediately ran down to the obstetrics unit and collected the sample in room 301. Upon collection, the patient asked why she was being stuck again. Rather than perform the venipuncture, the day shift phlebotomist contacted the lab supervisor regarding the statement and concern over the collection.

While the phlebotomist was explaining the situation to the lab supervisor, the charge nurse from OB called the lab to report concern over morning collections. The nurse stated that she was told the patient in room 303 had refused to be collected and that the phlebotomist stated he would return later to collect the samples. During morning rounds, the nurse stated that the patient in room 301 had been stuck and had not refused collection earlier. The lab supervisor immediately ran to the OB unit and performed venipunctures on both patients, returning to the lab and running tests in both collections. It was discovered that morning labels for room 301 were used to collect specimens on the patient in room 303 and that incorrect lab results were reported on the patient.

As a result of this mistake, testing personnel completed a variance report of the incident and forwarded the document to the lab supervisor. During this process, the staff amended the incorrect patient results promptly, reported the error to the primary caregiver, and thoroughly documented all steps in the correction. Unfortunately, patient care was adversely affected due to delay in the reporting of an elevated white blood cell count, and critically high potassium that was not reported to the provider promptly. The patient with the elevated lab results did not receive proper care and her condition deteriorated throughout the day. She was transferred to the medical intensive care unit where she expired 24 hours later. An investigation into this sentinel event began immediately through the lens of just culture.

PROBLEM ANALYSIS AND JUST CULTURE

Just Culture is a systematic approach to analyzing mistakes within workplace processes. This model considers both the organizational level of task execution and the task performance of the employee; however, initial assumptions, in a just culture, is that organizational processes may be the causative agent of error, not the employee. This vantage point establishes and ensures accountability of performance and support at all levels of the process and task execution (Boysen, 2013; Khatri et al., 2009; Petschonek et al., 2013).

In a just culture, problem analysis is examined in a very control, algorithmic manner that aligns with three main types of behavior associated with task performance - human error, at-risk behavior, and reckless behavior. The behavior of the caregiver is categorized according to five distinct classifications (Boysen, 2013). These include impaired judgment, malicious action, reckless action, risky action, unintentional error.

Impaired judgment warrants disciplinary action and evaluation into whether termination of caregiver is necessary. Malicious and reckless action calls for disciplinary action and verification that there are no legal ramifications associated with the caregiver's negligent behavior. Risky action requires additional coaching and for the caregiver to participate in a risk assessment to understand the consequences of their actions. Unintentional errors call for additional investigation (i.e. root cause analysis) to determine if there is a pattern associated with the occurrence of these errors.

These broad classifications serve alongside the algorithm to aid department leadership in determining problem cause and ultimately work toward problem resolution by accurately isolating the root cause of the error without placing blame for its occurrence (Boysen, 2013). This establishes equity and evidence-based determination of the cause of the error while providing the employee with the reassurance of a fair assessment of performance.

Because the nature of healthcare is rooted in the performance of individuals delivering patient care to other individuals, reason acknowledges that there are times when errant healthcare performance will negatively impact patient care (Kohn et al., 2000). Within a just culture of healthcare, employees are encouraged to report problems or potential problems, without the fear of immediate, severe repercussions; it is this occurrence reporting structure that can serve to improve patient care by mitigating mistakes and accurately and proactively addressing human performance situations. When employees operate within a safe reporting structure, near-miss events can be isolated and reported, knowing that discovery of the true cause of the problem can serve to prevent its future occurrence (Boysen, 2013; Khatri et al., 2009; Petschonek et al., 2013).

USING THE BEHAVIOR ENGINEERING MODEL TO IMPLEMENT PREVENTATIVE ACTIONS

In conjunction with a just culture, department leadership can utilize a systematic approach to analyze the error. Through the use of the Behavior Engineering Model (Gilbert, 1978), both the employee's performance and the working environment can be functionally and equitably examined, searching for potential conditions that would have contributed to the error.

Gilbert's Behavior Engineering Model (BEM) examines three components of both the worker's performance and the working environment. Table 1 explains the model. Two broad categories, Environment and Individual, specifically assess the factors of where and when the error happened and the performance of the individuals associated with the error. Using this model, from a just culture perspective, problem analysis can be completed fairly and systematically with clearly defined parameters with associated documentation and evidence. Aligned with a just culture, true causation for error can be placed upon either the construction of the process, procedure, and protocol or task execution of the individual (Boysen, 2013; Gilbert, 1978).

Common to both the environment and the individual are the three categories of information, instrumentation, and motivation. Viewing these categories as a check and balance system, employee performance can be directly aligned with the education and resources provided to accurately and reliably complete the work.

Table 1. Gilbert's behavior engineering model

	Information	Instrumentation	Motivation
Environment	*Data* Frequent feedback to the individual about performance. Clear directions and expectations of performance. Adequate performance support systems.	*Resources* Tools, resources, time materials provided to the individual that will facilitate expected performance.	*Incentives* Adequate monetary compensation for performance. Nonmonetary benefits and compensation. Career development opportunity Consequences for poor performance.
Individual	*Knowledge* Systematically designed training that aligns with performance expectations. Correct placement of training following expected performance outcomes.	*Capacity* Scheduling of performance to meet peak capacity. Visual aids and support devices to help achieve performance. Adaptation and flexibility to workplace needs and change	*Motives* Recruitment of people, placed in the correct positions. Assessment of workplace motives.

Furthermore, the Behavioral Engineering Model provides a mechanism for healthcare managers to identify factors that may have contributed to the caregiver's behavior. As a manager conducts a risk assessment and determines the type of training or level of coaching needed for remediation of the caregiver. The Behavioral Engineering Model helps the healthcare team examine the situation from the environmental level as well as the caregiver level. By examining these two levels, they can ensure that the appropriate infrastructure is in place to support a caregiver in their role and responsibilities.

Using this model, the lab supervisor can construct a series of questions used to investigate the incident before deciding on the cause of the problem and subsequent resolution steps. After construction of the questions, the investigative tool should be reviewed with another department manager for clarity, equity, and thoroughness. Table 2 provides an example of the tool constructed from the BEM, specific to the current case.

Table 2. Investigation tool created using Gilbert's BEM

Investigation Tool
1. What training is available that fully instructs the employee performing the task? 2. How has the employee received feedback on work performance, specifically for the task associated with the error? 3. What resources were required to complete the task, and were they readily available for the employee's use? 4. How did the employee demonstrate competency in utilizing the resources? 5. What benefits does the employee receive for satisfactory work performance? 6. How is the employee engaging in career development?
7. What documented evidence proves that the employee was adequately trained to perform the task and associated tasks? 8. Is the employee executing the task as instructed? 9. During the time the error was performed, was there sufficient staffing to cover the tasks required to be completed? 10. What task-specific performance support systems were available to the employee at the time of the error?

USING THE INVESTIGATION TOOL

The lab supervisor called a meeting with Alec, explaining that she wanted to discuss the situation and gather more relevant information. She told Alec that this discussion was in no way a punitive meeting or contained disciplinary action. Before the meeting, the lab supervisor took the time to use the created tool to examine the working environment and assess if potential causes for the error may have existed.

What training is available that fully instructs the employee performing the task?

The training that exists is a minimally structured cognitive apprenticeship that could last from 3 days to 3 weeks. New phlebotomists are paired with another employee and both perform collection rounds together. This takes place for as long as the new employee desires, up to 3 weeks. There is no instructional material associated with the training; however, there is a competency assessment and performance checklist completed at the end of the training period. The new employee is responsible for the completion of these documents.

How has the employee received feedback on work performance, specifically for the task associated with the error?

Alec did receive feedback on performance throughout his training; however, it was not immediate and not complete. Feedback was provided by the employees tasked to work with him and deliver his training.

What resources were required to complete the task, and were they readily available for the employee's use?

It was discovered that there were sufficient supplies, readily available the morning of the error. Alec had access to all equipment and resources required to accurately collect the samples.

How did the employee demonstrate competency in utilizing the resources?

Alec was observed collecting 10 patient samples before being deemed competent to work alone. This competency assessment was conducted during a weekday, day shift hours. There were no problems noted on Alec's competency assessment.

What benefits does the employee receive for satisfactory work performance?

Alec is a full-time employee of the lab with full benefits such as paid time off, healthcare insurance, and retirement. Additionally, Alec is on a consistent third shift schedule that rarely changes.

How is the employee engaging in career development?

On Monday, Wednesday, and Friday Alec has classes at the local community college where he is studying to be a nurse. His first class starts at 9:00 am and the last class ends at 1:00 pm. He is in his third semester of the program and anticipates being able to begin his clinical rotation next semester. Alec has plans to become a Registered Nurse and work in a Level 1 trauma center Emergency Department.

What documented evidence proves that the employee was adequately trained to perform the task and associated tasks?

The lab supervisor was able to locate Alec's initial competency assessment but did not locate the 6-month assessment. Since Alec is in his tenth month of employment, this document should have been completed at the end of his probationary period.

After an initial investigation into the work environment and general training information, the lab supervisory met with Alec and completed the investigation. This meeting lasted about 30-minutes, and Alec was very concerned about the patient care that was delivered, expressing contrition for the error.

Is the employee executing the task as instructed?

Alec was asked to explain his process for completing early morning lab collections. The lab supervisor asked him to begin from the point where specimen labels printed in the lab. Alec provided the following outline of his daily process.

1. Obtain the labels from the lab printer.
2. Separate patient labels from each other and place the patient label in the respective nursing unit stacks.
3. Restock the phlebotomy cart with ample supplies and place the labels on the cart in the order of anticipated collection. All patient labels are on top of the cart.
4. Starting with the Intensive Care Unit (ICU), he collects his patients, placing collected samples in the completed sample rack when finished.
5. To identify the patients, Alec stated that he memorizes the patient's name and date of birth before taking the collection supplies to the bedside.
6. At the bedside, he looks at the patient's armband to ensure the individual is the correct patient.
7. After the collection of the patient's samples, he moves to the next patient on the list.
8. Alec finishes up his morning by collecting the OB unit then the Med-Surg unit.
9. After collections are completed, he returns to the lab and delivers the samples to testing personnel.

During the time the error was performed, was there sufficient staffing to cover the tasks required to be completed?

The morning the error was made, Alec stated that he had been called to the Emergency Department four times during his morning rounds. This caused him to continually be pulled from the nursing floors and forced to regroup when he returned to the inpatient collection rounds. Due to the 07:30 completion time, Alec stated he felt rushed to complete on time.

What task-specific performance support systems were available to the employee at the time of the error?

The available support systems available to Alec would have been the testing personnel and an extra phlebotomist who generally reports for duty by 05:30. This particular morning, one of the two testing personnel and the other phlebotomist had called out sick, leaving Alec the only individual collecting the morning rounds, with only one employee in the lab to complete patient testing.

ANALYSIS OF INVESTIGATION IN A JUST CULTURE

After the lab supervisor completed her investigation of the environment and employee performance, she determined that multiple issues resulted in the errant performance of the employee: (1) unstructured new employee training program for phlebotomists, (2) lack of sufficient performance feedback, (3) employee work-school schedule, (4) incomplete competency assessment at 6-month mark, (5) workflow process, and (6) hospital staffing. Most of these issues are beyond the employee's control only one of these can be fully controlled by Alec, workflow process. In light of these issues, the lab supervisor decided that the error was not caused by at-risk behavior or impaired judgment but by unintentional error.

Due to the inadequate training and competency assessment program, low hospital staffing levels, and the employee's class schedule, it is apparent that these factors significantly contributed to the errors during the collection of the sample. Additionally, how Alec set up his collection labels and his performance of patient identification did, indeed, contribute to the error; however, without documentation of proper and full training, education on proper performance and technique cannot be ruled out as having been accurately completed. The decision was made to not place Alec on a disciplinary action plan. Instead, the lab supervisor decided to take a deeper look at the failed processes from this event and to include Alec in this project. Not only did this serve to improve performance for the entire lab but it empowered Alec to own and lead the change preventing this error moving forward.

CONCLUSION

Gilbert's Behavioral Engineering Model, systematically executed within a just culture of work, can serve to isolate opportunities for performance improvement amid human error. By purposefully examining how the employee performed the work and the environment in which the work was performed, the benefits are two-fold: employee performance can be enhanced and improved in alignment with the standard of work expected and a culture of continuous quality improvement can be created and maintained.

This framework allows for caregivers and healthcare managers to identify any discrepancies between the infrastructure (environment) and the caregiver related to information, instrumentation, and motivation. If this model is used to support risk assessments related to errors that occur within the healthcare system, managers will be better positioned to identify patterns of behavior and strategize initiatives to mitigate patient risk.

REFERENCES

Boysen, P. G. (2013). Just culture: A foundation for balanced accountability and patient safety. *The Ochsner Journal, 13*(3), 400–406. PMID:24052772

Creswell, J. W., & Creswell, J. D. (2017). *Research design: Qualitative, quantitative, and mixed methods approaches*. Academic Press.

Gilbert, T. F. (1978). *Engineering worthy performance*. Academic Press.

Gilbert, T. F. (2013). *Human competence: Engineering worthy performance*. John Wiley & Sons.

Hays, D. G., & Singh, A. A. (2011). *Qualitative inquiry in clinical and educational settings*. Academic Press.

Khatri, N., Brown, G. D., & Hicks, L. L. (2009). From a blame culture to a Just Culture in health care. *Health Care Management Review, 34*(4), 312–322. doi:10.1097/HMR.0b013e3181a3b709 PMID:19858916

Kohn, L.T., Corrigan, J.M., Donaldson, M.S., McKay, T., & Pike, K.C. (2000). To err is human. *Building a Safer Health System.*

Leighton, C., & McCabe, C. (2002). Performance Support for Complex Problem-Solving Tasks. *USE for 2002 USE for 2002*, 11.

Lowe, G. (2012). How employee engagement matters for hospital performance. *Healthcare Quarterly, 15*(2), 29–39. doi:10.12927/hcq.2012.22915 PMID:22688203

Mazur, L. M., McCreery, J. K., & Chen, S. J. G. (2012). Quality improvement in hospitals: Identifying and understanding behaviors. *Journal of Healthcare Engineering, 3*(4), 621–648. doi:10.1260/2040-2295.3.4.621

Pershing, J. A., Stolovitch, H. D., & Keeps, E. J. (2006). Handbook of human performance technology: Principles, practices, and potential. Academic Press.

Petschonek, S., Burlison, J., Cross, C., Martin, K., Laver, J., Landis, R. S., & Hoffman, J. M. (2013). Development of the Just Culture Assessment Tool (JCAT): Measuring the perceptions of healthcare professionals in hospitals. *Journal of Patient Safety, 9*(4), 190–197. doi:10.1097/PTS.0b013e31828fff34 PMID:24263549

Rossett, A., & Schafer, L. (2006). Job aids and performance support: The convergence of learning and work. *International Journal of Learning Technology, 2*(4), 310–328. doi:10.1504/IJLT.2006.011337

Rummler, G. A., & Brache, A. P. (1988). The systems view of human performance. *Training (New York, N.Y.), 25*(9).

Rummler, G. A., & Brache, A. P. (2012). *Improving performance: How to manage the white space on the organization chart.* Academic Press.

Simon, R. W., & Canacari, E. G. (2012). A practical guide to applying lean tools and management principles to healthcare improvement projects. *AORN Journal, 95*(1), 85–103. doi:10.1016/j.aorn.2011.05.021 PMID:22201573

van Tiem, D. M., Moseley, J. L., Dessinger, J. C., & O'Brien, C. (2002). Performance improvement interventions: Enhancing people, processes, and organizations through performance technology. *Performance Improvement, 41*(1), 45–49. doi:10.1002/pfi.4140410110

Villachica, S. W., Stone, D. L., & Endicott, J. (2006). Performance support systems. Handbook of human performance technology, 539-566.

Woodill, G. (2014). Performance Support as a Form of Mobile Learning. *Mastering Mobile Learning,* 171-173.

Chapter 11
Evaluation of Aerosolized Bronchodilator Protocol in a Large Urban Level II Hospital

Thomas W. Lamey
Salisbury University, USA

Lisa Joyner
Salisbury University, USA

EXECUTIVE SUMMARY

The purpose of this case study is to provide readers with an authentic experience of working alongside clinical care providers in a hospital environment. This case study walks the reader through the analysis, creation, implementation, and evaluation of a bronchodilator protocol initiative in a respiratory therapy department. Seeing the initiative from foundation to evaluation, the reader will experience the viewpoints, strengths, and weaknesses presented by all team members and stakeholders. By the end of this case study, the reader should be able to describe Kirkpatrick's Model of Evaluation and critique missteps the team took along the way.

SETTING THE STAGE

Walking out of the leadership meeting at Insley Medical Center the Pulmonary Services director, Barry Cones, was tasked with a simple directive: Decrease medication expenditure associated with his department. Barry was the director of a Pulmonary Services department that employed eighty-seven full-time Registered Respiratory Therapists, ten part-time Registered Respiratory Therapists, and three as-needed

DOI: 10.4018/978-1-7998-5092-2.ch011

(PRN) Registered Respiratory Therapists. His immediate task was to put together a team of respiratory therapist and stakeholders to analyze, create, implement, and evaluate *some* program that would immediately address the medication expenditure initiative. Since leadership met quarterly, Barry understood there was a three-month window to demonstrate an effective program. With that, Barry returned to his office and started to identify a team of respiratory therapists and stakeholders.

Dramatis Personae

Barry Cones: Pulmonary Services director
Dr. Blasilda Bells: Pulmonologist and Medical Staff director
Scott Robins: Pulmonary Services manager
Ami Flackson: Pulmonary Services dayshift supervisor
Patrick Kerry: Pulmonary Services nightshift supervisor
Sarah Kanatsey, Lead electronic chart and instructional design officer
Dr. Hemant Pharma, Pharmacist

After initial onboarding phone calls to discuss the initiative, Barry called the team together. He explained that Insley Medical Center respiratory therapists had delivered approximately 375,000 nebulized aerosol treatments to approximately 35,000 patients throughout the 2019 fiscal year. For the Pharmacy department, this amounted to a 1.7-million-dollar annual cost associated with nebulized aerosol medications. As Barry distributed a list of medications associated with the high annual cost, one class of medications stuck out: Bronchodilators. Bronchodilators consisted of 92% of all nebulized aerosol treatments administered for fiscal year 2019.

For staff respiratory therapists, administration of bronchodilators such as Albuterol and Levalbuterol is a time invasive procedure intended to control symptoms of asthma and/or chronic obstructive pulmonary disease (COPD), such as wheezing and shortness of breath (Egan, 2017). In its simplest form, administration of a bronchodilator consists of squirting a medicated liquid into a cup and exposing the liquid to a high velocity of air and/or oxygen. This exposure "blasts" the medicated liquid into small inhalable sized particles, and the patient inhales the medicated liquid particles into their lungs via slow deep breathing. In total, a respiratory therapist will spend approximately twelve minutes at the patient's bedside. At Insley Medical Center, the staff respiratory therapist will deliver approximately fifty aerosolized bronchodilators per twelve-hour shift.

"Good grief, that is a lot of Albuterol getting passed out daily throughout this hospital," said Dr. Pharma, "there's got to be a way to reduce the number of these we're giving patients without doing harm." "Well you know something," Scott replied, "we've been giving Albuterol for years and years knowing after about a day the patient is no longer receiving any benefit from it. We're just giving it because it's an order on the chart prescribed by a provider and there's nothing we can do to change that." Dr. Bells commented, "Well you know, at the facility I completed my residency the respiratory therapists used a protocol for all patients receiving a bronchodilator. After a provider would send an order to administer a bronchodilator like Albuterol, it was on the respiratory therapist to assess the patient and recommend how often it is given. I'm not certain, but I think it really cut down on the number of unnecessary bronchodilator treatments given. Can you imagine being a patient and being woken up at 3:00 am just to get a medication you totally don't need? I'd be so mad!" Sarah Kanatsey, the instructional designer, inquired, "What information would we need for this bronchodilator protocol? Like, current patient information or if they've ever taken this medication prior? Smoking history? I'm familiar with what a protocol is, but I need to know what information would need to be jammed into the electronic charting flowsheet for this." With that, Barry selected Sarah, Patrick, and Ami to form a sub-task team and design a bronchodilator protocol template with determinants of patient information driving the clinical decision making.

Analyzing and Creating a Plan

"Well, this is just terrible," said Patrick, "I've looked at a million bronchodilator protocols from other hospitals and all of them differ in some way." "I agree," said Ami, "somehow we're going to need to create a protocol that takes into consideration important information like breath sounds, perceived shortness of breath, chest radiograph results, and peak-expiratory flowrate. "OK," said Sarah, "so at the end of this you're going to give me a composed list of items for patient assessment that will make up the bronchodilator protocol. Each of these assessment items will be assigned a severity score, zero being *nonexistent* and three meaning *high to severe*." Ami asked, "So, if I listen to a patient's breath sounds and they're wheezing, that counts as a three since it's as bad as it gets?" "Correct," Sarah replied. "What about a chest radiograph," Patrick asked, "I'm not that good at interpreting chest radiographs so there's a good chance me or someone else would mess that up." Sarah answered, "Correct, but there's also an interpretation provided by the radiologist that you can use to guide the clinical decision making for that assessment." "Alrighty," said Patrick, "I just don't want to get in trouble with a doctor because I'm putting something down that they potentially wouldn't agree on." Indeed, protocols rely on scores from current objective information free as possible of bias from a care provider. After two days of deliberation and research, the small group led a presentation in front of the team to demonstrate their unique bronchodilator protocol (see Figure 1).

Figure 1.

Clinical Findings	0	1	2	3
Chest X-Ray	Clear or not indicated	Chronic changes	Infiltrates in more than one lung	Infiltrates + atelectasis or pleural effusion
Respiratory Pattern	Regular 12-20	Increased 21-25	Dyspnea or Irregular 26-30	Severe dyspnea, accessory muscles, respiratory rate > 30
Mental Status	Alert and oriented	Confused, follows commands	Lethargic, does not follow commands	Obtunded
Breath Sounds	Clear	Decreased unilaterally or bilaterally	Crackles in bases	Wheezing and/or rhonchi
Cough Effectiveness	Strong, spontaneous, non-productive	Strong and productive	Weak, non-productive	Weak, non-productive or rhonchi
Level of Activity	Ambulatory	With assistance	Temporarily non-ambulatory	Bed rest
Peak Flow Meter	80-100% of predicted normal	60-79% of predicted normal	40-59% of predicted normal	< 40% of predicted normal
O_2 required for SpO_2 > 92%	No oxygen	1-3 L/min	4-6 L/min	> 50%
		Total		
0-3	**4-7**	**8-12**	**13-17**	**>17**
As needed only	Two times a day and as needed	Three times a day and as needed	Four times a day and as needed	Every four hours and as needed

Figure 1-1 Insley Medical Center Aerosol Protocol

Sarah's Dilemma

Much to Sarah's surprise, the presentation of the bronchodilator protocol to the team was free of controversy from medical staff officers (i.e., Doctors Bells and Pharma) and was given the green light for implementation throughout the electronic medical record system at Insley Medical Center. However, Sarah had a dilemma: What would be the best way to implement the bronchodilator protocol to a respiratory staff of 100 that worked dayshift and nightshift? Some part-time and PRN respiratory therapists only worked two or three a month! Sarah decided to make Scott, Ami, and Patrick *superusers*. As a superuser, either of the three would be responsible for granting or denying the ability to perform a bronchodilator protocol on a patient in the electronic medical record system. For an employee to be granted access, the staff therapist would need to complete an instructional module in Insley Medical Center's Intranet system that detailed the protocol procedure. Upon completion, each employee would bring back two items of information to the superuser, 1) Likert style satisfaction survey, and 2) module questionnaire with an 80% or higher for granting access. With that, Sarah suggested to Barry that all respiratory therapists complete the module within the next two weeks. "Hehe, that will get the laggards moving," Sarah explained, "and we really need to jump on this before it's too late." Barry scoffed, "You're telling me. I don't think my staff realizes that their potential raises depend on if we can save the hospital money from these protocols." Sarah replied, "We'll know soon enough."

Kirkpatrick's Model of Evaluation

After two months of bronchodilator protocol implementation by staff respiratory therapists, Barry reconvened the team to discuss next steps. Barry asked, "Well, how does everyone feel like it's going?" Dr. Bells quickly chimed in, "I can tell you this much, my providers hate it and love it all at the same time. Sometimes we feel like the therapists are decreasing the number of aerosol treatments the patient receives just so he or she won't have to do more work. The majority of the time, we completely agree with how they're implementing the protocol and it saves us a headache, the hospital some money, and the patient unnecessary medication with gnarly side effects. You know, of course I'm going to make a big stink about the bad apples out there ruining it for everyone." Scott replied, "Sarah has recommended a strategy to evaluate that very issue Dr. Bells just brought up, and it'll also let the team know if we're moving in the right direction with this initiative. Sarah, can you explain to them what we discussed in the hall a few days ago?" "Absolutely," Sarah issued, "whether you realize it not we're halfway done with this evaluation, by design."

The rest of the team quizzically looked around to one another trying to assess who had done what. “It’s nothing you’ve done,” Sarah quickly added, “I just had the notion some form of quality assurance and return on investment would be coming down the pipeline. I implemented the initial stages Kirkpatrick’s Model of Evaluation (see Figure 2) from the very creation of the Intranet module that trained and signed-off your respiratory therapist (Mertens & Wilson, 2012). “Well, that’s exciting,” said Barry, “but how close are we from getting any hard data on this I can take back to leadership?” Sarah responded, “Scott, Patrick, Ami, and I will analyze the issue Dr. Bells raised, then we’ll address return on investment Dr. Pharma and Barry are so enthusiastic about.”

A timeline of one week was set by the team for evaluation of the first three stages. Scott, Ami, and Patrick would lead Sarah in data gathering throughout the week, and the following week would focus on results. “I guess I’ll see ya’ll bright and early tomorrow morning,” Sarah cheerily replied, “because we sure do have a lot of work to do!”

Figure 2.

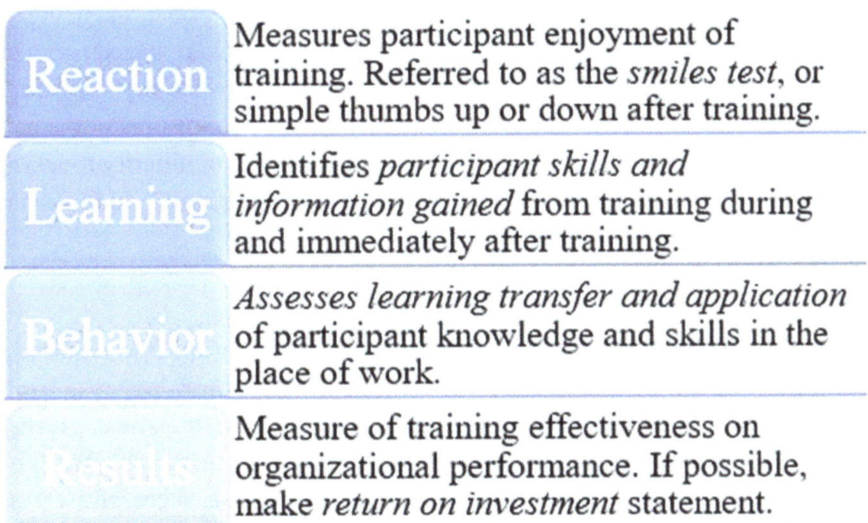

Note: A brief non-exhaustive description for each stage is provided. The highlighted sections are intended to demonstrate what the authors’ believe to be the most important evaluand during each stage.

Reaction Stage

Upon completion of the Intranet training module on conducting a bronchodilator protocol, each staff respiratory therapist was tasked to complete a reactionary survey, commonly referred to as a smiley rating questionnaire. A smiley rating questionnaire uses five emojis that represent each of the different states: extremely unsatisfied, unsatisfied, neutral, satisfied, and extremely satisfied. The smiley rating questionnaire Sarah created centered on satisfaction with the training, with the following examples listed:

- How satisfied are you with the content of the bronchodilator protocol training?
- How satisfied are you with your belief to competently perform a bronchodilator protocol?
- How satisfied are you with the user interface for this training module?
- How satisfied are you with navigation throughout this training module?

Taken as a whole, participants were satisfied with the training offered by the Intranet instructional module. Sarah noted that respiratory therapists over the age of fifty rated considerably lower (neutral or unsatisfactory) on user interface and navigation questions, leading to the belief this core group of therapists were unaccustomed to online delivery systems for learning or training. Conversely the highest satisfied group (very satisfied) were newer established respiratory therapist under the age of thirty, leading Sarah to believe this core group already held familiarity to learning management systems from college such as Canvas©, Blackboard©, and Moodle©.

Learning Stage

The second section upon completion of the Intranet training module required the respiratory therapists to successfully complete with an 80% or higher a 10-item multiple choice assessment centered on proper scoring of a patient given the appropriate information. Ninety-three of the 100 respiratory therapist scored above an 80% on their first effort, and the seven remaining therapists successfully passed the assessment upon remittance to the training module a second time.

Sarah noted that two items were missed at a higher rate than others on the assessment:

- What does the peak flow meter measure?
- Identify the correct chest radiograph interpretation in less than three minutes.

Consulting Scott, Ami, and Patrick, Sarah inquired as to why there were deficiencies in these two areas, and if they believed it would mitigate correct protocol administration. Scott explained, "For some of us older therapist we never used a peak flow meter at the bedside. We may have talked about it in school years ago, but that's it. Now, using one is the new standard and some of these older therapists need to dust back up on it and understand what it means beyond just a number on a scale." Ami further explained, "Sarah, you have to realize that some of the older therapist aren't going to just come right out and tell you he or she can't do something. That would mean admitting their ignorance, which is embarrassing since they're commonly viewed by young therapist as leaders or aides when they need help." Sarah nodded her head understandingly, "OK, I got it. I just want to bring this to your attention and this item may pop up again down the road once we investigate participant (therapist) behavior."

Sarah asked to Scott, Ami, and Patrick, "What do you think is going on with the chest radiograph interpretation? All therapists are on the electronic medical record every single day, so why couldn't some not tell us what the interpretation was in under three minutes?" Patrick jumped into the conversation, "I've been thinking about this and I think I got it. When you open up the electronic medical record and click on the radiology tab, it essentially is taking you to the embedded computer program PACS© (Picture Archiving and Communications Systems). PACS conveniently shows the chest radiograph that you want to see, but to read the radiologist interpretation you have to click on this tiny icon at the bottom of the screen. I bet some don't even know that's a thing or where it is, and that's why they didn't interpret the radiograph question correctly." Sarah looked dejected, "I may or may not have included that little tidbit of information in the training module, yikes!". Scott added, "Look, we're not going to catch everything so let's just move on and see how they're doing out on the hospital floor. I'm pretty happy with how this has gone thus far."

The evaluation team decided to meet in three days to begin investigating therapist's implementation of the bronchodilator protocol. In the meanwhile, Scott was tasked with randomly selecting up to three completed bronchodilator protocols from each therapist. Taking half a day to complete, Scott was ready for the team to reconvene with the information.

Behavior Stage

The list Scott provided to Sarah, Ami, and Patrick was comprised of 53 respiratory therapist who had completed between one to three bronchodilator protocols in the past two months. Splitting the list of bronchodilator protocols by respiratory therapists three ways, the small group split up to audit each protocol score, then reconvene with their results in two days. It should be noted that since Sarah was not a respiratory therapist, she tagged along with Scott to supply extra assistance and gain insight into clinical decision making. Before going their separate way, Scott spoke to the small group, "Let's call this what it is, an audit. Some therapists are going to be spooked when they see us, and especially spooked when they see we are going behind staff therapist's work and evaluating them." Ami spoke up, "Yeah, I'm kind of not looking forward to this because of exactly that. I'm kind of scared to go up there and maybe get into a confrontation with someone who thinks we are being sneaky and performing an evaluation on them that's going to effect their next paycheck." Sarah quizzically looked around to the group and inquired, "Is there not a time where ya'll can announce to the shifts as a whole what you're doing? I mean, you need to get it out into the open that there's nothing punitive about this and its only intention is to see if we're properly scoring patients on the protocol. This is going to turn really political really quick unless you get ahead of this!" Scott, Ami, and Patrick all looked at each other and said at the same time, "Huddle. Let's just postpone this until tomorrow and we'll communicate with our staff therapists."

Huddle was a hospital-wide strategy for each department to meet for ten to fifteen minutes and relay core patient safety goals, initiatives, and upcoming events. Scott, Ami, and Patrick announced during each shift's huddle that audits for the bronchodilator protocols were going to be conducted over the next two days. No concerns were expressed by the staff therapist, and fears were allayed after stressing the evaluation period was simply being used as a means for quality improvement with existing bronchodilator protocol instructional training. After the huddle meetings Ami, Patrick, Scott and Sarah finally went their separate ways to investigate.

Two days later, the small group met back to compile their audits. Scott and Sarah were quick to share what they've found. Scott explained, "So, out of the 27 respiratory therapists tracked we ended up looking at 61 protocols. That's great productivity by each therapist and is probably saving the department and patient a lot of money. With that though, we found that four therapists had misidentified the correct score for chest radiographs and one therapist completely forgot to score a peak flow meter reading. Lucky for them, what the score should've been would not have changed their overall score. Thank goodness." Sarah added, "Yeah, whenever we found these mistakes we kind of crossed out fingers and hoped it didn't effect the overall clinical decision-making score. Thank goodness it didn't!" It was then Ami and Patrick's turn to share what they've found.

Ami opened up first, "So I did 13 respiratory therapists and out of those 13 they did 48 bronchodilator protocols." Ami added, "However, I am a little confused as to why we don't have on the bronchodilator protocol a question asking if the patient already takes a medication like Albuterol or Levalbuterol. Think about it, if the patient already takes it at home and somehow it gets missed as a home medication then the poor patient would never get their bronchodilator unless they caused a fuss." Scott interjected, "Wow, that's a good find Ami! How in the world did we miss that the first go around? Sarah, can we please go ahead and add that assessment to the protocol immediately and just reconvene the sub-task team to reconfigure the score totals?" Sarah answered, "Yeah, I can do that immediately just understand for this evaluation we're just going to include the data we've already collected." All eyes then went to Patrick, who then threw his hands in the air and stated, "I didn't find a thing. I tracked 13 respiratory therapists and looked at 33 bronchodilator protocols and found nothing. Now, all my therapists are kind of young and scored high on the multiple-choice assessment and I don't know if that had anything to do with it." Scott added, "You know, come to think of it the respiratory therapists that fudged the chest radiograph scores were all older therapists." Scott smiled, "That's it, I'm taking all us old therapists to the optometrist for a new pair of glasses."

Sarah explained to the group that the audit period had accurately reflected the multiple-choice assessment scores, and that she was quite content with the behavioral performance of the staff respiratory therapists. Sarah left Ami and Patrick with these departing words, "Whenever you're committing an error less than 1% of the time with these bronchodilator protocols, you're doing a whole more correct then you are wrong. Great job as superusers and assisting with this." Sarah then walked with Scott back to Barry's office to deliver the information and begin the results stage. Sarah reluctantly asked Barry, "So Barry, how much do you really want to be a part of this next process?" Barry quickly replied, "I'm with you until the end when it comes to our department money and possible staff raises. Let's get this done."

Results Stage

At any given point in time, Insley Medical Center has three to five quality improvement initiatives underway focusing on improving patient outcomes, increasing care giver retention rates, and reducing unnecessary fiscal expenditures. Barry understood that to qualify the time-costs of developing, implementing, and evaluating the bronchodilator protocol he had to be able to demonstrate a return on investment for the initiative. With that, Barry met with Sarah to investigate the best method for obtaining and relaying this data to his stakeholders and Chief Financial Officer.

Sarah explained that their evaluation was conducted for the months of August and September of 2019, so she suggested to Barry pulling up September 2018 and 2017 data for comparison. At first glance the information was overwhelming positive (see Figure 3).

To restructure the information into digestible pieces of information, Barry simply created a bullet list that summarized the data provided in the table.

Figure 3.

Summary of August and September 2017, 2018, and 2019 number of bronchodilators administered throughout the hospital

	August 2017	September 2017	August 2018	September 2018	August 2019	September 2019
Number of Bronchodilators Administered	30,750	32,150	31,500	30,875	27,895	26,700
Total Cost	$140,000	$142,350	$141,000	$140,125	$122,050	$118,750
Cumulative Monthly & Yearly Cost	$282,350.00		$281,125.00		**$240,800.00**	

- Approximately $41,000.00 saved in August and September of 2019 in comparison to the last two years
- This $41,000.00 represented a decreased hospital expenditure of approximately 15% compared to previous years
- Approximately 13% decrease in number of bronchodilator medications being administered to patients

Sarah was quick to add, "Look Barry, this is with only 53 of your staff respiratory therapists onboard with performing the protocol. Imagine what this department can do and your estimates would look like if you had all 100 therapists fully onboard." Barry responded, "That's going to be the next initiative for this department, but I believe this is good enough information to make leadership and all stakeholders particularly pleased." Sarah smiled and said, "Well, good luck at our next meeting you know I got your back if there's any questions you feel uncomfortable with coming from the peanut gallery."

CONCLUSION

Before the meeting, Barry met with Scott, Sarah, Ami, and Patrick to ensure all stages of the evaluation would be represented in a correct and concise manner.

Dr. Bells and Dr. Pharma arrived to reconvene all members of the team, with Dr. Pharma stating, "I've only heard good things so folks let's get this done and over with." Dr. Bell replied, "I don't know, there's some skepticism still out there about all this." Sarah quickly answered, "Perhaps by the time Barry is done yours and anyone else's fears will be allayed."

Barry then reported summative evaluation stage findings, focusing on respiratory therapist's satisfaction level, lack of clinical decision-making errors, and return on investment. Stakeholders questioned why only 53 of the 100 staff respiratory therapists had completed any bronchodilator protocols. To that, neither Barry or Scott had an answer to. Hanging onto that question, Barry added that ensuring 100% participation in the bronchodilator protocol initiative would become a new employee performance marker and annually tracked. All agreed that adding bronchodilator protocol performance to bi-annual staff therapist evaluations would supply an impetus to start participation.

After the meeting, Sarah was walked out by Barry followed by small talk. Before Sarah left, Barry said, "Hey Sarah, next time we get a chance I want to hear more about this instructional design thing you said you can do." Sarah simply huffed and replied, "Barry, I was doing that the whole time with this project, you big galoot." Both laughed and quietly understood they'd be meeting over another a new department initiative soon enough.

IMPLICATIONS FOR INSTRUCTIONAL DESIGN PRACTICE

1. Why did Sarah structure the Intranet learning module the way she did? How would you have tracked 100 participant's reaction to and assessment of the instructional material?
2. What do you think could be causal factors to respiratory therapist reluctance for non-participating in conducting bronchodilator protocols?
3. Discuss the advantages and disadvantages of admitting in-the-field knowledge gaps in a hospital or transferrable setting.
4. What strategies would you recommend for increased therapist participation in conducting bronchodilator protocols?
5. How would you engage providers (i.e., MD, DO, PA, CRNP) to allay fears that bronchodilators are being administered in a *do no harm* manner?
6. Barry was blinded by fiscal savings associated with the bronchodilator protocol. What alternative forms of return on investment do you think Sarah should have included?
7. How can Scott and Sarah mitigate future concerns from physicians who may disagree with the bronchodilator protocol score?

ACKNOWLEDGMENT

The authors would like to extend a thank you to Dr. Robert Joyner, PhD, RRT, RRT-ACCS, FAARC, Director of the Richard A. Henson Research Institute at Peninsula Regional Medical Center in Salisbury, Maryland. Without his guidance, nuanced and topical conversational discussion points throughout this case study would not exist. Thank you!

REFERENCES

Kacmarek, R. M., Stoller, J. K., & Heuer, A. (2017). *Egan's fundamentals of respiratory care* (11th ed.). Elsevier Health Sciences.

Mertens, D. M., & Wilson, D. M. (2012). *Program evaluation theory and practice: A comprehensive guide*. The Guilford Press.

KEY TERMS AND DEFINITIONS

Electronic Medical Record: Digital version of a patient's medical record consisting of summative clinical data representing the total care-body of caregivers.

Evaluand: The subject matter being investigated during an evaluation.

Kirkpatrick's Model of Evaluation: A four stage model for evaluation of a new or existing program, with an emphasis on return on investment as a final determinant of program merit or worth.

Likert Scale: A point scale allowing for participant agreement or disagreement of certain statements.

Protocol: A bedside assessment tool commonly used to derive a clinical decision.

Return on Investment: A statement of program merit or worth that either qualifies or disqualifies continued program support.

Stakeholders: Supportive organizational personnel supportive of a new and/or existing program of operation.

Chapter 12
Leader Launch:
A Needs Assessment and Intervention for Effective Leadership Development in Healthcare

Candice Freeman
Old Dominion University, USA

EXECUTIVE SUMMARY

This case study examines how a rural healthcare system implemented LeaderLaunch, a leadership development program specifically supporting all front-line to director-level leaders employed within the organization's facilities. John DeJoria, the healthcare system's Director of Organizational Development, is a seasoned instructional designer and Certified Professional in Learning and Performance (CPLP) who was charged with the opportunity of determining the system's leadership development needs and responding with aligned performance improvement interventions, intended to build competency and capacity in current, new, and emerging leadership. This case explains how John and his team designed, conducted, and utilized a three phase needs assessment to select and design instructional and non-instructional interventions.

ORGANIZATION BACKGROUND

Samuel's Healthcare System (SHCS) is a 102-bed acute care hospital in Lynchburg, Kentucky, the county seat of Jamesin County. Lynchburg boasts a modest population of 16,000 and is the largest town within the small rural county. SHCS is the only hospital in Jamesin County and focuses on serving the entire community by providing quality valued-based healthcare to its residents. The hospital is affiliated with

DOI: 10.4018/978-1-7998-5092-2.ch012

Horton Health, a larger multi-site healthcare system based in Louisville which also serves as a research and teaching hospital for the University of Kentucky. Through this affiliation and partnership, SHCS can provide patients with extended services such as cancer treatment, robotic surgical procedures, and advanced neonatal care. The hospital was founded in 1946 and is owned by the community and managed by a local Board of Directors in conjunction with support from Horton. Over 800 healthcare professionals are employed by SHCS, and the Medical Staff is made up of 100 licensed clinicians who staff the main hospital, one ancillary urgent care facility, and 15 rural community health centers managed by the hospital. Comprehensively, SHCS has the capability to serve all healthcare needs of the residents of Jamesin County. The hospital is nationally accredited by The Joint Commission (TLC) and holds other specialty accreditations in chest pain, oncology, and cardiac rehabilitation. Most recently, SHCS received 5-star quality recognition by the Centers for Medicare and Medicaid and is currently striving to be a recipient of a Baldrige Award.

The mission of SHCS is to work with healthcare partners to create and operate a patient centered, integrated system to provide safe, high quality, compassionate, and sustainable healthcare to the people of Jamesin County. Its vision is to be recognized and chosen by patients and their families throughout Bluegrass region for the quality and value of the services provided. And at the heart of the organization are its core values of:

- Accountability and Transparency: As a community-owned healthcare system, SHCS believes in transparency and accountability to the community for the decisions made by the organization.
- Respect and Care: SHCS associates, physicians, other providers, and volunteers are its most important assets. Employees, patients and families are always treated with care, compassion, dignity and respect at all times.
- Value-added and Sustainable Healthcare: SHCS carries out all these principles in a financially prudent and sustainable manner to ensure the healthcare system stays focused on its mission.

SETTING THE STAGE

At the request of numerous department directors and leaders, the Chief Operating Officer (COO) of SHCS, Mike Biem, hosted a town hall series on various topics of concern expressed by front line managers and supervisory staff throughout all services lines of the organization. These topics included budgeting, performance improvement, human resource situations, payroll, scheduling, customer service, and many other department specific, managerial performance concerns. Mr. Biem hosted a total of 10 town hall meetings over a period of 5 days and across all shifts. These town halls were hosted in the hospital cafeteria, providing accommodation for up to 150 people. Early morning meetings were offered at 6am, and late evening meetings were offered at 8pm. Additionally, there was an early afternoon meeting at 1pm. Each town hall meeting lasted up to 60 minutes and was recorded for later viewing. Information Technology services also provided attendees the ability to join the meeting remotely using the organization's PolyCom conferencing system. During each meeting, attendees were asked to sign a log sheet showing attendance and were provided a meeting agenda for review and notetaking. All town hall meeting agendas contained the same information, and an administrative assistant was present to document meeting minutes and ensure the agenda focus remained consistent across all meetings. At the completion of the town hall meeting sessions, over 200 employees had documented attendance, spanning all healthcare system departments and service lines.

After all town hall meetings were concluded and all meeting notes were compiled, edited, and submitted to Executive Leadership for review, and several prevailing themes emerged from the feedback received from employees. One of the most impactful nuggets of information was that no formal leadership orientation or leadership development program existed designed to provide new leaders basic, foundational information needed to be successful in their roles. Consistently, meeting participants shared that they were never instructed on how to build a fiscal or a capital budget, human resource onboarding and out processing protocols, annual employee evaluation, or monitoring of daily productivity and FTE allocation. Additionally, employees stated that they would have benefited from having a mentor or peer guide them through their first few months in their new position.

Mr. Biem was not surprised by this information; in fact, it validated suspicions he had which led him to conduct the town hall meetings. With this information and disaggregated data, he could present the information to the hospital Board of Directors and recommend that the healthcare system design and develop a new and comprehensive leadership development program for all new and new-to-SHCS leaders for all departments within the organization. The Board agreed and approved Mr. Biem to move forward with this initiative under the expectation that a performance outcome measure of overall patient satisfaction be a metric utilized to assess the efficacy of the program.

Robin Morgan, the Vice President of Organizational Excellence, was charged by Mr. Biem with the task of developing a robust leadership development program that would comprehensively train new director-level leaders in their roles. Ms. Morgan leads several departments within SHCS, one of which is Organizational Development. It would be this department that was responsible for working with Ms. Morgan and the healthcare system on the creation of this leadership program, and John DeJoria,

Director of Organizational Development, was responsible for designing, developing, and deploying this program. Taking the Board's expectation of overall HCAHPS patient satisfaction scores, published by CMS, as one metric used to assess program effectiveness, John and Ms. Morgan suggested that employee satisfaction also be included as a performance outcome measure of director effectiveness within his/her respective department. This would assess both the micro and macro levels of program impact to the entirety of the healthcare system.

John was tasked with deploying this program by the start of the coming fiscal year, which was nine months from the date he was tasked with the project. His team of one instructional designer, three clinical nurse educators, and two credentialed Lean Analysts began planning, and John managed the project using Agile project management principles and strategies, assigned the instructional designer to be the Scrum Master.

CASE DESCRIPTION

As the project began, John planned to take a three-phase approach to understand the current state of leadership development at SHCS and how his team would use that information to create a program to meet the expectations of both the Executive Leadership of the organization and the system's Board of Directors. Table 1 explains the needs assessment which was based on Witkin and Altschuld's (1995) three phase needs assessment model. John utilized this model for the performance of this project.

Table 1. Needs assessment phase explanation

Phase 1	Phase 2	Phase 3
Planning and Data Gathering	*Data Collection*	*Design and Development of Interventions*
Known information will be obtained and reviewed. If further information is needed that is not present, planning for front-end analysis will include the design of data collection devices and strategies to obtain needed input.	Execution of needs assessment to uncover information that was not initially available from Phase 1. This may include focus groups with department leaders, interviews with employees and staff, or feedback from physicians and other clinicians.	Disaggregation of data from the analysis of the needs assessment. Information will be used as a foundation for the design and development of specific components of the Leadership Development program.

Planning and Existing Information: Phase 1

In Phase 1, John and his team gathered existing information from various resources within the healthcare system. In addition to the information from Mr. Biem's previous focus groups, the majority of this information was obtained by review of the current professional development courses and programs offered to managerial and leadership employees within the healthcare system. Additionally, the Human Resources department provided a list of all employees with direct reports or who manage employees; this included new and veteran leaders. This information provided the team an accurate list of employees to be included in the second phase of the project. Lastly, current employee and patient satisfaction scores were obtained to establish a baseline metric for the project. Table 2 provides information the team gathered during phase 1 of the needs assessment.

Table 2. Findings from Phase 1

Information Reviewed	Findings
Leadership development curriculum	Very few independent and specific leadership development courses exist, and there is no leadership orientation. Additionally, the learning management system is not utilized to its full capacity; no courses are offered in an online format.
Employee Roster	Approximately 100 employees are in a leadership role from front-line supervision to executive leadership. This represents approximately 12% of the organization's human capital.
Satisfaction scores	Hospital Consumer Assessment of Healthcare Providers and Systems (HCAHPS) scores indicate that SHCS is in line with national benchmarks for healthcare systems of comparable size and demographic. Current average patient satisfaction score for the organization is 74% compared to state and national averages of 76% and 79%, respectively. Employee satisfaction scores have declined over the past five years by, on average, 10% each fiscal year. Most of the employee survey responses point to dissatisfaction with immediate supervision appears to be a consistent theme across most of the organization departments.

Current Leadership Development Options

The team discovered that SHCS does not provide a dedicated leadership orientation program, specifically apart from general employee orientation which is required to be completed one the first day of employment. Current department leaders expressed the need to have a comprehensive class that covers, at a minimum, the basic, foundational information needed to be successful as a new leader within the organization. During the focus groups, new leaders took much of the allocated time to share their insight and opinions for this type of training. Suggestions included instruction on budgeting and fiscal information, Human Resource protocols and processes, and survey readiness and performance.

In addition to not providing a dedicated leadership orientation class, it was discovered that very few specific leadership courses are offered to department leaders. General courses offered did include courses such as Microsoft Excel, PowerPoint, and Access; however, only the basic levels of these courses were found in the course catalog. Most interviewed department leaders stated they need intermediate to advanced courses on various software programs, including programs used to monitor productivity and patient census activity.

Lastly, although the hospital system utilizes a learning management system, it is only used as a repository for presentations and documents. Employee transcripts are stored in this system, but no interviewed department leaders had knowledge of how to access employee education data. Leaders expressed the need to have an LMS platform that will allow all employees the capability to register for and complete self-paced, online courses.

Understanding Employee Perception

Front-Line Staff

Review of employee satisfaction scores suggests that front-line, nonsupervisory employees need greater professional development support, specifically related to mentorship from their immediate supervisors. When asked if their immediate supervisor routinely discussed professional growth plans with the employee, 76% of respondents stated this rarely happened. Also, 90% of the respondents expressed dissatisfaction with e-Learning options offered by the organization, consistently commenting that their preference is to have the option of choosing between face-to-face and online professional development course options. Table x provides an analysis of survey participant feedback.

Department Leadership

Part of the employee satisfaction surveys included managerial-specific formats that elicited feedback from department leadership, from front-line supervisors to department directors. Responses indicate that department leaders have very little extra day-to-day time to invest in their workplace professional development. Most leaders (73%) stated brief, asynchronous, online courses would be a beneficial, value-added component of their leadership development curriculum. When asked about specific topics they would like to see offered, 90% expressed the need for basic to advanced front-line budgeting and employee scheduling instruction, and 95% responded with a need for performance management development solutions, such as motivational strategies, for their department and staff. Synthesizing management satisfaction scores, the overall average for employee satisfaction was 45%, much lower than the industry benchmark of 59%.

New Information: Phase 2

After known data was gathered, reviewed, and analyzed, the team proceeded to plan Phase 2 of the project. This planning included the establishment of a project timeline and milestones, as well as the goals of the needs assessment and analysis. Figure 1 is a Gannt chart that displays the projected time of the project, and Table 3 lists established project goals that would be used to guide Phase 2 of the project.

Figure 1. Phase 2 project timeline presented in a Gannt chart

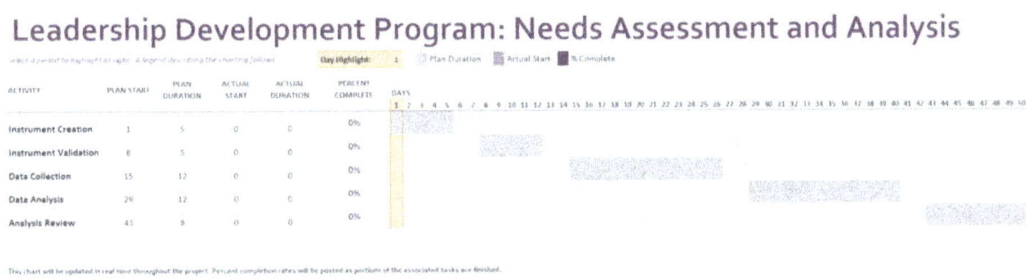

Table 3. Project goals for Phase 2

Goal
To isolate the desired state of leadership development training for the health system.
To articulate gaps in leader training and professional development.
To create relevant data used to design aligned performance improvement interventions.

This chart will be updated by the project Scrum Master throughout project entirety and in real time.

After completion of the timeline and goals, data collecting devices were created and tested for accuracy and reliability. These data collection devices were developed to uncover the reasons why employee satisfaction with professional development options was low and to understand the specific needs of department leaders with regard to providing developmental support to their employee staff. John knew that information would be needed from all employees that would be impacted by this leadership development initiative: front-line employees, middle management, and executive leadership.

The team, together, worked on the development of the data collection instruments. Understanding the nature of each stakeholder's job and work obligations, the team realized that the instruments must be mindfully created to be brief yet comprehensive to yield accurate and reliable information. For front-line staff, John know that the survey would need to be deployed to all nonmanagerial employees throughout the system, and the nature and diversity of the jobs required that the survey be brief, easily understood, and easily completed. It was determined that a 10-statement survey, score on a 6-point Likert scale, be used. Since all employees have email accounts but not all departments consistently used email as a means of communication, the team chose to create the survey using Microsoft Forms. SHCS used SharePoint and the suite of applications associated with the platform. making the administration of a Form easy and secure. To ensure that all employees received the survey, it was sent out via email, departmental communication flyers, and posted employee common areas within the hospitals such as time clocks, breakrooms, and Human Resources. Employees could access the Form through email, posted QR code or manual entry of a Bitly address. The survey was open for entry and submission for 14 days, at which it was closed for submission.

Focus groups would be used for middle management and executive leadership. Since the leadership development initiative would comprehensively provide support for new and current leaders, it was very important that current leader feedback by rich and expansive enough to ensure current perception and need was accurately captured. The focus group format was selected because highly descriptive information was designed to reveal how the current system works for the leaders. Open-ended inquiry prompted continued discussion between both middle management and executive leadership groups, of which both were conducted independently. Members of John's team facilitated the focus groups, using the created focus group template and question structures. Each facilitator was directed to take very detailed notes, including body language descriptions of the participants. This data would be used to create a thick, rich description of the focus group, which would be analyzed for common themes at the completion of data collection. Invitation to all middle management leaders was made, resulting in 20 directors volunteering. Two focus groups comprised of 10 participants each were held - one in the morning and one in the afternoon. All 10 members of the executive leadership team participated in their focus group session, which was held the day prior to the middle management sessions. Each group did not know when the other group sessions were held. Table 4 provides a brief overview of the data collection instruments created for the project.

Table 4. Phase 2 data collection instruments

Data Collection	Purpose	Intended Outcome
Employee Online Survey (Appendix A)	Multidisciplinary feedback on leadership and managerial performance.	To obtain anonymous feedback on the current state of front-line staff perception of the efficacy of leadership development within the healthcare system.
Middle Management Focus Group (Appendix B)	Uncover the current, expressed professional development needs of middle management.	To isolate specific support and instruction leaders within the healthcare system need and to also uncover opportunities to improve the current professional development offerings.
Senior Leadership Focus Group (Appendix C)	Identify the expectations Senior Leadership has of this project.	Align Senior Leadership expectations to the professional development needs of middle management and front-line staff

Data Analysis

After completion of the employee survey and focus group sessions, John and his team disaggregated and reviewed the data to uncover specific patterns and themes which could be used to design leadership development interventions. He assigned sets of his team specific tasks, including deadlines for completion and reporting to the group. Table 5 shows the teams and specific tasks of responsibility.

Table 5. Data analysis plan

Team	Team Members	Task and Deadline for Completion
Team Survey	Jill and Jimmy	Using the employee survey responses, provide percentage data on the frequency of statement ratings. Present this information in chart format. Deadline for completion is 7 days from the date of assignment.
Team Middle Management Focus Group	Jackson and Leo	Transcribe participant responses from the focus groups, and using primary and secondary coding methods, isolate themes in the participant responses and identify the most opportunities for improvement, specifically as related to leadership development strategies and initiatives. Deadline for completion is 14 days from the date of assignment.
Team Executive Leadership Focus Group	Kelly and Steve	Transcribe participant responses from the focus groups, and using primary and secondary coding methods, isolate themes in the participant responses and identify the most opportunities for improvement, specifically as related to leadership development strategies and initiatives. Deadline for completion is 14 days from the date of assignment.

Three weeks after the completion of data analysis, John met with his team to review their findings and present information within solely among the members of their team. Although all data was submitted to him on time, he took one week to review the information to ensure that no gaps were present in the analysis. His team had done an excellent job on the project.

During the meeting, John asked that each team present the information they discovered and engage in discussion about the emergent themes. This was done to brainstorm intervention planning and prepare for proposal to executive leadership and the Board of Directors. His intention in conducting analysis in this manner was to encourage ownership of the project and autonomy in performance of data analysis and knowledge acquisition; essentially, this manner of leadership builds confidence and ultimately ownership of the process, resulting in subject matter experts of the process at hand.

Team Survey

Team Survey, Jill, Kim, and Jimmy, presented their findings from the employee survey. To begin their presentation, they reminded their colleagues that this data came from an anonymous survey distributed to 564 non-managerial employees SHCS and was developed to investigate their satisfaction with professional support provided to them by their direct supervisor. The aim of this survey was to uncover the current effectiveness of leadership within the organization. Seventy-two percent (72%) of the surveys were returned, and from the team's analysis, data showed opportunities for improvement in leadership communication and meaningful feedback, professional growth and development of departmental staff, and employee acknowledgement of expertise and worker autonomy. Table 6 provides descriptive statistical information on frequency of employee response. Figure 2 graphically depicts this data, which was presented to the Organizational Development team.

Team Middle Management

"Both focus groups were wild,'' said Leo. "Yeah, I think that we caught the brunt of leader frustration in these two groups. I am worn out!", chimed Jackson. Both Leo and Jackson shared their experience in facilitating the middle management focus group, which provided a tremendous amount of information.

The first task the team had was to transcribe the focus group notes into a more readable, searchable format. Transcription software called Dragon was used to create the transcript, which was reviewed and edited by both Jackson and Leo prior to coding for common themes.

Table 6. Results of Employee Survey

Statement	1	2	3	4	5	6
I feel confident in my direct supervisor's ability to lead my department.	0%	3%	31%	25%	40%	1%
Communication within my department meets my expectations.	7%	45%	10%	14%	21%	3%
My direct supervisor encourages me to hold him/her accountable to their job and department responsibilities.	6%	35%	31%	3%	20%	5%
My direct supervisor cares about me both as a person and an employee.	10%	24%	12%	1%	45%	8%
I feel respected by my direct supervisor for the knowledge, expertise and ideas that I bring to the workplace.	0%	21%	35%	31%	12%	0%
Decisions my direct supervisor makes ensure the sustainability of my department.	6%	12%	19%	45%	16%	2%
I believe decisions made by my supervisor add value to the workplace.	10%	24%	14%	35%	10%	7%
I am working with my direct supervisor on a professional growth plan for future opportunities within the organization.	50%	28%	11%	9%	2%	0%
I get regular, useful feedback from my direct supervisor.	3%	35%	49%	6%	7%	0%
My direct supervisor makes me feel that I am an integral and valuable part of my department.	2%	4%	26%	58%	8%	2%

The second step in data analysis was to search for common themes between shared experiences of focus group participants. Open coding was used to isolate the most commonly encountered words or phrases the leaders shared. Figure 3 lists the outcomes of both open and axial coding.

The final step in the coding procedure was to examine the results of open coding and specifically induce themes from the focus group. This axial coding technique yielded 5 themes that defined the focus group data. Figure 2 includes these themes.

John asked Jackson and Leo to share some of the statements made during the middle-management focus group. Both were eager to read statements from the transcript.

"I was simply thrown into my position. One day I was a janitor and the next day I was a supervisor of 10 janitors. I was scared and so confused. Plus, they would not listen to what I had to say...it was not a fun time."

"I had this one employee who backed me up against a wall and told me that if I did not schedule her more hours, should would key my car. I could not help it; productivity numbers were low and I could not afford to schedule her. Sad thing is that after the conversation, I was too afraid to write her up because I had no clue what she would do to me. Some training on managing this type of situation would be helpful."

Figure 2. Graphical display of employee survey results

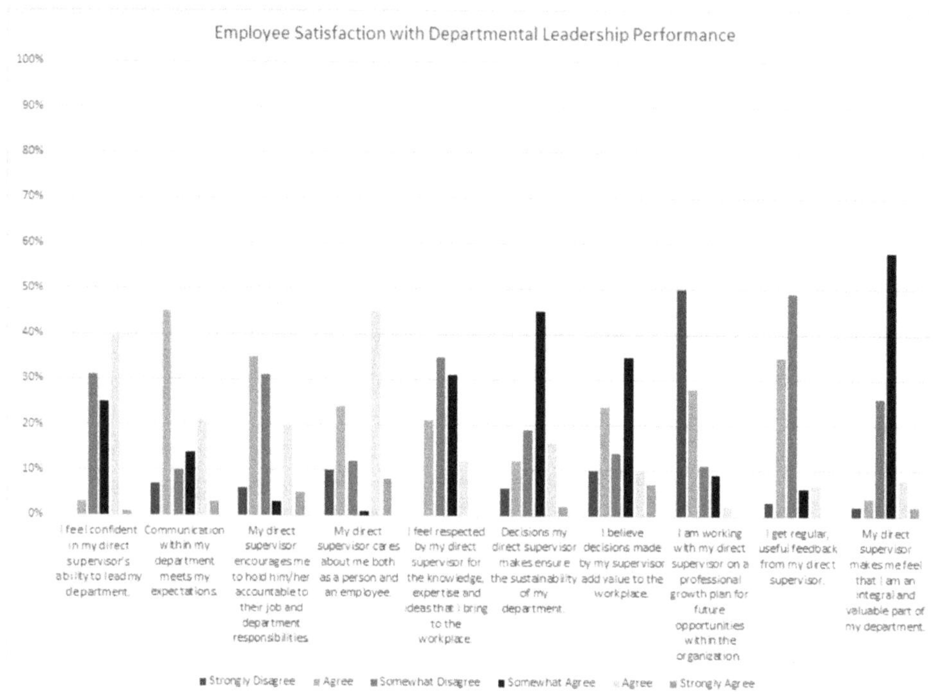

Figure 3. Coding scheme for middle management focus group

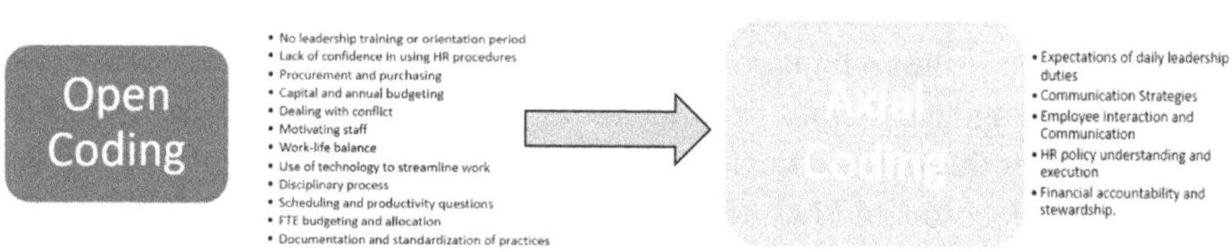

"I am paid for 40 hours but my typical work week is 65. I have no time for my family, and I still do not get all my work completed. I am seriously thinking about finding another job or stepping down. It is too much."

Team Executive Leadership

Kelly stated, "Well, at least you guys had a good showing for your focus group. We had to reschedule three times and still had to conduct one-on-one interviews with

Executive Leadership. They were never able to get their schedules to mesh." Kelly and Steve, Team Executive Leadership, were not able to conduct their focus group; Executive Leadership scheduling issues prevented finding a common time. However, they could conduct three interviews with the officers of the healthcare system. Mike Biem, Chief Operating Officer, Jack Gentry, Vice President of Human Resources, and Jessica Booker, Chief Executive Officer, were each individually interviewed using the prompting questions from the focus group template.

Kelly and Steve, like Jackson and Leo, transcribed their notes using transcription software and subsequently coded the data. using both open coding and axial coding methods, their study yielded three main themes from the interviews: value-added patient care, quality of care and patient safety through the support of all employees. These themes are rooted in the mission, vision, and values of the healthcare system. Steve shared some statements made during the interviews.

"My goal is to ensure that our leaders are well supported and can establish, maintain, and sustain a high quality of care for the people seeking our care. We place a huge emphasis on patient safety and want that to be in the forefront of our leaders' mindset."

"It would be helpful to provide our leaders with some sort of tiered support system, like a quick reference guide or something like that. I know they are busy, and we have to do more to ensure they are well equipped to take on the responsibilities of their roles."

"The LMS. The LMS is not utilized as much as it could be. When we purchased this system, we knew it had the capability to track employee training and to deliver it. In the future, my goal is to fully utilize the LMS to meet the needs of all SHCS employees."

Summary of Needs Assessment and Analysis

The team met for approximately 2 hours to review the data and discuss their findings. During this meeting, John captured minutes and compiled a summation of the finding; this information would be a critical component used to determine the most effective and organizationally aligned interventions that were (1) most appropriate for the system, (2) feasible and easily completed within the expected timeframe, and (3) sustainable and reliable to ensure desired outcomes over the coming years. Table 7 synthesizes the team's findings and informs the last phase of the needs assessment, intervention purpose, planning and proposal.

Table 7. Analysis of Needs Assessment

Data Collection	Findings
Employee Survey	Front-line staff expressed the need for more meaningful communication from their immediate supervisor, including regular feedback on performance. They also stated that more support with their own professional growth and development is a concern. Lastly, front-line seek more autonomy in the execution of workplace tasks performed within their scope of practice and areas of expertise. The overall focus of front-line staff is to safely and accurately deliver high quality patient care within their scope of practice, supported by the organization.
Middle Management Focus Group	Middle-management discussion resulted in the perceived need for leadership orientation and training that includes rich instruction on Human Resources policies and procedures, departmental budgeting and financial management, general duties of the department leadership role, and interpersonal and intrapersonal communication training to support the flow of information in their departments. The overall focus of middle management is to receive the training and instruction needed to utilize organizational resources that will ensure employee success in the delivery of patient care.
Executive Leadership Interviews	The interviews resulted in the expressed need of a redesigned, reorganized LMS. Additionally, the perceived need of a scaffolded leader support system, focused on patient safety and quality of care, aligned with the mission, vision, and values of the system, should be created to orient and train leadership on the basic to intermediate tasks related to a leadership role. These tasks include inter- and intradepartmental communication, fiscal responsibility, confidence in the utilization and practical application of organizational policies, and developmental support for departmental staff. The overall focus of executive leadership is to ensure value-added, quality care that ensures patient safety and positive medical outcomes.

Solutions and Recommendations: Phase 3

The last phase of the needs assessment and analysis was to utilize information learned from phases one and two to design aligned interventions that will take SHCS from its current state to its desired state. John explained to his team that it is vitally important to focus on the information known (from Phase 1) and the information learned (Phase 2) when planning interventions that will meet the needs of the healthcare system. Considering this information, John further explained that there would be two general classifications of intervention: instructional and non-instructional.

Instructional Interventions

Instructional interventions are focused on providing training to meet a need or fill a gap in a process or system. These intervention types are typically costly in both time and finances and require continual analysis of resources to ensure the training product is effective. John explained this to his team and asked for their feedback on what instructional interventions might be best choices for this specific situation.

"Well, I am fairly certain that we need a leadership orientation and one that takes place almost immediately once the employee takes on the leadership position; kind of like a leader launch course.," said Leo.

"I completely agree, and I like that title, LeaderLaunch. How long do you think it should be?" asked John.

"There is a lot of information about leadership responsibilities and policies to understand. I think 3 days would be realistic." offered Jackson.

"Maybe. But consider the financial aspect of training. Do you think the system could consistently sustain this over time? I am not sure that 3 days would be a timeframe that the Board would support. Let's talk about other options," said John.

Kelly chimed in, "Could the leadership orientation attendees complete online courses before coming to class?"

John, with a smile on his face, said, "Without a doubt! What leadership training could be effective online?"

Steve replied, "I think the instruction that focuses on communication and motivational strategies should not be online. It should be in the classroom and scenario-based."

"Without a doubt, my friend. That's the kind of instruction that can be fun to design and facilitate. We could have everyone engaged and laughing!", screeched Jill.

"So can we agree that the more procedural tasks, like how to enter payroll, complete online forms, and where to locate budgeting information can be taught through the LMS?" asked Leo.

"You guys are on a roll and right in line!", said John.

After extensive discussion, the team agreed that the instructional intervention would defined by two phases: (1) interactive e-learning modules self-paced and delivered through the LMS and (2) a one and a half day long collaborative classroom based orientation. Prerequisite for attendance to the classroom orientation would be completion of online training. Table 8 outlines components of both the online training and the classroom orientation.

Table 8. LeaderLaunch: Leadership Orientation Curriculum

SHCS LeaderLaunch Program: Leadership Orientation	
Self-paced, Online Training	*Interactive Classroom Training*
Managing the HR Basics	Communicating with the Team(s)
Payroll and Scheduling	Mitigating and Motivating
Fiscal Fundamentals	Resource Stewardship
Purchasing and Materials Management	Let's Build a Department

Non-Instructional Interventions

Non-instructional interventions are intended to support instruction and, essentially, become just-in-time, supportive resources to be accessed when and as needed (van Merriënboer & Kirschner, 2017). To augment the SHCS LeaderLaunch orientation program, the team decided to suggest the implementation of a mentorship program and an electronic performance support system (EPSS) delivered through a secure mobile application.

Mentorship programs provide employees the experience of engaging in workplace training that encourages and fosters critical thinking through the observation of tasks performed by experts in the field. This is one of the hallmarks of medical education; employees are trained through a cognitive apprenticeship model, whereby they engage in task completion alongside a guide who can provide immediate and relevant feedback (Lyons et.al., 2017). Mentor and mentee relationships in healthcare are not exclusive to bedside care and can be highly beneficial to leadership development. John's team recommended a mandatory mentorship program for all employees new to any leadership position within SHCS. After completion of leadership orientation, a new leader would be paired with veteran SHCS leader for a 12-month, structured mentorship program. The program is designed to introduce the employee to their leadership role responsibilities and to promote confidence and satisfaction in their task completion. The main goal of this program is to ensure new leaders are fully supported to successfully execute tasks associated with their roles the underlying intent of this program is to increase leader and employee retention within the healthcare system.

The second non-instructional intervention the team proposed was a mobile application used as an electronic performance support system (EPSS). This application would be developed by John's team and various stakeholders throughout SHCS. Just-in-time resources such as links to policies, scheduling, payroll assistance, and various department specific resources would be included in this EPSS, and all leaders would be granted access after completion of leadership orientation. Having immediate access to supportive resources, at the time and place of need, not only promotes safe and quality patient care but also aids in promoting employee satisfaction and retention (Shahmoradi et.al., 2017).

CURRENT CHALLENGES FACING THE ORGANIZATION

Employee Recruitment and Retention

It is a fact that small, rural healthcare facilities face a unique challenge in respect to recruiting and retaining medical professionals with a diverse and extensive background in their profession (Humphreys et al., 2012; McGrail et al., 2011; Weinhold & Gurtner, 2014), and SHCS is no exception. In the United States, approximately 1100 short term hospitals serve populations living outside of urbanized areas, comprising approximately 49% of the U.S. population. These rural areas often face shortages of highly qualified healthcare professionals trained to meet the needs of local communities (Weinhold & Gurtner, 2014). In addition, retaining these medical workers proves to be a significant challenge, resulting in chronic shortages of employees

Although many of these smaller hospitals, clinics, and medical practices located within these rural areas are affiliated with a larger healthcare system, some in urbanized areas, their remote, rural locations offer little in local incentives that draw professionals from larger metropolitan healthcare institutions (Frehywot et al., 2010). This tends to create one of two cultures: employees who are local and from the area who stay in positions for extended periods of time, or transient temporary staff who bring with them a varied background and diversified level of experience but provide little to no lasting human capital for the organization (Lowe, 2012). When the mission is doing what is best for patients who seek medical care from these facilities, oftentimes these two employee cultures create significant challenges when patient care is driven by problem solving.

Local Economic Outlook

Over the past 30 years, the local population has declined by approximately 20%, this being a direct result of the closure of many textile mills and manufacturing plants. What was once a local economy that brought jobs, people, and money, now repels it all. Although the hospital provides very high quality of care, the care that it most often provides is more for acute patient needs rather than preventive care. In 2010. over 30% of the county's residents reported household incomes below the poverty line, which, economically, equates to hard decisions to be made by households and families. Couple that with childhood food insecurity numbers running in line with these household incomes, the priority of preventative healthcare often takes a back seat to the two basic needs of life - food and shelter. And approximately 120 children in grades K-12 report living with their families in motel rooms, often moving weekly. Simply stated, financial security means easier access to preventative care. SHCS takes all this information into account when strategically planning for the future.

More acutely ill patients, specifically individuals lacking adequate preventive medical care, means provisions for this need must be made. SHCS provides a network of walk-in physician practices and even mobile care outreach programs that attempt to serve this great need.

Leadership development is planning for the future and creating a degree of succession that ensures sustainability of the department. Knowledge of the local economic outlook is very important when designing leadership development that is created to need the needs of the leader, the organization, and the community the organization serves. Past, present, and future history must be considered when planning for any form of professional development - if the learning and development product is to be effective and sustainable.

Healthcare Alliances and Partnerships

To ensure that the survival of many rural hospitals, organization leadership makes the decision to partner with larger, more comprehensive healthcare systems. The benefit of this is multi-faceted and not only creates and establishes a healthcare alliance with larger entities but provides local patients with access to more holistic healthcare through innovative and technologically advanced practices such as telemedicine, mobile cardiac and trauma care, and other services designed to promote preventative, rather than acute care. During the leadership development program initiative, SHCS entered talks with a local healthcare system regarding the formation of a health alliance partnership. This venture would provide SHCS access to resources that otherwise would have been prohibitive without the fiscal support and accountability of the larger system. John was pleased to receive this news and considered the planned interventions to be in alignment with this decision.

CONCLUSION

John opened the proposal presentation, thanking the hospital for the opportunity and investment in this effort and chose to have members of this team present findings of needs assessment and intervention plan to Executive Leadership and the Board of Directors. Jill and Leo willingly volunteered and were very honored to have this opportunity. The presentation was approximately 10 minutes in length, contained a digital presentation, and a handout for review. At the completion, members of leadership and the Board could ask questions, if needed. John closed out the meeting with additional thanks and an open door for further discussion if needed.

Samuel's Healthcare System adopted both the instructional and non-instructional interventions proposed by John's team, and the reason the interventions were well-received and ultimately adopted was a direct relation to the systematic and systemic approach taken by the needs assessment and analysis. John knew that for this initiative to be successful it had to touch every facet of the healthcare system, be considerate of challenges faced by both the hospital and the local community, and especially to be mindful of the needs and experiences of both the patients seeking care and the employees delivering care.

As with every metric driven process in healthcare, LeaderLaunch would need to be periodically assessed for effectiveness, revision, and, possibly, replacement. The Board initially requested that this program positively impact patient satisfaction scores; therefore, John's team planned an integral formative assessment plan to monitor program efficacy. This plan included feedback from leader program participants, annual employee satisfaction scores, and monthly monitoring of overall patient satisfaction scores, reported by CMS through HCAHPS survey analysis. The expectation of this program is that both employee and patient satisfaction scores will increase as more leaders complete this curriculum.

REFERENCES

Baron, A. E., & Orwig, G. W. (1995). *Multimedia technologies for training. Englewood*. Libraries Unlimited.

Chomeya, R. (2010). Quality of psychology test between Likert scale 5 and 6 points. *Journal of Social Sciences*, *6*(3), 399–403. doi:10.3844/jssp.2010.399.403

Christenberry, T. C., Training, C., & Vidali, C. A. (2003). *Continuous Learning Environments*. Academic Press.

Creswell, J. W., & Creswell, J. D. (2017). *Research design: Qualitative, quantitative, and mixed methods approaches*. Academic Press.

Florez-Arango, J. F., Iyengar, M. S., Dunn, K., & Zhang, J. (2011). Performance factors of mobile rich media job aids for community health workers. *Journal of the American Medical Informatics Association*, *18*(2), 131–137. doi:10.1136/jamia.2010.010025 PMID:21292702

Frehywot, S., Mullan, F., Payne, P. W., & Ross, H. (2010). Compulsory service programmes for recruiting health workers in remote and rural areas: Do they work? *Bulletin of the World Health Organization*, *88*(5), 364–370. doi:10.2471/BLT.09.071605 PMID:20461136

Gilbert, T. F. (2013). *Human competence: Engineering worthy performance*. John Wiley & Sons.

Gwee, M. C. E. (2009). Problem-Based Learning: A Strategic Learning System Design For The Education Of Healthcare Professionals in the 21ST Century. *The Kaohsiung Journal of Medical Sciences*, *25*(5), 231–239. doi:10.1016/S1607-551X(09)70067-1 PMID:19502143

Hannafin, M., McCarthy, J., Hannafin, K., & Radtke, P. (2001). Scaffolding performance in EPSSs: Bridging theory and practice. *EdMedia+ Innovate Learning*, 658-663.

Harless, J. (1975). Front-end analysis. *Training (New York, N.Y.)*, *12*(3), 27–29.

Harless, J. (1978). Motivation and Front-End Analysis. *NSPI Journal*, *17*(6), 5–6. doi:10.1002/pfi.4180170606

Harun, M. H. (2001). Integrating e-learning into the workplace. *The Internet and Higher Education*, *4*(3-4), 301–310. doi:10.1016/S1096-7516(01)00073-2

Hays, D. G., & Singh, A. A. (2011). *Qualitative inquiry in clinical and educational settings*. Academic Press.

Health and Rural Services Administration. (2019, January). Retrieved October 31, 2019, from https://data.hrsa.gov/tools/data-explorer

Humphreys, J., Wakerman, J., Kuipers, P., Russell, D., Siegloff, S., Homer, K., & Wells, R. (2017). *Improving workforce retention: Developing an integrated logic model to maximise sustainability of small rural and remote healthcare services*. Academic Press.

Humphreys, J. S., McGrail, M. R., Joyce, C. M., Scott, A., & Kalb, G. (2012). Who should receive recruitment and retention incentives? Improved targeting of rural doctors using medical workforce data. *The Australian Journal of Rural Health*, *20*(1), 3–10. doi:10.1111/j.1440-1584.2011.01252.x PMID:22250870

Issa, N., Schuller, M., Santacaterina, S., Shapiro, M., Wang, E., Mayer, R. E., & DaRosa, D. A. (2011). Applying multimedia design principles enhances learning in medical education. *Medical Education*, *45*(8), 818–826. doi:10.1111/j.1365-2923.2011.03988.x PMID:21752078

Kert, S. B., & Kurt, A. A. (2012). The effect of electronic performance support systems on self-regulated learning skills. *Interactive Learning Environments*, *20*(6), 485–500. doi:10.1080/10494820.2010.533683

Leighton, C., & McCabe, C. (2002). Performance Support for Complex Problem-Solving Tasks. *USE for 2002 USE for 2002*, 11.

Lowe, G. (2012). How employee engagement matters for hospital performance. *Healthcare Quarterly, 15*(2), 29–39. doi:10.12927/hcq.2012.22915 PMID:22688203

Lyons, K., McLaughlin, J. E., Khanova, J., & Roth, M. T. (2017). Cognitive apprenticeship in health sciences education: A qualitative review. *Advances in Health Sciences Education: Theory and Practice, 22*(3), 723–739. doi:10.100710459-016-9707-4 PMID:27544386

MacDowell, M., Glasser, M., Fitts, M., Nielsen, K., & Hunsaker, M. (2010). A national view of rural health workforce issues in the USA. *Rural and Remote Health, 10*(3), 1531. PMID:20658893

Mazur, L. M., McCreery, J. K., & Chen, S. J. G. (2012). Quality improvement in hospitals: Identifying and understanding behaviors. *Journal of Healthcare Engineering, 3*(4), 621–648. doi:10.1260/2040-2295.3.4.621

McGrail, M. R., Humphreys, J. S., Joyce, C., Scott, A., & Kalb, G. (2011). Rural amenity and medical workforce shortage: Is there a relationship? *Geographical Research, 49*(2), 192–202. doi:10.1111/j.1745-5871.2011.00690.x

Mihal, S., Center, F. L. E. T., Glynco, G. A., & Kirkley, S. (2003). *Continuous Learning Environments*. Academic Press.

Narayanamurthy, G., & Gurumurthy, A. (2018). Is the hospital lean? A mathematical model for assessing the implementation of lean thinking in healthcare institutions. *Operations Research for Health Care, 18*, 84–98. doi:10.1016/j.orhc.2017.05.002

Olagunju, A., Mokwe, M. D., & Anderson, J. (2012). *Effective Electronic Performance System Training for Supporting the Clinical Activities of Physicians*. Academic Press.

Pershing, J. A., Stolovitch, H. D., & Keeps, E. J. (2006). Handbook of human performance technology: Principles, practices, and potential. Academic Press.

Rossett, A. (1987). *Training needs assessment*. Academic Press.

Rossett, A., & Schafer, L. (2006). Job aids and performance support: The convergence of learning and work. *International Journal of Learning Technology, 2*(4), 310–328. doi:10.1504/IJLT.2006.011337

Rummler, G. A., & Brache, A. P. (1988). The systems view of human performance. *Training (New York, N.Y.), 25*(9).

Rummler, G. A., & Brache, A. P. (2012). *Improving performance: How to manage the white space on the organization chart*. Academic Press.

Saldaña, J. (2015). The coding manual for qualitative researchers. *Sage (Atlanta, Ga.)*.

Sandars, J., & Murdoch-Eaton, D. (2017). Appreciative inquiry in medical education. *Medical Teacher, 39*(2), 123–127. doi:10.1080/0142159X.2017.1245852 PMID:27852144

Shahmoradi, L., Safadari, R., & Jimma, W. (2017). Knowledge management implementation and the tools utilized in healthcare for evidence-based decision making: A systematic review. *Ethiopian Journal of Health Sciences, 27*(5), 541–558. doi:10.4314/ejhs.v27i5.13 PMID:29217960

Simon, R. W., & Canacari, E. G. (2012). A practical guide to applying lean tools and management principles to healthcare improvement projects. *AORN Journal, 95*(1), 85–103. doi:10.1016/j.aorn.2011.05.021 PMID:22201573

Strobel, J., & Van Barneveld, A. (2015). PBL effectiveness, tensions, and practitioner implications. *Essential readings in problem-based learning*, 355-372.

Tumosa, N., Horvath, K. J., Huh, T., Livote, E. E., Howe, J. L., Jones, L. I., & Kramer, B. J. (2012). healthcare workforce development in rural America: When geriatrics expertise is 100 miles away. *Gerontology & Geriatrics Education, 33*(2), 133–151. doi:10.1080/02701960.2012.661812 PMID:22490071

van Merriënboer, J. J., & Kirschner, P. A. (2017). *Ten steps to complex learning: A systematic approach to four-component instructional design*. Routledge.

van Tiem, D. M., Moseley, J. L., Dessinger, J. C., & O'Brien, C. (2002). Performance improvement interventions: Enhancing people, processes, and organizations through performance technology. *Performance Improvement, 41*(1), 45–49. doi:10.1002/pfi.4140410110

Villachica, S. W., Stone, D. L., & Endicott, J. (2006). Performance support systems. Handbook of human performance technology, 539-566.

Weinhold, I., & Gurtner, S. (2014). Understanding shortages of sufficient healthcare in rural areas. *Health Policy (Amsterdam), 118*(2), 201–214. doi:10.1016/j.healthpol.2014.07.018 PMID:25176511

Witkin, B. R., & Altschuld, J. W. (1995). Planning and conducting needs assessments: A practical guide. *Sage (Atlanta, Ga.)*.

Woodill, G. (2014). Performance Support as a Form of Mobile Learning. *Mastering Mobile Learning,* 171-173.

Zaber, M. A., Karoly, L. A., & Whipkey, K. (2019). *Reimagining the Workforce Development and Employment System for the 21st Century and Beyond.* Academic Press.

APPENDIX A

Employee Online Survey on the Impact of Leadership Development

Instructions:

Thinking about your professional working experience with your direct supervisor, rate the following statements based on your current opinion. (1= Strongly Disagree 2= Disagree 3=Somewhat Disagree 4= Somewhat Agree 5= Agree 6= Strongly Agree)

Table 9. Employee Online Survey

Rate each statement on a scale of 1 to 6	1	2	3	4	5	6
I feel confident in my direct supervisor's ability to lead my department.						
Communication within my department meets my expectations.						
My direct supervisor encourages me to how him/her accountable to their job and department responsibilities.						
My direct supervisor cares about me both as a person and an employee.						
I feel respected by my direct supervisor for the knowledge, expertise and ideas that I bring to the workplace.						
Decisions my direct supervisor makes ensure the sustainability of my department.						
I believe decisions made by my supervisor add value to the workplace.						
I am working with my direct supervisor on a professional growth plan for future opportunities within the organization.						
I get regular, useful feedback from my direct supervisor.						
My direct supervisor makes me feel that I am an integral and valuable part of my department.						

APPENDIX B

Department Leadership Focus Group

Instructions:

The following questions should be used to facilitate a department leadership focus group. Attendees should span a sample of leaders from front-line supervisors to department directors. Senior and executive leadership should not be included in this focus group. The focus group should be recorded via video, if possible. Detailed field notes should be taken and a transcript of the focus group should be drafted after completion.

To encourage participant-to-participant discussion, arrange the seating in a manner to promote active discussion.

Before beginning the focus group, read the following statement to the participants:

"Thank you for participating in this focus group on leadership development at SHCS. We appreciate your willingness to provide feedback that will improve the professional development courses and opportunities the system will provide in the future. This discussion should last no more than 45 minutes. All information provided in this focus group will be maintained in a confidential and anonymous manner; no participant names, titles, or department locations will be shared. You are encouraged to be as open in this group as you feel comfortable; you are not obligated to share any information that you are not willingly providing. At any time you may excuse yourself from the discussion with no questions asked or no repercussions. Your participation is entirely voluntary. Are there any questions before we begin?"

1. Let's open with discussion about the hospital's mission statement: The mission of SHCS is to work with healthcare partners to create and operate a patient centered, integrated system to provide safe, high quality, compassionate, and sustainable healthcare to the people of Jamesin County. Focusing on this statement, how does the healthcare organization work with department leadership to ensure patient-centered, safe, compassionate, and sustainable healthcare is delivered to the people treated within the system?
    a. What leadership development training does the healthcare system provide that aligns with this mission statement?
2. Discuss your experience when you first entered your leadership role. What professional development support did the healthcare system provide that set you up to be a successful leader in your department?
    a. What specific training did SHCS provide when you first entered your leadership role?
    b. What additional leadership development training have you completed since you took the leadership position?
3. The organization's vision is to be recognized and chosen by patients and their families throughout Bluegrass region for the quality and value of the healthcare services. How does your current position impact this vision, and how are you professionally supported to achieve this vision?

   a. What professional development courses have you completed that have trained you to execute a quality value-based, patient-centered care within your department?
4. Thinking about the professional development training you have received since you started in a leadership role, what are some strengths you have found with the leadership development program?
   a. What are some strategies you learned that have helped you in your leadership role?
5. What would you change about your leadership development training? If you could develop the ideal professional support, what would that training look like?
6. Reflect on your day-to-day working environment within your department and with your team, how would the employees reporting to you describe your leadership style?
   a. What would they say about your ability to create accountable and transparent communication, respect for their professional and personal life, and your ability to help them deliver value-added care to their patients?
7. Is there anything anyone would like to add to the discussion?

At the completion of the focus group, thank the attendees and remind them that everything shared in the discussion will remain confidential and anonymous. Also, tell them that a copy of the transcript will be available to them upon request.

APPENDIX C

Executive Leadership Focus Group

Instructions:

The following questions should be used to facilitate an executive leadership focus group. A sample of attendees should span the senior and executive leaders of the healthcare system, with representation from each service line. Front-line and department leadership should not be included in this focus group. The focus group should be recorded via video, if possible. Detailed field notes should be taken and a transcript of the focus group should be drafted after completion.

To encourage participant-to-participant discussion, arrange the seating in a manner to promote active discussion.

Before beginning the focus group, read the following statement to the participants:

"Thank you for participating in this focus group on leadership development at SHCS. We appreciate your willingness to provide feedback that will improve the professional development courses and opportunities the system will provide in the future. This discussion should last no more than 30 minutes. All information provided in this focus group will be maintained in a confidential and anonymous manner; no participant names, titles, or department locations will be shared. Your participation is entirely voluntary. Are there any questions before we begin?"

Let's open with discussion about the hospital's mission statement: The mission of SHCS is to work with healthcare partners to create and operate a patient centered, integrated system to provide safe, high quality, compassionate, and sustainable healthcare to the people of Jamesin County. Focusing on this statement, how does the healthcare organization work with department leadership to ensure patient-centered, safe, compassionate, and sustainable healthcare is delivered to the people treated within the system?

1. What is your opinion of how leadership development training aligns with this mission statement and supports the long-term vision of SHCS?
2. The organization's vision is to be recognized and chosen by patients and their families throughout Bluegrass region for the quality and value of the healthcare services. What are some aspects of training that you feel would build leaders within SHCS and promote the system's vision in the region?
    a. What are specific characteristics that you want SNCS leaders to hone that align with quality value-based, patient-centered care?
3. Thinking about the current leadership development initiatives, what are some strengths of the program and how would you recommend expanding upon them?
4. What would you change about leadership development courses and training? If you could develop the ideal professional support for new leadership, one that would support the organization's core values, what would that look like from an executive leadership perspective?
5. Is there anything anyone would like to add to the discussion?

At the completion of the focus group, thank the attendees and remind them that everything shared in the discussion will remain confidential and anonymous. Also, tell them that a copy of the transcript will be available to them upon request.

Chapter 13
Evaluating the Impact and ROI of Medical Education Programs

Timothy R. Brock
ROI Institute, USA

EXECUTIVE SUMMARY

Medical education programs must deliver valued results that stakeholders expect in return for their funding investments. In the past, healthcare organizations accepted reports about test results and participant perceptions of the program as adequate evidence of course outcomes. Today, program funders expect evaluations that provide evidence that medical education programs improve organizational excellence measures to justify ongoing funding. This chapter will explain four of the five elements required of a proven, comprehensive evaluation system. This five-element system is necessary to provide the desired organizational excellence evidence that medical educators can adopt to address the needs of stakeholders at different levels of an organization. Specifically, this chapter will overview an evaluation framework, a process model, and guiding principles that are crucial elements of this methodology. The chapter ends with a case study that shows how a medical education team used this measurement and evaluation methodology to plan how they would design and evaluate a medical education program requested by executives to solve an ICU central line infection problem.

INTRODUCTION

A well-known quote attributed to Yogi Berra states, "When you come to a fork in the road, take it." Medical education is standing at a fork in the road and must be ready to take it. Medical educators must be prepared to go left to create a traditional

DOI: 10.4018/978-1-7998-5092-2.ch013

classroom setting or go right to use learning technologies such as simulators, distance learning, mobile learning, or even virtual/augmented/mixed reality platforms. Today, this is more complicated. Even the forks have forks. Yogi was ahead of his time.

Medical educators place great emphasis on creating sound instructional programs that achieve the desired learning outcomes. These rigorous, theory-based programs are essential. However, they lead to other forks in the road. Should medical educators take the familiar path where the struggle to show value is more faith-based (i.e., have faith in us and what we do delivers value) than based on credible measures that resonate with stakeholders? Or should they take the other path where the challenge is to show the evidence-based value stakeholders want to see—the impact and return on investment (ROI) they expect?

The objectives of this chapter are:

1. Explain why medical educators must show the value of their programs using measures that matter to different stakeholders.
2. List the five elements required of a comprehensive evaluation system required to help stakeholders see and show the value of what medical educators deliver.
3. Describe the evaluation framework necessary to establish a chain-of-impact to measure different types of values that matter to stakeholders.
4. Explain the four-phase, 12-step process model used to collect and analyze the data to show the value of a medical education program.
5. Recall three common techniques used to isolate the effects of a medical education program.
6. List the 12 guiding principles used to implement the evaluation process model credibly.
7. Recall a case study showing how a medical education team used the ROI Methodology® to plan the design and evaluation of an education program requested by executives to solve an ICU central line infection problem.

BACKGROUND

Today, evaluation is about showing value that matters to key stakeholders. The challenge is "value" is in the eye of the beholder. Healthcare delivery executives and functional managers define value differently. Medical educators and healthcare providers also have unique definitions of value. When evaluating medical education programs, medical educators must have an evaluation methodology that shows the value of these programs in measures that matter to every stakeholder.

Medical educators value measures that indicate individuals or teams learned what was expected and had a favorable impression of the learning experience. Other stakeholders want to know if workplace performance improved. Executives want to know if the improved workplace performance subsequently improved the business measures they expect in return for the funding investment. This array of expectations requires a comprehensive evaluation framework showing a value continuum. This value continuum must balance six types of measures that do not reflect a single point-of-view or point-in-time perspective. These measures must provide financial and non-financial, quantitative and qualitative, tactical and strategic, and credible data to the stakeholders (Buzachero, Phillips, Phillips, & Phillips, 2013).

Even more, a comprehensive evaluation methodology must also answer the question, "How do you know the impact you are claiming is the result of your program and not something else?" The evaluation study must give impact credit where it is due and to claim credit with evidence (J. J. Phillips & Phillips, 2009). Finally, the medical educator must also know how to report the results of program evaluations in a way that executives, managers, and educators can take action to sustain and improve the learning program.

WHAT IS THE VALUE OF MEDICAL EDUCATION?

Medical educators claim medical education programs have value. Most people accept this assertion at face value. However, without data, this is a faith-based assertion. In today's new culture of impact and ROI, the triple-aim focus of healthcare systems drives accountability. Medical education programs must provide evidence showing they are investments (which are maintained, enhanced, and protected) rather than costs (which are controlled, reduced, or eliminated) (P. P. Phillips & Phillips, 2017). The challenge is how to show this value in a credible way to executives and other stakeholders.

Phillips and Phillips (2017) report a new path to increase an organization's perception of the value delivered by medical education programs using advanced learning technologies and design-thinking principles. These design thinking principles were developed in the innovation profession to plan, measure, and evaluate the results of learning programs supporting their strategic, important, and expensive programs.

A value claim begins with having a credible, comprehensive evaluation system. The evaluation system this chapter presents briefly explains the most used evaluation methodology in the world. Over 6,000 organizations use this methodology, including healthcare systems, colleges and universities, for-profit and not-for-profit organizations, government agencies, the United Nations, and the World Bank.

Even chaplains, providing spiritual care in healthcare settings, must now show measurable value contributing to the healthcare's bottom line—no more faith-based programs, even for chaplains. Chaplains are reporting that executives want them to show the value of what they do in business language to prevent the elimination of their positions. For the first time, using this measurement and evaluation methodology, chaplains are communicating the value of spiritual care in the evidence-based language of business. They are no longer considered a cost center. They are showing the organizational impact and ROI value of their spiritual care to patients, their families, and the healthcare staff using the five components of this measurement and evaluation system (P. P. Phillips, Phillips, Paone, & Gaudet, 2019). If chaplains can do it, so can medical educators.

THE FIVE EVALUATION SYSTEM COMPONENTS

Medical educators use different methods to evaluate their programs, projects, or initiatives. One or two have become the default evaluation favorite because they are familiar, or others are using it. Are these good reasons to use an evaluation methodology? Evaluations are supposed to help organizations see the value of their programs using measures that matter to all the stakeholders. Evaluation is supposed to identify what is and is not working with a program to achieve defined outcomes and results. It also should provide insights into how to improve the program. The evaluation results should help stakeholders make decisions to drive the organization. How does the medical educator select the most appropriate and credible method to do this?

Figure 1 shows the five critical components of a successful evaluation system that must fit together like a puzzle (P. P. Phillips, 2017). If you are missing a piece, the evaluation picture (and the credible evaluation practice of the medical educators) is incomplete and puzzling.

Figure 1. The Evaluation Puzzle

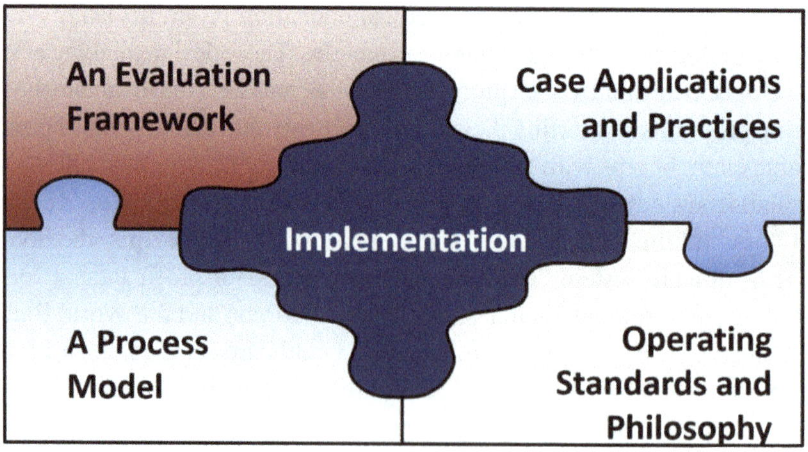

The evaluation framework establishes the data categorization schema. What types of data must the program evaluator collect, analyze, and report to tell a story and create an evidence-based value chain that various stakeholders will believe?

The process model provides the specific, necessary steps to collect and analyze the evaluation framework data. A famous statement by quality guru Deming states, "If you cannot explain what you are doing as a process, you do not know what you are doing."

The operating standards and philosophy element define the guardrails that provide a consistent practice using the process model to care program results on an apples-to-apples basis. These operating standards protect the evaluator's credibility with the stakeholders, especially the executives who control the fate of the program's funding.

The case applications and practices element of the evaluation system puzzle provide real-world examples of how organizations apply the process model in different disciplines, industries, and professions. More importantly, they provide evidence of program success using this evaluation methodology. The case study at the end of this chapter is an example of this puzzle piece. It shows how a medical education team applied this evaluation methodology to plan how they would create and evaluate an ICU intervention. This team wanted to ensure they focused on improving and evaluating the measures that mattered to the executives who directed this intervention action.

The implementation piece in the middle of the puzzle is the piece that holds everything together. Anyone can learn to collect data and evaluate programs. The key is to create sustainable change in how the medical education program adds value along a value chain from the intervention to organizational excellence results in exchange for funding.

This chapter will briefly review the first four evaluation categories of this evaluation puzzle to show how medical educators can implement this comprehensive evaluation methodology to see and show the value of what they do.

The Evaluation Framework

Figure 2 shows the six evaluation levels, along with the measurement focus and the typical measures different stakeholders want to see at each level. Level 0 Input and Indicators represent the Input-Activity-Output elements of a basic logic model (Kellogg Foundation, 2004). Evaluation levels 1 through 5 represent the outcome and result measures of this evaluation methodology's logic model foundation. This framework is essential because it establishes a chain of value (or evidence) that links the evaluation levels (P. P. Phillips & Phillips, 2007).

Figure 2. Evaluation Levels Framework. ©ROI Institute. Used with permission

Levels of Evaluation	Measurement Focus	Typical Measures
0. Inputs	The input into the program, including indicators representing scope, volume, time, costs and efficiencies	Types of programs, number of programs, number of people involved, hours of involvement, costs
1. Reaction & Planned Action	Reaction to the program, including participants' perceived value and planned action to make them successful	Relevance, Importance, Usefulness, Appropriateness, Intent to use, Motivation to take action, Recommend to others
2. Learning	Knowledge and success gained, learning how to develop concepts and how to use skills and competencies to drive program success	Skills, Learning, Knowledge, Capacity, Competencies, Confidences, Contacts
3. Application & Implementation	Application and use of knowledge, skills,, and competencies, including progress made and implementation success	Behaviors, Extent of use, Task completion, Frequency of use, Actions completed, Success with use, Barriers to use, Enablers to use
4. Impact	The impact of the programs and processes expressed as business impact measures	Graduation rates, infant mortality, crime rates, productivity, revenue, quality, jobs created, efficiency, incidents of disease, retention, customer satisfaction
5. ROI	Comparison of monetary benefits from project to project costs	Benefit-Cost Ratio (BCR), ROI%, Payback Period

For example, failure at a lower level will result in failure at higher levels. If the learners do not perceive the program as relevant, important, or useful (Level 1), they will not commit to learn it or use it. If they do not or will not learn it (Level 2), nothing will change in the workplace (Level 3). If nothing changes in the workplace, the Level 4 business impact measures will not improve. The impact is why the program was funded, (to sustain or improve one or more business measures). If medical education programs do not sustain or improve business measures, a negative Level 5 ROI will occur.

The impact measures are critical. These are the measures that executives expect to see improved or sustained for their healthcare education funding to continue. These impact measures are either hard or soft measures. Hard measures fall into four categories (i.e., output, quality, costs, and time). Soft measures are divided into five categories (i.e., work climate/satisfaction, customer services, employee development/advancement, initiative/innovation, and image).

Figure 2 lists some examples of these measures. Below are additional examples of hard and soft data measures to help medical educators understand the types of measures that executives want medical education programs to help improve.

Hard Data Examples:

- Output – inpatient/outpatient revenue, new patients, clinician productivity, screenings, births

- Quality – error rates, rework, medication event rate, bloodstream infections, incidents
- Costs – operating expenses, treatment costs, accident costs, budget variance, cost per case
- Time – length of stay, overtime, time to proficiency, response rate, patient wait times

Soft Data Examples:
- Work Climate/Satisfaction – grievances, complaints, satisfaction, engagement, intent to leave
- Employee Development/Advancement – promotions, readiness, performance appraisal ratings
- Customer Services – patient complaints/satisfaction, patient loyalty/retention
- Initiative/Innovation – suggestions, new products/services, innovation, process improvements
- Image – reputation, social responsibility, diversity, community awareness

Medical educators must provide evidence of a positive chain of impact by linking their program to the changed Level 3 workplace performance measures and the resulting changed Level 4 impact measures, when appropriate. This means the medical educator must evaluate specific programs beyond the course tests (Level 2) and end-of-course (Level 1) evaluations. Medical educators must plan to make this happen.

The Process Model

The ROI Methodology process model involves four phases—evaluation planning, data collection, data analysis, and optimize results. This process model puts into practice ten design thinking principles from the world of innovation (Mootee, 2013).

1. A problem-solving approach to handle problems on a systems level.
2. A mind-set for curiosity and inquiry.
3. A framework to balance needs and feasibility.
4. A way to take on design challenges by applying empathy.
5. A culture that fosters exploration and experimentation.
6. A fixed process and a tool kit.
7. A storytelling process to inspire Senior Executives.
8. A new competitive logic of business strategy.
9. A means to solve complex or wicked problems.
10. A means to reduce risks.

Phillips and Phillips (2017) transform these ten design thinking principles into the following twelve steps. A process model organizes these twelve steps into the four phases. The four process phases make it simpler for the healthcare educator to apply and explain their evaluation methodology to executives. The first three steps also follow Sinek's (2009) Golden Circle of *why?*, *how?*, *what?*.

Evaluation Planning Phase

1. Start with Why: Align programs with the business.
2. Make it Feasible: Select the right solution.
3. Expect Success: Plan for results.

Data Collection Phase

4. Make it Matter: Design for input, reaction, and learning.
5. Make it Stick: Design for application and impact.

Data Analysis Phase

6. Make it Credible: Isolate the effects of the program
7. Make it Credible: Convert data to monetary value
8. Make it Credible: Identify intangible measures
9. Make it Credible: Capture the costs of the program
10. Make it Credible: Calculate Return on Investment.

Optimize Results Phase

11. Tell the Story: Communicate the results to key stakeholders.
12. Optimize Results: Use black box thinking to increase funding.

These twelve steps use the design thinking principles to focus on delivering the results that stakeholders in the organization value and want from medical education programs. It enables the medical educator to evaluate how well the program is meeting the needs of the stakeholders at the different levels of the organization.

Figure 3 represents this process model (Phillips and Phillips, 2019). The process model demonstrates the importance of designing for results to show the value of medical education programs. Note how this process model includes the six evaluation levels (0 through 5) from the evaluation framework (see Figure 2).

The two most important phases of this process model are evaluation planning and optimizing results because they both focus on results rather than activities. Failing to plan for success by addressing organization and operational needs is a prelude to failure. Failing to report the results of the program evaluation can imply to the stakeholders that there was nothing positive worth reporting. Just as bad, the

Figure 3. ROI Methodology Process Model. © ROI Institute. Used with permission

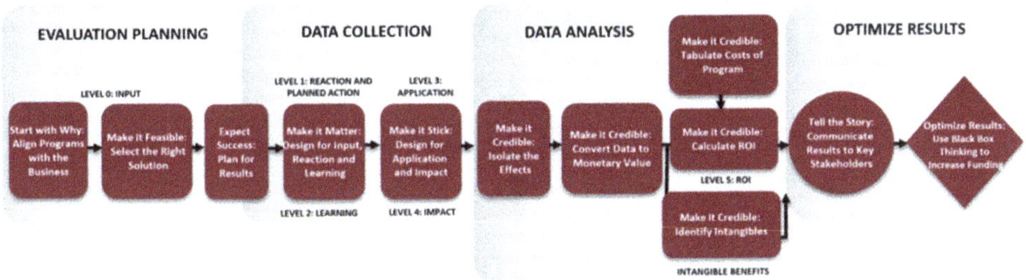

evaluation analysis offers no recommendations to improve the program. Executives will remember this when they must make budget cuts. What can prevent this?

The medical educator must collaborate with stakeholders during the evaluation planning phase to gain their support to implement this evaluation framework and process model to build a credible chain of impact. Figure 4 indicates how the chain of impact uses lower-level data (collected at the input, reaction, learning, and application levels) to show how each level influences the next higher level, ultimately influencing the impact level. This chain of impact also includes the critical data analysis step of isolating the effects of the program. The next section covers this crucial analysis step in greater detail.

After the four levels of data are collected as planned at step 3 of the process, the collected impact data is analyzed. The first analysis action is that crucial step to isolate the effect of the medical education program on the impact data collected. The next step is to convert this isolated impact measure into a monetized benefit (or tangible benefit, e.g., increased revenue) to include in the ROI calculation. If a cost-effective and credible way to convert the measure to monetary value does not exist, report the measure as an intangible benefit (e.g., improved nurse satisfaction). The costs of the program are then tabulated to calculate the ROI. These analyses steps complete the chain of impact with the isolated impact measures, the ROI, and the intangible measures.

The evaluation framework embeds the chain of impact into the process model. The first three steps ensure the evaluation plan links the chain of impact measures to focus on the business needs and results the funders expect in return for their investment. This focus allows the medical educator to tell an evaluation story the stakeholders want to hear during the last two steps of the process model.

Research related to this chain of impact indicates a correlation exists between breakdowns at one level that introduces process breakdowns at the higher evaluation levels (Aaron, 2005; Bledsoe, 1999). For example, if Level 1 Reaction survey data indicate participants did not find the medical education program relevant or useful,

Figure 4. Chain of Impact. © ROI Institute. Used with permission

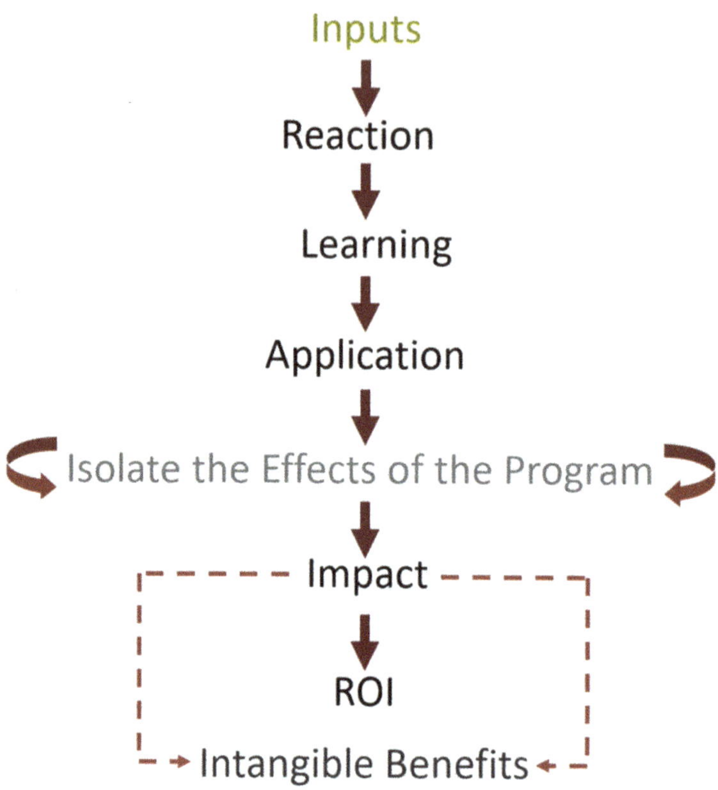

they will not learn. If they do not learn, they will not change how they perform their jobs. As expected, if they do not change how they do their jobs, the business measures will not improve. Even worse, if the business measures do not improve, there are no monetized benefits. Ultimately, with no monetized benefits, the program is all cost, and a negative ROI occurs. The program failed. The medical education professional must measure every level to identify red flags early to take corrective action early and report the whole story, both good and bad.

On the other hand, if the evaluation measures at levels 1 and 2 are positive, but the level 3 evaluation measures indicate nothing changed when they return to work, you have a chain of impact story to defend your medical education program. Level 2 measures tell you they can do what you want. Level 1 measures tell you that they want to change their workplace behaviors using what they learned. Therefore, something in the workplace is preventing them from applying what they learned and want to do. Find that barrier, or your impact measures will not improve. Executives do not want excuses. They want credible impact improvements and a positive ROI that is a direct result of the program.

Credible impact data and ROI calculations require credible isolation (J. J. Phillips, 1997). The only way to link a medical education program to actual organization results is to isolate its effects on defined organization measures (Russ-Eft & Preskill, 2001). Isolation is challenging yet necessary to establish a convincing case about the impact of a medical education program. It is not possible to *prove* impact. However, it is possible to develop defendable evidence that is acceptable to the key stakeholders through an evidence-based chain of impact at the isolation phase.

Program Isolation

Isolation is critical to the medical educator's credibility when reporting evaluation study impact results. This section provides a short overview of various techniques used to isolate the effects of a medical education program.

Everyone likes to claim credit for successful programs. On the other hand, who wants to claim credit for a negative 85% ROI? Furthermore, the rush to claim credit for successful programs can ignore other factors that influence the impact results, such as changes in a policy, work environment, resource, etc. It is essential to know how to give credit where credit is due. It is also vital to understand how to turn negative ROI results into opportunities for process improvement (Brinkerhoff, 2006; P. P. Phillips & Phillips, 2007). The only way to do this with credibility is to isolate the effects of your medical education program. This action requires the use of a systematic evaluation methodology that uses proven isolation techniques that can do this to an acceptable degree of accuracy and credibility (J. J. Phillips & Phillips, 2012). This isolation step allows the medical education professional to pinpoint the amount of improvement resulting from a medical education program and provide believable data to show evidence that your program is the cause of the impact results it claims.

Again, it is not possible to establish this isolation evidence and give credit where credit is due without a chain of evidence at the lower levels leading up to the impact level (P. P. Phillips & Phillips, 2019). This chain of impact positions the six levels of evaluation data to provide executives the data they want to see so they can decide if a medical education program is a worthwhile investment. The chain of impact also establishes a credible context for isolating the effects of a medical education program by considering the impact of other programs trying to improve the same measures (Elkeles, Phillips, & Phillips, 2014). Isolation requires measurable, targeted application data from the work environment after the medical education program occurs. The program's effectiveness data requires learning and reaction measures to link the training program to the application data (Hastings, 2010).

Isolation Techniques Overview

During the evaluation planning phase, the medical education professional collaborates with key stakeholders to plan how they will analyze the data they collect during the previous evaluation phase. The first analysis step is to select the appropriate isolation techniques based on the evaluation situation and available resources. The evaluator must isolate the impact measures to determine how well the medical education program did to achieve the program objective for each impact measure. That is what executives want to know.

There are a variety of analytical isolation techniques to use, ranging from research methods to estimates. ROI Institute conducts annual benchmarking studies of organizations applying the ROI Methodology to determine which isolation techniques practitioners use and their frequency of use (J. J. Phillips & Aaron, 2008). The benchmarking studies are conducted through questionnaires, as well as reviewing impact and ROI studies submitted to earn the Certified ROI Professional (CRP) credential. ROI Institute also reviews case studies submitted for publication consideration for these benchmarking studies. This benchmarking data indicates there are eight isolation techniques commonly used by organizations worldwide. Figure 5 lists of eight techniques in order of their accuracy and credibility, and how frequently practitioners use each one. This step is so crucial that it has a guiding principle. Guiding Principle 5 requires using at least one isolation method for every evaluation study at the impact level. The benchmarking research indicates the most used techniques are estimates, control groups, and trend line analysis.

For various reasons, practitioners use estimates most frequently. One reason is that they are used as backups when they select one of the first three methods in case the primary technique data becomes unusable (or contaminated). Another reason is the situation changes, and the technique is no longer appropriate. Additionally, estimates are useful when the organization does not support one of the first three options. Estimates are better than nothing, but only if they are obtained from credible sources and adjusted for bias (Guiding Principle 7).

A brief review of the three most used techniques will help bring clarity of how these techniques satisfy the isolation mandate.

Control Groups

Control groups represent the most accurate and credible approach to isolate the impact of programs because they establish an experimental design approach using staged events (Wang, Dou, & Li, 2002). There are four staged-event techniques: two variations of the classic control group technique, an ideal control group

Figure 5. ROI Institute Isolation Techniques Global Benchmarking Data

Method

1. Control Groups
2. Trend Line Analysis
3. Mathematical Modeling
4. Participant Estimates
5. Manager Estimates
6. Sr. Management Estimates
7. Expert Input
8. Customer Input

* Survey of Users, N = 235

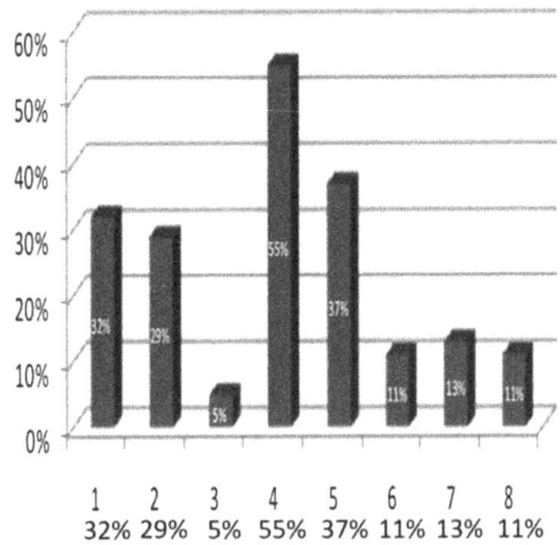

technique, and a staged control group technique. Each one involves control groups and experimental groups.

Figure 6 reflects the first design, where both groups are measured to establish a baseline for each group. The experimental group completes the medical education program, and then both groups are again assessed. The outcome provides evidence about the program's impact to change the behavior and capabilities of the experimental group that should not occur in the control group.

Figure 6. Classic Control Group Design with Pre-Measure

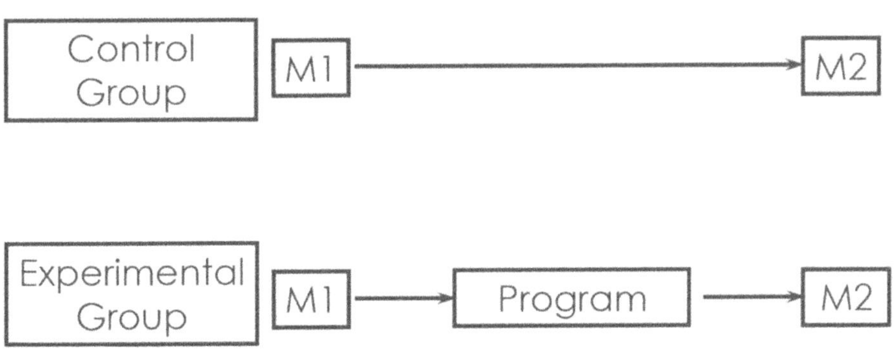

The second option for this design does not include a pre-measure (see Figure 7). This design addresses a concern that a pre-measure might influence the behavior of the control group, and thus contaminate it. Likewise, it might not be feasible or practical to conduct a pre-measurement assessment of both groups before the program. Therefore, a pre-measure is purposely not included.

Figure 7. Classic Control Group Design without Pre-Measure

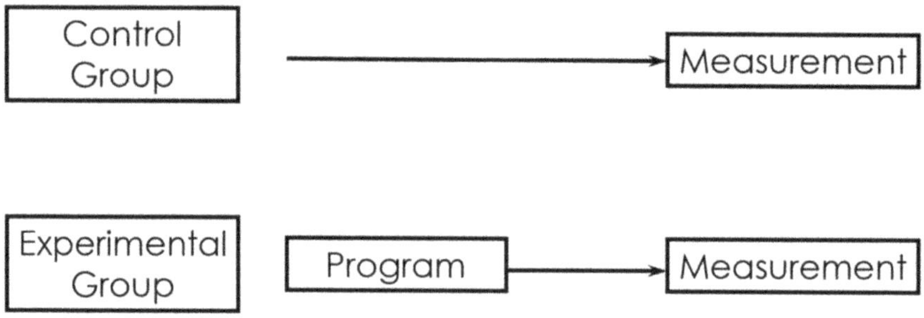

The ideal control group design involves three similar groups and combines the variations of the two classical control group techniques (see Figure 8). This option consists of designing a control group that includes a pre-measurement for the experimental and control group. Then adds a second control group that does not include the pre-measurement. This design allows the evaluators to account for any influence the pre-measurement may have had on the first control group. This approach is an ideal design but difficult to arrange with stakeholders and gain their support during the planning phase due to the additional resource requirements.

Figure 8. Ideal Classic Control Group Design

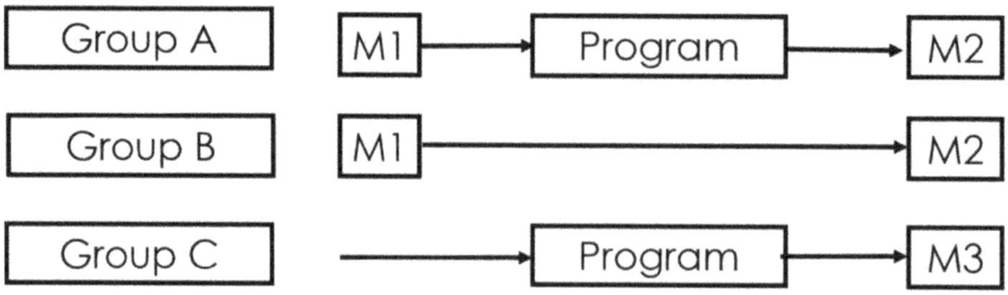

There are multiple potential problems involved with designing and implementing control groups to isolate the impact of a medical education program (Robinson, Robinson, Phillips, Phillips, & Handshaw, 2015). The first is the difficulty in selecting control groups that resemble the experimental group's key attributes, which make a difference with the results. Many factors can influence individual and team performance. Research suggests limiting the key variables requiring control to between four and six. Examples of key variables are location, supervisors, shift, job duties, etc. (Combs & Falletta, 2000).

Another potential problem is contamination. This contamination occurs when the control group learns what the experimental group is learning. The control group is contaminated because what they learn can influence their behavior and performance. It is best to set up the design to prevent contamination from occurring, such as having the groups at different locations, shifts, or floors of a building.

A third potential problem involves perception. No one likes to be considered an experiment. Therefore, use a term like a pilot group for the experimental group and the term comparison group for the control group. These terms are already part of the accepted medical education assessment and measurement lexicon.

Furthermore, if addressing a safety issue, do not give the impression that you are withholding safety-related content to conduct what some might perceive as an experiment. That is considered unethical.

Figure 9 represents how an extended, staged control group strategy could work to address some of these concerns. A staged control group technique uses the pilot group validation session as the first session, and then includes a follow-on group as the comparison group. Use the measure at the end of the second learning session of the control group to measure the initial pilot or trial group for continued improved performance to see if their proficiency matures or if their knowledge or skills decay from lack of use.

Figure 9. Extended Control Group Design

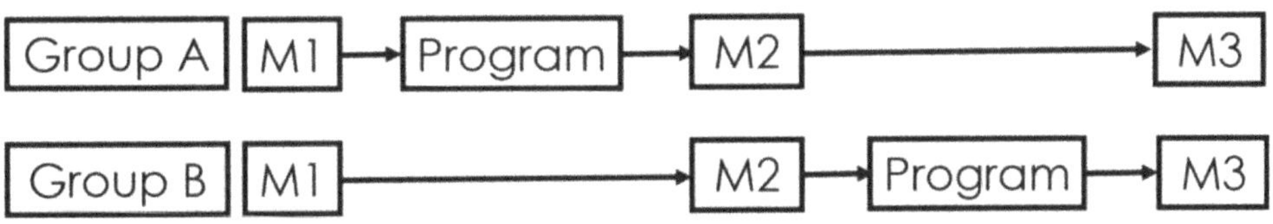

When it is not possible to use a control group for isolation, the next best options are trend line analysis and mathematical modeling. Both use real data generated before and after the medical education program to isolate its effect.

A trend line analysis is useful to approximate the impact of a program, using actual performance data before the medical education program, and extend the path of this data into the future. After the learning program occurs, actual performance data is plotted against the projected trend line data. This plotting of forecast and actual data points allows the medical education evaluator to compare the difference between the projected trend line and the actual data results following the training.

Trend lines are a simpler alternative to a control group using actual performance data. It is not an exact process, but when it is feasible to use this technique, it does establish a reasonable impact estimation of the medical education program. For example, pre-program data should be stable and not erratic. Likewise, stakeholders need to agree that the trend would continue without implementing the intervention. Finally, it is important to ensure no new variables occur during or after program implementation. If no new variables occur, it is reasonable to conclude that the trend would have continued as projected.

Figure 10 provides an example of a trend line analysis used to isolate the impact of a quality continuous performance improvement (CPI) program. The program was designed to decrease the number of acceptable syringes erroneously rejected as faulty. This graphic indicates that using the reject rate data from the first six months of the year (J, F, M = January, February, March, etc.), the trend line indicates a continued decrease through January of the following year. The error rate for rejecting syringes at the mid-point of the first six months is 1.85%. The *projected* rejection error rate at the mid-point of the second six months is 1.45%. Decision-makers wanted a medical education program to accelerate the decrease in costs associated with rejecting acceptable syringes.

Figure 10. Trend Line Analysis

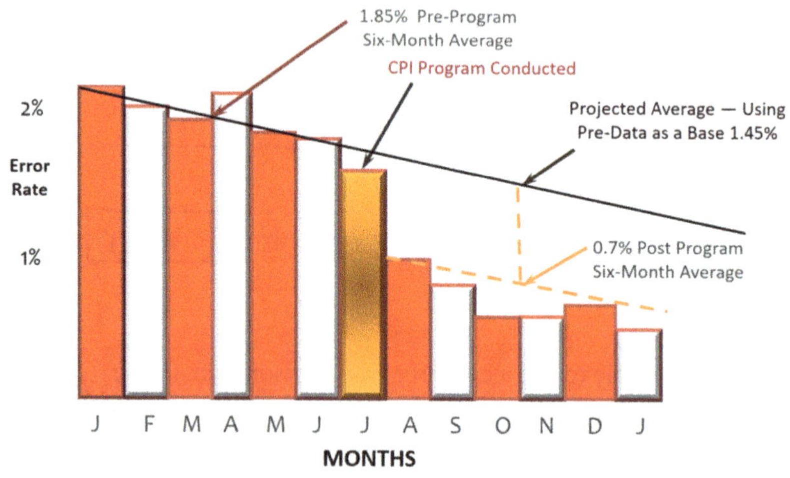

During July, the quality CPI program was implemented, seeking to decrease the number of erroneous rejects at a quicker pace. After implementing the CPI program, the *actual* average error rate for the next six months was 0.7% (established at the same mid-point as the *projected* 1.45% reject rate). The isolated decrease in error rate due to the CPI program is 0.75% (i.e., 1.45% - 0.7% = 0.75%). This trend line assumes that no other influences, other than the CPI program, occurred during the second six-month period.

The mathematical modeling technique is more analytical, using computations to develop a relationship for known output variables as a function of one or more known inputs. It can accurately predict measures using pre-program data if the required data and models are available. The actual performance data is compared to the forecasted data to derive an estimate of the impact. Without the input and output data, mathematical modeling is difficult to use. Further, it is challenging to use when multiple variables enter the process. This situation requires advanced statistical packages to identify the contribution of each variable.

ROI Institute global benchmarking results indicate mathematical modeling is the least used isolation technique (5%). Due to its complexity, it is best to reference other resources to learn how to use this isolation technique appropriately. Two reference resources are Armstrong (2001) or the International Institute of Forecasters (www.forecastingprinciples.com). If not done correctly, mathematical modeling can make a forecaster indistinguishable from a soothsayer.

Estimates are the third most used isolation technique. Three techniques rely on the estimates from the people directly affected by the program (participants, supervisors, and management). Additionally, there are two input estimates from experts and customers (see Figure 5). The methodology used to collect isolation data estimates for each of these five techniques is similar and adaptable to each source. Ideally, estimates are the option of last resort. However, global benchmarking results indicate they provide isolation data that is acceptable and credible to stakeholders and executives. When used, the evaluator must prepare to defend why these techniques are a viable option during the planning phase when stakeholders or situations prevent using control groups, trend line analysis, and mathematical modeling.

Some researchers do not like to use estimates, but isolation is not about research. Instead, isolation is about establishing reasonable evidence to support a claim. The real world is not inclined to fund "science projects" or wait for longitudinal studies to determine the wisdom of implementing an intervention to solve a business problem. The purpose of this evaluation step is to isolate the effect of the program and to do so within the constraints of limited resources and time. The goal is to produce reasonable and credible data that executives and other decision-makers consider "good enough," rather than scientifically pure. They must make decisions using the best data available within the dynamic environment and time constraints of a fast-paced' organizational tempo.

Estimates can generate credible results when following specific guidelines that include bias or error adjustments. Estimates are easy to use, which is why they are the most used technique. And estimates are better than having no isolation to support the data.

The most credible, expert estimate evidence comes from the people directly affected by the program—the participants. They know what is necessary to do their job and what is preventing them from doing it. Their voice is valuable and credible.

The second-most credible source of expert estimate evidence is the supervisors of the participants. Collect data from these individuals if you cannot collect the data from the participants. Another option is to compare the estimates of both groups and report the most conservative results. When using estimates, it is best to present the most conservative estimate to remain credible. This strategy is required by Guiding Principle 4 that tells us to select the most conservative alternative for calculations when analyzing data.

The third-most credible source of estimates is senior management. Their higher perspective might provide additional insights and reveal unconsidered factors not identified by the planned data collection instruments. This group can also provide new insights and perspectives to help claim the right level of isolated impact. The senior management group must believe what you report is credible and from reliable sources.

Two additional sources of evidence are experts and customers. Expert input (internal or external) can sometimes offer estimates to assign portions of the results to your training program. They should understand the process used to improve performance, including all the factors involved, and understand the situation surrounding the initiative. Internal experts are an excellent source to evaluate medical education programs provided by external vendors. Sometimes executives place more confidence in external experts than their internal staff.

Customer input is another source of isolation evidence. This technique focuses on the intended effect of the program. For example, after a medical education program, are patients satisfied with the quality of care received from their nurse? One drawback of this technique is customers are limited to comment on only what they know. Marketing departments have used this technique for years to determine the most effective marketing strategy by asking customers what influenced them most to purchase a product. Stakeholders and executives find these results credible.

Estimate data is typically collected using focus groups, interviews, and questionnaires. It seems logical to collect data from those most directly affected by the medical education program because they will know what had the most significant impact on their performance. Furthermore, while collecting this isolation data, it is also possible to include questions that indicate any barriers that prevent the participants from applying the knowledge or skills of the learning at the workplace and identify other environmental factors that affect performance.

Table 1 represents an estimated isolation example from a performance improvement initiative where the medication education program used simulation-based technologies. How does a medical education evaluator isolate the effect of the program when compared to the other contributing factors that could also produce improvement? One way is to ask the participants, supervisors, and managers directly affected how much influence the listed factors had on performance outcomes. Notice that space is included for the responders to add factors not considered when developing the list.

Table 1.

Factors that Influenced Improvement	Percent of Improvement Caused By	Confidence Expressed as a Percent	Adjusted Percent of Improvement Caused By
Medical Education Program	60%	80%	48%
System Changes	15%	70%	10.5%
Environmental Changes	5%	60%	3%
Process Changes	20%	80%	16%
Other	__%	__%	__%
Total	100%	N/A	N/A

In this example, the responses came from the participants of a medical education program. Their estimates about the medical education program indicate they believe, on average, that it was 60% responsible for the improved performance outcomes. They estimate other factors had a lesser impact but did contribute to the improved performance. These percentages must equal 100% to ensure the identification of all contributing factors.

Next, the medical education professional must adjust for errors in the estimates. People tend to overestimate impact, so it is important to remove this bias to establish a margin of error (Roulstone & Phillips, 2008). This adjustment begins by asking the participants to review their allocations, one at a time, and estimate their level of confidence in each allocation estimate on a scale of 0% representing no confidence and 100% representing certainty. These results will most likely vary based on their level of comfort with each allocation estimate. Collect the estimates and confidence levels from each participant, multiply the averaged improvement credit estimate by the averaged confidence level to calculate the adjusted attribution estimate for each factor.

In the medical education program example, the participants stated they were, on average, 80% confident in their averaged 60% allocation estimate. The final adjusted estimate allocation is the original averaged estimate of 60% multiplied by the averaged confidence level (80%). This calculation adjusts the estimate to 48%, a more conservative figure.

Of course, the error adjustment of 20% can also swing the other way. Put another way, the error rate (confidence) range is plus or minus (+/-) 12% (or 60% x 20%). This means the adjusted causal estimate could be between 72% (60% + 12%) or 48% (60 – 12%). One of the ROI Methodology guiding principles requires reporting the lower, more conservative result—48%. Performing this calculation for each allocation produces the results shown in Table 1 and allows for an apples-to-apples comparison. Executives routinely make decisions using data that have confidence, or error-adjusted, ranges due to their increased confidence levels in the adjusted data.

These isolation techniques collect estimate data from the most credible sources, who can comment on the level of impact each factor had on their improved performance. When these techniques are applied, you are giving credit where credit is due.

How important is including isolation when evaluating the impact of a program? Isolation was the main reason the United Nations officially adopted this evaluation methodology in 2008. Donors were questioning the impact of their investments in UN programs. These donors were asking how the UN knew their programs produced the improved results in developing countries that they were claiming. How did they know their program was the only one among others that made this improvement? This isolation question forced the UN to solve this credibility problem or risk losing financial support from donors. Their solution was adopting this measurement and evaluation methodology. Donor questions were answers to their satisfaction.

OPERATING STANDARDS AND PHILOSOPHY

This chapter has mentioned a few of the 12 guiding principles that establish the ROI Methodology's operating standards and philosophy. These principles provide the foundation that the process model is applied using the same underlying assumptions that ensure consistent decisions at each step to compare the evaluation results.

These guiding principles are (Phillips, 2017):

1. When a higher level of evaluation is conducted, it is <u>mandatory</u> to collect data at the lower levels.

This principle represents the chain of impact, which tells the complete story of the program. Failing to identify the outcomes of the lower levels and how they affect the following chain of impact level will cast doubt on the results claimed for the higher evaluation levels.

2. When the evaluation is planned for a higher level, the previous level of evaluation does not have to be comprehensive.

Because the evaluation costs increase at the higher levels, it is best to conserve resources at the lower levels to evaluate the data to a "good enough" state for the stakeholders. This is to ensure the necessary resources are available for higher-level evaluations. This "good enough" decision is made during the planning phase with the stakeholders.

3. When collecting and analyzing data, use only the most credible courses.

If people do not consider the evaluation sources credible, they will not believe your data or analysis outcomes or results. Sources the stakeholders will consider credible are defined during the planning phase.

4. When analyzing data, select the most conservative alternative for calculations.

Failing to choose the most fiscally conservative alternatives when analyzing data can lead to suspicions about the credibility of the numbers. The rule is for costs is, "when in doubt, include it." For monetized benefits, "when in doubt, do not include it." The goal is to minimize the calculated ROI, so it does not appear the numbers are inflated to make the program look better than it is. The data analysis calculation decisions are made with the appropriate stakeholders during the planning phase.

5. It is mandatory to use at least one method to isolate the effects of the program.

Failing to give credit where credit is due is a serious credibility issue with senior managers and with other programs seeking to improve the same measures. This is addressed during step 6 of the process model. The stakeholders approve the isolation techniques they will support for each impact measure during the planning phase.

6. If no improvement data are available for a population or from a specific source, assume that little or no improvement has occurred.

Make no assumptions for non-respondents. If 50% of the program participants do not provide data showing any improvement data, assume that no improvement occurred. This standard helps drive down the ROI and protect the integrity of the analysis and calculations.

7. Adjust estimates of improvement for the potential error of the estimate.

Estimates are typically overstated. It is human nature. Executives are used to working with estimates but want to see understated estimates rather than overly optimistic or overstated estimates. The estimates example in the previous section demonstrates this principle.

8. Do not use extreme data items or unsupported claims in the ROI calculation.

Good research omits extremes. Anything outside of two standard deviations is considered extreme. Also, if a claim is unsupported or not credible, do not include it.

9. Use only the first year of benefits (annualized) in the ROI analysis of short-term solutions.

Medical education programs typically support short-term programs because stakeholders do not want to wait two to three years to learn if their program is an effective and worthwhile investment. Therefore, the data analysis annualizes the ROI, so a year-to-year comparison is possible with other programs.

10. Fully load all costs of the solution for the ROI analysis.

The goal is to ensure every program cost is included in the ROI analysis to prevent someone from questioning the ROI calculation because a cost was not included. Including costs that others may not include protects the ROI analysis from accusations that the ROI calculation is inflated because certain costs were not included.

11. Intangible benefits are defined as measures that are purposely not converted to monetary value.

Intangible benefits connected to the program have value. Collect evidence of these impact measures and report them. However, if the cost to convert an impact measure to monetary value cannot be done with minimum resources or credibly, leave them as an intangible to protect the evaluation study's credibility.

12. It is mandatory to communicate the results of the ROI Methodology to all key stakeholders.

If the stakeholders do you know the outcomes and results of the evaluated medical education program, they will question whether the program delivered the value they expected in return for their investment. The story communicated is the evaluation results along the chain of impact.

In summary, these guiding principles are crucial for the medical education professional to apply during the process to ensure the evaluation methodology is applied consistently to earn the confidence of the stakeholder. These guiding principles ensure the evaluation results are credible and comparable to other studies using this methodology.

HOW TO DECIDE TO WHICH LEVEL TO EVALUATE

When using this evaluation methodology, decide with the stakeholders, what levels of evaluation are appropriate. Do not evaluate every program to the impact and ROI levels. That is unnecessary and not financially prudent. For example, for a short 30-minute lesson that educates a few people, evaluating the learning level, or possibly the application level, should be sufficient to determine if the program was effective. It is doubtful a program of that length would measurably impact a business indicator. One common criterion used by executives to select a program for evaluation at the impact or ROI levels is will the program solve an organization's problem or opportunity. Other criteria include will the program achieve a strategic objective, be of interest to management, have a high cost, or be highly visible, involve a large target population, or have a long life-cycle (Robinson et al., 2015).

Based on global benchmarking best practices, ROI Institute recommends the following evaluation targets for each level:

Level 1 Reaction and Planned Action 90-100%
Level 2 Learning 60-90%
Level 3 Application and Implementation 30-40%
Level 4 Impact 10-20%
Level 5 ROI 5-10%

Deciding which levels of evaluation are appropriate for medical education or operational performance improvement program depends on the purpose of the evaluation. For example, if your evaluation interest is limited to what occurs during the learning event, you evaluate to Levels 1 and 2. If you want to know if you changed workplace behaviors and performance, you evaluate to Level 3. If management wants to know how a program affects organizational measures, you evaluate to Levels 4 and 5.

CASE STUDY EXAMPLE

The following case study demonstrates how this comprehensive evaluation methodology process works in practice to plan how to design and evaluate a medical education program (Buzachero et al., 2013). A healthcare system was experiencing excessive central line blood infections that were dangerous to the patient and hard to treat. The executives asked the ICU team to take action to lower this infection rate. The rate was slowly declining over the previous three months but not at a fast enough pace for the executives. Therefore, the executives decided to engage the medical education team to accelerate the infection rate decline.

The medical education team started with learning why the executives wanted to take action to reduce this infection rate. It seemed apparent why action was required, but it was important to ask the executives for their reasons rather than presume them. They stated that this was a core mission issue involving patient safety and quality care. The medical education team asked the executives what business measures they were looking at that alerted them to this problem. There were four: number of infections, mortality rate, length of stay, and ICU costs. The medical education team then asked what the current numbers were for each of these four measures that caught their attention. The team asked the executive if a standard value existed for a central bloodline infection. The executives stated they had standard values for each of the business measures they want to be improved. They knew how much each measure was costing them.

After the executives defined the baseline "as-is state" numbers for each measure, the team asked the executives to tell them the "should-be state" numbers they had in mind. They asked how much improvement the executives expected from the intervention for each measure and by what date they wanted to see this improvement. The team then asked what minimum ROI the executives would like to see for the program.

Thinking ahead to how they would isolate the effect of their intervention, the medical education team realized that a control group approach was not appropriate. Which ICU would they delay improving through their intervention for the control group? They realized a trend line analysis would work since they would have at least six data points before implementing their intervention, and they could collect six data points afterward for the analysis. They asked the executives if the executives expected anything to occur after their intervention that would influence the ICU environment. Was it a stable environment? The answer was it was stable. As a result, the medical education team decided a trend line analysis would probably work best to isolate the effect of their program. To play it safe, they decided to use estimates as an isolation backup in case something unexpected did happen that would undermine their trend line analysis. Guiding Principle 5 that says to use at least one method to isolate the effect of a project drove their thinking.

The team left this meeting with a good understanding of the organizational perspective. The team also understood the expectations of the executives that the intervention had to address. Even more, they knew what measures they would use to evaluate the effectiveness of the program, as defined by the executives. They knew the ROI they were expected to achieve and had good insights about how they would isolate the program and convert the impact data to a monetary value so they could compute an ROI.

When they returned to their office, they created the high-level graphic at Figure 11. The first column defines the payoff and business needs of the executives. This is step 1 of the process model, to start with why. They knew the baseline needs, defined in terms of "as-is" measures, that explained why the executives wanted to fund this intervention. They also shifted over to step 3 of the process model to plan for a successful program. They did this by determining what the results of the intervention would have to achieve for the executives to consider it a success. These became their program objectives for the Level 5 Payoff Need and Level 4 Business Needs. The last column identifies the measures they will use to determine who well the program did to achieve the two program objectives for these two levels. They had a good idea of how they would isolate the impact measures and convert these measures to a monetary value. They could fill in other analysis blanks later. The arrows represent how the needs, objectives, and evaluation measures align. The team took this graphic to the executives and asked them if they agreed with their understanding of what the executives expected. It did.

With this data, the medical education and instructional design professionals knew the results their intervention had to achieve for the executives to classify it as a success and to justify continued funding.

The team then moved to step 2 of the process model to determine the most appropriate and most feasible solution to address these business and payoff needs and objectives.

The team shifted from an organizational perspective to an operational one. The focus was on ICU staff behaviors that were influencing the defined business measures. What had to change in the ICU for the staff to change, stop, or start doing in their daily practices to improve the defined business measures? What the team discovered was a problem with the current central line insertion procedure. As a result, staff members were working around this procedure deficiency in different ways. They

Figure 11. ROI Methodology Evaluation Planning Process Model Steps 1 and 3 for Levels 5 and 4

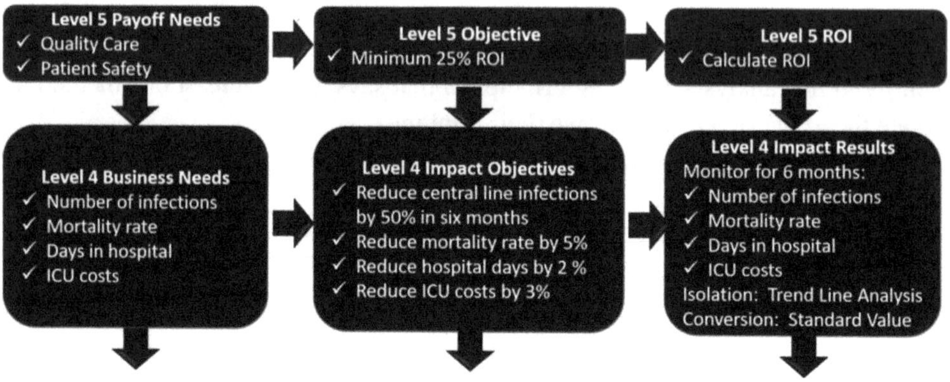

also learned that when someone was doing something incorrectly when inserting the central line, nobody said anything to advocate for the patient. This speak-up issue was especially true of nurses not questioning physicians.

Based on what they learned was happening, and not happening, in the ICU, the medical education team decided the solution was an instructional program that taught the ICU team to follow an approved procedure consistently and to say something when someone deviated from this procedure.

They decided to improve their current procedure and to add a "speak up" policy to increase the level of accountability in following the improved procedure. The ICU staff had to learn about the new speak-up policy and the new procedure and practice using it to develop their skills.

Figure 12 shows how each of the needs at the ICU workplace performance and learning levels translated into program objectives for each level. It also shows how everyone agreed to support evaluating the program to determine how well it did to meet these program objectives. The Level 2 Learning and Level 3 Performance needs were aligned to influence the Level 4 Business and Level 5 Payoff needs. So were the objectives. This logical approach helped the medical education team ensure that the instructional program they created was aligned to address the ICU operational issues to improve the business measures the executives wanted to resolve in return for the funding they are investing in the program.

They also had to decide how they would design the instructional course to increase the likelihood the ICU staff would react favorably to the course and use what they learned. Once again, step 2 of the process model addressed these needs for this to happen, while step 3 took care of the objectives and evaluation plan.

Figure 12. ROI Methodology Evaluation Planning Process Model Steps 2 and 3 for Levels 3 and 2

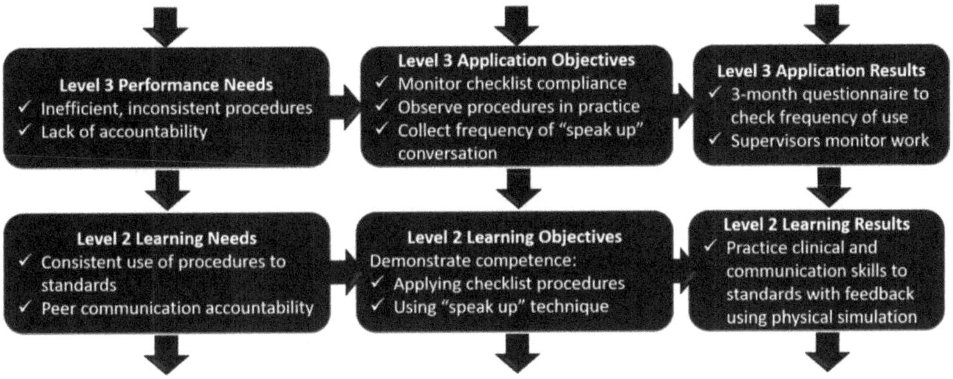

At level 1, they had to define the preference needs of the organization and the participants to ensure the designed and implemented a successful intervention. They decided the best way to get the buy-in of the ICU team was to have them improve the current procedure and practice using it through simulations. This approach allowed them to refine the procedures and develop their skills using them. They also practiced using the speak-up skills they learned. Figure 13 indicates the preference needs and the objectives they established that would tell them the likelihood the participants would learn the new procedures and apply them at the ICU. They also identified who should attend the instructional event to ensure the program's success. Again, the needs, objectives, and evaluation plan aligned vertically to the higher levels and horizontally to plan for operational and organizational results rather than on learning activities.

Figure 13. ROI Methodology Evaluation Planning Process Model Steps 1 and 3 for Levels 1 and 0

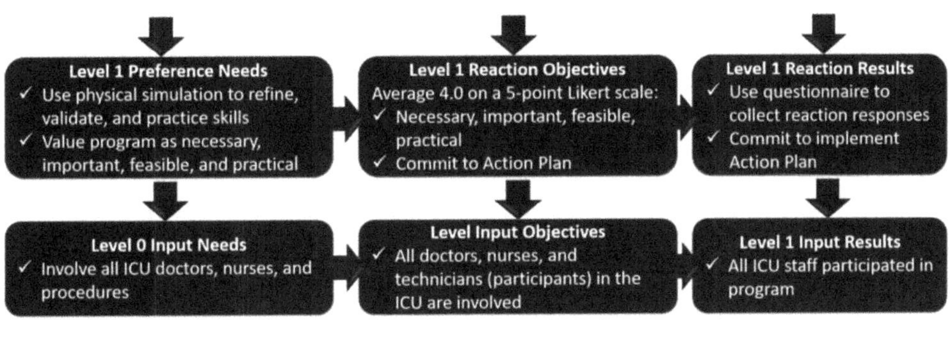

Once the medical education team finished defining the needs, objectives, and evaluation plan with the affected stakeholders at each level, the created a graphic that showed how the operational needs and objectives at Levels 0, 1, 2, and 3 were aligned to address the organizational needs and objectives at Levels 4 and 5. They used this graphic to communicate their plan to create the intervention to achieve the program objectives at each level and their plan to evaluate how well the program did to achieve these objectives. Figure 14 represents how this alignment model showed the agreed-upon plan to prove the value of the medical education program using measures that mattered to different stakeholders. Their plan was approved, funded, and implemented.

Figure 14. Business Alignment V-Model

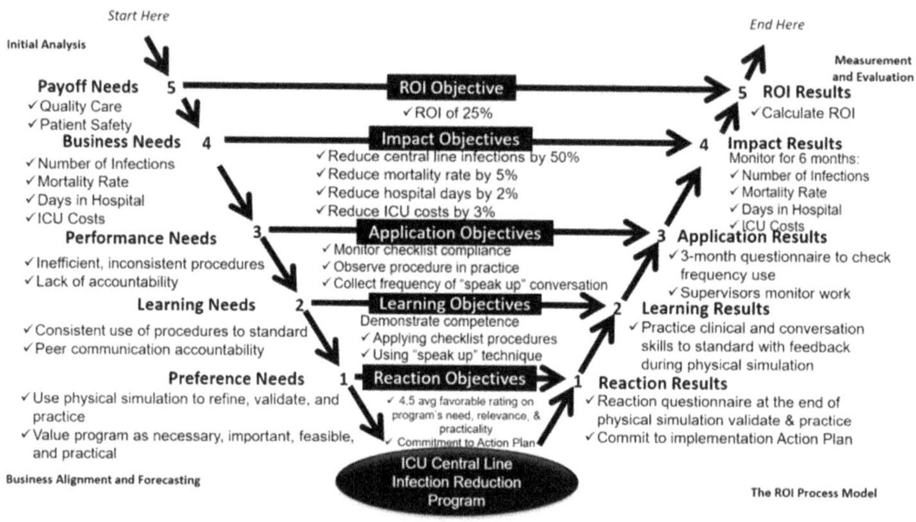

FUTURE RESEARCH DIRECTIONS

Many health care organizations have already adopted this evaluation methodology to demonstrate the value of their medical education programs. Medical educators who decide to use this methodology to evaluate a program are encouraged to write an ROI impact study for possible case study publication so others can learn from their evaluation efforts.

CONCLUSION

Healthcare educators have been evaluating programs for years. However, executives are now expecting more accountability in showing the value and results of medical education programs in the academic and healthcare provider environments (Buzachero et al., 2013). Healthcare educators must also have a way to show the value of using learning or workplace performance like simulation, virtual reality, augmented reality, and other emerging technologies (J. J. Phillips & Phillips, 2018). The ROI Methodology, briefly described in this chapter, provides healthcare professionals with a comprehensive, scalable evaluation system they can use with any program, project, or initiative. Using this methodology can answer the value-added questions about the impact and ROI of medical education program that stakeholders are asking more frequently.

REFERENCES

Aaron, B. C. (2005). *Use the chain of impact to leverage data and demonstrate roi.* Paper presented at the International Conference and Exposition of ASTD, Orlando, FL.

Armstrong, J. S. (2001). Principles of forecasting: A handbook for researchers and practitioners (J. S. Armstrong Ed.). New York: Springer Science+Business Media.

Bledsoe, M. D. (1999). *Correlations in kirkpatrick's training evaluation model* (9937553 Ed.D.). University of Cincinnati. Retrieved from https://search.proquest.com/docview/304510117?accountid=36783

Brinkerhoff, R. O. (2006). Using evaluation to measure and improve the effectiveness of human performance technology initiatives. In J. A. Pershing (Ed.), *Handbook of human performance technology: Principles, practices, and potential* (3rd ed., pp. 287–311). Pfeiffer.

Buzachero, V. V., Phillips, J. J., Phillips, P. P., & Phillips, Z. L. (2013). *Measuring roi in healthcare: Tools and techniques to measure the impact and roi in healthcare improvement projects and programs.* McGraw Hill Education.

Combs, W. L., & Falletta, S. V. (2000). *The targeted evaluation process.* American Society for Training & Development.

Elkeles, T., Phillips, P. P., & Phillips, J. J. (2014). *Measuring the success of learning through technology.* ASTD Press.

Hastings, N. B. (2010). Integrated evaluation: Improving performance improvement. In J. L. Moseley & J. C. Dessinger (Eds.), *Handbook of improving performance in the workplace: Measurement and evaluation* (pp. 240–255). Pfeiffer.

Kellogg Foundation. (2004). *W.K. Kellogg foundation logic model development guide*. Retrieved from https://www.wkkf.org/resource-directory/resource/2006/02/wk-kellogg-foundation-logic-model-development-guide

Mootee, I. (2013). *Design thinking for strategic innovation*. Wiley.

Phillips, J. J. (1997). *Handbook of training evaluation and measurement methods* (3rd ed.). Gulf Publishing Company.

Phillips, J. J., & Aaron, B. C. (2008). *Isolation of results: Defining the impact of the program* (Vol. 3). Pfeiffer.

Phillips, J. J., & Phillips, P. P. (2009). *Measuring for success: What ceos really think about learning interventions*. ASTD Press.

Phillips, J. J., & Phillips, P. P. (2012). An introduction to return on investment. In R. A. Reiser & J. V. Dempsey (Eds.), *Trends and issues in instructional design and technology* (3rd ed., pp. 105–115). Pearson.

Phillips, J. J., & Phillips, P. P. (2018). *The value of innovation: Knowing, proving, and showing the value of innovation and creativity*. John Wiley & Sons. doi:10.1002/9781119242413

Phillips, P. P. (2017). The bottomline on roi (3rd ed.). King of Prussia, PA: HRDQ.

Phillips, P. P., & Phillips, J. J. (2007). *The value of learning: How organizations capture value and roi and translate it into support, improvement, and funds* (1st ed.). Pfeiffer.

Phillips, P. P., & Phillips, J. J. (2017). *The business case for learning: Using design thinking to deliver business results and increase the investment in talent development*. HRDQ and ATD Press.

Phillips, P. P., & Phillips, J. J. (2019). *Roi basics* (2nd ed.). ATD Press and ROI Institute.

Phillips, P. P., Phillips, J. J., Paone, G., & Gaudet, C. H. (2019). *Value for money: How to show the value for all types of projects and programs in government, nongovernmental organizations, nonprofits, and business*. Scrivener Publishing. doi:10.1002/9781119322764

Robinson, D. G., Robinson, J. C., Phillips, J. J., Phillips, P. P., & Handshaw, D. (2015). *Performance consulting: A strategic process to improve, measure, and sustain organizational results* (3rd ed.). Barrett-Kohler.

Roulstone, D. B., & Phillips, J. J. (2008). *Roi in technology*. Butterworth-Heinemann.

Russ-Eft, D., & Preskill, H. (2001). *Evaluation in organizations: A systematice approach to enhancing learning, performance, and change*. Perseus.

Sinek, S. (2009). *Start with why: How great leaders inspire everyone to take action*. Penguin Group.

Wang, G. G., Dou, Z., & Li, N. (2002). A systems approach to measuring return on investment for hrd interventions. *Human Resource Development Quarterly*, *13*(2), 203–224. doi:10.1002/hrdq.1024

ADDITIONAL READING

Brock, T. R., & Holtschneider, M. (2016). Simulation operation, curriculum integration, and performance improvement. In L. T. Gantt & H. M. Young (Eds.), *Healthcare simulation: A guide for operations specialists* (pp. 56–77). Wiley & Sons, Inc. doi:10.1002/9781118949443.ch7

Gilbert, T. F. (1996). Human competence: Engineering worthy performance (Tribute ed.). Silver Spring, MD: International Society for Performance Improvement.

Guerra-Lopez, I. J. (2008). *Performance evaluation: Proven approaches for improving program and organizational performance*. Jossey-Bass.

Hale, J. (2012). *Performance-based evaluation: Tools and techniques to measure the impact of training*. Pfeiffer.

Kaufman, R., & Guerra-Lopez, I. (2013). *Needs assessment for organizational success*. American Society for Training and Development.

Phillips, J. J., & Aaron, B. C. (2008). *Isolation of results: Defining the impact of the program* (Vol. 3). Pfeiffer.

Phillips, J. J., & Phillips, P. P. (2007). *Show me the money: How to determine the roi in people, projects, and programs*. Berrett-Koehler, Inc.

Swanson, R. A. (2007). *Analysis for improving performance: Tools for diagnosing organizations and documenting workplace expertise* (2nd ed.). Barrett-Koehler.

Van Tiem, D. M., Moseley, J. L., & Dessinger, J. C. (2012). *Fundamentals of performance improvement: Optimizing results through people, process, and organizations* (3rd ed.). Pfeiffer.

KEY TERMS AND DEFINITIONS

Assessment: Defines the needs that justify funding a medical education program. A need is a gap between as-is and should-be results. An assessment also prioritizes those gaps based on their consequences and costs to the organization. An assessment differs from an analysis, which determines the causes of the gaps and identifies feasible solutions to address the identified program needs.

Evaluation: There are three evaluation phases. A formative evaluation occurs during the design and development of an intervention where the focus is to improve its input-process-output before it is implemented. A summative evaluation occurs during the intervention to determine how well the program did to close the immediate reaction, learning, and application gaps defined by program objectives for each of these program evaluation levels. A confirmative evaluation occurs after the intervention to determine how well the program did to close the lagging impact results gap and achieve the desired ROI efficiency objective. This last evaluation phase also recommends improvements to the program evaluated so decision-makers can act to address program shortcomings and improve program processes.

Evaluation Chain of Impact: A logic model that reflects how success or failure to address a need at a lower evaluation level affects the success or failure of the remaining evaluation levels to achieve program objectives. The evaluation chain of impact tells the complete story of the medical education programs success and shortcomings to achieve needs-driven program objectives.

Evaluation Guiding Principles: Provide guidance to ensure consistency in decisions made at each step of the process model to protect the credibility of evaluation results with all stakeholders and to allow a credible comparison between different evaluation studies.

Evaluation Levels: Categories of data that reflect both quantitative and qualitative, as well as financial and non-financial, measures that are collected at different times to make evidence-based decisions about the effectiveness and efficiencies of the medical education program.

Evaluation Impact Isolation: Provides evidence that allows the medical education program to take credit for impact measure improvements and to give credit elsewhere, where appropriate, since other variables can improve the same impact measures. Without isolation, an evaluation study is not valid when reporting the program's impact results.

Return on Investment: A financial metric that compares the monetary benefits of an investment against the program costs of the investment. It is considered the ultimate economic measure of program success used by executives and senior leaders to determine the value of a program, project, or initiative.

ROI Institute: Founded in 1992 to help organizations evaluate the success of projects and programs, including measuring the financial return on investment (ROI). ROI Institute provides workshops, consulting, coaching, hosting briefings and presentations, researching, and benchmarking. It operates through a network of partners and associates in the U.S. and in over 70 countries with the help of over 100 ROI consultants.

ROI Methodology® Process Model: A comprehensive measurement and evaluation process that generates six types of measures—reaction and planned action, learning, application and implementation, impact, return on investment, and intangibles. It is a balanced measurement approach that includes a step to isolate the effects of a program, project, or solution.

Compilation of References

Aaron, B. C. (2005). *Use the chain of impact to leverage data and demonstrate roi*. Paper presented at the International Conference and Exposition of ASTD, Orlando, FL.

Aaron, M., & Levenberg, P. (2014). The Millennials in Medicine: Tips for Teaching the Next Generation of Physicians. *Journal of Academic Ophthalmology*, *07*(01).

Accreditation Council for Pharmacy Education. (2015). *Accreditation Standards and Key Elements for the Professional Program in Pharmacy Leading to the Doctor of Pharmacy Degree ("Standards 2016")*. Retrieved from https://www.acpe-accredit.org/pdf/Standards2016FINAL.pdf

Ackerman, S. J., & Hilsenroth, M. J. (2001). A review of therapist characteristics and techniques negatively impacting the therapeutic alliance. *Psychotherapy (Chicago, Ill.)*, *38*(2), 171–185. doi:10.1037/0033-3204.38.2.171

Ackerman, S. J., & Hilsenroth, M. J. (2003). A review of therapist characteristics and techniques positively impacting the therapeutic alliance. *Clinical Psychology Review*, *23*(1), 1–33. doi:10.1016/S0272-7358(02)00146-0 PMID:12559992

Aggarwal, R., Ward, J., Balasundaram, I., Sains, P., Athanasiou, T., & Darzi, A. (2007). Proving the effectiveness of virtual reality simulation for training in laparoscopic surgery. *Annals of Surgery*, *246*(5), 771–779. doi:10.1097/SLA.0b013e3180f61b09 PMID:17968168

Aïm, F., Lonjon, G., Hannouche, D., & Nizard, R. (2016). Effectiveness of virtual reality training in orthopaedic surgery. *Arthroscopy*, *32*(1), 224–232. doi:10.1016/j.arthro.2015.07.023 PMID:26412672

Al Wahbi, A. (2014). The need for faculty training programs in effective feedback provision. *Advances in Medical Education and Practice*, *5*, 263–268. doi:10.2147/AMEP.S62889 PMID:25170287

Alaker, M., Wynn, G. R., & Arulampalam, T. (2016). Virtual reality training in laparoscopic surgery: A systematic review & meta-analysis. *International Journal of Surgery*, *29*, 85–94. doi:10.1016/j.ijsu.2016.03.034 PMID:26992652

American Medical Association. (2016). *AMA principles of medical ethics*. Retrieved October 1, 2019, from https://www.ama-assn.org/delivering-care/ama-principles-medical-ethics

American Psychological Association. (2014). *Guidelines for Clinical Supervision in Health Service Psychology*. Retrieved from http://apa.org/about/policy/guidelines- supervision.pdf

American Psychological Association. (2017). *Multicultural Guidelines: An Ecological Approach to Context, Identity, and Intersectionality*. Retrieved from http://www.apa.org/about/ policy/ multicultural-guidelines.pdf

Andersen, C., Winding, T. N., & Vesterby, M. S. (2010). Development of simulated arthroscopic skills. *Journal Acta Orthopaedica*, *82*(1), 90–95. doi:10.3109/17453674.2011.552776 PMID:21281257

Andersen, E. (2016). Enhancing the clinical reflective capacities of nursing students. *Nurse Education in Practice*, *19*, 31–35. doi:10.1016/j.nepr.2016.04.004 PMID:27428689

Andersen, S. A. W., Foghsgaard, S., Cayé-Thomasen, P., & Sørensen, M. S. (2018). The effect of a distributed virtual reality simulation training program on dissection mastoidectomy performance. *Otology & Neurotology*, *39*(10), 1277–1284. doi:10.1097/MAO.0000000000002031 PMID:30303946

Anderson, S. A. W., Mikkelsen, P. T., Konge, L., Cayé-Thomasen, P., & Sørensen, M. S. (2016). Cognitive load in mastoidectomy skills training: Virtual reality simulation and traditional dissection compared. *Journal of Surgical Education*, *73*(1), 45–50. doi:10.1016/j.jsurg.2015.09.010 PMID:26481267

Anderson, T., Rourke, L., Garrison, D. R., & Archer, W. (2001). Assessing Teaching presence in a Computer Conference Environment. *Journal of Asynchronous Learning Networks*, *5*(2), 1–17.

Ariza-Heredia, E. J., & Chemaly, R. F. (2018). Update on infection control practices in cancer hospitals. *CA: a Cancer Journal for Clinicians*, *68*(5), 340–355. doi:10.3322/caac.21462 PMID:29985544

Armbruster, B. B. (2000). Taking notes from lectures. In Handbook of college reading and study strategy research (pp. 175–200). Lawrence Erlbaum Associates.

Armstrong, J. S. (2001). Principles of forecasting: A handbook for researchers and practitioners (J. S. Armstrong Ed.). New York: Springer Science+Business Media.

Ashford, S. J., & Cummings, L. L. (1983). Feedback as an individual resource: Personal strategies of creating information. *Organizational Behavior and Human Performance*, *32*(3), 370–398. doi:10.1016/0030-5073(83)90156-3

Association for Educational Communications and Technology. (2013). Definition. In A. Januszewski & M. Molenda (Eds.), *Educational Technology: A Definition with Commentary* (pp. 1–14). Routledge. doi:10.4324/9780203054000

Atkinson, R. C., & Shiffrin, R. M. (1968). Human memory: A proposed system and its control processes. In K. W. Spence & J. T. Spence (Eds.), *The psychology of learning and motivation: II*. Academic Press. doi:10.1016/S0079-7421(08)60422-3

Austermann Hula, S. N., Robin, D. A., Maas, E., Ballard, K. J., & Schmidt, R. A. (2008). Effects of feedback frequency and timing on acquisition, retention, and transfer of speech skills in acquired apraxia of speech. Journal of Speech, Language & Hearing Research, 51(5), 1088-1113.

Ausubel, D. P. (1963). *The psychology of meaningful verbal learning*. Grune & Stratton.

Baker, J. P., Goodboy, A. K., Bowman, N. D., & Wright, A. A. (2018). Does teaching with PowerPoint increase students' learning? A meta-analysis. *Computers & Education, 126*(August), 376–387. doi:10.1016/j.compedu.2018.08.003

Bandura, A. (1977). *Social learning theory*. Prentice-Hall.

Bandura, A. (1986). *Social foundations of thought and action: A social cognitive theory*. Prentice-Hall.

Bandura, A., Ross, D., & Ross, S. A. (1963). Vicarious reinforcement and immitative learning. *Journal of Abnormal and Social Psychology, 67*(6), 601–607. doi:10.1037/h0045550 PMID:14084769

Barnett, J. E., Erickson Cornish, J. A., Goodyear, R. K., & Lichtenberg, J. W. (2007). Commentaries on the ethical and effective practice of clinical supervision. *Professional Psychology, Research and Practice, 38*(3), 268–275. doi:10.1037/0735-7028.38.3.268

Baron, A. E., & Orwig, G. W. (1995). *Multimedia technologies for training. Englewood.* Libraries Unlimited.

Barrouillet, P., Bernardin, S., Portrat, S., Vergauwe, E., & Camos, V. (2007). Time and cognitive load in working memory. *Journal of Experimental Psychology. Learning, Memory, and Cognition, 33*(3), 570–585. doi:10.1037/0278-7393.33.3.570 PMID:17470006

Beach, M. C., & Inui, T. (2006). Relationship-centered care: A constructive reframing. *Journal of General Internal Medicine, 21*(S1), S3–S8. doi:10.1111/j.1525-1497.2006.00302.x PMID:16405707

Beresin, E. V., Milligan, T. A., Balon, R., Coverdal, J. H., Louie, A. K., & Roberts, L. W. (2016). Physician Wellbeing: A Critical Deficiency in Resilience Education and Training. [PubMed]. *Academic Psychiatry, 40*, 9. doi:10.100740596-015-0475-x

Birkhäuer, J., Gaab, J., Kossowsky, J., Hasler, S., Krummenacher, P., Werner, C., & Gerger, H. (2017). Trust in the health care professional and health outcome: A meta-analysis. *PLoS One, 12*(2), e0170988. doi:10.1371/journal.pone.0170988 PMID:28170443

Bleakley, A. (2015). *Medical Humanities and Medical Education: How the medical humanities can shape better doctors*. Routledge. doi:10.4324/9781315771724

Bledsoe, M. D. (1999). *Correlations in kirkpatrick's training evaluation model* (9937553 Ed.D.). University of Cincinnati. Retrieved from https://search.proquest.com/docview/304510117?accountid=36783

Bligh, D. A. (2000). *What's the use of lectures?* (1st ed.). Intellect Books.

Bloom, B. S., Engelhart, M. D., Furst, E. J., Hill, W. H., & Krathwohl, D. R. (1956). *Taxonomy of educational objectives: The classification of educational goals*. Longmans.

Bordin, E. S. (1979). The generalizability of the psychoanalytic concept of the working alliance. *Psychotherapy (Chicago, Ill.)*, *16*(3), 252–260. doi:10.1037/h0085885

Bordin, E. S. (1983). A working alliance based model of supervision. *The Counseling Psychologist*, *11*(1), 35–42. doi:10.1177/0011000083111007

Borges, N. J., Manuel, R. S., Elam, C. L., & Jones, B. J. (2006). Comparing Millennial and generation X medical students at one medical school. *Academic Medicine*, *81*(6), 571–576. doi:10.1097/01.ACM.0000225222.38078.47 PMID:16728812

Bouton, M. E. (1994). Context, ambiguity, and classical conditioning. *Current Directions in Psychological Science*, *3*(2), 49–53. doi:10.1111/1467-8721.ep10769943

Boysen, P. G. (2013). Just culture: A foundation for balanced accountability and patient safety. *The Ochsner Journal*, *13*(3), 400–406. PMID:24052772

Brinkerhoff, R. O. (2006). Using evaluation to measure and improve the effectiveness of human performance technology initiatives. In J. A. Pershing (Ed.), *Handbook of human performance technology: Principles, practices, and potential* (3rd ed., pp. 287–311). Pfeiffer.

Bunney, H. S., & Dale, B. G. (1997). The implementation of quality management tools and techniques: A study. *The TQM Magazine*, *9*(3), 183–189. doi:10.1108/09544789710168966

Butler, A. C., Karpicke, J. D., & Roediger, H. L. III. (2007). The Effect of Type and Timing of Feedback on Learning from Multiple-Choice Tests. *Journal of Experimental Psychology. Applied*, *13*(4), 273–281. doi:10.1037/1076-898X.13.4.273 PMID:18194050

Buzachero, V. V., Phillips, J. J., Phillips, P. P., & Phillips, Z. L. (2013). *Measuring roi in healthcare: Tools and techniques to measure the impact and roi in healthcare improvement projects and programs*. McGraw Hill Education.

Cabrera, D., & Cabrera, L. (2015). *Systems thinking made simple: New hope for solving wicked problems*. Odyssean Press.

Caniza, M. A., Maron, G., McCullers, J., Clara, W. A., Cedillos, R., Dueñas, L., Arnold, S., Williams, B. F., & Tuomanen, E. I. (2007). Planning and implementation of an infection control training program for healthcare providers in Latin America. *Infection Control and Hospital Epidemiology*, *28*(12), 1328–1333. doi:10.1086/521655 PMID:17994511

Caniza, M. A., Odio, C., Mukkada, S., Gonzalez, M., Ceppi, F., Chaisavaneeyakorn, S., Nopporn Apiwattanakul, N., Howard, S. C., Conter, V., & Bonilla, M. (2015). Infectious complications in children with acute lymphoblastic leukemia treated in low-middle-income countries. *Expert Review of Hematology*, *8*(5), 627–645. doi:10.1586/17474086.2015.1071186 PMID:26211675

Cant, R. P., & Cooper, S. J. (2011). The benefits of debriefing as formative feedback in nurse education. *The Australian Journal of Advanced Nursing*, *29*(1), 37–47.

Cates, C. U., Lönn, L., & Gallagher, A. G. (2016). Prospective, randomised and blinded comparison of proficiency-based progression full-physics virtual reality simulator training versus invasive vascular experience for learning carotid artery angiography by very experienced operators. *BMJ Simulation and Technology Enhanced Learning*, *2*(1), 1–5. doi:10.1136/bmjstel-2015-000090

Center for Disease Control. (2020). *Infection prevention and control*. https://www.who.int/infection-prevention/publications/hh_evidence/en/

Chao, C. J., Wu, S. Y., Yau, Y. J., Feng, W. Y., & Tseng, F. Y. (2017). Effects of three-dimensional virtual reality and traditional training methods on mental workload and training performance. *Human Factors and Ergonomics in Manufacturing*, *27*(4), 187–196. doi:10.1002/hfm.20702

Charon, R. (2001). Narrative medicine: A model for empathy, reflection, profession, and trust. *Journal of the American Medical Association*, *286*(15), 1897–1902. doi:10.1001/jama.286.15.1897 PMID:11597295

Chipidza, F. E., Wallwork, R. S., & Stern, T. A. (2015). Impact of the doctor-patient relationship. *The Primary Care Companion for CNS Disorders*, *17*. Advance online publication. doi:10.4088/PCC.15f01840 PMID:26835164

Chomeya, R. (2010). Quality of psychology test between Likert scale 5 and 6 points. *Journal of Social Sciences*, *6*(3), 399–403. doi:10.3844/jssp.2010.399.403

Christenberry, T. C., Training, C., & Vidali, C. A. (2003). *Continuous Learning Environments*. Academic Press.

Clark, R. C. (2008). *Building expertise: Cognitive methods for training and performance improvement* (3rd ed.). Pfieffer.

Cliffe, T., Beinart, H., & Cooper, M. (2016). Development and validation of a short version of the supervisory relationship questionnaire. *Clinical Psychology & Psychotherapy*, *23*(1), 77–86. doi:10.1002/cpp.1935 PMID:25504780

Cohen, E. D. (2010). *Critical thinking*. Rowman & Littlefield.

Cohen, S. A. (1987). Instructional alignment: Searching for the magic bullet. *Educational Researcher*, *16*(8), 16–20. doi:10.3102/0013189X016008016

Combs, W. L., & Falletta, S. V. (2000). *The targeted evaluation process*. American Society for Training & Development.

CompuGroup Medical, Inc. (2019). *CGM webEHR*. CompuGroup Medical.

Concannon, B. J., Esmail, S., & Roduta Roberts, M. (2019). Head-Mounted Display Virtual Reality in Post-secondary Education and Skill Training. *Frontiers in Education*, *4*(August), 1–23. doi:10.3389/feduc.2019.00080

Constantino, M. J., Castonguay, L. G., & Schut, A. J. (2002). The working alliance: A flagship for the "scientist-practitioner" model in psychotherapy. In G. S. Tryon (Ed.), *Counseling based on process research: Applying what we know* (pp. 81–131). Allyn and Bacon.

Constantino, M. J., Morrison, N. R., MacEwan, G., & Boswell, J. F. (2013). Therapeutic alliance researchers' perspectives on alliance-centered training practices. *Journal of Psychotherapy Integration*, *23*(3), 284–289. doi:10.1037/a0032357

Creswell, J. W., & Creswell, J. D. (2017). *Research design: Qualitative, quantitative, and mixed methods approaches*. Academic Press.

Crits-Christoph, P., Gibbons, M. B. C., Crits-Christoph, K., Narducci, J., Schamberger, M., & Gallop, R. (2006). Can therapists be trained to improve their alliances? A preliminary study of alliance-fostering psychotherapy. *Psychotherapy Research*, *16*, 268-281. doi:500268557 doi:10.1080/10503300

Crits-Christoph, P., Crits-Christoph, K., & Gibbons, M. B. C. (2010). Training in alliance-fostering techniques. In J. C. Muran & J. P. Barber (Eds.), *The therapeutic alliance: An evidence-based guide to practice* (pp. 304–319). Guilford Press.

Daugherty, K. K. (2006). Backward course design: Making the end the beginning. *American Journal of Pharmaceutical Education*, *70*(6), 135. doi:10.5688/aj7006135 PMID:17332861

Davies, E. (1995). Reflective practice: A focus for caring. *The Journal of Nursing Education*, *34*(4), 167–174. PMID:7782884

Del Re, A. C., Flückiger, C., Horvath, A. O., Symonds, D., & Wampold, B. E. (2012). Therapist effects in the therapeutic alliance-outcome relationship: A restricted-maximum likelihood meta-analysis. *Clinical Psychology Review*, *32*(7), 642–649. doi:10.1016/j.cpr.2012.07.002 PMID:22922705

Dick, W., Carey, L., & Carey, J. O. (2015). *The systematic design of instruction*. Pearson.

Dobbelaer, M. J., Prins, F. J., & van Dongen, D. (2013). The impact of feedback training for inspectors. *European Journal of Training and Development*, *37*(1), 86–104. doi:10.1108/03090591311293301

Dobbie, A., Rhodes, M., Tysinger, J. W., & Freeman, J. (2004). Using a modified nominal group technique as a curriculum evaluation tool. *Family Medicine*, *36*(6), 402–406. PMID:15181551

Dorr Goold, S., & Lipkin, M. (1999). The doctor-patient relationship: Challenges, opportunities, and strategies. *Journal of General Internal Medicine*, *14*(S1), S26–S33. doi:10.1046/j.1525-1497.1999.00267.x PMID:9933492

Driscoll, M. P. (2005). *Psychology of learning for instruction* (3rd ed.). Pearson Education, Inc.

Dunbar, A., Tai, E., Nielsen, D. B., Shropshire, S., & Richardson, L. C. (2014). Preventing infections during cancer treatment. *Clinical Journal of Oncology Nursing*, *18*(4), 426–431. doi:10.1188/14.CJON.426-431 PMID:25095295

Dunlosky, J., Rawson, K. A., Marsh, E. J., Nathan, M. J., & Willingham, D. T. (2013). Improving students' learning with effective learning techniques: Promising directions. *Psychology Science in the Public Health Interest*, *14*(1), 4–58. doi:10.1177/1529100612453266 PMID:26173288

Eckleberry-Hunt, J., & Tucciarone, J. (2011). The Challenges and Opportunities of Teaching "Generation Y.". *Journal of Graduate Medical Education*, *3*(4), 458–461. doi:10.4300/JGME-03-04-15 PMID:23205190

Eckstrand, K. L., Eliason, J., St. Cloud, T., & Potter, J. (2016). The priority of intersectionality in academic medicine. *Academic Medicine*, *91*, 904–907. doi:10.1097/ACM.0000000000001231 PMID:27166867

Ekstrand, C., Jamal, A., Nguyen, R., Kudryk, A., Mann, J., & Mendez, I. (2018). Immersive and interactive virtual reality to improve learning and retention of neuroanatomy in medical students: A randomized controlled study. *CMAJ Open*, *6*(1), E103–E109. doi:10.9778/cmajo.20170110 PMID:29510979

Elkeles, T., Phillips, P. P., & Phillips, J. J. (2014). *Measuring the success of learning through technology*. ASTD Press.

Elvins, R., & Green, J. (2008). The conceptualization and measurement of therapeutic alliance: An empirical review. *Clinical Psychology Review*, *28*(7), 1167–1187. doi:10.1016/j.cpr.2008.04.002 PMID:18538907

Emory, J. (2014). Understanding backward design to strengthen curricular models. *Nurse Educator*, *39*(3), 122–125. doi:10.1097/NNE.0000000000000034 PMID:24743175

Ertmer, P. A., York, C. S., & Gedik, N. (2009). Learning from the Pros: How experienced designers translate instructional design models into practice. *Educational Technology*, *49*(1), 19–27.

Eubanks-Carter, C., Muran, J. C., & Safran, J. D. (2015). Alliance-focused training. *Psychotherapy (Chicago, Ill.)*, *52*(2), 169–173. doi:10.1037/a0037596 PMID:25150677

Evans, K. H., Ozdalga, E., & Ahuja, N. (2016). The Medical Education of Generation Y. *Academic Psychiatry*, *40*(382), 382–385. doi:10.100740596-015-0399-5 PMID:26283527

Evans, R. (2001). *The human side of school change: reform, resistance, and the real-life problems of school change*. Jossey-Bass.

Eveleigh, R. M., Muskens, E., van Ravesteijn, H., van Dijk, I., van Rijswijk, E., & Lucassen, P. (2012). An overview of 19 instruments assessing the doctor-patient relationship: Different model or concepts are used. *Journal of Clinical Epidemiology*, *65*(1), 10–15. doi:10.1016/j.jclinepi.2011.05.011 PMID:22118265

ExamSoft Worldwide, Inc. (2019). *ExamSoft* [assessment software]. Available from https://www.examsoft.com

Feldon, D. F. (2007). Cognitive load and classroom teaching: The double-edged sword of automaticity. *Educational Psychologist*, *42*(3), 123–137. doi:10.1080/00461520701416173

Fiorella, L., & Mayer, R. E. (2015). Introduction to learning as a generative activity. In *Learning as a generative activity: Eight learning strategies that promote understanding* (pp. 1–19). Cambridge University Press. doi:10.1017/CBO9781107707085.003

Fiorella, L., & Mayer, R. E. (2016). Eight ways to promote generative learning. *Educational Psychology Review*, *28*(4), 717–741. doi:10.100710648-015-9348-9

Fiorella, L., Van Gog, T., Hoogerheide, V., & Mayer, R. E. (2017). It's all a matter of perspective: Viewing first-person video modeling examples promotes learning of an assembly task. *Journal of Educational Psychology*, *109*(5), 653–665. doi:10.1037/edu0000161

Florez-Arango, J. F., Iyengar, M. S., Dunn, K., & Zhang, J. (2011). Performance factors of mobile rich media job aids for community health workers. *Journal of the American Medical Informatics Association*, *18*(2), 131–137. doi:10.1136/jamia.2010.010025 PMID:21292702

Flückiger, C., Del Re, A. C., Wampold, B. E., & Horvath, A. O. (2018). The alliance in adult psychotherapy: A meta-analytic synthesis. *Psychotherapy (Chicago, Ill.)*, *55*(4), 316–340. Advance online publication. doi:10.1037/pst0000172 PMID:29792475

Ford, C. R., Garza, K., Kavookjian, J., & Kleppinger, E. L. (2019). Assessing student pharmacist communication skills: Development and implementation of a communication rubric. *Currents in Pharmacy Teaching & Learning*, *11*(11), 1123–1131. doi:10.1016/j.cptl.2019.07.018 PMID:31783958

Fowler, C. (2015). Virtual reality and learning: Where is the pedagogy? *British Journal of Educational Technology*, *46*(2), 412–422. doi:10.1111/bjet.12135

Frehywot, S., Mullan, F., Payne, P. W., & Ross, H. (2010). Compulsory service programmes for recruiting health workers in remote and rural areas: Do they work? *Bulletin of the World Health Organization*, *88*(5), 364–370. doi:10.2471/BLT.09.071605 PMID:20461136

French, J. C., Colbert, C. Y., Pien, L. C., Dannefer, E. F., & Taylor, C. A. (2015). Targeted feedback in the milestones era: Utilization of the ask-tell-ask feedback model to promote reflection and self-assessment. *Journal of Surgical Education*, *72*(6), e274–e279. doi:10.1016/j.jsurg.2015.05.016 PMID:26123726

Frey, N., Fisher, D., & Hattie, J. (2018). Developing "assessment capable" learners. *Educational Leadership*, *75*(5), 46–51.

Friedlander, M. L. (2015). Use of relational strategies to repair alliance ruptures: How responsive supervisors train responsive psychotherapists. *Psychotherapy (Chicago, Ill.)*, *52*(2), 174–179. doi:10.1037/a0037044 PMID:25111380

Fuertes, J. N., Mislowack, A., Bennett, J., Paul, L., Gilbert, T. C., Fontan, G., & Boylan, L. S. (2007). The physician-patient working alliance. *Patient Education and Counseling*, *66*(1), 29–36. doi:10.1016/j.pec.2006.09.013 PMID:17188453

Fuertes, J. N., Stracuzzi, T. I., Bennett, J., Scheinholtz, J., Mislowack, A., Hersh, M., & Cheng, D. (2006). Therapist multicultural competency: A study of therapy dyads. *Psychotherapy (Chicago, Ill.)*, *43*(4), 480–490. doi:10.1037/0033-3204.43.4.480 PMID:22122138

Fuertes, J. N., Toporovsky, A., Reyes, M., & Osborne, J. B. (2017). The physician-patient working alliance: Theory, research, and future possibilities. *Patient Education and Counseling*, *100*(4), 610–615. doi:10.1016/j.pec.2016.10.018 PMID:27773600

Gagne, E. D. (1985). *The cognitive psychology of school learning*. Little, Brown.

Gagné, R. M. (1984). Learning outcomes and their effects: Useful categories of human performance. *The American Psychologist*, *39*(4), 377–385. doi:10.1037/0003-066X.39.4.377

Gagne, R. M. (1985). *The conditions of learning and theory of instruction* (4th ed.). Holt, Rinehart & Winston.

Garrison, D. R., Anderson, T., & Archer, W. (2000). Critical inquiry in a text-based environment: Computer conferencing in higher education. *The Internet and Higher Education*, *2*(2-3), 87–105. doi:10.1016/S1096-7516(00)00016-6

Gilbert, T. F. (1978). *Engineering worthy performance*. Academic Press.

Gilbert, T. F. (2007). *Human competence: Engienering worthy performance*. Pfeiffer.

Gilbert, T. F. (2013). *Human competence: Engineering worthy performance*. John Wiley & Sons.

Gooding, H. C., Quinn, M., Martin, B., Charrow, A., & Katz, J. T. (2016). Fostering Humanism in Medicine through Art and Reflection. *Journal of Museum Education*, *41*(2), 123–130. doi:10.1080/10598650.2016.1169732

Gordon, C., & Beresin, E. V. (2016). The doctor-patient relationship. In T. A. Stern, M. Fava, T. E. Wilens, & J. F. Rosenbaum (Eds.), *Massachusetts General Hospital Comprehensive Clinical Psychiatry* (2nd ed., pp. 1–7). Elsevier.

Górski, F., Bun, P., Wichniarek, R., Zawadzki, P., & Hamrol, A. (2017). Effective design of educational virtual reality applications for medicine using knowledge-engineering techniques. *Eurasia Journal of Mathematics. Science and Technology Education*, *13*(2), 395–416. doi:10.12973/eurasia.2017.00623a

Gurusamy, K., Aggarwal, R., Palanivelu, L., & Davidson, B. R. (2008). Systematic review of randomized controlled trials on the effectiveness of virtual reality training for laproscopic surgery. *British Journal of Surgery*, *95*(9), 1088–1097. doi:10.1002/bjs.6344 PMID:18690637

Gustafson, K. L., & Branch, R. M. (2002). *Survey of instructional development models* (4th ed.). ERIC Clearinghouse on Information & Technology.

Gwee, M. C. E. (2009). Problem-Based Learning: A Strategic Learning System Design For The Education Of Healthcare Professionals in the 21ST Century. *The Kaohsiung Journal of Medical Sciences*, *25*(5), 231–239. doi:10.1016/S1607-551X(09)70067-1 PMID:19502143

Haggerty, G., & Hilsenroth, M. J. (2011). The use of video in psychotherapy supervision. *British Journal of Psychotherapy*, *27*(2), 193–210. doi:10.1111/j.1752-0118.2011.01232.x

Half, R. (2015). *Get ready for generation Z.* Retrieved from https://www.roberthalf.com/blog/the-future-of-work/get-ready-for-generation-z

Hannafin, M., McCarthy, J., Hannafin, K., & Radtke, P. (2001). Scaffolding performance in EPSSs: Bridging theory and practice. *EdMedia+ Innovate Learning*, 658-663.

Haque, S., & Srinivasan, S. (2006). A meta-analysis of the training effectiveness of virtual reality surgical simulators. *IEEE Transactions on Information Technology in Biomedicine*, *10*(1), 51–58. doi:10.1109/TITB.2005.855529 PMID:16445249

Harden, R. M. (1988). What is an OSCE? *Medical Teacher*, *10*(1), 19–22. doi:10.3109/01421598809019321 PMID:3221760

Harden, R. M. (2015). Misconceptions and the OSCE. *Medical Teacher*, *37*(7), 608–610. doi:10.3109/0142159X.2015.1042443 PMID:26075956

Harless, J. (1975). Front-end analysis. *Training (New York, N.Y.)*, *12*(3), 27–29.

Harless, J. (1978). Motivation and Front-End Analysis. *NSPI Journal*, *17*(6), 5–6. doi:10.1002/pfi.4180170606

Harun, M. H. (2001). Integrating e-learning into the workplace. *The Internet and Higher Education*, *4*(3-4), 301–310. doi:10.1016/S1096-7516(01)00073-2

Hastings, N. B. (2010). Integrated evaluation: Improving performance improvement. In J. L. Moseley & J. C. Dessinger (Eds.), *Handbook of improving performance in the workplace: Measurement and evaluation* (pp. 240–255). Pfeiffer.

Hatcher, R. L., & Gillaspy, J. A. (2006). Development and validation of a revised short version of the Working Alliance Inventory. *Psychotherapy Research*, *16*(1), 12–25. doi:10.1080/10503300500352500

Hawkins, S. C., Osborne, A., Schofield, S. J., Pournaras, D. J., & Chester, J. F. (2012). Improving the accuracy of self-assessment of practical clinical skills using video feedback - The importance of including benchmarks. *Medical Teacher*, *34*(4), 279–284. doi:10.3109/0142159X.2012.658897 PMID:22455696

Haynes, C. (2010). Generation Gaps in Medical Education: Implications for Teaching and Learning. In *AAMC Annual Meeting*. Michigan State University.

Hays, D. G., & Singh, A. A. (2011). *Qualitative inquiry in clinical and educational settings.* Academic Press.

Health and Rural Services Administration. (2019, January). Retrieved October 31, 2019, from https://data.hrsa.gov/tools/data-explorer

Hemayattalab, R., & Rostami, L. R. (2010). Effects of frequency of feedback on the learning of motor skill in individuals with cerebral palsy. *Research in Developmental Disabilities*, *31*(1), 212–217. doi:10.1016/j.ridd.2009.09.002 PMID:19864110

Hendricks, S. M., Wallace, L. S., Narwold, L., Guy, G., & Wallace, D. (2013). Comparing the Effectiveness, Practice Opportunities, and Satisfaction of the Preceptored Clinical and the Traditional Clinical for Nursing Students. *Nursing Education Perspectives*, *34*(5), 310–314. PMID:24245381

Hilsenroth, M. J., Ackerman, S. J., Clemence, A. J., Strassle, C. G., & Handler, L. (2002). Effects of structured clinician training on patient and therapist perspectives of alliance early in psychotherapy. *Psychotherapy (Chicago, Ill.)*, *39*(4), 309–323. doi:10.1037/0033-3204.39.4.309

Hopkins, L., Hampton, B. S., Abbott, J. F., Buery-Joyner, S. D., Craig, L. T. B., Dalrymple, J. L., Forstein, D. A., Graziano, S. C., McKenzie, M. L., Pradham, A., Wolf, A., & Page-Ramsey, S. M. (2018). To the point: Medical education, technology, and the Millennial learner. *American Journal of Obstetrics and Gynecology*, *218*(2), 188–192. doi:10.1016/j.ajog.2017.06.001 PMID:28599897

Horvath, A. O., Del Re, A., Flückiger, C., & Symonds, D. (2011). Alliance in individual psychotherapy. *Psychotherapy (Chicago, Ill.)*, *48*(1), 9–16. doi:10.1037/a0022186 PMID:21401269

Horvath, A. O., & Greenberg, L. S. (1989). Development and validation of the Working Alliance Inventory. *Journal of Counseling Psychology*, *36*(2), 223–233. doi:10.1037/0022-0167.36.2.223

Huggard, J. (2013). Debriefing: A valuable component of staff support. *International Journal of Palliative Nursing*, *19*(5), 212–214. doi:10.12968/ijpn.2013.19.5.212 PMID:23971303

Hull, C. L. (1952). *A behavior system: An introduction to behavior theory concerning the individual organism*. Yale University Press.

Humphreys, J., Wakerman, J., Kuipers, P., Russell, D., Siegloff, S., Homer, K., & Wells, R. (2017). *Improving workforce retention: Developing an integrated logic model to maximise sustainability of small rural and remote healthcare services*. Academic Press.

Humphreys, J. S., McGrail, M. R., Joyce, C. M., Scott, A., & Kalb, G. (2012). Who should receive recruitment and retention incentives? Improved targeting of rural doctors using medical workforce data. *The Australian Journal of Rural Health*, *20*(1), 3–10. doi:10.1111/j.1440-1584.2011.01252.x PMID:22250870

Iacoboni, M. (2009). Immitation, empathy, and mirror neurons. *Annual Review of Psychology*, *60*(1), 653–670. doi:10.1146/annurev.psych.60.110707.163604 PMID:18793090

Institute for Healthcare Improvement (IHI). (2018). *Institute for healthcare improvement: Quality improvement essentials toolkit-Flow Chart*. doi:10.4102/hts.v71i1.2874

Issa, N., Schuller, M., Santacaterina, S., Shapiro, M., Wang, E., Mayer, R. E., & DaRosa, D. A. (2011). Applying multimedia design principles enhances learning in medical education. *Medical Education, 45*(8), 818–826. doi:10.1111/j.1365-2923.2011.03988.x PMID:21752078

Izard, S. G., Juanes, J. A., García Peñalvo, F. J., Estella, J. M. G., Ledesma, M. J. S., & Ruisoto, P. (2018). Virtual reality as an educational and training tool for medicine. *Journal of Medical Systems, 42*(3), 1–5. doi:10.100710916-018-0900-2 PMID:29392522

Jafari, S. M., & Setak, M. (2010). Total Quality Management Tools and Techniques: the Quest for an Implementation Roadmap. *Proceedings of the AGBA 7th World Congress, 1*(3), 1–12. 10.1111/conl.12206

Janeve, R., Desy, J. R., Wolansky, J., & Reed, D. (2017). Milestones and Millennials: A Perfect Pairing—Competency-Based Medical Education and the Learning Preferences of Generation Y. *Mayo Clinic Proceedings*. PMID:28160874

Jensen, L., & Konradsen, F. (2018). A review of the use of virtual reality head-mounted displays in education and training. *Education and Information Technologies, 23*(4), 1515–1529. doi:10.100710639-017-9676-0

Johnson, L., Adams Becker, S., Cummins, M., Estrada, V., Freeman, A., & Hall, C. (2016). *NMC Horizon Report: 2016 Higher Education Edition*. The New Media Consortium.

Joint Commission of Pharmacy Practitioners. (2014). *Pharmacists' Patient Care Process*. Retrieved from: https://jcpp.net/wp-content/uploads/2016/03/PatientCareProcess-with-supporting-organizations.pdf

Jonassen, D. H. (2009). Reconciling a human cognitive architecture. In S. Tobias & T. M. Duffy (Eds.), *Constructivist instruction: Success or failure* (pp. 13–33). Roultedge.

Jonassen, D. H., Tessmer, M., & Hannum, W. H. (1999). *Task analysis methods for instructional design*. Lawrence Erlbaum Associates.

Jones, D. S. (2014). A Complete Medical Education Includes the Arts and Humanities. *AMA Journal of Ethics, 16*(8), 636–641. doi:10.1001/virtualmentor.2014.16.8.msoc1-1408 PMID:25140687

Joyner, B., & Young, L. (2006). Teaching medical students using role play: Twelve tips for successful role plays. *Medical Teacher, 28*(3), 225–229. doi:10.1080/01421590600711252 PMID:16753719

Kacmarek, R. M., Stoller, J. K., & Heuer, A. (2017). *Egan's fundamentals of respiratory care* (11th ed.). Elsevier Health Sciences.

Kamińska, D., Sapiński, T., Wiak, S., Tikk, T., Haamer, R. E., Avots, E., ... Anbarjafari, G. (2019). Virtual reality and its applications in education: Survey. *Information (Switzerland), 10*(10), 1–20. doi:10.3390/info10100318

Kay, R., MacDonald, T., & DiGiuseppe, M. (2019). A comparison of lecture-based, active, and flipped classroom teaching approaches in higher education. *Journal of Computing in Higher Education, 31*(3), 449–471. doi:10.100712528-018-9197-x

Kellogg Foundation. (2004). *W.K. Kellogg foundation logic model development guide*. Retrieved from https://www.wkkf.org/resource-directory/resource/2006/02/wk-kellogg-foundation-logic-model-development-guide

Kert, S. B., & Kurt, A. A. (2012). The effect of electronic performance support systems on self-regulated learning skills. *Interactive Learning Environments*, *20*(6), 485–500. doi:10.1080/10494820.2010.533683

Khatri, N., Brown, G. D., & Hicks, L. L. (2009). From a blame culture to a Just Culture in health care. *Health Care Management Review*, *34*(4), 312–322. doi:10.1097/HMR.0b013e3181a3b709 PMID:19858916

Kirkpatrick Partners. (2020). *The Kirkpatrick Model*. https://www.kirkpatrickpartners.com/Our-Philosophy/The-Kirkpatrick-Model

Kirschner, P. A., Sweller, J., Kirschner, F., & Zambrano, J. R. (2018). From cognitive load theory to collaborative cognitive load theory. *International Journal of Computer-Supported Collaborative Learning*, *13*(2), 213–233. doi:10.100711412-018-9277-y PMID:30996713

Kohn, L.T., Corrigan, J.M., Donaldson, M.S., McKay, T., & Pike, K.C. (2000). To err is human. *Building a Safer Health System.*

Koven, S. (2016). *As hospitals go digital, human stories get left behind.* https://www.statnews.com/2016/04/06/electronic-medical-records-patients/

Ladany, N., Ellis, M. V., & Friedlander, M. L. (1999). The supervisory working alliance, trainee self-efficacy, and satisfaction. *Journal of Counseling and Development*, *77*(4), 447–455. doi:10.1002/j.1556-6676.1999.tb02472.x

Lam, M., Lechner, B., Chow, R., Chiu, L., Chiu, N., Lam, H., Popovic, M., Milakovic, M., DeAngelis, C., Chow, E., & Henry, B. (2015). A review of medical humanities curriculum in medical schools. *Journal of Pain Management*, *8*, 289–298.

Lavoie, P., Pepin, J., & Boyer, L. (2013). Reflective debriefing to promote novice nurses' clinical judgment after high-fidelity clinical simulation: A pilot test. *Dynamics (Pembroke, Ont.)*, *24*(4), 36–41. PMID:24616950

Leahy, W., & Sweller, J. (2016). Cognitive load theory and the effects of transient information on the modality effect. *Instructional Science*, *44*(1), 107–123. doi:10.100711251-015-9362-9

Lee, H., Lim, K. Y., & Grabowski, B. L. (2008). Generative learning: Principles and implications for making meaning. In *Handbook of research on educational communications and technology* (3rd ed., pp. 111–124). Routledge. https://aect.org/third_edition.php

Leighton, C., & McCabe, C. (2002). Performance Support for Complex Problem-Solving Tasks. *USE for 2002 USE for 2002*, 11.

Le, T., & Bhushan, V. (2018). *First Aid for the USMLE Step 1*. McGraw Hill Professional.

Lincoln, A. (2016, June). *Lincoln's second inaugural address*. Champaign, IL: Boulder, CO: Project Gutenberg;

London, M., & Smither, J. W. (2002). Feedback orientation, feedback culture, and the longitudinal performance management process. *Human Resource Management Review*, *12*(1), 81–100. doi:10.1016/S1053-4822(01)00043-2

Lowe, G. (2012). How employee engagement matters for hospital performance. *Healthcare Quarterly*, *15*(2), 29–39. doi:10.12927/hcq.2012.22915 PMID:22688203

Lurie, N. H., & Swaminathan, J. M. (2009). Is timely information always better? The effect of feedback frequency on decision making. *Organizational Behavior and Human Decision Processes*, *108*(2), 315–329. doi:10.1016/j.obhdp.2008.05.005

Lyons, K., McLaughlin, J. E., Khanova, J., & Roth, M. T. (2017). Cognitive apprenticeship in health sciences education: A qualitative review. *Advances in Health Sciences Education: Theory and Practice*, *22*(3), 723–739. doi:10.100710459-016-9707-4 PMID:27544386

MacDowell, M., Glasser, M., Fitts, M., Nielsen, K., & Hunsaker, M. (2010). A national view of rural health workforce issues in the USA. *Rural and Remote Health*, *10*(3), 1531. PMID:20658893

Mamykina, L., Vawdrey, D.K., & Hripcsak, G. (n.d.). How Do Residents Spend Their Shift Time? A Time and Motion Study With a Particular Focus on the Use of Computers. Academic Medicine, 91(6), 827–832. PubMed doi:10.1097/ACM.0000000000001148

Mandal, S. (2013). Brief introduction of virtual reality & its challenges. *International Journal of Scientific & Engineering Research*, *4*(4), 304–309.

Mann, S. (2017). *Focusing on Arts, Humanities to Develop Well-Rounded Physicians*. Retrieved from https://www.aamc.org/news-insights/focusing-arts-humanities-develop-well-rounded-physicians

Maresky, H. S., Oikonomou, A., & Ali, I. (2018). *Virtual reality and cardiac anatomy: Exploring immersive three-dimensional cardiac imaging, a pilot study in undergraduate medical anatomy education*. Clin Anat N Y N. doi:10.1002/ca.23292

Marsh, E. J., & Sink, H. (2010). Access to handouts of presentation slides during lecture: Consequences for learning. *Applied Cognitive Psychology*, *24*(5), 691–706. doi:10.1002/acp.1579

Mason, M. (2010). *Critical thinking and learning*. Wiley.

Mayer, R. E. (2009). *Multimedia Learning*. Cambridge University Press. doi:10.1017/CBO9780511811678

Mayer, R. E. (2010). Applying the science of learning to medical education. *Medical Education*, *44*(6), 543–549. doi:10.1111/j.1365-2923.2010.03624.x PMID:20604850

Mayer, R. E., & Moreno, R. (2003). Nine ways to reduce cognitive load in multimedia learning. *Educational Psychologist*, *38*(1), 43–52. doi:10.1207/S15326985EP3801_6

Mazur, L. M., McCreery, J. K., & Chen, S. J. G. (2012). Quality improvement in hospitals: Identifying and understanding behaviors. *Journal of Healthcare Engineering*, *3*(4), 621–648. doi:10.1260/2040-2295.3.4.621

McDonough, S. L. K., Kleppinger, E. L., Donaldson, A. R., & Helms, K. L. (2015). Going "high stakes" with a pharmacy OSCE: Lessons learned. *Currents in Pharmacy Teaching & Learning*, *7*(1), 4–11. doi:10.1016/j.cptl.2014.09.017

McGrail, M. R., Humphreys, J. S., Joyce, C., Scott, A., & Kalb, G. (2011). Rural amenity and medical workforce shortage: Is there a relationship? *Geographical Research*, *49*(2), 192–202. doi:10.1111/j.1745-5871.2011.00690.x

McKeown, J., Clarke, A., & Repper, J. (2006, July). Life story work in health and social care: Systematic literature review. *Journal of Advanced Nursing*, *55*(2), 237–247. doi:10.1111/j.1365-2648.2006.03897.x PMID:16866815

Mead, N., & Bower, P. (2000). Patient-centredness: A conceptual framework and review of the empirical literature. *Social Science & Medicine*, *51*(7), 1087–1110. doi:10.1016/S0277-9536(00)00098-8 PMID:11005395

Meara, J. G., Leather, A. J. M., Hagander, L., Alkire, B. C., Alonso, N., Ameh, E. A., Bickler, S. W., Conteh, L., Dare, A. J., Davies, J., Mérisier, E. D., El-Halabi, S., Farmer, P. E., Gawande, A., Gillies, R., Greenberg, S. L. M., Grimes, C. E., Gruen, R. L., Ismail, E. A., ... Yip, W. (2015). Global Surgery 2030: Evidence and solutions for achieving health, welfare, and economic development. *Lancet*, *386*(9993), 569–624. doi:10.1016/S0140-6736(15)60160-X PMID:25924834

Mercer, S. W., Maxwell, M., Heaney, D., & Watt, G. C. (2004). The consultation and relational empathy (CARE) measure: Development and preliminary validation and reliability of an empathy-based consultation process measure. *Family Practice*, *21*(6), 699–705. doi:10.1093/fampra/cmh621 PMID:15528286

Merriënboer, J. J. G., Kirschner, P. A., & Kester, L. (2003). Taking the load off a learner's mind: Instructional design for complex learning. *Educational Psychologist*, *38*(1), 5–13. doi:10.1207/S15326985EP3801_2

Merriënboer, J. J. G., & Sweller, J. (2010). Cognitive load theory in health professional education: Design principles and strategies. *Medical Education*, *44*(1), 85–93. doi:10.1111/j.1365-2923.2009.03498.x PMID:20078759

Merrill, M. D. (2013). *First principles of instruction: Identifying and designing effective, efficient, and engaging instruction*. Pfeiffer.

Mertens, D. M., & Wilson, D. M. (2012). *Program evaluation theory and practice: A comprehensive guide*. The Guilford Press.

Mihal, S., Center, F. L. E. T., Glynco, G. A., & Kirkley, S. (2003). *Continuous Learning Environments*. Academic Press.

Miller, A., & Mills, B. (2019). 'If They Don't Care, I Don't Care': Millennial and Generation Z Students and the Impact of Faculty Caring. *The Journal of Scholarship of Teaching and Learning, 19*(4). Advance online publication. doi:10.14434/josotl.v19i4.24167

Mission of the Office of Academic Affiliations. (2019). Retrieved from https://www.va.gov/oaa/oaa_mission.asp

Mitchell, J. D., Holak, E. J., Tran, H. N., Muret-Wagstaff, S., Jones, S. B., & Brzezinski, M. (2013). Are we closing the gap in faculty development needs for feedback training? *Journal of Clinical Anesthesia, 25*(7), 560–564. doi:10.1016/j.jclinane.2013.05.005 PMID:24008192

Mock, C. N., Donkor, P., Gawande, A., Jamison, D. T., Kruk, M. E., & Debas, H. T. (2018). Essential surgery: Key messages from Disease Control Priorities. *Lancet, 391*(10125), e11–e14. doi:10.1016/S0140-6736(15)60091-5 PMID:25662416

Mootee, I. (2013). *Design thinking for strategic innovation*. Wiley.

Morrison, G. R., Ross, S. M., Kalman, H. K., & Kemp, J. E. (2013). *Designing effective instruction*. Wiley.

Mueller, J. (2016). *Authentic Assessment Toolbox*. http://jfmueller.faculty.noctrl.edu/toolbox/whatisit.htm

Mukherji, B.R., Neuwirth, L.S., & Limonic. (2017, Apr.). Making the case for real diversity: Redefining underrepresented minority students in public universities. *Sage Open,* 1-10.

Mulford, K. F. (1999). *A multimedia paradigm of engaged learning: An intergenerational approach.* Retrieved from https://www.semanticscholar.org/paper/A-multimedia-paradigm-of-engaged-learning%3A-An-Mulford/79ebe86bd68c5951d243c8c490cf7599d1970957

Mullet, H. G., Butler, A. C., Verdin, B., von Borries, R., & Marsh, E. J. (2014). Delaying feedback promotes transfer of knowledge despite student preferences to receive feedback immediately. *Journal of Applied Research in Memory and Cognition, 3*(3), 222–229. doi:10.1016/j.jarmac.2014.05.001

Munoz, L. Q., O'Vyrne, C., Pugsley, J., & Austin, Z. (2005). Reliability, validity, and generalizability of an objective structured clinical examination (OSCE) for assessment of entry-to-practice in pharmacy. *Pharmacy Education, 5*(1), 1–12. doi:10.1080/15602210400025347

Muran, J. C., & Barber, J. P. (Eds.). (2010). *The therapeutic alliance: An evidence-based guide to practice*. Guilford Press.

Muran, J. C., Safran, J. D., & Eubanks-Carter, C. (2010). Developing therapist abilities to negotiate alliance ruptures. In J. C. Muran & J. P. Barber (Eds.), *The therapeutic alliance: An evidence-based guide to practice* (pp. 320–340). Guilford Press.

My Story, My Life. (2019). *VA Boston Education*. Retrieved from https://www.vabostoneducation.org/my-life-my-story

Narayanamurthy, G., & Gurumurthy, A. (2018). Is the hospital lean? A mathematical model for assessing the implementation of lean thinking in healthcare institutions. *Operations Research for Health Care*, *18*, 84–98. doi:10.1016/j.orhc.2017.05.002

Nathan, S., Fiore, L. L., Saunders, S., Vilbrun-Bruno, S. O., Hinrichs, K. L., Ruopp, M. D., Schwartz, A. W., & Moye, J. (2019, September 9). My life, my story: Teaching patient centered care competencies for older adults through life story work. *Gerontology & Geriatrics Education*, 1–14. Advance online publication. doi:10.1080/02701960.2019.1665038 PMID:31498034

Neuwirth, L. S., Ebrahimi, A., Mukherji, B. R., & Park, L. (2019). Addressing diverse college students and interdisciplinary learning experiences through online virtual laboratory instruction: A theoretical approach to error-based learning in biopsychology. Hershey, PA: IGI. doi:10.4018/978-1-5225-8179-6.ch025

Neuwirth, L. S., Dacius, T. F. Jr, & Mukherji, B. R. (2018). Teaching neuroanatomy through a historical context. *Journal of Undergraduate Neuroscience Education*, *16*(2), E26–E31. PMID:30057504

Neuwirth, L. S., Ebrahimi, A., Mukherji, B. R., & Park, L. (2018). Addressing diverse college students and interdisciplinary learning experiences through online virtual laboratory instruction: A theoretical approach to error-based learning in biopsychology. In A. Ursyn (Ed.), *Visual approaches to cognitive education with technology integration* (pp. 283–303). IGI. doi:10.4018/978-1-5225-5332-8.ch012

Norcross, J. C., & Wampold, B. E. (2011). Evidence-based therapy relationships: Research conclusions and clinical practices. *Psychotherapy (Chicago, Ill.)*, *48*(1), 98–102. doi:10.1037/a0022161 PMID:21401280

Olagunju, A., Mokwe, M. D., & Anderson, J. (2012). *Effective Electronic Performance System Training for Supporting the Clinical Activities of Physicians*. Academic Press.

Ong, L. M. L., de Haes, J. C. J. M., Hoos, A. M., & Lammes, F. B. (1995). Doctor-patient communication: A review of the literature. *Social Science & Medicine*, *40*(7), 903–918. doi:10.1016/0277-9536(94)00155-M PMID:7792630

Ormrod, J. E. (2008). *Human Learning* (5th ed.). Pearson Prentice Hall.

Oviatt, S. (2006). Human-centered design meets cognitive load theory: Designing interfaces that help people think. *Proceedings of the 14th AMC International Conference on Multimedia*, 871-880.

Paas, F., van Gog, T., & Sweller, J. (2010). Cognitive load theory: New conceptualizations, specifications, and integrated research perspectives. *Educational Psychology Review*, *22*(2), 115–121. doi:10.100710648-010-9133-8

Palomo, M., Beinart, H., & Cooper, M. (2010). Development and validation of the supervisory relationship questionnaire (SRQ) in UK trainee clinical psychologists. *British Journal of Clinical Psychology*, *49*(2), 131–149. doi:10.1348/014466509X441033 PMID:19457275

Panopto. (2019). *Panopto*™ [web-based video platform]. Available from https://www.panopto.com/

Patton, M. J., & Kivlighan, D. M. Jr. (1997). Relevance of the supervisory alliance to the counseling alliance and to treatment adherence in counselor training. *Journal of Counseling Psychology*, *44*(1), 108–115. doi:10.1037/0022-0167.44.1.108

Patton, M. Q. (2018). Facilitating evaluation principles in practice. *Sage (Atlanta, Ga.)*.

Pearce, C., Arnold, M., Phillips, C., Trumble, S., & Dwan, K. (2011). The patient and the computer in the primary care consultation. *Journal of the American Medical Informatics Association*, *18*(2), 138–142. doi:10.1136/jamia.2010.006486 PMID:21262923

Pershing, J. A., Stolovitch, H. D., & Keeps, E. J. (2006). Handbook of human performance technology: Principles, practices, and potential. Academic Press.

Peterkin, A. D., & Skorzewska, A. (Eds.). (2018). *Health Humanities in Postgraduate Medical Education: A Handbook to the Heart of Medicine*. Oxford University Press. doi:10.1093/med/9780190849900.001.0001

Peterson, J., & Shibley-Hyde, J. (2014). Gender-Related Academic and Occupational Interests and Goals. *Advances in Child Development and Behavior*, *47*, 43–76. doi:10.1016/bs.acdb.2014.04.004 PMID:25344993

Petschonek, S., Burlison, J., Cross, C., Martin, K., Laver, J., Landis, R. S., & Hoffman, J. M. (2013). Development of the Just Culture Assessment Tool (JCAT): Measuring the perceptions of healthcare professionals in hospitals. *Journal of Patient Safety*, *9*(4), 190–197. doi:10.1097/PTS.0b013e31828fff34 PMID:24263549

Phillips, P. P. (2017). The bottomline on roi (3rd ed.). King of Prussia, PA: HRDQ.

Phillips, J. J. (1997). *Handbook of training evaluation and measurement methods* (3rd ed.). Gulf Publishing Company.

Phillips, J. J., & Aaron, B. C. (2008). *Isolation of results: Defining the impact of the program* (Vol. 3). Pfeiffer.

Phillips, J. J., & Phillips, P. P. (2009). *Measuring for success: What ceos really think about learning interventions*. ASTD Press.

Phillips, J. J., & Phillips, P. P. (2012). An introduction to return on investment. In R. A. Reiser & J. V. Dempsey (Eds.), *Trends and issues in instructional design and technology* (3rd ed., pp. 105–115). Pearson.

Phillips, J. J., & Phillips, P. P. (2018). *The value of innovation: Knowing, proving, and showing the value of innovation and creativity*. John Wiley & Sons. doi:10.1002/9781119242413

Phillips, P. P., & Phillips, J. J. (2007). *The value of learning: How organizations capture value and roi and translate it into support, improvement, and funds* (1st ed.). Pfeiffer.

Phillips, P. P., & Phillips, J. J. (2017). *The business case for learning: Using design thinking to deliver business results and increase the investment in talent development*. HRDQ and ATD Press.

Phillips, P. P., & Phillips, J. J. (2019). *Roi basics* (2nd ed.). ATD Press and ROI Institute.

Phillips, P. P., Phillips, J. J., Paone, G., & Gaudet, C. H. (2019). *Value for money: How to show the value for all types of projects and programs in government, nongovernmental organizations, nonprofits, and business*. Scrivener Publishing. doi:10.1002/9781119322764

PioneerRx Pharmacy Software. (2019). *PioneerRx* [pharmacy dispensing software]. PioneerRx Pharmacy Software.

Popham, W. J. (1997). What's wrong - and what's right - with rubrics. *Educational Leadership*, *55*(2), 72–75.

Pories, S. E., Piawah, S., Abel, G. A., Mullangi, S., Doyle, J., & Katz, J. T. (2018, December). What is the Role of the Arts in Medical Education and Patient Care? A Survey based Qualitative Study. *The Journal of Medical Humanities*, *39*(4), 431–445. doi:10.100710912-018-9530-4 PMID:30076508

Posner, G. J., & Strike, K. A. (1976). A categorization scheme for principles of sequencing content. *Review of Educational Research*, *46*(4), 665–690. doi:10.3102/00346543046004665

QM Higher Education Rubric. Sixth Edition. (2018). MarylandOnline, Inc. Used under license. All rights reserved. Retrieved from https://www.qualitymatters.org/myqm

Quality Improvement Essentials Toolkit | IHI - Institute for Healthcare Improvement. (n.d.). Retrieved January 30, 2020, from http://www.ihi.org/resources/Pages/Tools/Quality-Improvement-Essentials-Toolkit.aspx

Ragan, E.D., Bowman, D.A., Kopper, R., Stinson, C., Scerbo, S. & McMahan, R.P. (2015). Effects of field of view and visual complexity on virtual reality training effectiveness for a visual scanning task. *IEEE Transactions on Visualization and Computer Graphics, 21*(7), 794-807.

Ramirez, A. (2015). Augmented Reality in Higher Education: Five Tips to Get Started. *Times Higher Education.* Retrieved from https://www.timeshighereducation.com/news/augmented-reality-in-higher-education-five-tips-to-get-started/2018933.article

Rasheed, A., Khan, S.-U.-R., Rasheed, M. F., & Munir, Y. (2015). The impact of feedback orientation and the effect of satisfaction with feedback on in-role job performance. *Human Resource Development Quarterly*, *26*(1), 31–51. doi:10.1002/hrdq.21202

Reigeluth, C. M., & Moore, J. (1999). Cognitive education and the cognitive domain. In C. M. Reigeluth (Ed.), Instructional design theories and models (vol. 2, pp. 51-68). Lawrence Erlbaum Associates.

Rentsch, J. R., & Klimoski, R. J. (2001). Why do 'great minds' think alike?: Antecedents of team member schema agreement. *Journal of Organizational Behavior*, *22*(2), 107–120. doi:10.1002/job.81

Richardson, D. (2008). Don't dump the didactic lecture; fix it. *American Journal of Physiology -. Advances in Physiology Education, 32*(1), 23–24. doi:10.1152/advan.00048.2007 PMID:18334564

Ringler, T., Ahearn, E. P., Wise, M., Lee, E. R., & Krahn, D. (2015, June). Using Life Stories to Connect Veterans and Providers. *Federal Practitioner, 32*(6), 8–14. PMID:30766066

Rivera-Chiauzzi, E., Lee, C., & Goffman, D. (2016). Debriefing after adverse outcomes. *Contemporary Ob/Gyn, 61*(2), 24–32.

Roberts, D., Newman, L. R., & Schwartzstein, R. M. (2012). Twelve tips for facilitating Millennials' learning. *Medical Teacher, 34*(4), 274–278. doi:10.3109/0142159X.2011.613498 PMID:22288944

Roberts, G. (2005). Technology and Learning Expectations of the Net Generation. In G. Oblinger Diana & J. L. Oblinger (Eds.), *Educating the Net Generation* (pp. 32–38). Educause.

Roberts, N. K., Williams, R. G., Kim, M. J., & Dunnington, G. L. (2009). The briefing, intraoperative teaching, debriefing model for teaching in the operating room. *Journal of the American College of Surgeons, 208*(2), 299–303. doi:10.1016/j.jamcollsurg.2008.10.024 PMID:19228544

Robinson, D. G., Robinson, J. C., Phillips, J. J., Phillips, P. P., & Handshaw, D. (2015). *Performance consulting: A strategic process to improve, measure, and sustain organizational results* (3rd ed.). Barrett-Kohler.

Roelle, J., & Nückles, M. (2019). Generative learning versus retrieval practice in learning from text: The cohesion and elaboration of the text matters. *Journal of Educational Psychology, 111*(8), 1341–1361. doi:10.1037/edu0000345

Rolfe, I., & McPherson, J. (1995). Formative assessment: How am I doing? *Lancet, 345*(8953), 837–839. doi:10.1016/S0140-6736(95)92968-1 PMID:7898233

Ros, M., & Neuwirth, L. S. (2020). Increasing global awareness of timely COVID-19 healthcare guidelines through FPV training tutorials: Portable public health crises teaching method. *Nurse Education Today, 91*(104479), 1–6. doi:10.1016/j.nedt.2020.104479

Ros, M., Trives, J. V., & Lonjon, N. (2017). From stereoscopic recording to virtual reality headsets: Designing a new way to learn surgery. *Neuro-Chirurgie, 63*(1), 1–5. doi:10.1016/j.neuchi.2016.08.004 PMID:28233530

Rosner, F. (1967). The Physician's Prayer Attributed to Maimonides. *Bulletin of the History of Medicine, 41*(5), 440–454. PMID:4865040

Rossett, A. (1987). *Training needs assessment.* Academic Press.

Rossett, A., & Schafer, L. (2006). Job aids and performance support: The convergence of learning and work. *International Journal of Learning Technology, 2*(4), 310–328. doi:10.1504/IJLT.2006.011337

Ross, M., & Stefaniak, J. (2019). Promoting a Holistic Approach to Delivering Performance Feedback: Introducing the Behavioral Analysis Feedback Model. *Performance Improvement, 58*(6), 17–27. doi:10.1002/pfi.21882

Roulstone, D. B., & Phillips, J. J. (2008). *Roi in technology*. Butterworth-Heinemann.

Roussou, M. (2000). Immersive interactive virtual reality and informal education. *Proceedings of i3 Workshop on Interactive Learning Environments for Children*, 1-9.

Ruiz, J. G., Mintzer, M. J., & Leipzig, R. M. (2006). The impact of e-learning in medical education. *Academic Medicine, 81*(3), 207–212. doi:10.1097/00001888-200603000-00002 PMID:16501260

Rummler, G. A., & Brache, A. P. (2012). *Improving performance: How to manage the white space on the organization chart*. Academic Press.

Rummler, G. A., & Brache, A. P. (1988). The systems view of human performance. *Training (New York, N.Y.), 25*(9).

Russ-Eft, D., & Preskill, H. (2001). *Evaluation in organizations: A systematice approach to enhancing learning, performance, and change*. Perseus.

Safran, J. D., Muran, J. C., & Eubanks-Carter, C. (2011). Repairing alliance ruptures. In J. C. Norcross (Ed.), *Psychotherapy relationships that work: Evidence-based responsiveness* (2nd ed., pp. 224–238). Oxford University Press. doi:10.1093/acprof:oso/9780199737208.003.0011

Saldaña, J. (2015). The coding manual for qualitative researchers. *Sage (Atlanta, Ga.)*.

Sandars, J., & Murdoch-Eaton, D. (2017). Appreciative inquiry in medical education. *Medical Teacher, 39*(2), 123–127. doi:10.1080/0142159X.2017.1245852 PMID:27852144

Santiago, C., & Abdool, S. (2011). Conversations about challenging end-of-life cases: Ethics debriefing in the medical surgical intensive care unit. *Dynamics (Pembroke, Ont.), 22*(4), 26–30. PMID:22279847

Schartel, S. A. (2012). Giving feedback – An integral part of education. *Best Practice & Research. Clinical Anaesthesiology, 26*(1), 77–87. doi:10.1016/j.bpa.2012.02.003 PMID:22559958

Schwartz, A. W., Abramson, J. S., Wojnowich, I., Accordino, R., Ronan, E. J., & Rifkin, M. R. (2009). Evaluating the impact of the humanities in medical education. *The Mount Sinai Journal of Medicine, New York, 76*(4), 372–380. doi:10.1002/msj.20126

Senge, P. M. (2012). *Schools that learn: A fifth discipline fieldbook for educators, parents, and everyone who cares about education*. Crown Business.

Sentz, J., Stefaniak, J., Baaki, J., & Eckhoff, A. (2019). How do instructional designers manage learners' cognitive load? An examination of awareness and application of strategies. In *Educational Technology Research and Development* (Vol. 67). Springer US. doi:10.100711423-018-09640-5

Shahmoradi, L., Safadari, R., & Jimma, W. (2017). Knowledge management implementation and the tools utilized in healthcare for evidence-based decision making: A systematic review. *Ethiopian Journal of Health Sciences*, *27*(5), 541–558. doi:10.4314/ejhs.v27i5.13 PMID:29217960

Shapiro, J., Bezzubova, E., & Koons, R. (2011, July). Medical Students Learn to Tell Stories about Their Patients and Themselves. *American Medical Association Journal of Ethics.*, *13*(7), 466–470. PMID:23134794

Sheik-Ali, S., Edgcombe, H., & Paton, C. (2019). Next-generation Virtual and Augmented Reality in Surgical Education: A Narrative Review. *Surgical Technology International*, *35*, 27–35. PMID:31498872

Shirwaikar, A. (2015). Objective structured clinical examination (OSCE) in pharmacy education – a trend. *Pharmacy Practice*, *13*(4), 627. doi:10.18549/PharmPract.2015.04.627 PMID:26759616

Silverman, E. (2017, Aug. 21). Sharing and Healing Through Storytelling in Medicine. *JAMA Intern Med*. doi: . doi:10.1001/jamainternmed.2017.2996

Simon, A., Ammann, R. A., Bode, U., Fleischhack, G., Wenchel, H. M., Schwamborn, D., Gravou, C., Schlegel, P.-G., Rutkowski, S., Dannenberg, C., Körholz, D., Laws, H. J., & Kramer, M. H. (2008). Healthcare-associated infections in pediatric cancer patients: Results of a prospective surveillance study from university hospitals in Germany and Switzerland. *BMC Infectious Diseases*, *8*(1), 1–10. doi:10.1186/1471-2334-8-70 PMID:18500998

Simon, R. W., & Canacari, E. G. (2012). A practical guide to applying lean tools and management principles to healthcare improvement projects. *AORN Journal*, *95*(1), 85–103. doi:10.1016/j.aorn.2011.05.021 PMID:22201573

Sinek, S. (2009). *Start with why: How great leaders inspire everyone to take action*. Penguin Group.

Skinner, B. F. (1938). *The behavior of organisms: An experimental analysis*. Prentice-Hall.

Smith-Hansen, L. (2016). The therapeutic alliance: From correlational studies to training models. *Journal of Psychotherapy Integration*, *26*(3), 217–229. doi:10.1037/int0000012

Smith, S. J., Farra, S. L., Ulrich, D. L., Hodgson, E., Nicely, S., & Mickle, A. (2018). Effectiveness of Two Varying Levels of Virtual Reality Simulation. *Nursing Education Perspectives*, *39*(6), E10–E15. doi:10.1097/01.NEP.0000000000000369 PMID:30335708

Soto, N. E. (2005). *Caring and Relationships: Developing a Pedagogy of Caring*. Retrieved from https://digitalcommons.law.villanova.edu/vlr/vol50/iss4/11

St. Jude Children Research Hospital. (2020a). *About us*. https://www.stjude.org/about-st-jude.html?sc_icid=us-mm-missionstatement#mission

St. Jude Children Research Hospital. (2020b). *Our history*. https://www.stjude.org/about-st-jude/history.html

St. Jude Children Research Hospital. (2020c). *St. Jude global*. https://www.stjude.org/global.html

Stefanou, C., Hoffman, L., & Vielee, N. (2008). Note-taking in the college classroom as evidence of generative learning. *Learning Environments Research*, *11*(1), 1–17. doi:10.100710984-007-9033-0

Strobel, J., & Van Barneveld, A. (2015). PBL effectiveness, tensions, and practitioner implications. *Essential readings in problem-based learning*, 355-372.

Sturm, L. P., Windsor, J. A., Cosman, P. H., Cregan, P., Hewett, P. J., & Maddern, G. J. (2008). A systematic review of skills transfer after surgical simulation training. *Annals of Surgery*, *248*(2), 166–179. doi:10.1097/SLA.0b013e318176bf24 PMID:18650625

Sugar, W. A., & Luterbach, K. J. (2016). Using critical incidents of instructional design and multimedia production activities to investigate instructional designers' current practices and roles. *Educational Technology Research and Development*, *64*(2), 285–312. doi:10.100711423-015-9414-5

Sulmasy, L. S., & Bledsoe, T. A. (2019). American College of Physicians ethics manual: Seventh edition. Annals of Internal Medicine, 170, S1-S32. doi:10.7326/M18-2160

Sunal, D. W., Hodges, J., Sunal, C. S., Whitaker, K. W., Freeman, L. M., Edwards, L., Johnston, R. A., & O'Dell, M. (2001). Teaching science in higher education: Faculty professional development and barriers to change. *School Science and Mathematics*, *101*(5), 246–257. doi:10.1111/j.1949-8594.2001.tb18027.x

Sutherland, J., Belec, J., Sheikh, A., Chepelev, L., Althobaity, W., Chow, B. J. W., Mitsouras, D., Christensen, A., Rybicki, F. J., & La Russa, D. J. (2019). Applying modern virtual and augmented reality technologies to medical images and models. *Journal of Digital Imaging*, *32*(1), 38–53. doi:10.100710278-018-0122-7 PMID:30215180

Sweller, J., Ayres, P., & Kalyuga, S. (2011). *Cognitive load theory*. Springer., doi:10.1007/978-1-4419-8126-4

Sweller, J., van Merriënboer, J. J. G., & Paas, F. (2019). Cognitive architecture and instructional design: 20 years later. *Educational Psychology Review*, *31*(2), 261–292. doi:10.100710648-019-09465-5

Szasz, T. S., Knoff, W. F., & Hollender, M. H. (1958). The doctor-patient relationship and its historical context. *The American Journal of Psychiatry*, *115*(6), 522–528. doi:10.1176/ajp.115.6.522 PMID:13595126

Taras, M. (2005). Assessment : Summative and formative : Some theoretical reflections. *British Journal of Educational Studies*, *53*(4), 466–478. doi:10.1111/j.1467-8527.2005.00307.x

Taylor, A., Lehmann, S., & Chisolm, M. (2017). Integrating humanities curricula in medical education: A literature review. *MedEdPublish*, *6*(2), 28. doi:10.15694/mep.2017.000090.2

The Role of Arts and Humanities in Physician Development: From Fun to Fundamental. (n.d.). Retrieved from: https://www.aamc.org/what-we-do/mission-areas/medical-education/humanities

Thompson, L., Exline, M., Leung, C. G., Way, D. P., Clinchot, D., Bahner, D. P., & Khandelwal, S. (2016). A clinical procedures curriculum for undergraduate medical students: The eight-year history of a third-year immersive experience. *Medical Education Online*, *21*(1), 29486. doi:10.3402/meo.v21.29486 PMID:27222103

Thorndike, E. L. (1913). *Educational psychology: The psychology of learning* (Vol. 2). Teachers College Press. doi:10.1037/13051-000

Thorndike, E. L. (1932). *The fundamentals of learning*. Teachers College Press. doi:10.1037/10976-000

Topor, D. R., AhnAllen, C. G., Mulligan, E. A., & Dickey, C. C. (2017). Using video recordings of psychotherapy sessions in supervision: Strategies to reduce learner anxiety. *Academic Psychiatry*, *41*(1), 40–43. doi:10.100740596-016-0605-0 PMID:27558629

Treadway, K. (2005). Notes to the Class— First Day. *The New England Journal of Medicine*, *352*(19), 1943–1944. doi:10.1056/NEJMp048298 PMID:15888691

Troester, K. (2018). How will we train generation Z? *Training Industry*. https://trainingindustry.com/blog/strategy-alignment-and-planning/how-will-we-train-generation-z/

Tufte, E. R. (2001). *The visual display of quantitative information* (Vol. 2). Graphics Press.

Tumosa, N., Horvath, K. J., Huh, T., Livote, E. E., Howe, J. L., Jones, L. I., & Kramer, B. J. (2012). healthcare workforce development in rural America: When geriatrics expertise is 100 miles away. *Gerontology & Geriatrics Education*, *33*(2), 133–151. doi:10.1080/02701960.2012.661812 PMID:22490071

Twenge, J. (2014). Generational changes and their impact in the classroom: Teaching Generation Me. *Medical Education*, *43*(5), 398–405. doi:10.1111/j.1365-2923.2009.03310.x PMID:19422486

Tyler, R. (2017). Basic principles of curriculum and instruction. In D. J. Flinders & S. J. Thornton (Eds.), *Curriculum studies reader* (4th ed., pp. 73–82). Routledge.

VA geriatric scholar uses the power of story to improve patient care. (2019). *VAntage Point blog*. Retrieved from: https://www.blogs.va.gov/VAntage/69524/va-geriatric-scholar-uses-power-story-improve-patient-care/

Van der Feltz-Cornelis, C. M., Van Oppen, P., Van Marwijk, H. W. J., De Beurs, E., & Van Dyck, R. (2004). A patient-doctor relationship questionnaire (PDRQ-9) in primary care: Development and psychometric evaluation. *General Hospital Psychiatry*, *26*(2), 115–120. doi:10.1016/j.genhosppsych.2003.08.010 PMID:15038928

Van Gog, T., Paas, F., Marcus, N., Ayres, P., & Sweller, J. (2009). The mirror neuron system and observational learning: Implications for the effectiveness of dynamic visualizations. *Educational Psychology Review*, *21*(1), 21–30. doi:10.100710648-008-9094-3 van Leusen, P., Ottenbreit-Lefwich, A. T., & Brush, T. (2016). Interpersonal consulting skills for instructional technology consultants: A multiple case study. *TechTrends*, *60*(3), 253–259. doi:10.100711528-016-0046-3

van Merriënboer, J. J., & Kirschner, P. A. (2017). *Ten steps to complex learning: A systematic approach to four-component instructional design*. Routledge.

Van Tiem, D. M., Moseley, J. L., & Dessinger, J. C. (2012). *Fundamentals of performance improvement: Optimizing results through people, process, and organizations* (3rd ed.). Pfeiffer.

van Tiem, D. M., Moseley, J. L., Dessinger, J. C., & O'Brien, C. (2002). Performance improvement interventions: Enhancing people, processes, and organizations through performance technology. *Performance Improvement*, *41*(1), 45–49. doi:10.1002/pfi.4140410110

Vankipuram, A., Khanal, P., Ashby, A., Vankipuram, M., Gupta, A., DrummGurnee, D., Josey, K., & Smith, M. (2014). Design and development of a virtual reality simulator for advanced cardiac life support training. *IEEE Journal of Biomedical and Health Informatics*, *18*(4), 1478–1484. doi:10.1109/JBHI.2013.2285102 PMID:24122608

Vaughan, N., Dubey, V. N., Wainwright, T. W., & Middleton, R. G. (2016). A review of virtual reality based training simulators for orthopaedic surgery. *Medical Engineering & Physics*, *38*(2), 59–71. doi:10.1016/j.medengphy.2015.11.021 PMID:26751581

Villachica, S. W., Stone, D. L., & Endicott, J. (2006). Performance support systems. Handbook of human performance technology, 539-566.

Wachter, A., & Lion, R. W. (2016). Multi-Rater Feedback: Improving Students' Readiness for the OR. *Techniques - American Vocational Association*, *91*(3), 44–49.

Walsh, T., Jairath, N., Paterson, M. A., & Grandjean, C. (2010). Quality and Safety Education for Nurses Clinical Evaluation Tool. *The Journal of Nursing Education*, *49*(9), 517–522. doi:10.3928/01484834-20100630-06 PMID:20672776

Wampold, B. E., & Imel, Z. E. (2015). *The great psychotherapy debate: The evidence for what makes psychotherapy work* (2nd ed.). Routledge. doi:10.4324/9780203582015

Wang, G. G., Dou, Z., & Li, N. (2002). A systems approach to measuring return on investment for hrd interventions. *Human Resource Development Quarterly*, *13*(2), 203–224. doi:10.1002/hrdq.1024

Ward, E. C. (2002). *Cultural competence, cultural mistrust, working alliance and racial ethnic minority clients' experience of counseling: A mixed methods study*. University of Wisconsin Press.

Watkins, C. E. Jr. (2014). The supervisory alliance: A half century of theory, practice, and research in critical perspective. *American Journal of Psychotherapy*, *68*(1), 19–55. doi:10.1176/appi.psychotherapy.2014.68.1.19 PMID:24818456

Watkins, C. E. Jr, & Scaturo, D. J. (2013). Toward an integrative, learning-based model of psychotherapy supervision: Supervisory alliance, educational interventions, and supervisee learning/relearning. *Journal of Psychotherapy Integration*, *23*(1), 75–95. doi:10.1037/a0031330

Weinhold, I., & Gurtner, S. (2014). Understanding shortages of sufficient healthcare in rural areas. *Health Policy (Amsterdam)*, *118*(2), 201–214. doi:10.1016/j.healthpol.2014.07.018 PMID:25176511

Weston, C., & Cranton, P. A. (1986). Selecting instructional strategies. *The Journal of Higher Education*, *57*(3), 259. doi:10.2307/1981553

Wiggins, G. P., & McTighe, J. (2008). *Understanding by design*. Association for Supervision and Curriculum Development.

Willis, J., & Cowie, B. (2014). Assessment as a generative dance: Connecting teaching learning and curriculum. In C. Wyatt-Smith, V. Klenowski, & P. Colbert (Eds.), *Designing assessment for quality learning* (pp. 23–38). Springer. doi:10.1007/978-94-007-5902-2_2

Wilson, Y., White, A., Jefferson, A., & Danis, M. (2019). Intersectionality in clinical medicine: The need for a conceptual framework. *The American Journal of Bioethics*, *19*(2), 8–19. doi:10.1080/15265161.2018.1557275 PMID:30784384

Witkin, B. R., & Altschuld, J. W. (1995). Planning and conducting needs assessments: A practical guide. *Sage (Atlanta, Ga.)*.

Wittrock, M. C. (2010). Learning as a generative process. *Educational Psychologist*, *45*(1), 40–45. doi:10.1080/00461520903433554

Wolfe, B. E., & Goldfried, M. R. (1988). Research on psychotherapy integration: Recommendations and conclusions from an NIMH workshop. *Journal of Consulting and Clinical Psychology*, *56*(3), 448–451. doi:10.1037/0022-006X.56.3.448 PMID:2899579

Wolters Kluwer Clinical Drug Information, Inc. (2019). *Lexicomp®* [web-based drug information resource]. Available from https://online.lexi.com/lco/action/home

Woodill, G. (2014). Performance Support as a Form of Mobile Learning. *Mastering Mobile Learning*, 171-173.

World Health Organization. (2020). *Cancer in children*. https://www.who.int/news-room/fact-sheets/detail/cancer-in-children

Worthington, D. L., & Levasseur, D. G. (2015). To provide or not to provide course PowerPoint slides? The impact of instructor-provided slides upon student attendance and performance. *Computers & Education*, *85*, 14–22. doi:10.1016/j.compedu.2015.02.002

Wright, B. M., Hornsby, L., Marlowe, K. F., Fowlin, J., & Surry, D. W. (2018). Innovating pharmacy curriculum through backward design. *TechTrends*, *62*(3), 224–229. doi:10.100711528-018-0283-8

Wroblewski, M. B., & Imran, I. A. (2017). *Teaching Millennials in the Clinical Environment. In Commitment to Excellence in Medical Education: Faculty Development Series*. University of Toledo.

Zaber, M. A., Karoly, L. A., & Whipkey, K. (2019). *Reimagining the Workforce Development and Employment System for the 21st Century and Beyond*. Academic Press.

Zickuhr, K., & Madden, M. (2012). Older adults and internet use. *Pew Internet & American Life Project*. Retrieved from https://pewinternet.org/Reports/2012/Older-adults-and-internet-use.aspx

Zigmont, J. J., Kappus, L. J., & Sudikoff, S. N. (2011). The 3D Model of Debriefing: Defusing, Discovering, and Deepening. *Seminars in Perinatology*, *35*(2), 52–58. doi:10.1053/j.semperi.2011.01.003 PMID:21440811

Zoom Video Connections, Inc. (2019). *Zoom* [web-based video conferencing system]. Available from https://zoom.us/signin

About the Contributors

Jill Stefaniak is Assistant Professor in the Learning, Design, and Technology program in the Department of Career and Information Studies at the University of Georgia, USA. Her research interests focus on the professional development of instructional designers, designer decision-making processes, and contextual factors that influence design in situated environments. Dr. Stefaniak has experience leading instructional design and performance improvement projects in healthcare, medical education, higher education, and safety.

* * *

Katie Asaro is an instructional designer for Kent State University. She has been with KSU since 2013 and has worked with a variety of programs to develop fully online courses. Her background is in Middle School Education and she earned her M.Ed. in Educational Technology from Ashland University.

Robin Bartoletti is an Instructional Designer and Project Manager for Indiana Tech University. She previously served as Assistant Director/Instructional Designer at the Center for Innovative Learning at the University of North Texas Health Science Center. As Assistant director and Instructional Designer, Dr. Bartoletti works with faculty and clinicians to plan and coordinate the design, development and implementation of curriculum for public heath, pharmacology, medical education, health professions and graduate biomedical science instruction. Dr. Bartoletti recommends instructional strategies in the development of healthcare related instructional design objectives, guidelines and procedures; conducts need analysis, and designs and produces instructional course modules that accomplish designated learning objectives. She also assists program deans and chairs in the scheduling of curriculum development, faculty development and other educational programs, and maintains the Center for Innovative Learning faculty and clinician focused website. Additionally, she serves as liaison and consultant in the curriculum design and documentation process to basic science, clinical faculty, and principal investigators. Dr. Bartoletti's experience includes over 15 years of experience in all levels of education with a focus on technology and has led numerous presentations and workshops around the country. She has served as co-investigator on projects with a focus on Faculty Development for Teaching Excellence and the Use of an Educational Tool Kit to Teach Mechanics of Materials in biomedical education. Dr. Bartoletti earned her Master of Information Science from the University of North Texas and Doctor of Education from Texas Woman's University as well as certificates in Interprofessional Education from the University of Washington and Principles of Medical Education from Harvard University.

Timothy R. Brock is the director of consulting services for the ROI Institute, the leading source of ROI competency building, implementation support, networking, and research. He helps organizations implement the ROI Methodology at more than 6,000 organizations in over 70 countries. Dr. Brock is also frequently invited to speak at association meetings and international conferences. He earned his Ph.D. in Education at Capella University with a specialization in training and performance improvement. Dr. Brock is a Certified ROI Professional (CRP), a Certified Performance Technologist (CPT), and a Certified Designer of Training with a specialization in Simulation and Labs (CDT[S&L+]).

Miguela Caniza is a pediatrician and infectious disease specialist with close to 20 years' experience in improving the standards for the prevention and care of infections in children at St Jude and globally. At St Jude, she cares for infected immunocompromised children, and mentors in-training pediatric specialists to deliver the best clinical care for this patient population. Across the globe, she directs the Global Infectious Disease Program to impact a wide clinical workforce audience. She designs and administers a variety of infection care and prevention training programs that are highly effective, and specifically tailored for the busy and diverse healthcare providers across the world.

Channing R. Ford, PhD, MPA, MA, is the Director of Assessment in the Department of Faculty Affairs and Strategic Initiatives. Prior to joining the Harrison School of Pharmacy at Auburn University in 2014, she served as the Education Program Director for the Division of Gerontology, Geriatrics, and Palliative Care at the University of Alabama at Birmingham (UAB). While at UAB, Dr. Ford worked closely with faculty from a variety of health professions to create, implement, and evaluate student learning experiences. Currently, Dr. Ford dedicates most of her time to the integration of performance-based assessments across the first three years of the Doctor of Pharmacy degree program, collaborating with faculty to development, implement, evaluate and refine these assessments to foster best assessment practices within the curriculum.

Candice Freeman is a Clinical Laboratory Scientist with over 20 years of leadership experience in healthcare, specifically in rural hospital systems. Additionally, she is an Instructional Designer and doctoral candidate at Old Dominion University in Norfolk, Virginia. Her research focuses on instructional design and human performance initiatives in healthcare, situated in promoting positive patient experience and employee satisfaction in underserved and underrepresented populations.

Brooke Happ, MPH, is an epidemiologist with experience in both public health and global health. In her role at St. Jude Children's Research Hospital, she coordinates the development and delivery of infection prevention and control educational courses, facilitates capacity building initiatives with partner sites and global networks, and supports other efforts of the Global Infectious Diseases Program.

Maysam R. Homsi, MPH, CCRP, is the project coordinator for the Global Infectious Diseases Program at St. Jude Children's Research Hospital. She currently manages the development, implementation and evaluation of infection care and prevention initiatives worldwide, including team-based mentoring and capacity-building projects; regional and global-focused training and education programs; and collaborative research and quality improvement projects.

Lisa Joyner, M.Ed, RRT, RRT-NPS, is the Program Chair for the Respiratory Therapy program at Salisbury University in Salisbury, Maryland. Lisa is a Registered Respiratory Therapist (RRT) and Neonatal & Pediatric Specialist (RRT-NPS). She brings over 30 years of respiratory therapy knowledge both in the clinical and classroom setting.

Erika L. Kleppinger, Pharm.D., BCPS, is an Associate Clinical Professor in the Department of Pharmacy Practice. Since joining the faculty at the Harrison School of Pharmacy in 2003, she has practiced in several ambulatory care practice settings, coordinated and taught in a variety of skills laboratory activities, and worked passionately on curriculum development and revision. Currently Dr. Kleppinger dedicates most of her time to skills activity coordination and assessment with Objective Structured Clinical Exams (OSCEs) and other performance-based assessments. She teaches in many areas of the Practice-Ready Curriculum, including patient assessment skills, communication skills (specifically assessing patient understanding and new prescription counseling), the pharmacists' patient care process, self-carc, dermatology, cough and cold management, and immunization certification training. She also serves as a Skills Coordinator and a Learning Experience Coordinator for the first professional year of the PharmD program.

Thomas Lamey is the Director of Clinical Education for the Respiratory Therapy program at Salisbury University in Salisbury, Maryland. Thomas is a Registered Respiratory Therapist (RRT) and Certified Asthma Educator (AE-C), focusing research and outreach efforts on asthma awareness and self-management strategies. Prior to Salisbury University, he worked in a 600+ bed Level II urban hospital for 10 years.

Kim Meyer graduated from the University of Texas at Galveston as a Physician Assistant. While practicing clinically as a PA, she earned her Masters of Physician Assistant Studies degree with specialization in neurosurgery from the University of Nebraska. She began her teaching career as a PA faculty member at the Louisiana State University Health Sciences Center in Shreveport from 2002 – 2005 and served as PA Program Director there from 2005 - 2015. At LSU, she maintained a part-time clinical practice in neurosurgery and earned a PhD in Education from Capella University with specialization in Higher Education Leadership. In 2015, her family moved to Fort Worth, Texas where she accepted a faculty appointment at UNTHSC as an Associate Professor in the PA Program and later accepted an additional position as Director of the Center for Innovative Learning (CIL) in January of 2017. She now leads a talented and diverse group of educational innovators in the support of academic excellence at UNTHSC. Dr. Meyer maintains academic appointments in PA Studies and in the Osteopathic Medical School (TCOM) Department of Medical Education.

Nicholas R. Morrison, Ph.D., is a Postdoctoral Fellow in the Interprofessional General Mental Health Track at the VA Boston Healthcare System and holds an appointment as a Clinical Fellow of Psychology at Harvard Medical School. He completed his doctoral training in Clinical Psychology at the University of Massachusetts Amherst. Dr. Morrison's research interests center around psychotherapy process, outcome, integration, and training.

Susan Nathan, MD. is a Geriatrician and Hospice and Palliative Medicine physician at VA Boston Healthcare System. She is an Instructor in Medicine at Harvard Medical School and an adjunct Instructor in Medicine at Boston University School of Medicine and serves on the steering committee of the Harvard Medical School Arts and Humanities Initiative. She is the site director for the My Life, My Story Project at VA Boston. She is interested in the role of patient story in healthcare as well as education around serious illness communication.

Lorenz S. Neuwirth, Ph.D. is an Assistant Professor of Psychology at the SUNY College at Old Westbury and a member of the SUNY Neuroscience Research Institute (SUNY-NRI). Dr. Neuwirth is a neuroscientist who studies developmental behavioral neurotoxicology and its relationship to developmental disabilities. He is a proponent of increasing underrepresented minority undergraduate student participation in both the physical and social sciences. He is a first generation minority male who has benefitted greatly from programs dedicated towards reducing and/or attempting to eliminate the academic achievement gap (i.e., STEP, C-STEP, LSAMP, and AGEP). He received his Ph.D. in Biology/Neuroscience at The CUNY Graduate Center in 2014. He completed a two year postdoctoral NIEHS fellowship in developmental neurotoxicology and molecular epigenetics at Thomas Jefferson University's Department of Anatomy, Pathology, and Cell Biology in Philadelphia, PA before joining the faulty at SUNY-OW. His research is focuses on understanding the effects of environmental neurotoxicants and their relationship to dysexecutive functions as they related to goal-directed attention and memory dependent neurobehavioral disorders. His other research interests are directed towards using technology to teach neuroscience and research methodology to a wide range of students.

Maxime Ros is a neurosurgeon passionate about the way skills are transmitted around the globe. After his residency, Maxime performed fellowships in different cities. This experience made him realize how different skills are being taught, for the same procedure, which drove his exploration of Virtual and Augmented Reality. He also holds a Master 2 in biomechanical engineering, is graduated in medical teaching, and is now working on a PhD in teaching science. He has been elected member of the French Academy of Surgery for his works about surgical training. Maxime developed Revinax, initially, to allow medical professionals to share their skills, in a new, engaging, and efficient way, using video-based VR in first person view. Revinax's approach to VR has been used at first by Fortune 100 companies in the Medical Device industry, and now by several other industries requiring experiential training. Revinax is willing to create a Foundation to deliver an affordable and efficient way to train healthcare professionals in remote area.

Melanie Ross, Ph.D., is an instructional designer for Northrop Grumman where she develops and manages content and delivery of learning programs for a diverse audience ranging from business and operations personnel to engineers and technicians. She received her Ph.D. from Old Dominion University in Instructional Design & Technology in 2018 where she developed the Behavioral Analysis Feedback Model – a model designed to deliver behavior-specific feedback by focusing on the environmental and individual elements that can influence a performer's behavior. Previously, she received her Master of Arts in Instructional Technology from Virginia Tech in 2012 and a Bachelor of Science in Liberal Studies with a teaching license in PreK-8 from Longwood University in 2007. Dr. Ross's current research interests focus on delivering frequent, behavior-specific feedback and the effects of instructional and non-instructional interventions on performance outcomes.

Andrea Wershof Schwartz, MD, MPH, MA, is an Assistant Professor of Medicine at Harvard Medical School (HMS) and serves on the steering committee of the HMS Arts and Humanities Initiative. Dr. Schwartz earned her MD from Mount Sinai School of Medicine's Humanities and Medicine program, her MPH from the Hebrew University of Jerusalem, and her MA from the Jewish Theological Seminary. She is Medical Director of the Geriatrics Consult Clinic at the VA Boston Healthcare System and an Educator in the New England Geriatric Research Education and Clinical Center and she serves as Associate Program Director for the Harvard Multicampus Geriatrics Fellowship.

Bethany Simunich is the Director of Online Pedagogy and Research for Kent State University, and has worked in online education for over fifteen years. She has held positions in learning technology, instructional design, online teaching, and faculty development, and has also worked in the area of research and evaluation of online quality and effectiveness. Her research interests include presence in the online classroom, online student and instructor satisfaction, and rigor and outcome achievement in online courses. Bethany received her bachelor's and two master's degrees from the University of Pittsburgh, and her doctorate from The Ohio State University. She is a regular presenter of workshops and sessions at online learning conferences, and also facilitates custom presentations and workshops on online teaching and design for educational audiences.

Suha R. Tamim, EdD, MPH, is a Clinical Assistant Professor in the Curriculum Studies program in the department of Instruction and Teacher Education at the University of South Carolina. Previously, she taught at the University of Memphis in the Instructional Design and Technology program and at the American University of Beirut in the Faculty of Health Sciences. She also worked as an instructional design and educational consultant for health and corporate organizations.

David R. Topor, Ph.D., MS-HPEd, is a Clinical Psychologist and the Associate Director for Healthcare Professional Education at the VA Boston Healthcare System. He is an Assistant Professor in the Department of Psychiatry at Harvard Medical School. He holds a Ph.D. in Clinical Psychology and a Master's of Science degree in Health Professions Education. He has expertise in faculty development, interprofessional education evaluation and research, educational leadership, and in teaching and mentoring.

Lorraine Weaver worked as an Aerospace Engineering Officer in the Canadian Armed Forces for twenty years. During this time she worked in aviation maintenance, aerospace test and evaluation, aircrew standards, airworthiness certification, junior officer training/personnel management and training design and development. Working as the Airworthiness Training – Team Lead for the Directorate Technical Airworthiness and Engineering Support, she oversaw course design, development and implementation using the Canadian Forces Individual Training and Education framework. As the team lead, she also created and lead a customized goal-based instructor professional development program as well as developing and implementing a memory booster program for in-class courses. She also enjoyed applying instructional design methodologies when revising the Human Factors course in the Aerospace Systems Program to make it more engaging and enhance discovery learning. Lorraine Weaver has completed her BSc in Math, MSc in Human Factors and a Graduate Diploma in Technology-Enhanced Learning and Design. She is currently enrolled in the Masters of Education program at Thompson Rivers University.

Nicole Yoder joined Kent State University as an Educational Technology Designer in 2017. Prior to working for KSU, Nicole worked as an Adult Services Librarian for four years and a K-12 Librarian for two. She has always had a strong interest in higher education, however, and truly enjoys working with faculty and subject matter experts to design high quality online courses. Nicole holds a Master's degree in Library and Information Science and a Master's degree in Digital Sciences with a concentration in Digital Training Technology.

Index

H

I

K

L

M

N

O

P

Q

R

www.ingramcontent.com/pod-product-compliance
Lightning Source LLC
LaVergne TN
LVHW080901300926
849162LV00003B/512
* 9 7 8 1 7 9 9 8 5 0 9 2 2 *